Rhetoric in Detail

Discourse Approaches to Politics, Society and Culture (DAPSAC)

The editors invite contributions that investigate political, social and cultural processes from a linguistic/discourse-analytic point of view. The aim is to publish monographs and edited volumes which combine language-based approaches with disciplines concerned essentially with human interaction – disciplines such as political science, international relations, social psychology, social anthropology, sociology, economics, and gender studies.

General Editors

Ruth Wodak and Greg Myers
University of Lancaster

Editorial address: Ruth Wodak, Bowland College, Department of Linguistics and English Language, University of Lancaster University, LANCASTER LA1 4YT, UK
r.wodak@lancaster.ac.uk and g.myers@lancaster.ac.uk

Advisory Board

Volume 31

Rhetoric in Detail. Discourse analyses of rhetorical talk and text
Edited by Barbara Johnstone and Christopher Eisenhart

Rhetoric in Detail

Discourse analyses of rhetorical talk and text

Edited by

Barbara Johnstone
Carnegie Mellon University

Christopher Eisenhart
University of Massachusetts at Dartmouth

John Benjamins Publishing Company
Amsterdam / Philadelphia

™ The paper used in this publication meets the minimum requirements of
American National Standard for Information Sciences – Permanence of
Paper for Printed Library Materials, ANSI z39.48-1984.

Library of Congress Cataloging-in-Publication Data

Rhetoric in detail : discourse analyses of rhetorical talk and text / edited by Barbara
     Johnstone and Christopher Eisenhart.
    p. cm. (Discourse Approaches to Politics, Society and Culture, ISSN 1569-9463 ; v. 31)
    Includes bibliographical references and index.
      1. Discourse analysis. 2. Rhetoric. I. Johnstone, Barbara. II. Eisenhart, Christopher.
    P302.R49   2008
401'.41--dc22   2008035988
ISBN 978 90 272 0619 0 (Hb; alk. paper)

John Benjamins Publishing Co. · P.O. Box 36224 · 1020 ME Amsterdam · The Netherlands
John Benjamins North America · P.O. Box 27519 · Philadelphia PA 19118-0519 · USA

for Alton L. Becker and Richard E. Young

Table of contents

PART I

Introduction

CHAPTER 1

Discourse analysis and rhetorical studies

Christopher Eisenhart and Barbara Johnstone
University of Massachusetts, Dartmouth / Carnegie Mellon University

Overview

This book brings together twelve studies, all written by scholars who identify themselves primarily as rhetoricians, that employ theory and/or method from linguistic discourse analysis. The studies make use of a variety of discourse analytic resources, including those of critical discourse analysis, interactional sociolinguistics, narrative analysis, and computer-aided corpus analysis. They illustrate the utility of discourse analysis in research in a variety of rhetorical sites, including discourses of public memory and collective identity, rhetoric of science and technology, vernacular argumentation, media discourse, and immigration studies. The method these projects share begins in close attention to the linguistic details of records of discourse, be they written texts or transcripts of talk. The authors take a mostly qualitative, interpretive approach, but one that differs from the approaches often taken in rhetorical studies in being data-driven rather than theory-driven. Working upward from particular, situated instances of text and talk rather than downwards from abstract models of discourse, they take systematic approaches to exploring why particular utterances take the particular shapes they do. The approach involves beginning with an attitude attuned to multiple sources of contextual constraint, rather than beginning with theory and seeking evidence for it. While the studies in these chapters deal with various rhetorical issues in a variety of ways, they all share three methodological characteristics: They are *empirical*, in the sense that they are based in observation rather than introspection alone; they are *ethnographic*, in that they seek to understand the rhetorical workings of discourse and context through the eyes and minds of those engaged in them; and they are *grounded*, returning again and again to their data as they build theory to account for it.

Originating in an analytical heuristic rather than in a pre-chosen theoretical framework, these studies illustrate the potential of discourse-based, observation-driven theory building for rhetorical studies and criticism. As the focus of rhetoric widens from the planned to the spontaneous and from the public to the private, rhetoricians acknowledge the need for new methods, and they will find some illustrated here. Discourse analysts may likewise discover some new tools. The first theorists of discourse in the Greco-Roman intellectual tradition were the philosophers and sophists who described and taught public speaking to those citizens whose voices mattered in a newly democratic fifth-century BCE Athens, and the authors whose work appears here represent the reinvigoration of this tradition, particularly in North America, in the "new rhetoric" of the later twentieth century. In new ways, many of these studies draw on the traditional analytical tools of rhetoric – figures of speech, topoi, lines of argument; invention and style; ethos, logos, and pathos – showing how they can inform and be informed by discourse analysts' attention to how lexicon and syntax can evoke styles, genres, and prior texts and speakers, and thereby create social relations and experiential worlds in talk and writing.

Methods and issues in North American rhetorical studies

Rhetoricians have always taken an inclusive approach to analytic method. In addition to using the analytic vocabulary of classical rhetoric, practitioners have borrowed and adapted methods from other disciplines, taking intuition-based reasoning from philosophy, for example, and *explication de texte* techniques and a variety of critical-theoretical lenses from literary and sociological theory. These tools were developed to answer questions about the carefully planned, often institutional genres that were the primary object of rhetorical critique. The focus of rhetoricians' attention is widening, however, from public to private spheres, from official to vernacular rhetoric, from oratory to written and multimedia discourse, from the carefully crafted to spontaneous discourse emerging from fleeting everyday rhetorical situations. Now we are asking not just about the rhetoric of politics, but also about the rhetoric of history and the rhetoric of popular culture; not just about the rhetoric of the public sphere but about rhetoric on the street, in the hair salon, or online; not just about the rhetoricity of formal argument but also about the rhetoricity of personal identity. To address these new concerns and sites, we need to continue to supplement traditional modes of work with new techniques for analyzing the language of text and talk and with ways of describing the sociocultural and material contexts of discourse.

Since at least as long ago as the Wingspread conference in 1970, evaluations of the health of rhetoric as a discipline have stressed the widening, deepening object of rhetorical study and the need for appropriate methods and conceptual frameworks for exploring this object. In the proceedings of that conference (Bitzer & Black 1971), particularly in articles by Becker, Brockriede, and Henry

Johnstone discussing trends in the field, the momentum in rhetoric was observed to be moving out from a speaker-audience dyadic, text-bounded model of study toward studies of communication processes and interactions, situated and constituted in rich, real-world settings. Rhetorical analysis and criticism were no longer being applied only to historical works, but also to contemporary communication. Rhetorical scholarship no longer focused only on institutionalized speech situations, but was increasingly turning to experiments, to interactive and everyday speech genres, and to other studies of meaning-making as situated activity.

As Brockriede (1971) observed, this trajectory would require the conceptual and methodological flexibility needed to "let the transaction [under study] itself suggest its own analytic categories," while maintaining lively connections with established theoretical inquiry so as not to become isolated and trivial. This trajectory in the discipline, acknowledged again in more recent reflections (cf. Benson 1993; Enos & McNabb 1996; Gross & Keith 1997; Cherwitz & Hikins 2000; Schiappa et al. 2002; Simons 2003), has demanded the development of conceptual and methodological frameworks beyond, while not wholly independent from, those already institutionalized, such as the Burkean and Neo-Aristotelian. Where these traditional approaches to rhetorical criticism have been discussed as heuristics for invention and interpretation as much as they are methods for systematic analysis (Nothstine et al. 1994), some rhetoricians have turned to linguistic discourse analysis for that sought-after conceptual and methodological flexibility. Tracy (2001) describes the connections that have emerged between communication studies and discourse analysis. Scholars in rhetoric and composition studies have also issued calls for the inclusion of discourse analytic methods. MacDonald has termed discourse studies "the interconnected fields of rhetoric and composition and applied linguistics" (2002). Barton (2002) has suggested that composition studies can benefit from discourse analytic approaches particularly in "connections between texts and contexts, with a focus on the repeated use of linguistic features ... and the associated conventions that establish their meaning and significance in context" (285).

One way of describing the contribution this volume makes is in terms of a set of general issues that are both current and fertile for rhetorical theory-building: context, agency, and the relationship between style and argument. In the following discussion, we sketch trajectories within these issues toward grounded analyses of discourse, demonstrating how rhetoricians have and can further benefit from discourse analytic approaches.

Context and agency

Among rhetoric's most fundamental disciplinary practices has been the study of discourse in context. In his treatise on rhetoric, Aristotle discussed the components of a speaking situation and very clearly established the connection of rhetoric to public, civic discourse. Rhetoric's self-imposed limitation to civic discourse alone has passed, but its central premise that discourse must be shaped by context has not.

Similarly foundational is rhetoric's interest in the power and choices a rhetor – a speaker or writer – brings into a situation. Some definitions of rhetorical discourse distinguish it primarily through the assumption that it is discourse that is intended to change, and capable of changing, the situation for which it was designed. Hence, agency is an essential feature of rhetorical problem spaces. Leff, for example, discusses agency as a source of tension between enlightenment conceptualizations of the self and post-modern critiques of these conceptualizations, in a sophistic and Ciceronian tradition which he renames "humanistic rhetoric":

> The humanistic approach entails a productively ambiguous notion of agency that positions the orator both as an individual who leads an audience and as a community member shaped and constrained by the demands of the audience. ... [This tradition may] include a suspicious attitude toward abstract theory not only in respect to rhetoric, but also to ethics and politics, a conviction that discourse, especially discourse that allows for argument on both sides of an issue, has a constitutive role to play in civic life; a valorization and idealization of eloquence that entails a strong connection between eloquence and virtue; and a conception of virtue that is decisively linked to political activity.   (Leff 2003: 135, 136)

Attempting to define and study rhetorical spaces, and the tensions between presumed rhetorical agency and acknowledged constraints of context, has proven to be one of contemporary rhetoric's most productive theoretical problems (cf. Bitzer 1968; Vatz 1973). And it is in relation to this problem space that rhetorical studies have engaged the challenge of describing the interaction of rhetorical agency and context. In the last few decades, work stemming from Habermasian public sphere theory (1989) has provided a productive way of thinking about this intersection. In rhetorical studies, a central concern is with the study of concrete, agentive discourse in the public sphere. As Hauser has written,

> At its best, a democracy's rhetoric is untidy by Enlightenment standards of reason. Consequently, some thinkers, such as Habermas, who have been the staunchest champions of discourse as democracy's anchoring concept, have found the strategic impulses of rhetoric problematic. But excluding rhetorical processes from our assessment of democracy's ongoing conversation also excludes the agency by which democratic decisions are reached. Before we can rehabilitate public life, we first must understand the way actually occurring discourse shapes it. Otherwise, whatever critique we advance or remedy we propose is entirely analytic, producing conclusions that follow logically from *a priori* assumptions about the rational/ideological standards for "valid" assent but that lack an empirical referent in the actual discursive method that members of publics employ. (Hauser 1999: 273)

Hauser's positive program, then, is to adopt an empirical attitude toward the study of how rhetors act in publics, valorizing the study of vernacular discourses over theoretical generalizations based on the solitary reading of institutional discourses. This resonates with Asen's (2004) admonition to develop a sense of the democratic citizen by shifting "from *what* constitutes citizenship to *how* citizenship proceeds," and with Simons' (2000) admonition to "proceed to the particular, the local, the unique – to a theory of the specific event – out of which one could then derive a sense of limits and possibilities and of the tradeoffs involved in selecting this option rather than that" (448–9). Illustrating this pursuit, Johnstone (1996) uses discourse analysis to investigate how the complex of rhetorical agency and context is constituted in discourse, and McCormick (2003) focuses rhetorical analyses on vernacular discourses which could benefit from CDA.

Style and argument

Throughout its history, rhetoric's fraught relationship with style has drawn it in and out of favor with other disciplines. The scope of this perpetual interest in style has shifted, of course. Much of the conflict between sophist and Platonic/Aristotelian traditions revolved around the significance of style and of style's role as a central component in rhetorical practice, teaching, and theory. During the Middle Ages, when philosophers such as Ramus deemed invention to be the realm of dialectic and philosophy, rhetoric retained a position as the art overseeing style, alongside delivery (Conley 1990). More recently, the mid-twentieth century's "new" rhetoric (Perelman & Olbrechts-Tyteca 1969) can be distinguished in part by its interest in style as constitutive rather than merely ornamental. Several conceptual developments, which did not so much occur in the mid-twentieth as disciplinarily cohere then, mark the current rhetorical attitude toward style. For example, Burkean treatments of metaphor (Burke 1945, 1950) depart rather dramatically from the Aristotelian (1991) discussion of metaphors as other names, into an appreciation for the knowledge-making work of metaphor and the essentially metaphoric nature of rhetorical practices.

Rhetorical studies of style should include levels of analysis that discourse studies can inform, still engaging the resonances for which style remains a useful concern in rhetorical studies (MacDonald 2002). Herndl, Fennell, and Miller (1991) demonstrate the need to study texts at multiple levels (linguistic, semantic, argument) to engage both the evidence and the critical framework of discourse adequately. In rhetorical analyses of political discourse, concerns for style are often attached to constitutive force. Several studies have followed Charland's (1987) influential discussion of how language choices in significant political texts constitute agents and agentive communities. One recent example is Cordova's (2004) study of a Puerto Rican populist campaign of the mid-twentieth century.

Rhetoric's interest in invention – the finding and creating of arguments, and more generally the making of meaning – has been both a part of its foundation and also, during some periods of its history, banished from its discipline. Contemporary rhetorical studies have renewed the interest in invention (cf. Young & Liu 1994), both in relation to composition studies and in terms of epistemic rhetoric, or the study of how meaning or knowledge is made via rhetorical processes. Several studies have advocated discourse analytic methods for analyzing invention behaviors in composition classrooms (Sperling 1994; Hodges 1994), and some focus on micro-rhetorical features in these moments as opportunities for studying classroom invention and invention in writing pedagogy (Hillocks 1994; Strauss & Xiang 2006).

Further connecting the rhetor to the community, many rhetoricians and communications scholars have used the intersection of style and argument as a way to typify rhetorical discourse and characterize types of practices. The Aristotelian classification of public discourses as forensic, epideictic, and deliberative included components of types of appeals being made (and the types of proofs on which they operated), but also discussed expectations of stylistic features which would typify each mode. This tradition persists in studies of genre or typification, often through combined attention to style and argument. Dunmire's work, for example, (2005, 2000, this volume) examines the role of constructions of temporality in genres that involve shaping the future. Illustrative studies of typical practices within disciplines include Winsor (2000, 1999), Bazerman (2000), Myers (2003) and Fahnestock and Secor (1991).

What is discourse analysis?

Linguists who refer to themselves as discourse analysts explore what can be learned about language and about speakers by studying language in use. Unlike generative linguists in the Chomskyan tradition, they examine written texts or transcripts of spoken or manually signed discourse rather than relying on their own intuitions about grammatical possibilities. They are interested in the structure and function of pieces of talk or text that are larger than a single sentence, and in how the structure of sentences is influenced by how they function in the linguistic and social contexts in which they are deployed. By "discourse," they mean actual instances of talk, writing, or linguistic communication in some other medium. Some discourse analysts explicitly try to link features of discourse in this sense with aspects of what scholars in the Foucauldian tradition call "discourses": circulating sets of ideas and social practices that may include ways of talking. Other discourse analysts have other agendas. Some are interested in the kinds of questions linguists have always asked: questions about how language is represented in the mind, how the production and interpretation of discourse can best be modeled, how languages change, how language is acquired, and so on. Others explore the linkages between discursive and social phenomena in a wide variety of contexts, including institutional communication, the discursive construction of identity and memory, political discourse, organizational behaviour, communication in families, and so on.

Along with other strands of contemporary linguistics, discourse analysis has historical roots in nineteenth-century philology, in other words in diachronic (historical) language study aimed at the exegesis of texts. Following Ferdinand de Saussure's (1916) call to refocus language study on synchronic structure, dominant approaches for most of the twentieth century attended to sounds, phrases, and clauses rather than connected discourse. Beginning in the 1960s, however, linguists working in several intellectual traditions began to converge on two related ideas about discourse: (1) the idea that the structure of phrases and sentences is shaped in part by how they function in conversations and texts, and (2) the idea that texts and conversations are shaped, just as sentences are, by repeatable patterns of structure that could be called "grammar." In the U.K., M. A. K. Halliday, building on work by J. R. Firth, began to develop "systemic-functional grammar" and to ask about how sentences cohere with others in texts (Halliday 1994; Eggins 1994). In the U.S., Kenneth Pike and other linguists associated with the Summer Institute of Linguistics developed a similarly function-based way of understanding sentence and discourse structure, which they called tagmemic grammar (Pike 1967). At the same time, the emergence of variationist sociolinguistics, Conversation Analysis, and interactional sociolinguistics, and the ethnography of communication brought discourse into the purview of students of language change, the sociology of language, and anthropological linguistics, respectively (Labov 1963, 1972; Sacks, Schegloff, & Jefferson 1974; Ten Have 1999; Gumperz 1982; Gumperz & Hymes 1972).

In France, Marxist linguists began to explore how ideology is constructed in and revealed through discourse (Pêcheux 1969). Somewhat later, linguists influenced by Birmingham-school social theory brought a similarly critical approach to discourse to Anglophone attention, proposing that, since discourse analysis could never be simply descriptive, its goal should be to uncover how power circulates, usually invisibly, in discourse (Fairclough 1992, 2003; Wodak 1996, 2005, see also the introduction to Section II of this volume,). This approach, usually called Critical Discourse Analysis, remains influential, and several of the chapters in this volume draw on it. Other current work by discourse analysts is more eclectic, drawing on pragmatics, sociolinguistics, and interactional linguistics and on various strands of argumentation, rhetorical, sociological, literary, and anthropological theory. Many discourse analysts, particularly those whose disciplinary homes are in linguistics, continue to be interested primarily in questions about language, but the use of discourse analysis, however defined, as a systematic, grounded method of analysis has become increasingly interdisciplinary. Textbooks no longer presuppose that all discourse analysts are linguists; instruction in discourse analysis is offered, sometimes in the context of programs in "discourse studies," in various academic specialities; and journals such as *Discourse Studies*, *Discourse in Society*, *Discourse and Communication* and *Text and Talk* publish the work of people with a variety of disciplinary affiliations.

A heuristic approach to discourse

The discourse analyses illustrated in the chapters in this volume all start in work by A.L. Becker (1995, see also Johnstone 2008). We begin our work with a heuristic technique, a particularistic, interpretive, but systematic approach to unpacking why a given text is the way it is. Discourse analysts work with material of many kinds, including transcripts of audio- or videorecorded interactions, written documents, texts transmitted via oral tradition such as proverbs, and printouts of online communication. Their material sometimes consists of words alone and sometimes includes pictures, gestures, gaze, and other modalities. But no matter what sort of discourse we consider, the basic question a discourse analyst asks is "Why is this stretch of discourse the way it is? Why is it no other way? Why these particular words in this particular order?"

To answer these questions, we obviously need to think about what our "text" is about, since clearly what a person is talking about has a bearing on what is said and how it is said. We also need to think about who said it, or who wrote it or signed it, who is thought, in its particular sociocultural context, to be responsible for what it says, who the intended audience was and who the actual hearers or readers were, because who the participants in a situation are and how their roles are defined clearly influences what gets said and how. We need to think about what motivated the text, about how it fits into the set of things people in its context conventionally do with discourse, and about what its medium (or media) of production has to do with what it is like. We need to think about the language it is in, what that language encourages speakers and writers to do and what is relatively difficult to do in that language. We need to think about the text's structure and how it fits into larger structures of sets of texts and sets of interactions.

We can divide the questions that need to be asked about a text into six broad categories. Each of these categories corresponds to one way that contexts shape texts and texts shape contexts. Each of these aspects of text-building is both a source of constraint – a reason why texts are typically some ways and not others – and a resource for creativity, as speakers, signers, and writers express themselves by manipulating the patterns that have become conventional.

– Discourse is shaped by the world, and discourse shapes the world.
– Discourse is shaped by language, and discourse shapes language.
– Discourse is shaped by participants, and discourse shapes participants.
– Discourse is shaped by prior discourse, and discourse shapes the possibilities for future discourse.
– Discourse is shaped by its medium, and discourse shapes the possibilities of its medium.
– Discourse is shaped by purpose, and discourse shapes possible purposes.

Figure 1. How discourse is shaped by and shapes its context

Figure 1 lists these six aspects of the shaping of texts. These six observations about discourse constitute a heuristic for exploring, in a systematic way, what is potentially interesting and important about a text or a set of texts. A *heuristic* is a set of discovery procedures for systematic application or a set of topics for systematic consideration. Unlike the procedures in a set of instructions, the procedures of a heuristic do not need to be followed in any particular order, and there is no fixed way of following them. A heuristic is not a mechanical set of steps, and there is no guarantee that using it will result in a single definitive explanation. A good heuristic draws on multiple theories rather than just one. The heuristic we use here forces us to think, for example, about how discourse is shaped by ideologies that circulate power in society, but it also forces us to think about how discourse is shaped by people's memories of previous discourse, along with other sources of creativity and constraint. We may end up deciding, in a particular project, that the most useful approach will be one that gives us ways of identifying how ideology circulates through discourse, or that the most useful approach will be one that helps us describe "intertextuality," or that the most useful approach will be one that helps uncover the relationships between the text and its medium, the language it is in, or its producers' goals or social relationships. The heuristic is a first step in analysis which helps the analyst see what sorts of theory are needed in order to connect the particular observations about discourse made as one uses the heuristic with general statements about language, human life, or society. It is a way to ground discourse analysis in discourse, rather than starting with a pre-chosen theory and using texts to test or illustrate the theory.

Locating the heuristic in rhetorical theory

Each of the six elements of our analytical heuristic draws on a body of thought about language and communication that is, at least in part, already familiar to rhetoricians. The claim that texts and interpretations of texts are shaped by the world and shape the world is rooted in rhetorical and linguistic theory about the role of reference in the production and interpretation of discourse. Discourse arises out of the world or worlds that are presumed to exist outside of discourse, the worlds of the creators and interpreters of texts. Whether or not discourse is thought to be about something is relevant to how it is interpreted. Discourse that is thought not to refer to anything may be seen as nonsensical or crazy; it may be the result of a linguistic experiment like Dadaism in poetry; it may be required in ritual. The Western tradition of thought about language has tended to privilege referential discourse and to imagine that discourse (at least ideally) reflects the pre-existing world. But as twentieth-century philosophers (Foucault 1980), rhetoricians (Burke 1945), and linguists (Sapir 1949; Whorf 1941) showed us again and again, the converse is also true, or perhaps truer: human worlds are shaped by discourse.

When we point to how texts and their interpretations are shaped by the structural resources that are available, we are adducing the fact (well known to rhetoricians interested in style and arrangement) that there are conventionalized ways of structuring texts on all levels. Speaking a language, such as English or Korean, means using conventional ways of structuring syllables (a new English word could start with the syllable *pri* but not with *ngi*), conventional ways of structuring words (the *-s* that shows that an English word is plural goes after the stem, not before), conventional ways of structuring sentences (in declarative written English sentences, the subject typically precedes the predicate). Likewise, there are conventional ways of structuring larger chunks of discourse, some culturally specific and others resulting from what human cognition is like. They include ways of moving from familiar information to new information, for example, or moving from examples to general claim or from general claim to examples, or moving from question to response.

The claim that discourse is shaped by interpersonal relations among participants and helps shape interpersonal relations should bring to mind traditional ways of thinking about audience and rhetorical ethos, as well as newer ways of thinking about how speaking positions and roles are mutually shaped and enabled, in the context of larger structures of power. The interpersonal relations connected with discourse include the relations among the speakers and writers, audiences, and overhearers who are represented in texts, as well as the relations among speakers and writers, audiences, and overhearers who are involved in producing and interpreting texts.

The observation, next in the heuristic, that discourse is shaped by expectations created by familiar discourse, and new instances of discourse help shape our expectations about future discourse, should also be familiar to rhetoricians engaged with contemporary theory about genre (Miller 1984; Swales 1990) and intertextuality (Bakhtin 1986). Intertextual relations among texts enable people to interpret new instances of discourse with reference to familiar activities and familiar categories of style and form. The uses of discourse are as varied as human cultures are, but often-repeated activities involving discourse give rise to relatively fixed ways of proceeding with the activities, and these ways of proceeding often include relatively fixed, routinized ways of talking and types of texts.

Visual rhetoricians (Handa 2004; Prelli 2006) and others interested in multi-modality (Hodge & Kress 1988; Levine & Scollon 2004; Scollon & Scollon 2003) should also be sympathetic to the claim that discourse is shaped by the limitations and possibilities of its media, and the possibilities of communications media are shaped by their uses in discourse. Finally, the observation that discourse is shaped by purpose is at the root of the discipline of rhetoric, and the idea that discourse also shapes possible purposes should resonate with anyone who thinks about how epideictic or deliberative rhetoric works in contemporary contexts.

Starting out by interrogating texts in all the ways suggested by the heuristic means that analysis starts with the texts and a systematic way of thinking about possibly relevant contexts. This results in a broad, multidimensional, "thick" description (Geertz 1983). Having done that, the analyst is in a position to focus on one or two questions, taking any of a number of approaches to fleshing out the details. The papers in this volume illustrate some of these approaches, some of the ways in which linguistic discourse analysis can provide a grounded, rigorous set of analytical methods for answering a variety of rhetorical questions. Different authors focus on different elements of the heuristic. In each case, though, the authors pay systematic attention to the ways that texts and discourses are shaped and enabled, in the context of close attention to the structural and semantic characteristics of particular instances of text and talk.

Discourse analysis in contemporary research in rhetoric

Although many rhetorical critics are not familiar with discourse analysis, they have colleagues who are. English department rhetoric-and-composition specialists have long looked to linguistics as a source of ideas and methods (cf. Cooper & Greenbaum 1986; Raskin & Weiser 1987). Compositionists Barton and Stygall note that "the analysis of discourse is basic to the enterprise of composition studies: Every study in the field is based implicitly or explicitly on the analysis of texts and/or talk in their various contexts" (Barton & Stygall 2002: 1). Barton and Stygall's volume collects work by linguists and rhetoricians (and scholars who are both) having to do with writing in general, academic writing, second-language writing, and scientific and professional discourse, as well as analyses of discourse in writing classrooms. Bazerman and Prior's (2004) volume focuses on methods for studying writing, including linguistic discourse analysis. Students interested in quantitative text analysis can turn to Geisler's (2004) textbook, and Kaufer and his colleagues (Kaufer & Butler 2000; Kaufer et al. 2004) have developed an automated text-analysis system based on rhetorical principles. Critical discourse analysis has also resonated with students of literacy (Gee 2005).

In North American communications departments, discourse analysis is often practiced not by rhetoricians but by people studying interpersonal or organizational communication, media discourse, or argumentation. Ethnographers of communication like Philipsen (1992) and Carbaugh (2005) do discourse analyses, as do scholars like Tracy (2002) and Fitch (1998) in the "language in social interaction" tradition. Jacobs and Jackson (1982) have developed a theory of argumentation based on the principles of Conversation Analysis, and Critical Discourse Analysis is popular in communications programs. However, people who think of their work as rhetorical criticism or rhetorical theory have yet to see a collection of articles that introduce discourse analysis to them and show them its utility for answering the kinds of questions they ask. The approaches to discourse analysis we offer and exemplify in this book are meant to illustrate the many productive ways close, rigorous attention to language can pay off for rhetoricians.

Chapter themes

We have arranged the book topically. Section II consists of studies of style and legitimation in carefully crafted and relatively formal political discourse. Section III consists of studies of identity and agency in media discourse and in interaction, both face-to-face and computer-mediated. Section IV consists of studies of the ways controversy is entextualized and enacted, in media discourse as well as in interactions in mundane public spaces. Each section begins with an introduction focused on the analytic methods the section's authors employ. These introductions are meant to provide brief overviews of some of the ways discourse analysts work, together with references to key sources.

The four chapters in Section II all focus on sentence- and paragraph-level features of discourse which would fall within the traditional rhetorical canon of style. They explore how small grammatical and rhetorical choices contribute to the political activity of legitimation, or the discursive representation and reification of institutional power and its exercise. Patricia L. Dunmire and Susan Lawrence discuss the ways linguistic constructions constitute particular kinds of claims and evidence, typifying or confounding the conceptual categories of deliberative and epideictic genres. Dunmire's chapter has to do with how the future is linguistically represented in political discourse and with the rhetorical functions of such representations. Dunmire sees the future as a discursive construct which rhetors embed within and project through the linguistic design of their texts, and, which thereby functions in deliberative discourse to ground and legitimate specific calls to action. Lawrence explores how the design of the amnesty hearings that were part of the South African Truth and Reconciliation Commission's work affected how responsibility was talked about. Lawrence draws together the rhetorical concepts of epideictic discourse, to describe the TRC's intention that the hearings help create social cohesion in South Africa, and figuration, to catalog the ways that applicants' testimony was shaped by the TRC's rules about what could count as a valid argument for amnesty. She explores how amnesty applicants named and otherwise characterized their victims, often in ways that made the victims appear to share responsibility for their abuse.

Andreea Deciu Ritivoi and Christopher Eisenhart each discuss how stylistic moves and variations constitute political agents and political actions. Ritivoi explores how, during the Cold War, the leader of a would–be Romanian government in exile used the sorts of micro-rhetorical strategies traditionally thought of as stylistic choices to project an aura of political legitimacy. Her analysis shows how letters he wrote to representatives of the U.S. government made strategic use of *transitivity*, to convey assertiveness and self-confidence, and *modality*, to depict the Romanian refugees as united under his leadership and committed to the fight against communism. Eisenhart compares the official reports of two U.S. government agencies involved in a 1993 standoff between government agents and the members of a religious community near Waco, Texas. He shows how both reports draw on conventional features of bureaucratic genre and style to represent the events in such a way as to reassert the government's control over the story. In particular, Eisenhart examines how the characters in the story were construed through choices about transitivity and naming and how the metadiscursive framing of the reports – the talk in them about how they were created, and by whom – also serves to apportion responsibility and blame.

The four studies in section III illuminate the context-agency problem space. Studying media discourse, computer-mediated communication, and face-to-face talk, the authors focus on identity and agency, issues that are of current concern across the humanistic and social scientific disciplines. In his study of the debate surrounding a controversial medical treatment for deafness, the cochlear implant, Sean Zdenek shows how the representation of others' voices and languages can deprive them of rhetorical agency. Zdenek's chapter asks "Who has the right to speak for deaf people? To what extent are deaf voices spoken for by the mainstream media?" He finds that members of the Deaf community are regarded as lacking a recognizable rhetorical voice. Like Zdenek, Amanda Young considers a population that sometimes lacks a rhetorical voice. Young's research site is an after-school program for girls at risk of unplanned pregnancy, where Young developed and tested an interactive computer program meant to encourage the girls to re-imagine themselves as rhetorical agents, ready to make themselves heard.

Martha S. Cheng and Neeta Bhasin each study ways that identity formation arises as a response to rhetorical exigency. In her analysis of an online chatroom that was part of a distance-learning course for software–development managers, Cheng shows how brief narrative allusions to personal experience help construct professional identities for students and their teacher. Bhasin explores the rhetorical usefulness of the nonce concepts of "Indian humor" and "American humor," which arise in a conversation among students from India in the U.S. Elaborating on this fleetingly imagined contrast helps Indian students differentiate themselves from their American colleagues and constructs them as an ethnic community, even though they would be seen as culturally and ethnically diverse in their home environment.

The three chapters in Section IV examine the ways controversy (and debate) arise and are bounded in their own participants' discourse. As Cramer suggests in his chapter, rhetorical conceptions of "controversy" have often borrowed commonsensical definitions of the term and treated it as an *a priori* conceptual frame applied to certain kinds of discourse. The three chapters here each spotlight the constitution of controversy and debate from within, as it is built and bounded in media discourse and in everyday public spaces.

Craig O. Stewart's study of a scientific controversy problematizes the rhetorical conception of argumentative spheres, reconceptualizing normative, clearly bounded spheres in terms of looser, less stabilized orders of discourse (a concept he borrows from Foucault via critical discourse analysis). Stewart's analysis of how arguments about "reparative therapy" for homosexuality cross from the scientific order of discourse to the popular and back demonstrates the permeability of the boundaries between ways of speaking. In his study of a corpus of print media accounts about an art exhibition in Brooklyn, New York, Peter A. Cramer explores how media representations call a controversy into being by creating it as an "event category." Genre, he argues, is rhetorically constructed or assigned by being made relevant in discourse. Questioning the perceived lack of functional public discourse in the U.S., Susan Gilpin systematically observed mundane public spaces, examining the discourse therein for substantive engagement with significant and controversial public topics. Gilpin's participant-observational study of clients and stylists interacting in hair salons explores the conditions under which people engage in the kind of open-minded, exploratory discourse about public issues that can result in change rather than entrenchment.

The intellectual history of this book

As we have noted above, all the authors whose work appears here are in some way affiliated with the Rhetoric Program in the English Department at Carnegie Mellon University. Ritivoi and Johnstone are on the program's faculty, and the others earned their Ph.D.s in Rhetoric there between 1996 (Dunmire) and 2007 (Bhasin).

At Carnegie Mellon, the tradition of exploring the links between rhetoric and discourse studies has a history dating to the 1970s and early 1980s, when discourse analysis was just being proposed in linguistics and when rhetoric was just being rediscovered in English studies. In 1975, Richard Young, then on the faculty of the Humanities Department in the School of Engineering at the University of Michigan, and A.L Becker, his friend and colleague in the Department of Linguistics there, together with Kenneth Pike, Becker's mentor and one of the first American theorists of discourse, published an extremely influential textbook for writing courses (Young, Becker, & Pike 1975). *Rhetoric: Discovery and Change* was one of the first such texts to be based on rhetorical principles and one of the first to expect students to approach texts in somewhat the way a field linguist might.

Partly on the strength of that book, Young was hired by Carnegie Mellon's English Department to start an undergraduate program in professional and technical writing. He also founded the Ph.D. program that accepted its first students in 1980, one of the first such programs in Rhetoric. Students in the program would address questions about writing and writing instruction in richly interdisciplinary ways, combining ideas from classical Greco-Roman rhetorical theory with ideas from cognitive psychology, computer science, design, organizational sociology, and linguistics. Since then there has always been at least one discourse analyst on the program's faculty, and close attention to the details of language and text have always been a hallmark of its students' and faculty's work.

A.L. Becker was a continuing influence, visiting Young often and lecturing to the students in the Rhetoric Program. At the University of Michigan, Becker's students in linguistics were encouraged to think in innovative interdisciplinary ways, just as Becker does (Becker 1995). As early as the 1970s, they read Pike's work and the work of a growing number of other linguists about the structural characteristics of discourse, but they also read discourse theory from anthropology (such as Geertz), critical theory (Ricoeur, Propp, Derrida), sociology (Goffman), and cognitive psychology (Shank and others on frames and schemas). Becker's students from that era were among the first linguists to call themselves discourse analysts, and they have been able to watch the field mature in theoretical nuance and intellectual stature. Johnstone, this volume's senior editor, was one of those students. Her interest in persuasive discourse across languages led her, with Becker's encouragement, to courses in the history and theory of rhetoric. Johnstone's move to Pittsburgh in 1997 thus retraced the intellectual route between linguistics and rhetoric, and between the University of Michigan and Carnegie Mellon University, that had been mapped decades earlier by Young and Becker.

A more recent impetus was a panel at the 2002 meeting of the Rhetoric Society of America that was meant to illustrate how discourse analysis could be of use to rhetorical critics. Audience members were interested, but if "discourse" had any prior resonance with them, they were thinking of Foucault and structures of power, taking a macroscopic view without connecting it to a microscopic one. We sensed that there was a gap our work could fill in rhetorical studies, and since then we have heard more and more explicit calls from rhetoricians for new ways of thinking about new modes of discourse. We are happy to find ourselves positioned to describe and illustrate some of these.

Above all, this project was made possible by the Rhetoric Program at Carnegie Mellon, where interdisciplinary collaboration, close attention to language and to method, and a generous sense of the purview of rhetorical studies are unremarkable. We are grateful to department head David Kaufer for encouraging faculty and students alike to think around disciplinary boundaries and beyond the rhetorical canon, and to the rest of our colleagues and students at CMU for asking us to explain what we do and why and being interested in our answers. We are grateful too for the support and feedback from colleagues at UMass Dartmouth, particularly from Catherine Houser and Jerry Blitefield. We are also grateful to Ruth Wodak and Greg Myers, editors of the series in which this book appears, for seeing its potential; to two anonymous reviewers they recruited; and to Isja Conen at Benjamins in Amsterdam for seeing the manuscript into production.

References

Aristotle and George A. Kennedy. 1991. *On Rhetoric: A Theory of Civic Discourse*. New York: Oxford UP.

Asen, Robert. 2004. "A Discourse Theory of Citizenship." *Quarterly Journal of Speech*. 90: 2. 189–211.

Bakhtin, Michael. 1986. *Speech Genres and Other Late Essays*, C. Emerson and M. Holquist, eds. Austin: University of Texas Press.

Barton, Ellen. 2002. "Resources for Discourse Analysis in Composition Studies." *Style*. 36: (4)575.

_____ and Gail Stygall. 2002. *Discourse Studies in Composition*. Cresskill, NJ: Hampton Press.

Bazerman, Charles, and Paul Prior, eds. 2004. *What Writing Does and How it Does it: An Introduction to Analyzing Texts and Textual Practices*. Mahwah, NJ: Lawrence Erlbaum.

_____. 2000. *Shaping Written Knowledge: The Genre and Activity of the Experimental Article in Science*. Madison: University of Wisconsin Press.

Becker, A. L. 1995. *Beyond Translation: Essays toward a Modern Philology*. Ann Arbor: University of Michigan Press.

Benson, Thomas, ed. 1993. *Landmark Essays on Rhetorical Criticism*. Davis, Calif.: Hermagoras Press.

Bitzer, Lloyd. 1968. "The Rhetorical Situation." *Philosophy and Rhetoric*. 1: 1–14.

_____ and Edwin Black, eds. 1971. *The Prospect of Rhetoric*. Englewood Cliffs, N.J.: Prentice Hall.

Brockriede, Wayne. 1971. "Trends in the Study of Rhetoric: Toward a Blending of Criticism and Science." *The Prospect of Rhetoric*. Lloyd Bitzer and Edwin Black, eds. Englewood Cliffs, N.J.: Prentice Hall.

Burke, Kenneth. 1945. *A Grammar of Motives*. Berkeley: University of California Press.

_____. 1969. *A Rhetoric of Motives*. Berkeley: University of California Press.

Carbaugh, Donal. 2005. *Cultures in Conversation*. Mahwah, NJ: Lawrence Erlbaum.

Charland, Maurice. 1987. "Constitutive Rhetoric: The Case of the Peuple Quebecois." *Quarterly Journal of Speech*. 73: 133–150.

Cherwitz, Richard A. and Hikins, James W. 2000. "Climbing the Academic Ladder: A Critique of Provincialism in Contemporary Rhetoric." *Quarterly Journal of Speech*. 86: 4. 375–385.

Conley, Thomas M. 1990. *Rhetoric in the European Tradition*. Chicago: University of Chicago Press.

Cooper, Charles R., and Sidney Greenbaum, eds. 1986. *Studying Writing: Linguistic Approaches*. Vol. 1, *Written Communication Annual*. Beverly Hills, Calif.: Sage.

Cordova, Nathaniel. 2004. "The Constitutive Force of the Catecismo del Pueblo in Puerto Rico's Popular Democratic Party Campaign of 1938–1940." *Quarterly Journal of Speech*. 90: 2. 212–233.

Dunmire, Patricia L. 2005. "Preempting the Future: Rhetoric and Ideology of the Future in Political Discourse." *Discourse and Society*. 16: 4. 481–513.

_____. 2000. "Genre as Temporally Situated Social Action: a Study of Temporality and Genre Activity." *Written Communication*. 17: 1.93–138.

Eggins, Suzanne. 1994. *An Introduction to Systemic Functional Linguistics*. London and New York: Pinter.

Enos, Theresa and Richard McNabb, eds. 1997. *Making and Unmaking the Prospects for Rhetoric*. Mawah, NJ: Lawrence Erlbaum Associates.

Fahnestock, J. and Secor, M. 1991. "The Rhetoric of Literary Criticism." *Textual Dynamics of the professions: Historical and Contemporary Studies of Writings in Professional Communities*. C. Bazerman and J. Paradis. eds. Madison: University of Wisconsin Press. 76–96.

Fairclough, Norman. 1992. *Discourse and Social Change*. Cambridge UK: Polity.

_____. 2003. *Analysing Discourse: Textual Analysis for Social Research*. London: Routledge.

Foucault, Michel. 1980. *Power/Knowledge: Selected Interviews and Other Writings, 1972–1977*. Edited by C. Gordon. New York: Pantheon.

Fitch, Kristine. 1998. *Speaking Relationally: Culture, Communication and Interpersonal Connections*. London: Guilford Press.

Gee, James Paul. 2005. *An Introduction to Discourse Analysis: Theory and Method*. 2nd ed. London: Routledge.

Geertz, Clifford. 1983. *Local Knowledge: Further Essays in Interpretive Anthropology*. New York: Basic Books.

Geisler, Cheryl. 2004. *Analyzing Streams of Language: Twelve Steps to the Systematic Coding of Text, Talk, and Other Verbal Data*. New York: Pearson Longman.

Gross, Alan G. and William M. Keith, eds. 1997. *Rhetorical Hermeneutics: Invention and Interpretation in the Age of Science*. Albany: State University of New York Press.

Gumperz, John J. 1982. *Discourse Strategies*. Cambridge: Cambridge University Press.

_____ and Dell Hymes eds. 1972. *Directions in Sociolinguistics: The Ethnography of Communication*. New York: Holt Rinehart Winston.

Habermas, Jürgen. 1989. *Structural Transformation of the Public Sphere*. Tr. by Thomas Burger. Cambridge, Mass: MIT Press.

Halliday, M. A. K. 1994. *An Introduction to Functional Grammar*. 2nd ed. London: Edward Arnold.

Handa, Carolyn, ed. 2004. *Visual Rhetoric in a Digital World: A Critical Sourcebook*. Boston: Bedford/St. Martins.

Hauser, Gerard. 1999. *Vernacular Voices: The Rhetoric of Publics and Public Spheres*. Columbia: University of South Carolina Press.

Herndl, Carl, Barbara Fennell, and Carolyn Miller. 1991. "Understanding Failures in Organizational Discourse: The Accident at Three Mile Island and the Shuttle Challenger Disaster," *Textual Dynamics of the Professions*. ed. by Charles Bazerman and James Paradis. Madison: University of Wisconsin Press. 279–30.

Hillocks Jr., George. 1994. "Interpreting and Counting: Objectivity in Discourse Analysis." *Speaking About Writing: Reflections on Research Methodology*. Peter Smagorinsky ed. Thousand Oaks, Calif.: Sage Publications. 185–204.

Hodge, Robert, and Gunther Kress. 1988. *Social Semiotics*. Cambridge, UK: Polity.

Hodges, Elizabeth. 1994. "What's all this Talk I Hear?: Using Sociolinguistic Analysis to Locate and Map Themes in Teacher/Student Talk About Writing." *Speaking About Writing: Reflections on Research Methodology*. ed. by Peter Smagorinsky. Thousand Oaks: Sage Publications: 225–246.

Jacobs, Scott, and Sally Jackson. 1982. "Conversational Argument: A Discourse Analytic Approach." In *Advances in Argumentation Theory and Research*, ed. by J. R. Cox and C. A. Willard. Carbondale and Edwardsville, Ill.: Southern Illinois University Press.

Johnstone, Barbara. 1996. *The Linguistic Individual: Self-Expression in Language and Linguistics*. New York: Oxford UP.

_____. 2008. *Discourse analysis,* 2nd. ed. Oxford: Blackwell.

Kaufer, David S., and Brian S. Butler. 2000. *Designing Interactive Worlds with Words: Principles of Writing as Representational Composition*. Mahwah, NJ: Lawrence Erlbaum.

_____, Suguru Ishizaki, Brian Butler, and Jeff Collins. 2004. *The Power of Words: Unveiling the Speaker and Writer's Hidden Craft*. Mahwah, NJ: Lawrence Erlbaum.

Labov, William. 1963. "The Social Motivation of a Sound Change." *Word* 19:237–309.

_____. 1972. *Sociolinguistic Patterns*. Philadelphia: University of Pennsylvania Press.

Leff, Michael. 2003. "Tradition and Agency in Humanistic Rhetoric." *Philosophy and Rhetoric*. 36: 2. 135–147.

Levine, Philip, and Ron Scollon, eds. 2004. *Discourse and Technology: Multimodal Discourse Analysis*. Washington, D.C.: Georgetown University Press.

MacDonald, Susan Peck. 2002. "Prose Styles, Genres, and Levels of Analysis." *Style*. 36:4. 618–39.

McCormick, Samuel. 2003. "Earning One's Inheritance: Rhetorical Criticism, Everyday Talk, and the Analysis of Public Discourse." *Quarterly Journal of Speech*. 89(2): 109–131.

Miller, Carolyn. 1984. "Genre as Social Action." *Quarterly Journal of Speech*. 70:151–167.

Myers, Greg. 2003. "Discourse Studies of Scientific Popularization: Questioning the Boundaries." *Discourse Studies*. 5:2.265–279.

Nothstine, William L., Carole Blair, and Gary A Copeland. 1994. "Invention in Media and Rhetorical Criticism: A General Orientation." *Critical Questions: Invention, Creativity, and the Criticism of Discourse and Media*. Nothstine, Blair, and Copeland, eds. New York: St. Martin's Press. 3–14.

Pêcheux, M. 1969. *Analyse Automatique du Discours*. Paris: Dunod.

Perelman, Ch. and L. Olbrechts-Tyteca. 1969. *The New Rhetoric: A Treatise on Argumentation*. Translated by John Wilkinson and Purcell Weaver. Notre Dame, Ind.: University of Notre Dame Press.

Philipsen, Gerry. 1992. *Speaking Culturally: Explorations in Social Communication*. Albany, N.Y.: State University of New York Press.

Pike, Kenneth L. 1967. *Language in Relation to a Unified Theory of the Structure of Human Behavior*. The Hague: Mouton.

Prelli, Lawrence J., ed. 2006. *Rhetorics of Display*. Columbia: University of South Carolina Press.

Raskin, Victor, and Irwin Weiser, eds. 1987. *Language and Writing: Applications of Linguistics to Rhetoric and Composition*. Norwood, N.J.: Ablex.

Sacks, Harvey, Emanuel A. Schegloff, and Gail Jefferson. 1974. "A Simplest Systematics for the Organization of Turntaking for Conversation." *Language* 50:696–735.

Sapir, Edward. 1949. *Selected Writings of Edward Sapir in Language, Culture, and Personality*. D. G. Mandlebaum, ed. Berkeley: University of California Press.

Saussure, Ferdinand. 1916. *Cours de Linguistique Générale*. Paris: Payot.

Schiappa, Edward, Alan G. Gross, Raymie E. McKerrow, and Rober L. Scott. 2002. "Rhetorical Studies as Reduction or Redescription? A Response to Cherwitz and Hikins." *Quarterly Journal of Speech*. 88:1. 112–120.

Scollon, Ron and Suzie Wong Scollon. 2003. *Discourses in Place: Language in the Material World*. London: Routledge.

Sperling, Melanie. 1994. "Discourse Analysis of Teacher-Student Writing Conferences: Finding the Message in the Medium." In *Speaking About Writing: Reflections on Research Methodology*. Peter Smagorinsky. ed. Thousand Oaks: Sage Publications. 205–224.

Simons, Herbert W. 2003. "The Globalization of Rhetoric and the Argument from Disciplinary Consequence." *Poroi*. 2: 2. http://inpress.lib.uiowa.edu/poroi/papers/simons031101.html

_____. 2000. "A Dilemma-Centered Analysis of Clinton's August 17th *Apologia*: Implications for Rhetorical Theory and Method." *Quarterly Journal of Speech*. 86: 4. 438–453.

Strauss, Susan, and Xiang, Xuehua. 2006. "The Writing Conference as Locus of Emergent Agency." *Written Communication*. 23: 4.355–396.

Swales, John M. 1990. *Genre Analysis: English in Academic and Research Settings*. Cambridge: Cambridge University Press.

Ten Have, P. 1999. *Doing Conversation Analysis: A Practical Guide*. London: Sage Publications.

Tracy, Karen. 2002. *Everyday Talk: Building and Reflecting Identities*: London: Guilford.

_____. 2001. "Discourse Analysis in Communication." *The Handbook of Discourse Analysis*. Deborah Schiffrin, Deborah Tannen, and Heidi E. Hamilton, eds. Malden, MA: Blackwell Publishers. 725–750.

Vatz, Richard E. 1973. "The Myth of the Rhetorical Situation." *Philosophy and Rhetoric*. 6: 154–161.

Winsor, Dorothy. 2000. "Ordering Work: Blue-Collar Literacy and the Political Nature of Genre," *Written Communication*, 17:2. 155–84.

_____. 1999. "Genre and Activity Systems: The Role of Documentation in Maintaining and Changing Engineering Activity Systems." *Written Communication*. 16.2. 200–24.

Whorf, Benjamin Lee. 1941. "The Relation of Habitual Thought and Behavior to Language." In *Language, Culture, and Personality: Essays in Memory of Edward Sapir*, ed. by L. Spier. Menasha, WI: Sapir Memorial Publication Fund.

Wodak, Ruth. 1996. *Disorders of Discourse*. London: Longman.

_____. 2005. *A New Agenda in (Critical) Discourse Analysis*. Amsterdam and Philadelphia: John Benjamins.

Young, Richard E., Alton L. Becker, and Kenneth L. Pike. 1970. *Rhetoric: Discovery and Change*. New York: Harcourt, Brace, and World.

_____ and Yameng Liu, eds. 1994. *Landmark Essays on Rhetorical Invention in Writing*. Davis, Calif.: Hermagoras Press.

PART II

Style and legitimation

Studying style and legitimation

Critical Linguistics and Critical Discourse Analysis

Sean Zdenek and Barbara Johnstone
Texas Tech University / Carnegie Mellon University

The chapters in this section all use methods associated with **Critical Linguistics** (CL) and **Critical Discourse Analysis** (CDA) to explore questions about one of the traditional foci of rhetorical scholarship, political discourse. Some of the chapters bring analytical categories from rhetorical studies, such as genre and figuration, into CDA. In this introduction to the section's methods, we sketch the history of Critical Linguistics and Critical Discourse Analysis and provide an overview of their key techniques, which typically involve looking systematically at one or more of the often unnoticed details of grammar or word choice. These details can help the critic understand not only how texts give presence to a particular picture of the world but also how linguistic choices signal one or more of the authors' possible underlying motives.

As rhetoricians have always known, all discourse – spoken or written, highly planned or completely spontaneous – requires choices about how to present things, and these choices are never neutral. Contemporary rhetorical studies have focused mainly on choices of the more global sort, choices about what persuasive strategies and lines of argument to adopt and how to structure texts. In traditional rhetorical theory, these levels of choice are referred to with Aristotle's terms "invention" and "arrangement," respectively. For various historical reasons, what Aristotle called "style" became identified with the ornamentation of already-planned talk or writing, the flourishes that could be added to make already-persuasive discourse sound elegant. In the 20th century, the study of style came to be seen as less important than the study of invention and arrangement, to the point that some influential approaches to the teaching of writing and to rhetorical criticism ignored sentence-level grammar and word choice altogether. Although this gap was being criticized as early as the 1950s (Bryant 1957; Redding 1957), rhetorical theory has only slowly moved away from an approach to criticism focused more on history and biographical context than on rhetorical texts themselves (Mohrmann & Leff 1974) and toward a broader conception of style that emphasizes its ideological dimensions and the ways in which it is connected with identity (Hariman 1995; Carpenter 1994; Murphy 1997).

Meanwhile, almost the opposite was happening in linguistics. People whose primary expertise had to do with syntax and semantics became interested in talk and texts, at first in the context of what is traditionally known as "descriptive" linguistic research. Descriptive discourse analysis aims to show how utterances and texts are structured across languages, and to explore what new conceptual tools, in addition to already available models for words and sentences, are needed to understand conversations and paragraphs. Work of this kind is based in the idea that the primary goal of scholarly research is to describe the world, or whatever bit of the world the researcher is interested in.

The beliefs that underlie pure descriptivism have been called into question more and more urgently across the disciplines, under the influence of philosophical relativism and critical social theories such as Marxism. Relativism leads to skepticism about the possibility of "scientific truth" and encourages researchers to take a critical, self-conscious (or "reflexive") stance vis-à-vis their own work and the claims they make. Critical social theory describes the human world as characterized by dominance, exploitation, struggle, oppression, and power. People whose grounding is in theory of this sort attempt to show what is wrong with the status quo. They tend to be interested in the dominated groups rather than in those who dominate them; their research about struggles over power is (at least in principle) meant to help empower the relatively powerless.

Discourse analysis is now often used in the service of critical goals as well as descriptive ones. Two groups of researchers who are particularly identified with this trend have called their ways of working Critical Linguistics, or CL (Fowler, Hodge, Kress, & Trew, 1979; Hodge & Kress 1979) and Critical Discourse Analysis, or CDA (Fairclough 1985, 1992; van Dijk 1993; Wodak 1996). It should be stressed that there is far more research using discourse analysis that is critical in this sense than just the work explicitly associated with these two schools. Critical approaches to texts have a long tradition in North American anthropology and linguistics (Adams 1999), and these approaches have had considerable influence. More generally, discourse analysis is, at root, a highly systematic, thorough approach to critical reading (and listening), and critical reading almost inevitably leads to questioning the status quo and often leads to questions about power and inequality.

Although CDA has become increasingly eclectic, drawing analytical categories and methods from a variety of sources, CL and CDA both have their roots in Systemic Functional Linguistics, or SFL, a theory of grammar developed by British linguist M. A. K. Halliday (1994; Eggins 1994). The influence of SFL continues to be unmistakable (see Wodak 2001:8), because Halliday offers "clear and rigorous linguistic categories for analyzing the relationship between discourse and social meaning" (Blommaert & Bulcaen 2000:454).

SFL proposes that sentences take the forms they do for reasons that are neither arbitrary nor the result of innate mental structures, but rather for reasons connected with the functions utterances serve. One of these functions involves representing the world, or "ideation." In addition to representing the world, every utterance must also claim or signal something about who its speaker, its audience, and other participants in the communicative event should be taken to be (this is its "interpersonal" function) and how it is to be understood in the context of preceding and following discourse (its "textual" function). Halliday identified aspects of grammar that can serve each of these functions.

To give just one example of how choices among grammatical possibilities can make a difference, let us take a brief look at one of the key grammatical resources for ideational (world-representing) work, namely *transitivity*. A transitive clause is one that has a direct object. *Pete rides his bike to campus* has the direct object *his bike*, so it is a transitive clause. *Pete rides to campus*, on the other hand, is an intransitive clause, because it lacks a direct object. Speakers and writers can sometimes choose whether to use a transitive or an intransitive clause, and the choice can have ideational force. A child whose mother has just asked what happened to the glass bowl that was on the sideboard could say either "I dropped it" (transitive) or "It fell" (intransitive). Alternatively, the child could say "It got dropped," using a passive-voice construction. The transitive choice makes the responsibility for the accident clear; in the intransitive choice and the passive-voice choice, responsibility does not enter the picture.

CDA is not a set of tools or a methodology per se (see Fairclough 2001:121; Meyer 2001:14) but "a complex cluster of practices and approaches at the crossroads of several disciplines" (van Noppen 2004:108). Indeed, the theoretical foundations of CDA are rich, varied, and selectively applied among CDA practitioners. Yet despite the multiplicity of both approaches and underlying social theories, proponents tend to share a set of assumptions about discourse, readers, texts, and social reality:

– CDA "starts from prevailing social problems, and thereby chooses the perspective of those who suffer most" (van Dijk 1986:4). Critics advocate for those with limited power, limited or non-traditional forms of agency, oppressed groups, "the losers" (Fairclough 2001:125), and those deemed outside the mainstream.

– CDA is "emancipatory" (Fairclough 2001:125) and works for social change and social justice. "CDA scholars play an advocatory role for groups who suffer from social discrimination" (Meyer 2001:15).

- Problems of interest to CDA critics therefore intersect with areas where power and ideology are likely to circulate discursively (albeit not always visibly): "Gender issues, issues of racism, media discourses or dimensions of identity have become very prominent" (Wodak 2001:3). Popular also are studies of political discourse and economic discourse (especially globalization and economic change), advertising, institutional discourse (bureaucracy, governance), and education and literacy (see Blommaert & Bulcaen 2000:450–1). This list is by no means exhaustive: "What is problematic and calls for change is an inherently contested and controversial matter" (Fairclough 2001:125).
- Social problems may become naturalized, sedimented, conventionalized, invisible. The challenge for the CDA critic is to "'demystify' discourses by deciphering ideologies" (Wodak 2001:10). CDA "endeavours to make explicit power relationships which are frequently hidden" (Meyer 2001:14). "[D]iscourse is an opaque power object in modern societies and CDA aims to make it more visible and transparent" (Blommaert & Bulcaen 2000:448).
- Power, ideology, and history are key terms in CDA (Wodak 2001:3). Ideology "refers to social forms and processes within which, and by means of which, symbolic forms circulate in the social world" (Wodak 2001:10). CDA critics are particularly interested in the link between hegemonic ideologies and language. Power is typically defined, in keeping with Foucault's work, as both repressive and productive – and also "entwined" in language (p. 11). According to Jan Blommaert and Chris Bulcaen (2000:451), "A fundamental aspect of CDA is that it claims to take its starting point in social theory." In their review of CDA, they list a number of social theorists who have been influential to CDA critics, including Foucault ("orders of discourse," "power/knowledge"), Gramsci ("hegemony"), and Althusser ("ideology," "interpellation"). The focus on history is reflected, for example, in Ruth Wodak's "discourse-historical" approach (Wodak 2001; see also Krzyżanowski 2005 and Oberhuber 2005), which is "intent on tracing the (intertextual) history of phrases and arguments" across a wide range of discourses and practices (Blommaert & Bulcaen 2000:450). Also popular are theorists who have made explicit the link between discourse and power, such as Laclau (p. 450; see Jäger 2001:42).
- CDA is aggressively interdisciplinary and pluralist in both method and theory (Wodak & Weiss 2005:124). Fairclough (2005:53) has argued that interdisciplinary research should seek to transcend the particularities of each discipline through "dialogue." Wodak and Gilbert Weiss (2005:123) concur: "We believe that the interdisciplinary approach allows for some innovative and creative proposals, which the perspective from inside one traditional field might restrict."
- Social and linguistic categories are "basically not compatible" (Wodak & Weiss 2005:124), and need to be translated so that they can be channeled into a

common framework. Even when linguistic categories are identical in name to social categories, meanings may differ. How to move back and forth between macro views of society and micro views of discourse is the so-called "mediation problem" (124): "No such uniform theoretical framework of mediation has been proposed in CDA to date" (125).

- Discourse is a form of social practice. Accordingly, discourse is not merely a reflection of society but shapes and is shaped by it. This view is referred to as "dialectical" (Fairclough 2005:66). "It is an important characteristic of the economic, social and cultural changes of late modernity that they exist as discourses as well as processes that are taking place outside discourse, and that the processes that are taking place outside discourse are substantively shaped by these discourses" (Chouliaraki & Fairclough 1999:4, qtd. in Blommaert & Bulcaen 2000:448).

- The dialectical view entails a dynamic relationship between structure and agency (Blommaert & Bulcaen 2000:452). CDA avoids structuralist determinism by inscribing in local practices the power to shape (and potentially resist) hegemonic structures of control and domination. A slightly different way of putting it: "readers/hearers are not passive recipients in their relationship to texts" (Wodak 2001:6).

This list of common features in CDA is not exhaustive, and many of these features are shared by other approaches taken in this book and in rhetorical studies at large, but it does begin to suggest the contours of a CDA-inspired way of analyzing discourse.

In their chapters in this section, Andreea Deciu Ritivoi and Christopher Eisenhart show how transitivity can function in a constitutive, ideational way, to shape the world readers are meant to imagine. Eisenhart shows, for example, how the report about a review of a botched law-enforcement operation sometimes represents the review process, rather than any particular human agents, as the producer of the report: "the Review made factual determinations;" "[human agents'] expertise enabled the Review to conduct a comprehensive examination." Ritivoi shows how the would-be leader of a government in exile makes dissent among members of the group he represents invisible via passive-voice constructions: "The following lists of members was agreed on"; "It was decided that all the members would."

These chapters, and the other two in this section, also explore other aspects of grammar and vocabulary choice suggested by CL and CDA: modality, naming, nominalization, and tense and aspect, as these resources are deployed to shape depictions of agency, responsibility, time, identity, and, most generally, political and rhetorical legitimacy. In addition, Eisenhart and Susan Lawrence bring analytical categories and categorization schemes from rhetorical studies to the CDA table. Bringing to bear rhetorical genre theory, Eisenhart shows how the rhetorical exigencies created by the immediate purposes of official government reports shape the ideational work that texts of this sort can do in shaping events for subsequent rhetorical deployment. In her study of amnesty hearings during South Africa's Truth and Reconciliation process, Lawrence uses the traditional rhetorical notion of figuration to describe patterns of intertextuality linking an individual's testimony with the law that stipulates the intended scope of the testimony. She shows how the language of the actual testimony reflected the language of the law not just by repeating it, but also through metonymy, hyperbole, synecdoche, and metaphor.

Challenging an Aristotelian distinction between rhetorical (political) and arhetorical (natural) futures, Patricia Dunmire explores representations of the future in deliberative discourse. Analyzing the construction of natural futures in a government report on sea level rise, Dunmire shows how nominalization and modality play a role in the rhetorical construal of future outcomes of action and inaction. Analyzing the construction of political future in a US national security report and proposal, Dunmire illustrates how tense and aspect construe future risks and outcomes with relative certainties and in relative proximity and distance.

References

Adams, Karen L. 1999. "'Critical Linguistics': Alternative Approaches to Text in the American Tradition." In *Theorizing the Americanist Tradition*, R. Darnell and L. Valentine (Eds.), 351–64. Toronto: University of Toronto Press.

Blommaert, Jan and Bulcaen, Chris. 2000. "Critical Discourse Analysis." *Annual Review of Anthropology* 29: 447–66.

Bryant, Donald C. 1957. "Of Style." *Western Speech* 21: 103–110.

Carpenter, Ronald H. 1994. "The Stylistic Persona of Bill Clinton. From Arkansas to Aristotelian Attica." In *Bill Clinton on Stump, State, and Stage*, S. Smith (Ed.), 101–132. Fayetteville: The University of Arkansas Press.

Chouliaraki, L. and Fairclough, Norman. 1999. *Discourse in Late Modernity: Rethinking Critical Discourse Analysis*. Edinburgh, UK: Edinburgh University Press.

Eggins, Suzanne. 1994. *An Introduction to Systemic Functional Linguistics*. London and New York: Pinter.

Fairclough, Norman L. 1985. "Critical and Descriptive Goals in Discourse Analysis." *Journal of Pragmatics* 9: 739–63.

_____. 1992. *Discourse and Social Change*. Cambridge UK: Polity.

_____. 2005. "Critical Discourse Analysis in Transdisciplinary Research." In *A New Agenda in (Critical) Discourse Analysis*, R. Wodak and P. Chilton (Eds.), 53–70. Amsterdam and Philadelphia: John Benjamins.

Fowler, Roger, Hodge, Bob, Kress, Gunther, and Trew, Tony. (Eds.) 1979. *Language and Control*. London: Routledge and Kegan Paul.

Halliday, M. A. K. 1994. *An Introduction to Functional Grammar*, 2nd Ed. London: Edward Arnold.

Hariman, Robert. 1995. *Political Style: The Artistry of Power.* Chicago: The University of Chicago Press.

Hodge, Robert, and Kress, Gunther. 1979. *Language as Ideology.* London, Boston: Routledge and Kegan Paul.

Jäger, Siegfried. 2001. "Discourse and Knowledge: Theoretical and Methodological Aspects of a Critical Discourse and Dispositive Analysis." In *Methods of Critical Discourse Analysis*, R. Wodak and M. Meyer (Eds.), 32–62. London, UK: Sage.

Krżyzanowski, Michał. 2005. "'European Identity Wanted!' On Discursive and Communicative Dimensions of the European Convention." In *A New Agenda in (Critical) Discourse Analysis*, R. Wodak and P. Chilton (Eds.), 137–163. Amsterdam and Philadelphia: John Benjamins.

Mohrmann, G. P. and Leff, Michael C. 1974. "Lincoln at Cooper Union: A Rationale for Neo-Classical Criticism." *Quarterly Journal of Speech* 60: 459–467.

Murphy, John M. 1997. "Inventing Authority: Bill Clinton, Martin Luther King, Jr., and the Orchestration of Rhetorical Traditions." *Quarterly Journal of Speech* 83. 71–89.

Meyer, Michael. 2001. "Between Theory, Method, and Politics: Positioning of the Approaches to CDA." In *Methods of Critical Discourse Analysis*, R. Wodak and M. Meyer (Eds.), 14–31. London: Sage.

Oberhuber, Florian. 2005. "Deliberation Or 'Mainstreaming'? Empirically Researching the European Convention." In *A New Agenda in (Critical) Discourse Analysis*, R. Wodak and P. Chilton (Eds.), 165–187. Amsterdam and Philadelphia: John Benjamins.

Redding, W. Charles. 1957. "Extrinsic and Intrinsic Criticism." *Western Speech* 21: 96–103.

Van Dijk, Teun A. 1986. *Racism in the Press.* London, UK: Arnold.

———. 1993. "Principles of Critical Discourse Analysis." *Discourse & Society* 4: 249–83.

Van Noppen, John-Pierre. 2004. "CDA: A Discipline Come of Age?." *Journal of Sociolinguistics* 8: 107–26.

Wodak, Ruth. 1996. *Disorders of Discourse.* London: Longman.

———. 2001. "What CDA Is About – A Summary of its History, Important Concepts and its Developments." In *Methods of Critical Discourse Analysis*, R. Wodak and M. Meyer (Eds.), 1–13. London, UK: Sage.

——— and Gilbert Weiss. 2005. "Analyzing European Union Discourses: Theories and Applications." In *A New Agenda in (Critical) Discourse Analysis*, R. Wodak and P. Chilton (Eds.), 121–135. Amsterdam and Philadelphia: John Benjamins.

CHAPTER 2

Talking the (political) talk

Cold War refugees and their political legitimation through style

Andreea Deciu Ritivoi
Carnegie Mellon University

At the beginning of the Cold War, with the advent of communism in Soviet-controlled Eastern Europe, many members of the former political elites in the region defected to the United States. Here they hoped to organize movements that would overthrow the regimes at home and allow them to return and resume their disrupted existence. But with several groups and individuals contending for recognition, it was often difficult to know whose claims to leadership were legitimate.[1] Legitimation, a key aspect of modern political life, is a process that determines the extent to which leaders, organizations, parties, or governments are perceived by their constituencies as justified in their attempts to acquire and exercise their power. (Weber 1978; Major & Jost 2001; Zelditch Jr. 1998; Coicaud 2002; Schechter 2005). While power can be obtained and maintained through force, political legitimacy requires discursive strategies rather than physical coercion (Chilton & Schaffner 1997: 212–13). The need for effective legitimating strategies was acutely felt by Cold War immigrant lobby groups trying to form governments-in-exile – "opposition groups that struggle from outside their home territory to overthrow the regime in their independent, occupied, or claimed home country" (Shain 1999: 2). For such groups, persuasion was the main, if not the only weapon, since recourse to physical coercion was not available. In this chapter I examine how Cold War refugees won political legitimacy through discursive means so that officials of the host society allowed them to represent their country's interests.

---

1. Examinations of Eastern European Cold War diasporas have revealed that, despite the ethno-national factor that organized them, the communities they formed were often torn apart by internal strife and power struggles (cf. Jaroszynska-Kirchmann 2004).

The discursive aspect of political legitimation has been a topic of concern for rhetoricians and discourse analysts trying to understand how power is achieved and maintained when various groups compete for it (Bostdorff 1994; Zarefsky 1986; Chilton & Schaffner 1997). Recent work in discourse analysis (Jaworski & Galasinski 2000) argues that an important tool in achieving legitimacy is the reliance upon well-established ideologies – those beliefs and representations that are shared by the members of a community and that act as providers of meaning for their everyday practices. Rhetorical scholars have shown that Cold War ideology relied heavily on an image of the United States as rescuer of all nations, morally compelled and uniquely qualified to intervene in the international arena to oppose the spread of communism (Brockriede & Scott 1970; Medhurst 1987; Wander 1984; Ivie 1999). Refugees from the countries behind the Iron Curtain contributed to the legitimation of this ideology: their stories of escape from oppressive regimes were deftly used as "touching symbols around which to weave the legitimacy needed for foreign policy," particularly when it came to pushing for more armaments or immigration reform (Shain 1999:40). This chapter argues that the refugees were also able to take strategic advantage of the Cold War ideology prevalent at the time in the United States to achieve their goals.

In rhetorical studies, scholarship on the Cold War commonly ignores the way that the refugees exploited the dominant ideology not only to legitimate their goals but also to lobby successfully for the creation of special government refugee aid programs and agencies (Medhurst 1990; Ivie 1990; Wander 1990). Historians and sociologists studying the immigrant communities forming during this period have documented several cases in which the refugee groups were able to form effective movements and organizations designed to carry out a nationalist agenda (Jakobson 1997; Jaroszynska-Kirchmann 2004). While it is difficult to make generalizations about this issue, immigration scholars have repeatedly found that refugee communities are less likely to lobby effectively for their home country's interests if they are not recognized in the host country as legitimate spokespersons. For this reason, immigrant communities strive to prove their legitimacy through official channels of U.S. foreign policy – "the electoral system and the lobbying of decision makers" (Shain 1999:199). This chapter builds on such work by showing specific ways that official lobbying can become effective. I focus on the ability of the refugees to tap into the dominant ideology through stylistic choices that cause them to be perceived as legitimate politicians.

I discuss the case of Constantin Visoianu, the leader of a Romanian group that sought to fashion itself as a legitimate government-in-exile operating from the United States between 1949 and 1978. Visoianu had been Minister of Foreign Affairs in the pre-communist governments in their home country. Abroad, he no longer held official political titles, and his entry visas assigned him merely the status of refugee, one among so many other Eastern Europeans in American territory. In order to approach United States government officials on behalf of the Romanian nation and to make demands and argue for a particular course of action in the war against communism, Visoianu needed to be recognized as a statesman. His legitimation, then, involved the forging of a particular subjectivity[2] – that of an authentic political actor who could claim the right to be obeyed and followed. In his communications with American officials, the invention of such a subjectivity relied heavily on his ability to sound like a politician by making particular grammatical and lexical choices.

The documents I analyze in this chapter are three letters sent by Visoianu to two successive presidents of the Free Europe Committee, C. D. Jackson and Whitney H. Shepardson, and to D. Leverich, undersecretary at the State Department, in charge with Eastern European affairs.[3] In all three documents, Visoianu sought to secure (or ensure the continuation of) financial support from the United States government and to gain political recognition both for the organization he headed, as representative of the Romanian people's (rather than merely the Romanian refugees') interests, and for himself as their legitimate leader. I chose such a small sample for analysis for two reasons. First, the approach I take, which draws on both rhetorical criticism and critical discourse analysis, is specifically designed to offer close readings of texts; it therefore works best when dealing with fewer and shorter ones (Black 1978; Leff 1980; Fairclough 1992). Second, critical discourse analysis recommends as a selection strategy *cruces* or "moments of crisis," when the result of the discursive act becomes especially important to the speakers (Fairclough 1992). These letters marked "moments of crisis" in the history of the Romanian diaspora, as each triggered, or responded to, a sea change in American

---

2. "Subjectivity" is a fraught concept, with a long and complex intellectual history. As I use it here, the term refers to the identity of an individual as it is constructed through social and political interaction. I have chosen to use "subjectivity" over other candidates, such as "identity" or "selfhood," because it is the term employed by most scholars who study legitimation, as well as those who examine style in connection with the identity of individuals. The term "subjectivity" seems especially apt given its Althusserian legacy, which stresses the situated, contractual aspect of identity formation. These Althusserian roots also make "subjectivity" an appropriate choice for a project such as mine, relying on Critical Discourse Analysis as its main method of research.

3. The documents I analyze in this paper are available in the archives of the Hoover Institution at Stanford University (collection title Comitetul National Roman) and have also been published in Visoianu 2000. References in this paper are to the published volume. The original language of the documents is Romanian, and the documents were translated into English before being sent to the American addressee. Because I focus on the intention of the writer, I have used my own translation into English. In analyzing these documents, I have sought to avoid interpretations that would only apply to the English version. I have not had access to the official English translations.

relations with, and attitudes toward, Eastern European immigrants in general, and Romanians in particular.

I seek to make a two-fold contribution to this volume: first, a theoretical and methodological comparison between two approaches that share many goals and assumptions, yet also differ significantly, and second, an application of the insights resulting from this comparison to a particular analysis – that of Visoianu's political legitimation through style. In the first part of the chapter, I present the theoretical and methodological underpinnings of my analytic framework by reading the strengths and limitations of rhetorical analysis from the perspective of critical discourse analysis and forming my own, cross-fertilized, approach. I focus particularly on forging an understanding of style and ideology which can shed light on the legitimation efforts of political refugees in Cold War America.

The importance of style for politics is well captured by the definition of political life as "a mixture of persuasive techniques, aesthetic norms, and political relationships working together in cohesive patterns of motivation activated through speech" (Hariman 1995:53). Traditionally interested in style as a collection of ornamental devices and figures, rhetorical theory has gradually moved toward a broader conception that emphasizes the ideological dimension of style and its role in forging subjectivity (Hariman 1995; Carpenter 1994; Murphy 1997). My focus is on the role played by style in creating political relationships that establish a particular subjectivity – that of a legitimate political actor. This particular function of style, though recognized in rhetorical studies, remains less developed in our field than the more traditional emphases on style as aesthetic norm and technique of persuasion. While I approach the study of Visoianu's legitimation strategy as a rhetorician, I argue that in this case an adequate rhetorical analysis (RA) requires some methodological and theoretical amendments at the level of how style is conceived in relation to ideology. I offer such amendments by drawing on critical discourse analysis (CDA).

Both RA and CDA share a specific explanatory concern in that they are equally committed to tracing the connection between the way texts are constructed and their conditions of production and reception (Leff 1980; Mailloux 1989; Fairclough 1992). RA and CDA are also similar in their emphasis on context: both rhetorical scholars and discourse analysts recognize that the political and social setting of communication shapes the form and the meaning of messages. Both therefore argue that the material dimension of discourse should be an important analytic concern. According to rhetorical scholars, in studying Cold War rhetoric the analytic task "cannot be accomplished ... apart from the historical, critical, archival, and field research that allows the critic to reconstruct the strategic motives that give birth to Cold War discourse" (Medhurst 1990:21). From the perspective of critical discourse analysis, to understand discursive interactions and the way in which they position groups toward one another requires an analysis that relates discourse "to the particular economic, political and institutional settings within which discourse is generated" (Fairclough 1992:71).

Among critical discourse analysts, Ruth Wodak has paid particular attention to the heuristic significance of a contextualization of discursive acts, creating a special approach called the "discourse-historical method." This method attempts to "integrate systematically all available background information in the analysis and interpretation of the many layers of a written or spoken text" (Fairclough & Wodak 1997:266). Wodak's methodological recommendations match those offered by rhetorical scholars, who insist that "to analyze Cold War rhetoric the critic must first become a strategist, seeking to understand the goals being pursued and the precise situational configuration – the situation . . . as it existed at the time a particular decision was made or symbolic action undertaken" (Medhurst 1990:20).

In keeping with these methodological recommendations, in the second part of the paper I reconstruct the post-World War II political climate in the United States, paying particular attention to the role played by Eastern European refugees in the anti-communist ideology of the Cold War period. Within this historical and political setting, I analyze the letters sent by Visoianu, focusing on stylistic choices that shape the political authority of the author as a statesman consulting with peers, exchanging views, and offering recommendations, carefully avoiding a supplicatory tone even when approaching American officials with requests for financial and political support.

Political legitimacy across disciplines: From rhetoric to critical discourse analysis

Rhetorical scholars interested in Cold War ideology have showed that it relied heavily on an image of the United States as appointed by God to save other nations, particularly those threatened by communism, as well as on insisting upon an imminent global danger posed by the Soviet Union and its allies (Scott 1990; Medhurst 1990; Ivie 1990). But these studies ignore how Cold War ideology could be appropriated for purposes other than justifying American politics, especially by immigrant lobby groups with their own agendas. The broader implication of such an omission is that the rhetorical work of official ideologies is limited to those who create them, suggesting that ideologies are impossible to resist, while obscuring the fact that they can be used strategically to further the goals of those who seek power.

To remedy this deficiency one must do more than simply reorient case studies toward situations in which the Eastern European refugees promoted or advanced the American political agenda. The analysis must be theoretically and methodologically re-framed so that it neither reduces the refugees to the status of mere pawns in Cold War propaganda nor assumes that their own goals and interests were entirely subservient to the official American agenda. The analysis cannot assume uncritically that the main role of this discourse was to echo official American talk, but should instead strive to understand the former's own goals and strategies, and to consider its relation to the American agenda. But the theoretical underpinnings of the existing studies by rhetorical scholars working on the Cold War make it difficult to go beyond the official discursive arena, because one of the theoretical tenets of this work is that ruling ideologies must always be the target of study and critique (McGee 1980; McKerrow 1989). Written primarily by experts in presidential rhetoric, this scholarship tends to focus on the discourse of political officials – members of the government and Congress, politicians with a well-established authority in the public arena. Such an approach inevitably ignores interventions coming from those who have no official authority, as was the case for most immigrants and refugees. Operating with a conception of ideology as the discursive product of those in power, this body of work requires the rhetorical critic to identify and expose the hold of ideology on political practices (Wander 1990:132). This goal makes it hard to see how ideologies can be challenged and modified by those outside the official political spectrum.[4]

Critical discourse analysts have argued, on the other hand, that ideologies do not automatically legitimate ideas and agendas, but involve constant negotiations and transformations that can bestow legitimacy on interventions from outside the official political arena. With its Althusserian roots, CDA has employed a conception of ideology not as "a nebulous realm of 'ideas' but as tied to material practices embedded in social institutions" and capable of "positioning people in particular ways as social 'subjects'" (Wodak & Fairclough 1997:261). Norman Fairclough's contributions to critical discourse analysis, in particular, have stressed the role of ideology in constituting subjectivities in a site of struggle (Fairclough 1992:87). Fairclough sees "discourse as a political practice [that] establishes, sustains and changes power relations, and the collective entities (classes, blocs, communities, groups) between which power relations obtain" (Fairclough 1992:67). Thus understood, discourse becomes an essential tool in the legitimation of particular actors and their agendas.

But legitimation is not a one-way street, from discursive to social practices. CDA focuses on the mutual impact of language and the social structures in which language is used (Titscher et al. 2000:147). For Fairclough, discourse represents "one form in which people may act upon the world and especially upon each other,

---

4. The understanding of ideology in rhetorical studies is not limited to these perspectives, and my critique does not imply that all rhetorical treatments of ideology are faulty.

as well as a mode of representation" (Fairclough 1992:63). Discursive practices, by this logic, are both conventional and creative insofar as they can reproduce existing beliefs while also shaping and eventually transforming them. This way of understanding discourse is particularly relevant to the study of refugees' rhetoric because it allows us to focus on the strategic ways that refugees can subscribe to their new social and discursive environment, while simultaneously making subtle changes in it and leaving their own mark.

Through this alternative understanding of ideology, CDA equips us better than rhetorical scholarship does to assess the role of Eastern European refugees as active players in the Cold War political arena and to examine their use of the anti-communist ideology dominant in America. This understanding of ideology draws attention to the way that stating an idea or a belief through certain stylistic choices can legitimate particular actors by situating them in certain relations toward one another and defining the roles they assume. The extent to which refugees adopt discursive practices associated by the members of the host society with the specific norms and beliefs of a ruling ideology can determine whether they are perceived as potential allies or enemies, as legitimate or illegitimate representatives of their nation. Perhaps most important, this process of social and political positioning assumes that discourse is a site of struggle; it therefore acknowledges that refugees may strategically choose how to employ the discursive practices used in their host society and how the meaning and social relevance of that practice is ultimately negotiated among its users.

This negotiated meaning and significance is "closely intertwined with the form of texts, and formal features of texts at various levels may be ideologically invested" (Fairclough 1992:89). Stylistic choices can enable certain representations of those who make them, whether subscribing to particular norms or challenging them, recognizing the authority of others or questioning it, accepting or contesting a particular ideology. Style has been recognized by discourse analysts and rhetorical theorists alike as an important category for understanding how subjectivities take shape in interaction with others – legitimating particular identity choices or giving credence to particular agendas (Hariman 1995; Johnstone 1996). Among the rhetorical theorists who explicitly argue against the "handbook of techniques" approach, Robert Hariman has insisted that we think of style as a set of "specific rules of usage for the composition of self and others in relations of equality and subordination" (Hariman 1995:7). Hariman thus emphasizes the role played by style in forging subjectivity, by articulating individuals' goals and dispositions and then relating them to others' interests and dispositions.

Such an understanding of style plays out in rhetorical analyses that systematically link discursive features to the mark of a particular subjectivity, as in Ronald Carpenter's study of President Clinton's style as a charismatic leader (Carpenter 1994). As a marker of subjectivity, style functions as a strategy of legitimation insofar as it allows individuals to step into socially or politically potent roles and thus to articulate certain positions that could otherwise be dismissed as illegitimate. A case in point is John Murphy's examination of the way in which President Clinton was able to modify his own style and adopt another one, that of the Reverend Martin Luther King Jr., in order to address an African-American audience successfully and to appear to them as a legitimate leader (Murphy 1997). Style, by this account, becomes a way of signaling membership in a community, and stylistic choice a way of using strategically the discursive conventions of the group in order to legitimate particular actors and allow them to pursue their goals and interests.

Rhetorical scholarship, then, explicitly links style to political legitimacy and authority. But the studies that do so still tend to equate style with figuration and to limit the investigation to discourses that display a certain form of eloquence, rich in tropes and elaborate uses of language (Fahnestock 1999; Bostdorff 1994; Hariman 1995). For my purposes here, the disadvantage of such an approach is that it seems unlikely to ponder a discourse whose mechanisms of persuasion are not reducible to figuration. At the same time, rhetorical approaches that are willing to locate style in common usage, such as ideographic criticism, are disadvantaged by their lack of recourse to a well-defined set of techniques and strategies, a clearly identifiable category under which various examples can be subsumed. Ideographic criticism has produced compelling analyses of the political legitimation made possible by the use of words like "equality" or phrases like "family values" in American public discourse (Condit & Lucaites 1993; Cloud 1998). But such studies are hard to emulate in the absence of a method that guides the investigation and explains how to identify an "ideograph" in the first place. CDA provides a remedy for both of these methodological limitations of rhetorical criticism. On the one hand, it operates unencumbered by a tradition of figures and is declaredly interested in discourses across a wide stylistic spectrum (Kress 1988). On the other hand, CDA offers a systematic way of investigating discourse, employing well-defined heuristic categories.

Drawing on M. A. K. Halliday's Systemic Functional Linguistics, Fairclough views discourse as fulfilling several functions at once, including the ideational and the interpersonal, which anchor discourse in social practices and institutions, orienting speakers and their communications toward one another. Fairclough uses the label *modality* to define the "dimension of the grammar of the clause which corresponds to the 'interpersonal' function of language" (Fairclough 1992:158). Modality is the linguistic feature that reveals the speakers' attitude toward the propositional content of their statements – an attitude that can vary from certainty to uncertainty, depending on whether the content is conveyed in direct, strongly endorsing forms, or in a more cautious, hedging manner. The ideational dimension, on the other hand, is captured through the linguistic feature of *transitivity*, which concerns "the types of processes which are coded in clauses, and the types of participant involved in them" (Fairclough 1992: 177–78). Transitivity reveals the extent to which particular actions are identified, along with the agents involved, and can thus background or foreground causal connections among events as well as particular individuals' responsibility for them. Linguistically, modality can be conveyed through the use of modal verbs (*should, must, need to, may, could*), the historic present tense, certain adverbials (*definitely, certainly, surely, probably, allegedly*) and adjectives (*evident, imperative, necessary, uncertain, probable*), but also through recourse to presuppositions. Transitivity, in turn, involves the use of verbs and their objects and the types of processes they convey. While both modality and transitivity have been discussed by other language theorists and philosophers of language, in this chapter I rely upon Fairclough's analytic schema and upon his particular vocabulary and distinctions.

Case study

Historical context

In asserting political legitimacy, Visoianu faced a two-fold challenge. On the one hand, he had to address American officials as a statesman in order to be recognized as a legitimate representative of the entire Romanian nation, not just a handful of Romanian immigrants. On the other hand, he had to draw attention away from the discord within the Romanian immigrant community, so he could be recognized as its sole legitimate representative, and the National Committee under his leadership as the legitimate government-in-exile. In order to avoid seeming like a refugee, he presented himself as the leader of a cohesive Romanian refugee community.

From the American perspective, Eastern European political refugees had the potential to be crucial allies in disseminating anti-communist ideology in the Soviet- controlled region. Even in 1946, before the Cold War was in full swing, George Kennan – diplomat and political advisor to Harry Truman – organized a small private group that offered aid and employment to Eastern European refugees, as well as helping them stay in touch with their homelands. In June of 1949 this group became the Free Europe Committee (FEC). The FEC was placed under the jurisdiction of the State Department, with supervising authorities that included some of the major political figures of the day, such as Allen Dulles and Dwight Eisenhower. The goal of the FEC was to foment unrest among the people in the "captive nations" of Eastern Europe and to encourage them to rebel against the Soviet occupation (Kovrig 1991). In September of 1954 the FEC organized a conference in New York and invited the more prominent political refugees from Eastern Europe to attend and express their views regarding the fight against communism. The conference resulted in the founding of the Assembly of Captive

European Nations, with each "captive nation" represented by a National Commit-tee. The members of these committees were encouraged by the State Department "to regard themselves as virtual governments-in-refuge" (Kovrig 1991:66), even though the committees did not have any diplomatic status and were not consulted in any systematic way in foreign policy matters.

Constantin Visoianu, who immigrated to the United States in 1945 and re-mained until his death in 1977, was the president of the Romanian National Com-mittee, which claimed to represent the interests of Romanian Cold War refugees and fashioned itself as a government in exile. The initial membership list identi-fies participants by their former official political titles and positions in Romania. From the main headquarters in Washington, D.C., Visoianu oversaw activities in the entire Romanian diaspora, and even opened "embassies" wherever Romanians emigrated in significant numbers – in France, Germany, Italy, Greece, Turkey, and the United Kingdom, but also Brazil, Argentina, and Israel. Under the patronage of the FEC, the Romanian organization received moral, political, and financial sup-port for various activities, including public appearances during which the refugees got to plead for their cause.

Unlike other Eastern European refugee groups, the Romanian politicians in exile had served various regimes at home, in some cases governments that had ve-hemently contested and then violently replaced each other. Visoianu's leadership was contested from the very beginning; other former political elites in the Ro-manian diaspora not only refused to join the Romanian National Committee but even actively boycotted it. By 1953 the dissent among Romanian immigrants had increased and intensified to the point where the American officials became con-cerned that these conflicts would render the refugees inefficient in the fight against communism. The FEC asked the Romanian National Committee – as the repre-sentative group under its patronage – to resolve disputes within the Romanian diaspora. When Visoianu's group failed to do so, the FEC withdrew its financial support. Visoianu restored the relation with the FEC. The funding resumed.

Visoianu adopted a rhetorical style that empowered him to represent himself as a legitimate statesman who should be carefully listened to and obeyed. He suc-ceeded in fending off the Americans' attempts at imposing their own policy in the running of the national committees. Emboldened by this success, he even sought to influence the internal organization of the FEC to further his own purposes. In what follows, I analyze Visoianu's strategic use of modality and transitivity, the two main techniques he used to represent his political legitimacy.

Modality

As mentioned earlier, modality reveals the attitude speakers have toward the con-tent of their communication, an attitude that can vary from strong endorsement and complete assurance to hesitation and tentativeness. Attitudes towards one's own words and sentences reflect particular worldviews, as well as relationships to one's audience. Speakers can sound forceful and confident or timid and tentative, depending on whether the ideas they convey are widely accepted or controversial and on whether their audience is accepting and open or authoritative and intimidating. As such, modality is "a point of intersection in discourse between the signification of reality and the enactment of social relations" (Fairclough 1992:160). A high degree of affinity with one's mode of communication constitutes, according to Fairclough, *categorical modality*, which can be either *objective*, when no individual consciousness assuming the beliefs is mentioned, or *subjective*, when the attitude is explicitly attributed to a speaker.

In Visoianu's correspondence with the American officials, categorical modality is a key characteristic of his assertive style. Categorical modality functioned as a strategy of legitimation by portraying him as a political leader authorized to represent the Romanian people and negotiate with the representatives of the U.S. government. Using categorical modality, Visoianu conveyed self-assurance rather than subservience, while also aligning the requests he was making on behalf of the exiles with the central tenets of the US government's ideological agenda. Visoianu used modality to tap strategically into the Cold War anti-communist ideology by emphasizing his status as a refugee from totalitarianism – someone who could legitimately ask for the help of a government that defined its historic mission primarily as a fight against communism. At the same time, by expressing a strong affinity with the tenets of the anti-communist ideology of the United States, he hoped to be seen as an ally and an associate, addressing his interlocutors from a position of equality in the name of shared ideals.

In the first document, a letter addressed to C. D. Jackson, the President of the FEC, Visoianu asks for financial support for the Romanian National Committee – support that had already been extended to the other National Committees representing Eastern Europeans in exile. By its very nature, the request is likely to position Visoianu in a relationship of inferiority to his addressee, and by extension, to depict the Romanian exiles as dependent on the benevolence of the U.S. government. But Visoianu avoids (and to some extent even inverts) this position by accompanying the request with a strongly expressed certainty that the Free Europe Committee will grant it.

(1)   *Convinced* that the Free Europe Committee, which *was born* out of the American people's generosity and love of freedom in order to aid the liberation of the countries behind the Iron Curtain, *could not intend* to extend a favorable treatment to some of the captive people, while discriminating against others, we take the liberty of requesting, on behalf of the future activities of the Romanian National Committee, the generous help of the Free Europe

> Committee, to the same extent and according to the same criteria as those currently used for other European National Committees (183).

Rather than presenting the reasons the Romanian National Committee needs funding, describing the financial need in more specific terms, or articulating a specific political program that would benefit from the money, Visoianu introduces the request as an entitlement – a claim that is legitimate not because of a particular program the RNC has, but because of the mission the FEC has announced and in part fulfilled: to offer financial aid to Eastern European refugees. More specifically, Visoianu manages to avoid any specific argumentation by advancing the highly modalized (that is, strongly endorsed) presupposition that the Romanian National Committee will respond positively to the request. According to Fairclough, pre-suppositions take "factuality for granted" (Fairclough 1992:161). Visoianu could not know whether the State Department would be willing to extend its financial support to *this* particular Romanian organization, but it is important for him to speak as if operating on such an assumption. This presupposition, advanced with high epistemic modality, allows him to issue the request not as a petition, but rather as a requirement for the fulfillment of the FEC's own agenda. Visoianu, then, taps into the ideological resources available to him, especially the image of a mythical America, savior of all nations and moral guarantor of universal freedom, to ensure that his request would be seen as legitimate. At the same time, he ensures that the request for financial aid does not mark political servitude, but rather endorsement of an ideological tenet.

Another important tenet of Cold War ideology was opposition to communism. By emphatically stating his commitment to the shared cause of anti-communism, Visoianu situates himself in Jackson's frame of reference, signaling solidarity and commonality. As Fairclough explains, "producers often indicate commitment to propositions in the course of interactions with other people, and the affinity they express with propositions is often difficult to disentangle from their sense of affinity, or solidarity, with interactants. ... expressing high affinity may have little to do with one's commitment to a proposition, but a lot to do with a desire to show solidarity." (Fairclough 1992:160). United by their common anti-communist fervor, Visoianu and Jackson are no longer in a relationship of victim and savior, but one of partners and allies. By relying on emphatically expressed anti-communist views, Visoianu's style informs his subjectivity in relation to that of the American official, rhetorically bestowing the same official status upon Visoianu himself.

We have seen that Visoianu addressed the president of the FEC as a political equal and partner rather than as a refugee and supplicant. Categorical epistemic modality enacted a particular social relation, one designed to eliminate the distance that existed between the interlocutors. It is in the name of such a relation that

Visoianu could afford to accompany the request with a strong warning. Through his disavowal of the possibility that the FEC might *not* offer financial support to the Romanian organization, he warns that turning down the request would constitute a discriminatory act, incompatible with the Committee's original agenda and with the American people's vision. Visoianu thus uses to his advantage the Cold War ideology that insisted upon America's moral duty to spread freedom to *all* nations, and to save victims of totalitarian oppression *everywhere*. Indeed, because he relied on the power of ideology to naturalize claims and reject objections, Visoianu was able to express high confidence that the request will be granted,

Categorical modality is an efficient tool for instituting and maintaining ideologies, insofar as it constitutes a strategy for introducing personal opinions and idiosyncratic interpretations as universally recognized facts (Fairclough 1992: 160–61). Rhetorical scholars, too, have documented the role played by the elimination of hedging in reducing nuanced, complex arguments to evidentiary statements, thus obscuring uncertainty or diverting attention away from the possibility of multiple meanings (Fahnestock 1986). Visoianu's use of categorical modality in the letter to Jackson allowed him to gloss over more complex and controversial issues – such as his contested status as leader of the Romanian National Committee within the Romanian exile community – for the sake of presenting to the addressee a clear and compelling message. The main goal of this message is to place the Romanian National Committee in the category of the other Eastern European committees under the financial patronage of the FEC, and Visoianu does not defend the legitimacy of the RNC within the Romanian exile community.

But after the FEC became aware of the dissent within this community, and in response threatened to withdraw funding for the activities of the Romanian National Committee, Visoianu found himself facing a different, more difficult, exigency. His task was now to renew the relationship with the American organization, yet at the same time to limit its involvement in the organization of the Romanian National Committee in order to make it impossible for the Americans to demand changes in the working and leadership of the committee (which might have included Visoianu's replacement). Under these circumstances, the second document, a letter sent to Leverich, who had replaced Jackson as the president of the FEC, had an even more assertive style that allowed Visoianu to claim the political autonomy of the Romanian National Committee as representative of the Romanian nation. Visoianu presented the decision of the FEC as an illegitimate intervention in the affairs of another country, which allowed him to reject it. Here Visoianu is challenging the official ideology of the time, which emphasized the mission of the United States as global rescuer of nations. The delegitimation of the FEC is conveyed by a series of negative modifiers placed in evidentiary statements that express his disapproval of the FEC decision to withdraw the funding. The FEC decision is described as follows:

(2) *shocking*, not only based on *completely mistaken* considerations that reveal an *inadmissible* position assumed by the Free Europe Committee, but also amounting to a moral and material pressure, which I [Visoianu] deem *incompatible* with the generous and just objectives of American politics (184).

At the beginning of the letter, Visoianu criticizes the FEC from a generic perspective, without specific reference to the individual consciousness behind it:

(3) *It is quite evident* that no one can fight properly for the freedom of his enslaved country unless he himself feels dignified and independent (184).

The criticism is expressed forcefully and unambiguously through objective categorical modality conveyed by the present tense of the verbs and the adjective "evident." This objective modality obscures the existence of a particular perspective on the events to suggest that the events in question would be universally regarded in such negative terms. By omitting the reference to himself ("it is quite evident to me"), Visoianu strengthens the validity of his claim and intensifies its weight, but in so doing he implicitly also asserts his legitimacy as critic. Fairclough claims that "the use of objective modality often implies some form of power" (1992: 159). Indeed, by making such statements, Visoianu assumes the authority not merely to complain about the decision but to render it invalid.

Visoianu's legitimacy as a critic of the FEC is asserted overtly in the second part of the letter, in which the objections are explicitly represented as his own personal reactions:

(4) Should I still stress *my own personal revulsion* at such methods? My memory from Romania of fighting against the brutal pressures of a foreign power [the Soviet Union] is still alive. I am also *totally aware* that such methods are at the opposite of the spirit and the workings of the American people and the American government (187).

Here Visoianu introduces a subjective position (as indicated by the heavy use of personal pronouns), but the subjectivity is (for the moment) not that of the president of the Romanian National Committee, but rather of a generic political refugee who has experienced the Soviet invasion in Romania. This is a powerful symbolic affiliation in light of Cold War ideology, an efficient way of asserting the deontic legitimacy to issue moral imperatives. Likewise, within Cold War ideology the transparent allusion to the Soviet Union, to which the Romanian National Committee is likened, is the most emphatic way of delegitimating the FEC's decision. Visoianu makes the FEC accountable to its own ideological credo, forcefully sanctioning its departure from the set of beliefs that define it. This departure is announced through the use of modality ("I am totally aware") in expressing another assumption – his belief that the Free Europe Committee could not be acting in accordance with the views of the American government and the American people. Here Visoianu is exploiting a leitmotif in the official American ideology, which systematically claimed to be representing the views of millions of Americans, in order to attack one of the main carriers of this ideology, the FEC.

Let us take stock of the stylistic progression that shaped how Visoianu's subjectivity appears in these documents. In the first letter, in which he requested funds from FEC, Visoianu did not speak in his own name but on behalf of the Romanian people. In the second letter, in which he protested against the cessation of funding, he began by speaking as a refugee and then inserted his own individuality into the discourse, as a legitimate political actor who expects to be consulted and respected by the American officials. His subjectivity, then, shifted from a symbolic anti-communist stance (which would have been available to almost any Eastern European exiled politician) to a specific political position, that of the president of the Romanian National Committee. The political legitimacy of the second letter is crucially informed by the moral legitimacy of the first. As the president, he can identify the challenges facing the Romanian exiles, point out mistakes, and even admit to particular errors or failures, without risking a disparagement of the organization. For instance, Visoianu prefaces incriminating accounts of various activities within the Romanian community with forms of deontic modality:

(5)   I *am bound* to say (192)

to place himself in a position of responsibility that also reinforces his legitimacy as political leader. (Someone cannot be held responsible unless also seen as legitimately occupying that position to begin with.) Likewise, when he does acknowledge the dissent among Romanian immigrants, Visoianu uses modality expressed through emotions: his attitude toward the dissent is one of

(6)   *much pain* and *embarrassment* at watching such a shameful spectacle (192).

In this paragraph the use of modality allows Visoianu to formulate self-criticisms that legitimate him just as much as it delegitimates any foreign organization that would seek to make similar criticisms. Insofar as there are problems in the Romanian immigrant community, the leader is well aware of them and can therefore find a solution. But an outside intervention by the Free Europe Committee is both unnecessary and unjustified.

The stylistic strategies of these two letters were apparently successful. Obtaining and then renewing funding for the RNC were important achievements for Visoianu, and they emboldened him to try an even more assertive approach in later exchanges with U.S. officials. In 1954, with the change in American relationships with the Eastern European immigrants (marked by the Assembly of the Captive Nations conference and reflected in the change in the leadership of the Free Europe Committee), Visoianu seized the opportunity to approach the new president with a whole new set of demands. He sent to Whitney H. Shepardson a set of guidelines for the re-structuring of *all* the national committees under the FEC's patronage. The memo also contains recommendations for how the collaboration between FEC and the national committees should proceed. While the recommendations reflect Visoianu's personal views, he formulates them in deontic modality, which gives them the force of an imperative:

(7)   National Committees *must* be formed in accordance with the traditions and institutions of each country (193).

(8)   It is *not advisable* that the Committees follow the same model (193).

(9)   The Committees *should be* inclusive within the limits imposed by patriotism, democracy, and decency (194).

(10)   The Committees *must* be centers of national solidarity in exile (194).

(11)   In the structuring of each Committee, it *must be taken into account* the extent to which the membership is trustworthy in the home country (194).

(12)   For a Committee to be harmonious and to work efficiently, it *must* not be homogeneous or too large (195).

(13)   The Free Europe Committee *must* collaborate with the National Committees, not with their individual members (195).

(14)   It *is necessary* that the management of Radio Free Europe consult on a regular basis with the National Committees (196).

(15)   Each Committee *may* delegate one or more of its members to represent it on the Radio Free Europe broadcasts (196).

(16)   The committees *ought* to be consulted by the Mid-European Center, when the latter wants to solicit contributions from a scholar in exile (197).

(17)   It *is highly desirable* that the president of the Free Europe Committee meet regularly with the presidents of each National Committee (197).

Modal verbs are the most emphatic way in which speakers can signal their endorsement of the statements they make. Throughout the third document, the pervasiveness of statements with modal verbs, or constructions that function as modal verbs, conveys self-assuredness and assertiveness. By now Visoianu speaks as someone confident enough to claim the legitimacy to issue commandments to the entire Eastern European exile community and to promote his views as obligatory norms for the proper functioning of the FEC. This marks a new stage in his subjectivity and a reversal of roles; instead of seeking help and guidance, Visoianu can now offer them.

Transitivity

Fairclough explains that "a social motivation for analyzing transitivity is to … work out what social, cultural, ideological, political, or theoretical factors determine how a process is signified in a particular type of discourse" (1992:180). Fairclough distinguishes two kinds of processes in the category of transitivity: intransitive or relational clauses, which represent a relationship between participants (being, having, becoming, etc.), and transitive, or action, clauses, in which an agent acts upon a goal (1992:178). By focusing on the actions of the Romanian National Committee as a group rather than on the actions of individual members, thus endowing the group and not its members with a high degree of agency, Visoianu presented the organization as a monolith. By doing so, he shifted attention away from disputes within the Romanian diaspora and claimed various rights for his organization in the name of the Romanian nation. The extent to which Visoianu's exchanges with American high officials represent processes in relational or action terms varies depended on his strategic purpose, on whether he wanted to appear as sharing the predicament of all Soviet Bloc refugees or whether he tried to advance a personal agenda, sometimes one markedly departing from that of other Eastern European exiles.

In the first letter, which solicits funds from FEC president C. D. Jackson, Visoianu had to depict the Romanian National Committee as an organization worthy of American financial and political support. He did so by featuring the RNC in transitive constructions, as an agent, yet without providing any information about its individual members:

(18)   The Romanian National Committee, legitimate representative of the people of Romania, to whose liberation it *dedicates all of its means and energy,*

(19)   *takes this opportunity*

(20)   to *convey once again its sincere desire* for a strong and harmonious collaboration with the Free Europe Committee

(21)   we take the liberty of *requesting* on behalf of the future activities of the Romanian National Committee, *the magnanimous help* of the Free Europe Committee, to the same extent and according to the same criteria as those currently used for other European National Committees (183).

As Fairclough explains, directed action realized as a transitive construction (subject-verb-object) identifies an agent acting upon a goal. By presenting the Committee as an agent with a goal, Visoianu reifies a collection of individuals into a cohesive organization, which is depicted as acting in unison for the liberation of the Romanian nation. The ideological tenet that everyone must be against communism works in his favor, and allows him to make claims without defending them. Note that Visoianu does not offer in this introductory paragraph any concrete information about the Romanian National Committee (such as duration of existence, membership, or mission). He merely asserts that the organization represents the Romanian nation, and attributes to it the generic (i.e., valid for all Eastern Europeans) goal of freeing the home country. Suppressing more specific information about the Committee enables Visoianu to introduce the organization to the reader as a particular kind of political agent, identical to the other Eastern European committees that had already received support from the Romanian National Committee. At the same time, such a focus on the Romanian National Committee as a legitimate agent makes the request for funding appear legitimate, rendering any additional justification superfluous.

Transitivity, then, reinforces the rhetorical effect of modality. While Visoianu's letter asks for money, the request is presented as a political statement – Romanian refugees are united against communism – which is closely aligned with the ideology promoted by the FEC. In reality, while the FEC was interested in supporting refugees' organizations, it had no *a priori* reason to prefer this particular Romanian group over others. Visoianu establishes the political legitimacy of his group by also advancing the request through action processes, which unambiguously identify commitment to the anti-communist agenda through transitive constructions, as in examples (1)–(4) above (*convey desire, request help, take opportunity, dedicate energy*). But these transitive constructions alternate with intransitive relational ones:

(22)   the Free Europe Committee was born out of the American people's generosity (183).

(23)   the Romanian national committee is entirely dedicated to the Romanian people (183).

(24)   The national committees are willing to cooperate with one another (184).

These constructions point to the link between the Free Europe Committee and its Romanian counterpart. The relational processes put Visoianu and the RNC on a par with the American officials to whose generosity they are appealing, thus making the appeal seem an entitlement. Situating the RNC and the FEC on the same level also allows Visoianu to describe the relationship between them as one of collaboration rather than of supervision – and thus to avoid a position of political subservience.

Visoianu also represents the request for money as a mental process (through the noun "desire") in a transitive construction that involves a distinction between a "senser" (the Romanian National Committee), or what Fairclough (1992:76) calls "the entity that experiences the mental process" and "the target of that experience," which in this case is the Romanian National Committee. This type of construction creates the assumption that there is a relationship between the two committees before the financial nature of the request is even mentioned. The relationship functions as another justification for the request and makes further arguments by Visoianu unnecessary.

Visoianu made astute efforts to represent the RNC as a united political organization that was unanimously recognized among the Romanian refugees. This representation was hardly accurate, however, and required further work. In the second letter, in which he complained to Leverich about the FEC's withdrawal of funding, he tries to consolidate this discursive representation of the Romanian National Committee by backgrounding and minimizing the internal dissent in the Romanian community. To this end, Visoianu features the Romanian National Committee only in passive constructions like

(25)   The following list of members *was agreed* upon... (193).

(26)   *It was decided* that all the members would... (194).

(27)   *It is well known* that several appointments were made ... (192).

The use of the passive voice glosses over the differences of opinion among the immigrants, shifting the attention away from individual dissenters to the diaspora as a community. A similar function is performed by Visoianu's ambiguous use of the first- person plural pronoun. Throughout the letter, he employs "we" to perform four different referential acts that in his rhetoric are (for strategic reasons) difficult to keep apart. Visoianu uses "we" to refer to (1) refugees from the captive nations, (2) Romanian immigrants in general, (3) members of the Romanian National Committee, and (4) specific, named individuals. Only once does he add an appositive phrase that specifies the identity of the referent, in "we, the current members of the Romanian National Committee," and then the qualification occurs in the context of an agreement reached among the Romanian immigrants:

(28)   It is clear that, when the list was put together, we, the current members of the Romanian committee, agreed to include more representatives of the New York-based group (213).

Yet Visoianu could not completely avoid any reference to the conflicts within the Romanian diaspora, given that these conflicts had been explicitly cited by the Free Europe Committee as the reason for its withdrawal of funds. When he addresses the issue of internal dissent, Visoianu employs transitive constructions that unambiguously identify the culprits and their deeds:

(29)   *Mr. Gafencu maintained* an unacceptable position. He *demanded* the formation of two Romanian Committees, one in the United States and another one in France, under his own presidency (215).

(30)   *Mr. Farcasanu insisted on* a disproportionate number of seats for the former members of the Liberal Party (216).

(31)   *Nicolae Malaxa made* every effort, through corruption and slander, to block the formation of the Romanian National Committee (216).

By naming names and mentioning specific activities in transitive constructions, Visoianu tries to contain the dissent and to salvage the idea that the Romanian National Committee is a stable organization. At the same time, note the contrast between these transitive constructions with unambiguous content, which isolate and condemn the dissenters, and the passive constructions, which gloss over the identity and number of the immigrants who agree with one another. Through its explicitness and directness, the first category contributes to the force of Visoianu's critical stance, further presenting him as outraged and blunt, unafraid to recognize problems, and solely concerned with the truth. Thus, the transitive constructions reinforce the rhetorical effect of modality, reinforcing the assertive style of a speaker who has strong beliefs and is willing to express them firmly. In the context of such a style, his accusations appear all the more justified, while his claims to entitlement go unquestioned.

In the third letter, which issued recommendations for the organization of the FEC, Visoianu uses impersonal or passive constructions that identify actions without designating the actors who would be responsible for them:

(32)   A system of periodical consultations between the Radio services and the committees *must be established* (218).

(33)   Conditions for cooperation *should* also *be established* for the activities of the national committees (218).

(34)   The Committees lose their efficiency if they *are not taken seriously* (219).

(35)   The supervision of compromised immigrants [those who served in fascist organizations in the home country] *must be pursued* carefully and wisely (220).

(36)   The compromising of the United States [which would occur if the national communities failed to reach their purpose] *should be avoided* at all costs (220).

The FEC was the organization responsible for immigrant activities in the United States, and by extension for carrying out the re-structuring proposed by Visoianu. But this is the organization that had already given the Romanians trouble, so Visoianu tries to limits its control by obscuring its agency. In conjunction with the deontic modality featured in his recommendations, the de-emphasizing of the agency of the Free Europe Committee represents an important emancipatory gesture. It is the discursive attempt of a refugee to assert his subjectivity as a legitimate political actor and thus to assert the rights and autonomy of the organization he is representing. Such emancipation, though, must be carefully controlled so as not to be confused with a rejection of American patronage. The use of the passive voice allows Visoianu as the agent to maintain a presence, but one that is strategically toned down; it also allows the Free Europe Committee to remain readily available for identification as the group responsible for supporting the political life of the refugees. Intransitivity, then, gives Visoianu a discursive form for expressing two rhetorical goals that would otherwise work against each other: to insist on continued support from the American government, and to also keep it (or its main representative) at arm's length.

Throughout the three documents, transitivity informs a subjectivity that aspires to both political independence and a clientele relationship with the United States. This subjectivity redefines the terms of the encounter, making it more like a diplomatic negotiation between state officials and politicians than a plea for help. But Visoianu was a political refugee with no official responsibility. He was entirely dependent on the American government – not just for support for the activities of Romanian refugees, but also for his own residence visa in the United States. He and others like him were the recipients of decisions made by the American officials, both regarding the national group to which they belonged, and their own situation as individual immigrants. It is this relation of political subordination that Visoianu sought to modify. His strategic use of language functions as an attempt to engage the interlocutor – in each case a powerful official – from a position of equality and to speak as an official himself.

Conclusion

The Cold War saw a massive increase in political immigration to the United States, and among the newly arrived, many wanted to use the resources of the host country to influence the fate of their homeland and to return there safely, rather than stay and start a new life. My analysis has focused on how refugees can assert political legitimacy in order to be able to pursue their goals. Using the case of Constantin Visoianu, leader of the Romanian National Committee, I have shown how political legitimacy can be derived from stylistic mechanisms that bestow upon the agent a particular subjectivity, that of a statesman. My analysis has also revealed that what gave his stylistic choices weight and effectiveness was their strategic connection to the official ideology of the period.

In Visoianu's case, style allowed him to act discursively as a statesman negotiating with a peer rather than as a refugee-supplicant. As a statesman, he could protest too much intervention in the affairs of his organization from U.S. officials while continuing to negotiate for financial support. As a statesman, he could issue guidelines for the "cooperation" between his group and the American government. But as a statesman he also had to project a unified image of his organization in order to avoid, or rebut, the criticism that he and the RNC did not speak for the Romanian nation.

To pursue my investigation of Visoianu's legitimation through style and ideological alignment with official American discourse, I have relied on insights from rhetorical studies of Cold War ideology. But I have also had to amend the theoretical assumptions on which these studies are based with regard to the problem of ideology. Much of this rhetorical scholarship tends to equate ideology with official political discourse, and to pay little or no attention to discourse from outside of, or from the margins of, the official political arena. Conversely, critical discourse analysis offers an understanding of ideology that focuses on the negotiation, rather than the imposition, of beliefs and values between those in power and those who challenge power from the margins or even outside the political spectrum. The emancipatory agenda of the CDA, which sets out to expose injustices or manipulations of social categories and individuals by institutions and people in power, is well suited for the study of the legitimation of refugees who are used in the political battles of their host countries, as Eastern European refugees were during the Cold War.

My analysis also departs from the more common course taken in rhetorical studies, because it argues that studying style as critical discourse analysts do is more productive in this situation. Where RA still tends to operate under the dictate of a long tradition that equated style with figures and persuasion with eloquence, CDA is more oriented toward common speech and completely disavows the figurative-literal distinction. Visoianu's style resides not in figures but in his use of particular grammatical constructions. I study the role played by modality and transitivity in defining his style, the former by conveying assertiveness and self-confidence, and the latter by depicting the Romanian refugees as united under his leadership and committed to the fight against communism.

Immigration scholars have argued that the successful mobilization of immigrants on homeland-related affairs can lead to the "assimilation or reinforcement of basic American values" (Shain 1999:199). My analysis suggests that the political mobilization of refugees during the Cold War amounted to more than merely an assimilationist project. Visoianu's success in keeping America's interest in his country alive for the first two decades of the Cold War – even when American politicians began to argue for a policy of containment – depended on his ability not simply to "assimilate" the American ideology, but also to put it to strategic use in their discursive practices. Visoianu's references to anti-communism and to America's fight for freedom played an important role in legitimating him as a political actor who could demand to be consulted, obeyed, and respected. Visoianu's use of modality as a way to assert his authority as president of the RNC, and thus as a statesman, exploited American anti-communist feelings. In more general terms, this analysis suggests that immigrants' political agenda should not be uncritically assumed to be merely a reduplication of the host country's goals and values, or slavishly to follow its foreign policy desiderata, in order to be successful.

References

Black, Edwin. 1978. *Rhetorical Criticism: A Study in Method*, 2nd ed. Madison: University of Wisconsin Press.

Bostdorff, Denise. 1994. *The Presidency and the Rhetoric of Foreign Crisis*. Columbia: The University of South Carolina Press.

Brockriede, Wayne and Robert L. Scott. 1970. *Moments in the Rhetoric of the Cold War*. New York: Random House.

Carpenter, Ronald H. 1994. "The Stylistic Persona of Bill Clinton. From Arkansas to Aristotelian Attica". *Bill Clinton on Stump, State, and Stage*. Stephen A Smith, ed., 101–132. Fayetteville: The University of Arkansas Press.

Chilton, Paul and Christina Schäffner. 1997. "Discourse and Politics". In *Discourse as Social Interaction*. Teun A. van Dijk, ed., 206–231. Thousand Oaks, Calif.: Sage.

Cloud, Dana. 1998. "The Rhetoric of Family Values: Scapegoating, Utopia, and the Privatization of Social Responsibility". *Western Journal of Communication* 62. 387–419.

Coicaud, Jean-Marc. 2002. *Legitimacy and Politics: A Contribution to the Study of Political Right and Political Responsibility*. Cambridge: Cambridge University Press.

Condit, Celeste Michelle and John Louis Lucaites. 1993. *Crafting Equality: America's Anglo-African Word*. Chicago: University of Chicago Press.

Fahnestock, Jeanne. 1986. "Accommodating Science: The Rhetorical Life of Scientific Facts". *Written Communication* 3. 275–296.

———. *Rhetorical Figures in Science*. New York: Oxford University Press.

Fairclough, Norman. 1992. *Discourse and Social Change*. Cambridge: Polity Press.

Hariman, Robert. 1995. *Political Style: The Artistry of Power*. Chicago: The University of Chicago Press.

Ivie, Robert. 1999. "Fire, Flood, and Red Fever: Motivating Metaphors of Global Emergency in the Truman Doctrine Speech". *Presidential Studies Quarterly* 29. 570–592.

Jaroszynska-Kirchmann, Anna. 2004. *Exile Mission: The Polish Political Diaspora and the Polish Americans, 1939–1956*. Columbus: Ohio University Press.

Jaworski Adam and Dariusz Galasinsky. 2000. "Vocative Address Forms and Ideological Legitimation in Political Debates". *Discourse Studies* 2. 35–53.

Johnstone, Barbara. 1996. *The Linguistic Individual*. Oxford: Oxford University Press.

Jost, Brenda and John T. Major. 2001. *The Psychology of Legitimation: Emerging Perspectives on Ideology, Justice, and Intergroup Relations*. Cambridge: Cambridge University Press.

Kovrig, Bennet. 1991. *Of Walls and Bridges: United States and Eastern Europe*. Oxford: Oxford University Press.

Kress, Gunther. 1988. "Textual Matters: The Social Effectiveness of Style". *Functions of Style*. Ed. By David Birch and Michael O'Toole 126–142. London: Pinter Publishers.

Mailloux, Steven. 1989. *Rhetorical Power*. Ithaca: Cornell University Press.

McGee, Michael Calvin. 1980. "The 'Ideograph': A Link Between Rhetoric and Ideology". *Quarterly Journal of Speech* 66. 1–16.

McKerrow, Raymie E. 1989. "Critical Rhetoric: Theory and Praxis". *Communication Monographs*. 56. 91–111.

Medhurst, Martin J. 1987. "Eisenhower's 'Atoms for Peace' Speech: A Case Study in the Strategic Use of Language". *Communication Monographs*. 54. 204–220.

_____. 1990. "Rhetoric and Cold War: A Strategic Approach". *Cold War Rhetoric. Strategy, Metaphor, and Ideology*. Edited by Martin J. Medhurst et al, 19–28. Westport: Greenwood Press.

Murphy, John M.1997. "Inventing Authority: Bill Clinton, Martin Luther King, Jr., and the Orchestration of Rhetorical Traditions". *Quarterly Journal of Speech* 83. 71–89.

Schechter, Darrow. 2005. *Beyond Hegemony: Towards a New Philosophy of Political Legitimacy*. Manchester: Manchester University Press.

Scott, Robert L. "Cold War and Rhetoric: Conceptually and Critically". *Cold War Rhetoric. Strategy, Metaphor, and Ideology*. Ed. by Martin J. Medhurst et al, 1–18. Westport: Greenwood Press.

Shain, Yossi. 1999. *Marketing the American Creed Abroad: Diasporas in the United States and their Homelands*. Cambridge: Cambridge University Press.

Shanks, Cheryl. 2001. *Immigration and the Politics of American Sovereignty, 1890–1990*. Ann Arbor, Mi: University of Michigan Press.

Titscher, Stefan, et. al.. 2000. *Methods of Text and Discourse Analysis*. Thousand Oaks: Sage.

Visoianu, Constantin. 2000. *Din misiunile mele*. Bucuresti: Editura Ministerului de Externe.

Wander, Philip. 1990. "Critical and Classical Theory: An Introduction to Ideology Criticism". *Cold War Rhetoric. Strategy, Metaphor, and Ideology*. Ed. by Martin J. Medhurst et al., 131–152. Westport: Greenwood Press.

_____. 1984. "The Rhetoric of American Foreign Policy". *Quarterly Journal of Speech* 70. 339–361.

Weber, Max. 1987. *Economy and Society: An Outline of Interpretive Sociology*. Berkeley: University of California Press.

Webner, Pnina. 1999. "The Fiction of Unity in Ethnic Politics: Aspects of Representation and the State among British Pakistanis". *Black and Ethnic Leadership. The Cultural Dimensions of Political Action*. Ed. By Pnina Webner, 113–145. London: Routledge.

Wodak, Ruth. 1989. *Language, Power, and Ideology*. Amsterdam: John Benjamins.

Zelditch, Morris Jr.. 1998. *Status, Power, and Legitimacy*. New Brunswick, N.J.: Transaction Publishers.

CHAPTER 3

Reporting Waco

The constitutive work of bureaucratic style

Christopher Eisenhart

University of Massachusetts, Dartmouth

On February 28, 1993, agents of the Bureau of Alcohol Tobacco and Firearms (the ATF) attempted to execute search-and-arrest warrants for Vernon Howell, also known as David Koresh. The ATF attempted to raid the Mt. Carmel Center outside Waco, Texas, which served as the residence for Koresh's religious sect, the Branch Davidians. The raid failed, and the ensuing gunfight killed four ATF officers and at least five Davidians and injured many on both sides. After a ceasefire was negotiated, law enforcement jurisdiction was turned over to the FBI, who oversaw a 51-day siege. The negotiations during that time did yield some results: several adults and children left the Mt. Carmel Center. However, on April 19, when the FBI attempted to drive the Davidians out with tear gas, roughly 90 members were still inside. During the course of that day, a fire consumed the building, killing at least 70 Davidians.

For all the publicity surrounding the event, there were few signs of great public outcry or of the beginnings of a broad public controversy immediately after the fire. There were, however, calls for the agencies to review and report on their own actions. In fact, the Treasury Department began the process of reviewing ATF involvement following the Feb. 28 attempt to serve warrants well before the siege ended.[1] In addition, the Justice Department conducted a review of the involvement of the FBI at Waco almost immediately following the catastrophic outcomes of April 19. The reports that were the primary discursive products of these reviews

---

1. "Clearly, there needed to be a comprehensive review of the events of February 28, and of the process that lead up to the raid. The Treasury Department began planning for such a review during the 51 -day stand- off that followed the failed raid." October 31, 1995, from the statement of H. Geoffrey Moulton Jr., Associate Professor, Widener University School of Law; Project Director, Department of the Treasury Waco administrative review before the Senate Judiciary Committee body

eventually received considerable attention; however, government statements to the public immediately after the Waco conflict were framed as accounts of the disaster rather than as condemnations of its handling by law enforcement.

Once the Justice Report and Treasury Report were published, Congress scheduled no additional investigations of the Waco incidents. In terms of the public record, it appeared that the reports submitted by the Departments of Treasury and Justice would be the final governmental word on Waco. For two years, Waco was only a tangential subject in public House and Senate hearings. It was not until July of 1995 that Congress held ten days of joint hearings, kicking off a one-year joint Congressional Review of government involvement in Waco. During the time between the publication of the initial government reports and the summer of 1995, a controversial climate had built around Waco. That controversy appears to have been focused largely around the representation of Waco in the government reports and, most tragically, around the bombing of the Murrah Federal building in Oklahoma City in April of 1995, on the two-year anniversary of the Waco fire, which inevitably linked the two events.[2]

The two government reports generated immediately after the Waco event are the primary texts analyzed in this study. Neither report has clearly demonstrable authorship; each presents itself as the collective findings of reviewer personnel. The involvement of the Bureau of Alcohol, Tobacco, and Firearms (the ATF) was reviewed by the Treasury Department, because it was then a law enforcement arm of that department. The Justice Department reviewed the involvement of the Federal Bureau of Investigations (FBI) and remains its parent organization. Together, these reports constitute a single narrative whole, and for at least two years after the Waco event, constituted the government's single most authoritative word on what happened at Waco.

The government report as genre

In the wake of highly public and controversial events, American government institutions such as congressional committees, agencies, and presidential commissions often generate a staggering volume of reporting, hearings, and accounting. In some instances, these may be recognized among the most authoritative of accounts. For example, the 9/11 Commission has been among the most authoritative voices in any public debate about that event, and the 9/11 Commission Report has

---

2.   Timothy McVeigh quoted in the Boston Herald, "If there would not have been a Waco, I would have put down roots somewhere and not been so unsettled with the fact that my government ... was a threat to me. Everything that Waco implies was on the forefront of my thoughts. That sort of guided my path for the next couple of years."(Mashberg, June 10, 2001)

been the Commission's most significant discursive act. The 9/11 Commission Report, published by Norton and sold at every Barnes and Noble, made its way into American public discourse to a degree perhaps matched only by the 1964 Warren Commission Report about the assassination of President John F. Kennedy in 1963. The 9/11 Commission's decision to use a private press and bookseller usurped the usual process of printing and distribution by the U.S. Government Press Office (GPO) claiming a role for the government report as a means of public information, and as a source in and for public debate.

In a retrospective account of his involvement as a special investigator into the Waco event in 2000, John Danforth discussed the exigence for such work.

> The situation, before I became special counsel, was this. In December of 1999, *Time* Magazine had a poll, and the poll said that 61 percent of the American people believed that the FBI started the fire at Waco. Now, when 61 percent of the American people believe such a dire thing as that federal agents started a fire that killed some 80 people, that is a real breakdown in public confidence in their government. That's why I believed the Waco investigation was so important. We looked into some very dark charges that had been made against the FBI, that the FBI started the fire, that FBI agents fired guns into the complex when the building was on fire to pin people into it. And in our investigation, which lasted 14 months and cost \$17 million, we proved, with absolute certainty, that these dark thoughts about the FBI were definitely not true (Federal News Service 2001, under "Hearing of the Senate Judiciary Committee").

Government hearings and reports enter into climates of public contention over a disputed past, attempting to create rhetorical *presence* for certain aspects of an event while simultaneously silencing others.[3] As in any other accounting for or commemoration of a controversial event, some voices are given priority over others.[4] Expensive to conduct and produce, government hearings, commissions, and reports expend political and economic resources toward the creation of a univocal and monolithic representation of an event. Such acts, often framed within a mandate of "providing a full account" of what went wrong, are constitutive forces attempting to render a controversial event as a more univocal icon in public discourse.[5]

---

3.   On "presence," see Perelman (1982) and Perelman and Olbrechts-Tytecha (1969).

4.   See Wells (1990) and Sauer's discussion (2000) of how not only different voices, but also different modes of discourse are granted priority in institutional accounting for risk and disaster.

5.   A contrastive example of a report which apparently preserves tension and multiple voices can be found in Erik Doxater's discussion of the TRC's Final Report as part of the reconciliation process in South Africa (2003:274).

Following Max Weber, rhetorical theorist Robert Hariman (1995) argues that bureaucratic style is an enactment of bureaucratic logic attempting to co-opt its audiences. For an audience to take the bureaucratic account of an event seriously, they must assume the problems posed by the event were potentially avoidable or manageable with the apt and efficient performance of government structure (Wells 1990). Bureaucratic accounting for these kinds of events operates against a standard of a catastrophe-free or disaster-free existence. Granting these accounts as authoritative presumes that the events they recount constitute a hiccup in an otherwise normalized and bureaucratically regulated existence.

When events such as assassinations, terrorist attacks, and national disasters are included within the jurisdiction of bureaucratic accounting, they are thereby framed as problems that the government and its bureaucratic structure should be able to solve (or prevent). Hearings and reports are a primary discursive means of recovering the control manifestly "lost" in the tragedy, disaster, catastrophe, attack, etc. Retroactively, government reports and hearings bring these types of events back under governmental and bureaucratic control. This work re-establishes the sense of all-pervasive bureaucratic control, care, and oversight after an upsetting event.

Hariman (1995) discusses the features of a bureaucratic style in perpetuating bureaucratic structures. For his example, he takes the characterization of bureaucratic society in the fiction of Franz Kafka:

> Under the illusion of critique, the reader reinscribes the terms of bureaucratic legitimacy. If the officials appear laughable because they are inefficient and prevaricating, it is only because one has assumed the legitimacy of the corresponding norms of efficiency and precision. We laugh at them, but the joke finally is on us (147).

Hariman's discussion of bureaucratic style exemplifies the North American rhetorical approach to style as constitutive meaning-making, wherein variations in performance that might be considered stylistic variations are recognized not merely as coloration, but as the construction of meaning.[6] In what follows I explore the details of how these types of texts do the rhetorical work of constituting and reinscribing bureaucratic control. Following Hariman, I ask, "What are the characteristic manners, modes of manipulation, or persuasive appeals embedded within bureaucratic organizations" (148)? My analysis uncovers three ways that these reports re-establish and reify bureaucratic control: (1) through the entextualization of an event into bureaucratic logic (2) through stylistic choices that create and authorize characters in the event and in the accounting for the event, and (3) through stylistic choices that locate responsibility for the event.

---

6.   Charland (1987) provides a landmark discussion of "constitutive rhetoric."

Entextualizing bureaucratic structure

Silverstein and Urban (1996) argue that studies of discourse should consider the exertion of power taking place when events are de-contextualized as they are discursively created or "entextualized":

> To turn something into a text is to seem to give it a de-contextualized structure and meaning; that is, a form and meaning that are imaginative apart from the spatiotemporal and other frames in which they can be said to occur (1).

Other treatments of "textualization" explicitly discuss the creation of institutions through discursive practices as an essential function in organizational life (Anderson 2004; Geisler 2001). These treatments develop a Foucauldian critique, wherein inscription is taken as the creation of structure, eliding or eliminating individual agency. To study (en)textualization is to ask the question, "In what ways is the creation of this event-as-text an imposition of organization, order, structure, or logic onto the event?" To answer that question, I discuss the ways the government reports on Waco both followed and imposed a logic, parsing the events' outcomes along lines of organizational authority and responsibility.

The two government reports on Waco – one focused on the ATF and the other on the FBI – were both created by institutional mandate. These two reports overlap very little, which is consistent with the logic of independent institutional structures of the law enforcement agencies. Although both are part of the executive branch of government, the FBI and ATF were not then members of the same department (the ATF was then a law enforcement agency of the Treasury Department, the FBI an agency of the Justice Department). The framework of this bureaucratic structure implies that their internal reviews should distinguish rather than synthesize the events of February 28 – the initial raid – and April 19 – the final raid and fire. Indeed, the two agencies create parallel distinctions between the events, as they set bounds around events' beginnings and ends based on the separate involvement of each.

Institutional structures within the Departments of Treasury and Justice appear to have dictated the framework for their reports, and the resulting narratives reinforce the underlying logic of those structures. The Treasury Report focuses on the telling and retelling of events leading up to, and including, some events of March 1, 1993, the day after the ATF's abortive raid. Then, the Report's narrative ends abruptly, with the transfer of authority from the ATF to the FBI.

(1) The next day, March 2, the HRT [Hostage Rescue Team] took control of the inner perimeter from ATF agents, who by then had supplanted local law enforcement officials. In turn, the ATF agents took the positions of the outer perimeter previously held by local law enforcement... Transfer to the FBI of

control of the inner perimeter effectively ended ATF's authority over and responsibility for the standoff (118).

By ending here, the Treasury Report frames the event within the bureaucratic structure of the law enforcement agency. As the audience, we are encouraged to imagine that the ATF had no responsibility for anything that happened after March 1. By the logic of the report structure, at the moment when the ATF no longer had legal authority over the siege, the moment when authority had been transferred to the FBI, there was an end to the ATF's responsibility for the conflict, regardless of what followed. Put another way, within its bureaucratic structure, it makes absolute sense to end the Treasury Report's narrative here, and to leave the accounting of events, and the attribution of responsibility for all the events from March 2 to April 19, to the Justice Department.

This logic is reinforced by the Justice Department Report, which glosses events leading up to and including the ATF raid only to introduce the account of FBI involvement.

> (2)   On February 28, 1993, at approximately 9.30 A.M., Central Time, agents
>   of the Bureau of Alcohol, Tobacco, and Firearms (ATF) came under heavy
>   gunfire while attempting to execute an arrest warrant for Vernon Howell,
>   otherwise known as David Koresh. The warrant authorized Koresh's arrest
>   for federal firearms and explosives violations. An accompanying search war-
>   rant authorized the ATF agents to search the compound where Koresh and
>   his followers, known as the Branch Davidians, lived near Waco, Texas. Four
>   ATF agents were killed and sixteen were wounded during the shootout with
>   the Branch Davidians on February 28. Additionally, a number of individuals
>   inside the compound were killed and injured; however, the number killed by
>   ATF gunfire cannot be precisely determined.
>
>   Within a few hours of the incident, and at the request of ATF officials, the
>   FBI dispatched trained negotiators to the scene in Waco. By that afternoon,
>   the FBI, in cooperation with the ATF and Department of Treasury officials,
>   had also sent in advance units of its elite Hostage Rescue Team. The next day
>   (March 1, 1993), also at the request of Treasury Department officials, the FBI
>   became the lead agency responsible for resolving the standoff with the Branch
>   Davidians. (1)

Here the Justice Department Report briefly recreates the early events at Waco un-der ATF control to set the scene for the FBI's assumption of control, the point when this report begins. These two reports overlap very little, which is consistent with the logic of independent institutional structures of the law enforcement agencies.

This entextualization reinforces distinctions between institutional involve-ment and responsibility in Waco. In the two reports, the events from March 2 (two days after the initial raid) through April 19 have nothing to do with the ATF. Likewise, the events leading through to March 1 have nothing to do with the FBI. In this way, the violent outcomes of Feb. 28 and April 19th are dispersed. By ending the review of ATF involvement on March 1, the ATF is made distinct from the outcomes of April 19, and in fact the two events themselves are made distinct from one another. Rather than highlighting what might be considered gaps in law enforcement practice and policy, this reporting structure along bureaucratic lines tends to reinforce the view that each agency acted appropriately in dealing with the events under its purview. But the entextualization of the Waco story and its use to buttress these institutions also has more subtle effects. It encourages a fragmented, bureaucratic way of seeing an event that otherwise might be viewed – and has largely been commemorated elsewhere – in a narrative whole.

Characters, actions, and responsibilities in the reports

Sentence-level choices about how to represent "how things are" is another means by which bureaucratic logic is discursively perpetuated. As Johnstone suggests, "Choices about the metaphorical representation of people and events both reflect and create ways of imagining what is normal"(2002:49). Hodge and Kress (1996) discuss the potential "ideological effect" of the non-agentive representation of a character by grammatical means to maintain power relations or ideological structures. They suggest that through grammatical positioning, actors become the affected, and vice-versa:

> The effect of this linguistic process is to reassign the actor roles in the two conflated models. The real actor of the process is denied credit and responsibility for the action he performs, and this credit is assigned to the syntactic participant who is regarded as more powerful. It is a thing not lightly done (60).

According to Hodge and Kress, *non-transactive* structures are semantic structures which confuse cause and effect relations. They discuss the effect of this structuring:

> The intrinsic limitations of the non-transactive model in all this are clear. The direction of causality, who is doing what to whom, what is acting on what, is left uncertain. As a result, no causal chain can be envisaged, since in terms of the model there is no distinction between causer/actor and affected, the beginning and end of the causal unit. A whole set of questions about causality are unaskable, or receive only pseudo-answers, answers which essentially restate the vagueness of the model (42).

Much of the Treasury Report on the ATF at Waco is a highly active and agentive narrative representing "what happened" at Waco. However, the *metadiscursive* sections – sections, that is, in which the report describes its own authorship, the process of the review, and the credibility of its account – possess features typical of bureaucratic style in the sense that they work to represent and reify the institutions involved. The metadiscursive text of the Treasury Report works to establish the credibility of the reviewers and the report. This credibility is partly established through the representation of three groups of characters: (1) President Bill Clinton, Treasury Secretary Lloyd Bentsen, and Assistant Secretary Ronald Noble (2) outside experts and independent reviewers, and (3) "the Review," which is a compilation of all those who conducted the nuts-and-bolts work of investigation, analysis, and authorship. The representation of the first two groups of characters shifts individual authority and agency toward the bureaucratic institution of the review process. It is through this representation that "the Review" becomes authorized to bring the controversial event under the bureaucratic umbrella.

The Treasury Review's metadiscourse highlights President Clinton's mandate and the authorization by Treasury Secretary Lloyd Bentsen, and passes that credibility to Assistant Secretary Ronald Noble as the director of the project and to the review. The Report represents high-ranking characters as agents ("President Clinton promptly directed"; "Secretary of the Treasury Lloyd Bentsen asked Ronald. K Noble, who was then designated to be Assistant Secretary of the Treasury for enforcement, to focus on "; Charged by Secretary Bentsen to examine "whether procedures policies and practices were adequate and whether they were followed," "Assistant Secretary Noble promised"; "Secretary Bentsen selected"). This agentive representation establishes the hierarchy of authority: Clinton's mandate, Bentsen's authorization, and Noble's introduction with title and endorsement. Identifying these three as particular agents within the metadiscourse emphasizes their authority over and influence on the review process.

The second group of characters in the Treasury Report metadiscourse consists of the "experts" and "independent reviewers" brought in to contribute analyses of the materials, to make recommendations, and in some cases to replicate the work of the Treasury's own report with individual reports, some of which were included as appendices. In the metadiscourse of the Treasury Report, however, participating experts and independent reviewers are grammatically represented as objects, a representation that semantically transfers their admirable qualities to the review process.

The following excerpt demonstrates the representation of the role of experts and reviewers in the review process:

(3)   In addition, on May 3, 1993, the Department further announced *the selection of three independent reviewers* to ensure that the Department's administrative review was comprehensively and impartially conducted. These *reviewers were selected* because of their national *prominence, integrity* and law enforce-

ment *expertise*. The *reviewers are responsible* for *providing* guidance to the investigation, *reviewing* the investigative team's findings and *providing* an independent assessment of the information contained in the final report (ix, emphasis added).

In this passage, the "independent reviewers" are co-opted by the review process more than participants with agency in it. They are introduced as grammatical objects in the first sentence of the passage ("the Department further announced the selection of three independent reviewers to ensure"). Rather than saying that "reviewers ensure," which would make them somewhat agentive, the Report uses the nominalized act of "selection" by "the Department" as what "ensures." In sentences in which reviewers are the subject, ("reviewers are responsible for"), the structure is relational. The *relational* semantic structure relates attributes to a category, in this case, the category, "reviewers" with the attributes, "responsibility." These responsibilities (providing, reviewing, and providing) are gerund phrases, each begun with these abstract, but generally positive verbs. In each, more active verbs are nominalized as objects the reviewers possess. Each of these choices minimizes the action and reduces the agency of the reviewers.

Both the non-transactive sentence and the relational sentence cast the reviewers as containers of categories (prominence, integrity, and expertise) controlled within the larger agency of the review. The implication is that the experts' and independent reviewers' virtues are appropriated by other, more powerful agents within the review process and the report, subsuming any agency the experts and independent reviewers had in either the review or the report. Unsurprisingly, as institutional or organizational higher-ups authorize, the figures lower on the institutional totem pole do the work for less credit.

Finally, "the Review" incorporates the Treasury Department officers and others who constitute the working force of the review process and the writers of the report. This character is more complex than the previous two character groups, in part because this character is the lynchpin of the report. The character receives all the credibility assigned by and borrowed from the previous two character groups, operating as an agentive, but ultimately supra-human investigator and author. "The review" takes the actions of investigating, interviewing, analyzing and interpreting to provide this text's final word on Waco.[7] This work is done in two ways: naming conventions and the use of spatial metaphors to establish relations among characters.

---

7.   For another discussion in which federal reviews and reports play prominent character roles, see Miller (2003).

Naming conventions and spatial relations

Naming conventions are used in the Report's metadiscourse to create the character of "the Review." It is initially spelled out in full title, ("Department of the Treasury's Waco Administrative Review") reduced ("the Review") and repeated ("I established the Review"), which makes it an efficient moniker. For example,

> (4)   To assure that the *Waco Administrative Review*, conducted by the Treasury Department, would fulfill its promise of objectivity and comprehensiveness, Secretary Bentsen selected three prominent individuals with expertise in law enforcement and experience in media relations to guide *the Review's* investigation and report to the public on its findings (2).

This example contains the most straightforward of the naming strategies: the reduction of all investigation, administration, and reporting into "the Review."

Example (4) also illustrates one way that bureaucratic structure is established using spatial relations. The relationship of all three character groups is sketched out with Bentsen, again as the most active character or agent, having selected experts to guide the investigation and the report of the Review.[8] This top-down structure of the review is repeated, with the Department's mission and Assistant Secretary Noble as the powers sequentially and figuratively positioned in a space above the work and workers of the review (e.g., "Under the overall supervision of ... Noble"). This top-down structure permeates the metadiscourse of the Report, as the construction of the Review-as-character operates on the combination of naming and spatial relations.

Example (5) illustrates the ways "the Review" itself is constituted as an agent of action, and the way the authority of this metonymic character is established through naming conventions and spatial relations. Here again, spatial relations represent institutional relations, and reinforce the sense that credible figures are in control of the Review. In addition, this "Project Statement" uses a series of nominalizations, passive verbs, prepositional phrases, and positioning of human characters as objects to represent the agent, "the Review."

---

8.   We might note the phrase "selected three prominent individuals with expertise in law enforcement and experience in media relations to guide the Review's investigation and report to the public on its findings." It is somewhat ambiguous in this sentence whether the "three prominent individuals" guide the Review's investigation and report, or if the individuals guide and report on the investigation. The ambiguity need not be explained away here; however, I should note that it might be taken as an indication of a less carefully constructed subject structure, and should remind us that this analysis teases out potential rhetorical effects and ways of structuring experience and relations within discourse, but makes no claims to authors' intentions.

(5)   The mission of the Treasury Department Office of Enforcement was to conduct a comprehensive inquiry into the ATF operation, from the initiation of its investigation of Koresh's activities through the raid at the Branch Davidian Compound on February 28 and its aftermath. Under the overall supervision of Assistant Secretary Noble, a team of attorneys and law enforcement agents conducted interviews, obtained primary source materials and exhibits, viewed the compound and other key sites near Waco, and analyzed the materials and information gathered. Based on this investigation, including the credibility assessments and circumstantial evidence, the review made factual determinations and analyzed those facts. Assistant Secretary Noble provided final oversight of the report before its submission to Secretary Bentsen.

The review's day-to-day operations were supervised by the project director, H. Geoffrey Moulton, Jr., Associate Professor at Widener University School of Law in Delaware, and the assistant project directors, Lewis C. Merletti, Deputy Assistant Director of the U.S. Secret Service, and David L. Douglass, an attorney on leave from Wiley, Rein & Fielding in Washington, D.C. The review's investigators included 17 senior agents from the Secret Service, the Customs Service, the Internal Revenue Service (both the Criminal Investigation Division and the Internal Security Division), and the Financial Crimes Enforcement Network. These agents, whose names and bureau affiliations are listed at the front of this report, brought to the review an extraordinary range of investigative and tactical experience from law enforcement and the military. Their collective expertise enabled the review to conduct a comprehensive examination of ATF's investigation of Koresh.

In addition, the review was assisted by a computer expert from the Federal Law Enforcement Training Center, an intelligence research specialist from the Customs Service, and clerical support from several Treasury agencies. These agents and other personnel were detailed to the review full-time. Four other attorneys were also assigned to the review: two from Treasury's Office of General Counsel, another detailed to Treasury from the Interagency Council on the Homeless, and one who had recently completed a federal district court clerkship.

The investigative team maintained offices at the Department of the Treasury's main building. Access to these offices, the review's computers, and records compiled by the review was restricted to ensure the confidentiality and integrity of the investigation (3–4).

In the first sentence, the review has already begun to be represented as an entity rather than as an action, although the ambiguity of *review* as verb or nominalization remains in play throughout the text. The first of several names given the review in this section is the nominalization "comprehensive inquiry" in the first sentence. In the second sentence, the relationship between Noble and the review is established by placing the "team of attorneys and law enforcement agents" "under" him ("Under the overall supervision of Assistant Secretary Noble, a team of attorneys and law enforcement agents conducted interviews"). This sentence also represents individuals taking actions as a collective, in this case the "team" that undertook the activity of investigation: conducted, obtained, viewed, analyzed. All of those actions are then immediately recast as an entity under the nominalization "investigation," which becomes the basis for the review. This is part of the pattern of developing the review as a metonymic subject subsuming human workers and human work: a part of the review entity does work, and the review is able to operate on that work as a fixed object.

As a character, "the Review" is composed of individuals unified under collective noun synonyms: ("team of attorneys and law enforcement agents"; "The Review's investigators included 17 senior agents"; "Those agents. . . brought to the Review"; "The investigative team maintained offices"). The Review and its other names are consistently collective nouns, and except perhaps for "agents" are non-human nouns, emphasizing a sense of the review as supra-human entity. The text casts the participation of those individuals as passive or as a possession or a quality of the review.

In the second and third paragraphs of the mission statement, individual agents are identified, but their actions are represented in passive clauses ("The Review's day-to-day operations were supervised by H. Geoffrey Moulton, Jr. "; "The Review was assisted by a computer expert"). In addition to topicalizing "the Review," these passive constructions diminish the agency of those individuals by subsuming their actions to those of the review. Further, attributes of individuals, rather than the individuals themselves, contribute to the review's actions ("their collective expertise enabled the Review to conduct a comprehensive examination of ATF's investigation of Koresh"). Here, because "collective expertise" and "the Review" are the only grammatical subjects of verbs, the actions of the individuals contributing that expertise are subsumed under the collective review.

These lexico-grammatical features cast "the Review" as an agent that takes actions. The review co-opts the effort and credibility of actual, individual agents, without the audience ever seeing those individuals taking actions. The objectivity and comprehensiveness of the review as a character determining "what happened at Waco" is reinforced by its linguistic representation; because the review encompasses all efforts and makes all acts seamlessly, the review is never an individual assessing evidence, identifying facts, or reporting them with individual bias. Rather, it is the collective effort, expert perspective, and authoritative account.

Eliding expertise and authorship

The metadiscourse in the Justice Report is a few scant paragraphs in the introduction and one as a closing. Unlike the intricate representations establishing
the character and credibility of the Treasury Review, the Justice Report states its
aims but creates almost no meta-discursive embodiment of itself, as it obliter-
ates almost entirely investigator, source, evidence, and authorial hand, developing
an omniscient narrative perspective from which it recounts events at Waco from
March 1 through April 19. This authorship is created largely through two moves:
the marginalizing of identifiable, expert voices, and the elision of individual investigators, researchers, and authors in the department's investigation and reporting.

In the metadiscourse of the Justice Report, as in the Treasury report, a category
of agents is created for experts and independent reviewers ("An additional report
has been prepared by Edward S.G. Dennis, Jr., a former Assistant Attorney General of the Criminal Division and former United States Attorney for the Eastern
District of Pennsylvania, containing his analysis"; "Finally, nine noted and highly
respected experts have prepared reports with their recommendations concerning
what we as law enforcement, and we as citizens, can learn from this tragedy").
Here, the Justice Report subtly marginalizes the participation of "experts." It does
so in the first example by distinguishing the report from independent reviewer
Dennis. The use of the modifier "additional" together with its separate publication removes it somewhat from the Justice Report. In the second example, the
discourse marker "finally" introduces the unnamed experts as again distinct from
the Justice Department's review. All these independent reviews were also published in separate volumes, further distinguishing them from the main Justice
Department account.

Individual FBI reviewers and authors are absent in the scant metadiscourse of
the Justice Report. Through a series of agentless passives, actions of review and
actions of authoring are mentioned but given no agent: ("as will be discussed later
in this report"; "He will be referred to throughout this report as David Koresh"; "it
can be anticipated"; "interviews were conducted, and tens of thousands of pages
of documents and transcripts were read and analyzed"; "documentation will be
made available to the public"). Elsewhere, participants in the Justice's review process are included only as the objects of prepositional phrases, subordinating their
participation rather than characterizing them as the agents of action ("This report
has been prepared with the cooperation of literally hundreds of individuals").

The report authors do represent an authorial "we" both to testify to the credibility of the report and to offer a disclaimer for the eventuality of further, unre-
ported evidence which might surface ("we believe this report to be accurate and
based upon solid evidentiary grounds; we expect additional details to be revealed
at trial"). However, the "we" here cannot be identified, beyond perhaps referring

to the entire Justice Department or FBI, or at least all the unidentified individuals who worked on the Justice Report. Where the report is described in some detail, it is an authorial agent, rather than its authors ("The report begins with"; "the report will address"). The effect of this obliterated author is to imply an unidentifiable authorial voice, similar to the Treasury Report's representation of "the Review." But where "the Review" was carefully constructed under the credibility of named superiors, borrowing the authority and actions of agents and experts, the authorial voice here is everyone and no one. More than a sum of subordinated and forgotten individual parts, it is always only an anonymous, omniscient voice.

Distinct causal narratives: Institutional v. individual

This analysis focuses on a subset of the stylistic choices within what might be considered the "rhetorical depiction" of the Waco event in these two government reports (Osborn 1986; Gring-Pemble 2001). In her discussion of the role of narratives as a form of rhetorical depiction in political discourse, Gring-Pemble problematizes as overly idealistic the notion that narratives facilitate a more open and multivocal deliberative discourse. "Fisher's insistence upon audiences' ability to judge a text critically based on its narrative rationality ... discounts the power of discourse to shape and position audiences' understanding of their world in particular ways"(359). This conception of the potential power of organizational narratives follows Faber's (1998) discussion of narrative as the means of discursively (re)constructing organizational identity through the act of representing organizational experiences. As do grammatical choices at the sentence level, choices of narrative styles affect the ways agency, authority, and responsibility are assigned for what happened at Waco. The analysis of narratives shows how differing styles can attribute agency primarily to the individual or primarily to the institution. The Treasury Report tells a story of individual ATF agents as named characters acting out investigative roles and driving the narrative. The Justice Report, on the other hand, tells the story of the FBI as an institutional character. The Treasury Report account represents individual characters' actions; the Justice Report account represents an institution very much in control of the situation.

Institutional authority, action, & responsibility in the Justice Report

The Justice Report conveys a strong chain of command, where commanders are the only named agents in the account, and the commanders' decisions are represented as largely or entirely determined by policy set in place before the raid. Agency for Waco is placed at the institutional level through four primary stylistic moves: (1) only supervisors, decisionmakers and negotiators are individually identifiable

(2) individual actions on the ground in Waco are elided in passives, nominalizations, and through attribution to institutional policy and plans (3) those actions which are represented on the ground are attributed to collective noun categories or non-human agents (4) Davidians are represented as a collective, positioning the conflict as between two institutions.

The following examples include these moves, which I discuss further below.

(6)   At 5.59 A.M. SSRA Sage called into the compound and told the person answering the telephone that it was very important that he speak with Schneider or Koresh. Another individual came to the telephone and Sage informed him that gas was about to be introduced; that it was not an assault; that no FBI agents would enter the compound; and that no one should fire weapons. The individual hung up the phone. Two CEVs, or Combat Engineering Vehicles, approached the compound to begin methodically injecting tear gas through spray nozzles attached to their booms.

At this point, SSRA Sage began reading a message over the loudspeaker system to those inside the compound, advising them to come out immediately and that they were now under arrest. The plan to insert the gas was initiated at 6:02 A.M. At 6:04 A.M., the Davidians began shooting at, and hitting, the CEVs. Once the Davidians opened fire, the FBI was authorized to insert gas into the entire compound. The FBI began deploying "ferret" rounds (canisters containing gas) through the windows.

SSRA Sage continued broadcasting his announcement over the loudspeaker system while the armored vehicles continued to insert CS gas at intervals. The intervals occurred during the approximate one-hour period that it took to reload the gas canisters in the vehicles. During these intervals Sage urged the people to come out before more gas was inserted. The Davidians continuing [sic] firing at the FBI vehicles (110–11).

(7)   On Monday morning, the Attorney General and several senior Justice Department representatives gathered with senior FBI officials in the FBI SIOC, where they monitored events throughout the morning via CNN footage and a live audio feed directly from the FBI forward command post in Waco.

The weather conditions in Waco that morning did not work in the FBI's favor. Strong, gusty winds prevailed, which probably helped to disperse the tear gas and fan the flames once the fire started.

The tear gas action began at 5:55 A.M. when HRT Commander Rogers ordered the two CEVs deployed to the compound, with CEV-1 proceeding to the front-left corner of the building and CEV-2 proceeding to the right side of the building. At 5:56 A.M. lead negotiator Byron Sage telephoned the compound and asked to speak with Schneider. It took approximately three minutes for Schneider to come to the phone (285).

(8)   When the Davidians started shooting the scope and pace of the operation changed. Although envisioned originally as an incremental operation that could take as long as two to three days to complete, the operations plan took account of the possibility that the Davidians might respond to the limited nature of the initial gassing operations by opening fire. Under that operations plan, as approved by the Attorney General, "If during *any* tear gas delivery operations, subjects open fire with a weapon, then the FBI rules of engagement will apply and appropriate deadly force will be used. Additionally, tear gas will immediately be inserted into all windows of the compound utilizing the four BV's as well as the CEVs." The FBI opted to escalate the gassing operation but <u>not</u> to shoot back at the compound. In fact, *the FBI did not fire a shot during the entire operation*[42] (emphasis in original).

Between 6:07 and 6:31 the HRT escalated the pace of tear gas delivery pursuant to the "compromise" order from Rogers. The CEVs inserted gas at their designated positions, while the four Bradleys deployed ferret rounds through the windows into the building. At 6:14 and 6:18, the Sierra One post reported that the Davidians were still shooting at the CEVs. At 6:31 the HRT reported that the entire building had been gassed. Rogers halted the gas insertions and ordered his units to stand by. The CEVs were sent to reload the Mark-V systems, a process requiring approximately one hour (289).

Only supervisors, decisionmakers and negotiators are individually identifiable. The only named law enforcement agent taking action in example (6), chief FBI negotiator Byron Sage, does have an individual role in this section ("Sage called. . .and told"; "Sage informed him"; "Sage began reading"; "Sage continued broadcasting"). However, as chief negotiator, Sage is not an actor in Waco's violence. In addition, Sage's actions are represented as following an institutional script. Similarly, example (7) represents only the highest department authority, Attorney General Janet Reno, as a recognizable individual monitoring the event ("the Attorney General and several senior Justice Department representatives gathered with Senior FBI officials in the FBI SIOC"). On the ground in Waco, only the two on-site commanders (Rogers commanding the HRTs and Sage leading the negotiation teams) are identifiable as implementing the authorized plan. Throughout, only the highest authorities, both in Washington, D.C. and at the scene in Waco, are individually recognizable actors.

Individual actions on the ground in Waco are elided in passives, nominalizations, and attribution to institutional policy and plans. Example (6) connects every action to the Justice Department plan and the contingencies of that plan by positioning the FBI as subordinate to the plan ("The plan to insert gas was initiated. . .") and

by implying the presence of an unseen authority ("the FBI was authorized to insert gas...."). The account is of a carefully orchestrated action, where non-human
entities or commanders follow the script of a plan initiated by higher authorities.

In example (7), violent actions are repeatedly connected back to the plan and
policy established by higher authorities, not to the decisions of on-the-ground
commanders or agents. At its most summary levels, the account dilutes these actions by nominalizing violent action on the ground ("Initial Implementation of
the Tear Gas Plan"; "The tear gas action began..."). In addition, the actions of
both commanders and unnamed FBI agents are reconnected to the plan by naming their actions and by positioning the plan and its contingencies as the real forces
driving FBI action. For example, lead negotiator Sage's repeated plea to the Davidians to leave is not represented in the account as negotiation, nor even apparently
as his own words. ("Sage began broadcasting the following message, read from a
prepared script"; "Sage repeated this message, over and over again, until the fire
finished burning later that day"). Sage, as the commander of communications with
the Davidians, follows the authorized script throughout the events of the day.

In example (8), the plan determines the actions the FBI agents should take in
response to gunfire from the Davidians. The plan is represented here as the stand-
in for higher authorities and their decision making ("the operations plan took
account of the possibility"; "Under that operations plan, as approved by the Attorney General"). In addition, the plan and FBI policy determines FBI escalation
in response to Davidian violence ("If subjects open fire with a weapon, then FBI
rules of engagement will apply and appropriate deadly force will be used.") FBI
actions here are in the grammatical passive ("deadly force will be used") distancing FBI agents from violent action yet again. The only decision for commanders
to make on the ground, by this representation, is what force constitutes "appropriate deadly force," and in this account, the FBI – not any single commander or
individual agent – determined that the least deadly force available was appropriate ("The FBI opted to escalate the gassing operation but not to shoot back at the
compound. In fact the FBI did not fire a shot during the entire operation"). The
footnote to this section further reinforces this representation of the FBI escalation
as determined by the plan and authorized from on high, and that their response
was the least violent option available to them.[9]

---

9. "Some observers, including FBI employees who were not privy to the operations plan, have
questioned whether it was proper for the FBI to escalate the operation once the Davidians
opened fire, given that the HRT agents were not threatened by the gunfire while they were inside
the CEVs and Bradleys. First, the FBI had the Attorney General's prior approval to escalate the
operation if the Davidians engaged in hostile conduct. Second, the HRT agents were not completely immune from the hostile fire, as the possibility existed that a round could penetrate an
opening in an armored vehicle and strike one of the occupants. Third, it must be remembered

Also in Example (8) is the institutional, anonymous representation of the FBI in Waco. This institutional or supra-human representation stems from the nominalizing or making passive the actions of agents on the ground ("the scope and pace of the operation changed"; "... deadly force will be used. Additionally, tear gas will immediately be inserted"). Again we see the actions which might be attributed to individual agents or groups of agents attributed instead to non-human entities or institutions ("The FBI opted..."; "the FBI did not fire a shot"; "the HRT escalated the pace of tear gas delivery"; "The CEVs inserted gas...while the four Bradleys deployed Ferret rounds"; "the Sierra One post reported"; "the HRT reported"). This representation belies a sense of individuals taking actions on the ground for which they might be individually responsible. The overall effect of these features is the establishment of a top-down, plan-over-action, institution-over-individual sense of the actions and forces at work at Waco.

Actions are attributed to collective noun categories or non-human agents. In example (6), the FBI vehicles ("Combat Engineering Vehicles" or "CEVs") are given agency ("CEVs ... approached the compound to begin methodically injecting"; "the armored vehicles continued to insert CS gas"). In others, the FBI is, again, characterized as a single entity taking actions in the narrative ("The FBI began deploying 'ferret rounds'"). In example (7), the CEVs and Bradleys, or tank-like vehicles, are the actors on the ground ("The CEVs inserted gas "; "the four Bradleys deployed Ferret rounds through the windows into the building"; "the CEVs were sent to reload"; "CEV-1 approached the front-right corner, time [sic] breaching the front side of the building ... as it injected the gas"; "CEV-2 breached a hole"; "CEV-2 was experiencing mechanical trouble"; "CEV-1 should enlarge the opening in the middle of the front side of the building to provide a larger opening"). Much more than the human FBI agents who manned them, these vehicles become the characters executing the plan, or taking the actions on the ground to deploy tear gas and induce the departure of the Branch Davidians, arguably the most violent actions taken by the FBI during the siege.

Davidians are primarily represented as a collective. In example (8), the representation of escalating violence follows Davidian aggression and fit with the contingencies of the plan. The actions of the Davidians instigate the escalation of the gas plan. Representation of the Davidians ("When the Davidians started shooting"; "the Davidians might respond ... by opening fire"; "Davidians were still shooting") as active characters instigating violence is the catalyst for the change in FBI action, necessitating the response of increased violence from the FBI. In this feature, the Davidians are represented as the cause for escalated violence of

that the FBI exercised remarkable restraint, as it did not fire a single shot during the entire 51 days of the standoff, including the last day."(footnote on 289)

April 19. Davidian actions cause a change in the FBI actions, in accordance with the plan and "rules of engagement." In addition, this collective representation of "the Davidians" frames the conflict as between institutions, rather than as between individuals.

Individual agency in the Treasury Report

The style of the Treasury Report account of events in Waco on February 28 represents named ATF agents as the characters taking actions in Waco. This individual agency is represented through two primary moves: (1) identifiable, individual field agents and their specific actions are represented, (2) omniscient authorship assigns intent and value to actions. The following excerpts illustrate these moves:

(9)   Rodriguez [an undercover ATF agent inside Mt. Carmel shortly before the raid] was shocked. As Koresh repeatedly looked out the window and said, "They're coming," Rodriguez wondered whether the raid was beginning even though he was still in the compound. Needing an excuse to leave, Rodriguez told Koresh he had to meet someone for breakfast, but Koresh did not respond. Other male cult members entered the room, effectively if not intentionally coming between Rodriguez and the door. Fearing that if he did not leave he would be trapped in the compound, Rodriguez contemplated jumping through the window. He repeated that he had to leave for a breakfast appointment. Koresh approached him, and in a manner Rodriguez believed highly uncharacteristic, shook Rodriguez's hand and said, "Good luck, Robert." Rodriguez left the compound, got into his truck and drove to the undercover house.

Agents in the undercover house recall that Rodriguez was visibly upset when he returned from the compound. He complained that the windows of the undercover house were raised and that he could see a camera in one of them. Cavanaugh asked Rodriguez what had happened in the Compound. Rodriguez announced that Koresh was agitated and had said ATF and the National Guard were coming. Cavanaugh asked Rodriguez whether he had seen any guns, had heard anyone talking about guns, or had seen anyone hurrying around. Rodriguez responded in the negative to all three questions. Cavanaugh then told Rodriguez to report his observations to Sarabyn (89).

(10) Similarly, agents inside the civic center recall Sarabyn [the Tactical Commander of the ATF raid teams] running in and calling for their attention. He announced, "Robert has just come out. Koresh knows that ATF and the National Guard are coming." Sarabyn told the agents they would proceed immediately. Sarabyn exhorted the agents to move quickly, repeatedly telling them to hurry, to get their gear because Koresh knew they were coming. There

was no formal briefing, discussion, or evaluation of Rodriguez's information. Several agents report having had qualms about going forward, especially since Koresh had mentioned the National Guard, yet they also felt questioning the decision would be inappropriate (91).

(11)   At the arms room, Agent Jordan managed to "break and rake" the window and Agent Buford threw a distraction device into the room. Buford, Constantino and Jordan entered. Inside, Agent Buford saw a person armed with an assault rifle backing out of a doorway in the far left corner of the room. That individual began firing into the room from the other side of the thin walls. The agents returned fire, but without automatic weapons, which are used to deliver a defensive spray of gunfire, they could not suppress the attacker's fire. The shots fired at the agents inside the room passed through the wall to where Special Agent Millen was positioned on the roof. Shots were also fired at Millen from the first floor up through the roof. He escaped the attacks by sliding down the ladder to the ground.

Inside the room, Buford was shot twice in the upper thigh. Agent Constantino provided cover for Buford and Jordan while they ran back for the window, dove out onto the pitched roof and then dropped to the ground. As Agents Chisolm and Bonaventure dragged Buford out of the line of fire, they were fired upon. A bullet creased Buford's nose. Agent Chisolm threw his body over Buford to protect him.[26] When the shooting stopped, Chisolm and Bonaventure pulled Buford to a safe position. Chisolm, the medic for the team, observed Buford's wounds and began administering an IV to him (99–100).

Identifiable, individual field agents and their specific actions are represented. The Treasury Report account of Feb. 28 moves from an individual character-centered story of the preparations for the raid through an individual character-centered story of the raid itself. The preparations for the raid, as represented in example (9), focus on the actions of individual agents, often placing individuals in specific locations and describing both their actions and their words. As this excerpt shows, the narrative tends to employ very active language, depicting the actions of named individuals, at times down to the level of direct quotations among interlocutors. This style of focusing on the individual conveys both a more dramatic scene and a scene that suggests greater agency in the recognizable individuals on the ground driving the action.

In example (11), the actions of the individual agents absolutely dominate this section of the account. In the manner of an action drama, the account identifies characters exchanging gunfire and taking care of other ATF officers. Most of the action is recounted with individual, named agents in active constructions ("Jordan managed to 'break and rake'"; "He escaped the attacks"; "Constantino provided cover"). Proper noun subjects (or clearly attributable pronouns) and active verbs represent the action of the gunfight. Where there are passive constructions or unidentifiable characters, they refer to violence perpetrated by unidentified Branch Davidians against the agents ("Shots were also fired"; "The shots fired at the agents"; "That individual began firing"). Individual characters are not identified in this narrative only when their identities presumably cannot be verified.

Authorship assigns intent and character to those actions. In excerpt (10), not only are the actions and words of individual characters part of the narrative, but values are also assigned to those actions by their characterization. Sarabyn, a character in a position to decide whether to go ahead or not go ahead with the raid, is portrayed not only individually and actively, but also as hurried in his actions and his words. Sarabyn is "running and calling for their attention". The sections that paraphrase his words repeatedly focus on his hurried behavior (immediately, exhorted, quickly, hurry). These modifiers assign values to those individual actions, actions that are later condemned as contributing to the dire outcomes of February 28.

In example (11), the third-person narrative describes what the agents saw and assigns intent to their actions. At this point, the Treasury Report account is a story of individual law enforcement officers attempting to arrest subjects who resist and of the violence that ensues. The focus of the action and agency for those actions lies in the characters on the ground in Waco. The account represents not only what agents did, but also what they saw. In addition, ATF agents' actions are characterized in laudatory language ("Agent Constantino provided cover for Buford and Jordan"; "Agent Chisolm threw his body over Buford to protect him"). In the footnote (26) to this section, this particular passage is characterized as one of many acts of heroism too numerous to catalog. These evaluative and either critical comments (in the case of example (9)) or laudatory comments (in the case of example (11)) do the work of not only creating agentive characters driving the action of February 28, they also do the work of assigning praise and blame, a framework of culpability for further evaluation, focused at the level of individual characters.

Differences between the two reports

The narrative style of the Treasury Report reflects and reinforces a logic that individual culpability led to the outcomes of February 28, initiating the standoff at Waco. Because we can see the individual characters – agents, commanders, decisionmakers – each taking actions within the narrative account, their roles, and therefore responsibilities and accountability are dramatically highlighted. It is not surprising that the Treasury Department, which produced this report, also made administrative moves to hold individual agents accountable.

On the other hand, the institutional narrative of the Justice Report places agency and culpability only at the institutional and highest decision-making levels (and with the Davidians). The FBI on the ground at Waco was not, for the most part, individually agentive, but was institutionally empowered and functional. Attorney General Janet Reno was individually identified as culpable for the April 19 outcomes at Waco in a way Treasury Secretary Bentsen was not, and she received both credit and blame for her role as *the* lone individual figure among this institutional action.

In the post-hoc accounting for Waco, these are the lines on which blame was largely assigned among these agencies. Individual ATF agents and decision-makers were identified and singled out for praise and blame, but individual FBI agents largely were not. In fact, authors of the Treasury report criticized the Justice Report for not creating a adequate standard of accountability, for not "naming names" as they had.[10] This analysis does not to suggest that these reports caused assignments of responsibility – both praise and blame – after Waco; such a relationship would be impossible to demonstrate. However, there does appear to be a correlation here between the representation of authority, responsibility, and agency in these reports and the perceptions of how those agencies' roles were perceived in the subsequent hearings.

Conclusion

The aim of this study was to highlight the discursive means by which government reporting – an increasingly influential genre in public discourse – represents "what happened" following controversial events. The analysis highlights how the performance of a bureaucratic style brings tragic events under the aegis of institutional control. Through acts of (en)textualization, the events are described in the bureaucratic logic of the agencies that account for them. The authority of reviewing and reporting these acts is established through the institutional discourse that creates "the Review" from the authority and expertise of others. By means of large-scale decisions about where to begin and end the narrative, lexico-grammatical choices about representing actors and agency, and choices about how to tell the story, causal agency during the tragedy is established, assigning culpability at the individual or institutional level, perhaps laying the groundwork for punitive action or deliberative recommendation. These relatively mundane, institutional acts of bureaucratic style work to mend the break in bureaucratic orderliness created by events like Waco. This chapter also illustrates how categories and techniques drawn from Critical Linguistics and other strands of discourse analysis can be used to

---

10.   For a further discussion of the context of these reports and their reception, see Eisenhart (2003).

provide an in-depth account of the inner workings of the constitutive rhetoric of this important genre.

References

Anderson, Donald L. 2004 "The Textualizing Functions of Writing for Organizational Change." *Journal of Business and Technical Communication.* (18) 2: 141–164.

Charland, Maurice. 1987. "Constitutive Rhetoric: the Case of the People Quebecois." *Quarterly Journal of Speech.* 73: 133–150.

Doxater, Erik. 2003. "Reconciliation – A Rhetorical Conception." *Quarterly Journal of Speech.* 89(4): 267–393.

Eisenhart, Christopher. 2003. *Waco Decade.* Unpublished dissertation. Carnegie Mellon University.

Faber, Brenton. 1998. "Toward a Rhetoric of Change: Reconstructing Image and Narrative in Distressed Organizations." *Journal of Business and Technical Communication.* (12) 2: 217–237.

Federal News Service. "Hearing of the Senate Judiciary Committee." June 20, 2001.

Fisher, Walter. 1984. "Narration as Human Communication Paradigm: The Case of Public Moral Argument." *Communication Monographs.* 51, 1–22.

Geisler, Cheryl. 2001. "Textual Objects: Accounting for the Role of Texts in the Everyday Life of Complex Organizations." *Written Communication,* 18: pp 296–325.

Gring-Pemble, Lisa. 2001. "'Are We Going to Now Govern By Anecdote?': Rhetorical Constructions of Welfare Recipients in Congressional Hearings, Debates, and Legislation, 1992–1996." *Quarterly Journal of Speech* (87) 4: 341–365.

Hariman, Robert. 1995. *Political Style.* Chicago: University of Chicago Press.

Hodge, R. & Kress, G. 1996. *Language as Ideology.* London: Routledge Press.

Johnstone, Barbara. 2002. *Discourse Analysis.* Malden, MA: Blackwell Publishers.

Mashberg, T. 2001. "Passion, Not Insanity, Fueled McVeigh's Fury." *Boston Herald.* June 10, 2001. 4.

Miller, Carolyn. 2003. "Presumption of Expertise: the Role of Ethos in Risk Analysis." *Configurations,* 11:163–202.

Osborn, Michael. 1986. "Rhetorical Depiction." *Form, Genre, and the Study of Political Rhetoric.* Ed. By Simons, H. W. and Aghazarian, A. Columbia, SC: University of South Carolina Press. 79–107.

Perelman, Ch, & Olbrechts-Tytechca. 1969. *The New Rhetoric.* trans. Wilkinson & Weaver. Notre Dame: University of Notre Dame Press.

Perelman, Ch. 1982. *The Realm of Rhetoric.* Notre Dame: Notre Dame Press.

Silverstein, M. & Urban, G. eds. 1996. *The Natural History of Discourse.* University of Chicago Press.

US. Department of Justice. 1993. *Report to the Deputy Attorney General on the Events at Waco, Texas.* GPO.

US. Department of the Treasury. 1993. *Report of the Department of Treasury on the BATF Investigation of Vernon Wayne Howell a.k.a David Koresh.* GPO.

Wells, Susan. 1990. "Narrative Figures and Subtle Persuasions: The Rhetoric of the MOVE Report." *The Rhetorical Turn: Invention and Persuasion in the Conduct of Inquiry.* Herbert W. Simons, ed. Chicago: University of Chicago Press. 208–237.

CHAPTER 4

The rhetoric of temporality

The future as linguistic construct and rhetorical resource

Patricia L. Dunmire
Kent State University

Introduction

This chapter is concerned with the ways the future is linguistically represented in political discourse and the rhetorical functions those representations serve. The future, I contend, is a discursive construct that rhetors embed within and project through the linguistic design of their texts, and, which, thereby, functions as a means of persuasion. In slightly different terms, I see representations of the future in policy documents as a type of legitimation device (van Dijk 1998) used in institutional contexts to shore up an institution's call for particular near-term policies and actions. Like Murray Edelman (1971), I see this process as both rhetorical and political as political actors "create perceived [future] worlds that in turn shape perceptions and interpretations of current events and therefore the behavior with which people respond to them" (7).

Using a systemic-functional analytic framework, I examine representations of the future within two texts: *Climate Change and Human Health*, 'CCHH' (McMicheal et al. 1996) and *The National Security Strategy of the United States*, 'NSS' (United States National Security Council 2002).[1] CCHH reports on the future impact of global warming on human health and the ecosystem; the NSS outlines the Bush Administration's strategy for ensuring the military and economic security of the United States. The apparent incongruity of these two texts – one about the natural world, the other about the political world – enables me to illustrate the complex and disparate ways in which the future is represented and

---

1. I provide further explication of these data sources in the "Analytic Framework and Data" section below.

functions within texts. As a text about the natural world, CCHH concerns what Aristotle conceived of as *arhetorical futures*: events and phenomena that "will exist inevitably" (34). As a text concerned with government policy and action, the NSS represents *rhetorical futures*: events and phenomena that "ultimately depend upon ourselves" (35). Within this scheme, rhetorical futures are the only appropriate subject matter for the rhetor; arhetorical futures are outside the domain of deliberative rhetoric.

My analysis, however, challenges this dichotomy by illustrating the discursive nature and rhetorical function of both inevitable, natural futures and possible, manmade futures within the domains of science and politics. I demonstrate the nuanced yet deliberate ways that both the CCHH and NSS linguistically construe particular future events and phenomena in ways that serve particular rhetorical ends and purposes. Briefly, representations of the future in the CCHH text take the form of explicit factual claims about distant future "realities." These "facts" about the future, in turn, function evidentially in arguments for more immediate policies and actions. In contrast, the NSS text comprises much less overt representations of the future. My analysis demonstrates how the linguistic construal of historical precedents and present circumstances embed and project representations of the future that legitimate a policy that prescribes specific national security strategies.

My analysis of these documents will prove useful to both rhetorical critics and discourse analysts. For rhetoricians, I illustrate both the various ways in which the future figures in deliberative arguments and the consequential role that the linguistic construal of claims and evidence plays in argumentation. For discourse analysts, this chapter further demonstrates the importance of the future as a site for critical analyses of politics and ideology. I build on previous work (Dunmire 1997, 2005, 2007) to demonstrate the ideological nature and function of representations of the future and to show how discourse analysts can demystify those representations and the ideology they embed and sustain.

The future in discourse

In previous work I have argued that the means by which the future is represented in and projected through political discourse is an important, though neglected, focus for critical discourse analysis (Dunmire 2005). Briefly, work in critical studies of politics and culture has recognized the future as both a site for analyzing and a framework for critiquing dominant political practices (e.g., Alessandrini 2003; de Saint-Georges 2003; Grosz 1999; Levitas 1993; Morris 1998; Scollon 2001; Scollon & Scollon 2000). Although this work has called attention to the material and ideological stakes embedded in representations of the future, as well as the stakes involved in demystifying those representations, there has not been sufficient analytic attention to the discursive means by which representations of the future are embedded in political discourse. By focusing on the discursive nature and rhetorical function of representations of the future, I add my voice to Scollon and Scollon's (2000) call for discourse analysts to attend to the ways social agents position themselves, and are positioned by others, with respect to the future. Such a temporal orientation is needed, they contend, to counterbalance the past orientation that typifies most discourse analytic projects. Fairclough (2005), for example, assumes a past orientation in his analysis of Tony Blair's discourse concerning globalization. He examines how Blair moves "from 'is' to 'must', from descriptions (narratives) of the world and world change to prescriptions for policy, from actualities to imaginaries" (44). In contrast, by taking a future orientation, my study asks: How do political discourses move from "will be'" to "must"? How do political actors argue from distant future "realities" to more immediate future actions? As Hebdige (1993) argues, such attention to "how particular discursive strategies open up or close down particular lines of possibility" is important "if we are to begin really exploiting the actively performative (not just referential) functions of communication" (275).

In this paper, I extend this call to rhetoricians by considering the ways in which temporality, generally, and futurity, specifically, have figured in rhetorical studies. Although temporality has been an important component of rhetorical theory and analysis, it has generally been conceived of as external to texts, as an element of contexts which impinges upon the rhetor's production of, and the audience's interpretation of, texts. For example, in classical and contemporary rhetorical studies, *kairos* and *exigence* are the key concepts for conceiving of and analyzing the temporal aspects of discourse.[2] Both are understood as dimensions of rhetorical context, or situation, which rhetors must attend to in composing rhetorically efficacious texts. Poulakos (1983) explains that *kairos* – "rhetorical timing" – requires that a rhetorical act "show respect for the temporal dimensions of a situation," that it must attend to and be guided by "the temporality of the situation within which it occurs" (30). Bitzer (1968) argues that exigence, that is, an "imperfection marked by urgency," is a necessary element of rhetorical situations (6). The responsibility of the rhetor is to observe this exigence and remedy it through her rhetorical act.

What is lacking, I contend, is an approach to temporality that focuses on the temporal landscape of texts themselves, on the rhetorical nature and function of elements of lexico-grammar having to do with temporality. My specific point of intervention is Aristotle's conception of *deliberative rhetoric* – political speech that is concerned with the efficacy or harmfulness of particular policies and courses of

---

2.   See Dunmire (2000) for a more extensive review of how temporality has figured in rhetorical studies.

action. I begin by examining Aristotle's conception of the types of future events and situations appropriate for rhetorical deliberation, as well as the rhetorical strategies he outlines for constructing arguments about the future. Then, using a discourse analytic framework, I explicate the linguistic means by which representations of the future are embedded within two particular texts and argue that these representations function rhetorically as legitimation devices within their particular political and institutional contexts.

The future in deliberative rhetoric

In his treatise on classical rhetoric Aristotle notes the key role temporality plays in rhetorical discourse. Each genre of discourse in his tripartite scheme – forensic, epideictic, and deliberative – corresponds to different kind of time – past, present, and future, respectively (32).[3] Within this scheme the future is the temporal domain of deliberative rhetoric, as political speaking "urges us either to do or not to do something ... [it] is concerned with the future: it is about things to be done hereafter" (32). Of particular interest here is Aristotle's conception of the types of future events and situations appropriate to rhetorical deliberation and also the strategies a rhetor should use in constructing arguments about the future. Regarding content, Aristotle explains that the deliberative orator only deals with:

> such [things] as may or may not take place. Concerning things which exist or will exist inevitably, . . . no counsel can be given ... Clearly counsel can only be given on matters about which people deliberate; matters, namely, that ultimately depend on ourselves, and which we have it in our power to set going (34–35).

Aristotle's conception of deliberative rhetoric makes a clear distinction between possible, man-made future events that depend on human agency and inevitable, "natural" future events that are outside of human agency, a distinction that resides in the events themselves. As future events that may take place, possible, manmade futures are within the rhetor's purview; as futures that will take place, inevitable, natural futures are not.

Aristotle also lays out various principles and lines of argument for a rhetor to use in making arguments about possible futures. In short, he looks at the past as "a guide to the future and at the future as a natural extension of the present" (Poulakos 1984: 223). Aristotle contends that arguments for particular policies and actions should be grounded in examples from the past "for we judge of future events by divination from past events" (63). Rhetors are further advised to quote

---

3.   Forensic rhetoric is the rhetoric of the law courts and is oriented toward the past; epideictic rhetoric is used in various ceremonial contexts and is oriented toward the future.

"what has actually happened, since in most respects the future will be like what the past has been" (134). Within Aristotle's scheme, the future serves solely as the end point of deliberation, since the goal of deliberative rhetoric is to establish "the expediency or harmfulness of a proposed course of action" (33). In sum, the future is understood to be the terminus of deliberation, rather than a means of persuasion within deliberative rhetoric.

This rhetorical structure is evident in contemporary scholarship. Weaver (1994), for example explains, "Rhetoric depends on history. All questions that are susceptible to rhetorical treatment arise out of history and it is to history that the rhetorician turns for his means of persuasion" (75). Scott (1967) similarly contends that to make ethical decisions about the future we "must be prepared to look at the past" (17). Finally, Kaufer and Butler (1996) contend that rhetorical plans are a "speaker's construction of the historical world and the means by which that world should evolve in the future. Plans are used to build the world that the speaker has inherited" and "to project future worlds on the normative basis of these alternatives" (47).

The present paper seeks to expand and complicate classical and contemporary conceptions of the types of futures appropriate for deliberation and the functions those futures serve in the production and interpretation of deliberative discourse. Aristotle's distinction between rhetorical futures and arhetorical futures can be understood in discourse analytic terms as a distinction between deontic and epistemic modality. *Deontic modality* is concerned with future actions and policies. Through modal auxiliaries such as "ought," "should," and "must," deontic modality expresses notions of obligation, conviction, and permission. *Epistemic modality* is concerned with knowledge and belief concerning "reality." Through modal auxiliaries such as "will," "might," and "would," epistemic modality expresses judgments about the status and/or certainty of that knowledge and belief. For Aristotle, deliberative rhetoric is solely concerned with futures within deontic modality since it speaks only to actions of human agents. Epistemic futures – those concerned with what will, could, or might *exist* at some future moment – are outside human agency and thus outside the province of deliberative rhetoric. The rhetor's task, then, is to perceive these different futures and to debate the possible and ignore the inevitable.

I contend, however, that questions about what will exist at some future moment – that is, epistemic futures – are also within the domain of deliberative rhetoric. Moreover, I understand the future as a multi-faceted and variable temporal domain that locates various types of events predicated in a text and that functions rhetorically as a means, rather than as solely an end, of persuasion. I ground this conception in Fleischman's (1982) linguistic categories of "proximal" and "distal" future events that represent the temporal location of a particular future moment relative to the speech moment: proximal futures are represented as relatively close to the speech moment and distal futures are represented as relatively distant from the moment of speech (17). Taken together, the concepts of proximal/distal and deontic/epistemic futures enable an understanding of the future not as a monolithic, unified whole but as comprising various interconnected and dynamic temporal moments.

Analytic framework and data

I have conducted the following analysis within a systemic-functional linguistic framework, or SFL (Halliday 1978; Halliday & Martin 1993; Kress 1995), which derives largely from Halliday's theories of language as social semiotic and functional linguistics (Halliday 1978, 1985). SFL theorizes language as a resource for meaning rather than as a system of abstract, decontextualized rules (Halliday & Martin 1993). As an instance of language use, the lexico-grammatical structure of texts represents the choices a speaker or writer makes from within the meaning potential of language. That is, because any given event, action, or process can be represented grammatically in a number of ways, the meaning of that event, action, or process can be construed in a variety of ways. The actual lexico-grammatical structure of a text, then, is of analytic and rhetorical significance because it manifests the particular choices of a speaker or writer working within a particular social context and with a particular purpose.

Within an SFL perspective, language and context are related in two primary ways. They are reciprocally related as each semiotic system "redounds" with the other, "language construes, is construed by and (over time) reconstrues and is reconstrued by social context" (Halliday & Martin 1993:24). They are further related through the process of realization. Texts, a relatively concrete plane of semiosis, realize particular elements of social context, a relatively abstract plane of semiosis. More specifically, what Halliday has termed the metafunctions of language – ideational, interpersonal, and textual – realize particular dimensions of social context – field, tenor, and mode, respectively. The ideational function construes physical reality, the interpersonal function enacts and creates social roles and relationships, and the textual function creates texts that cohere with their internal and external contexts. These metafunctions, in turn, are realized in texts through specific lexico-grammatical systems. The ideational meaning of a text is realized in the transitivity system, which construes material, verbal, mental, and relational processes. Interpersonal meaning is realized through mood system, including modality, and construes the speaker or writer's attitude toward the content of the text and the social status and relationships of the participants in the communicative transaction. Finally, the resources for textual meaning include deixis, markers of coherence and cohesion, and theme/rheme.

Systemic-functional linguistics is useful for my consideration of temporality for a couple of reasons. First, with its attention to the grammatical and lexical features of texts, SFL provides a means for examining at a fine level of detail the ways arguments about the future are constructed, in part, through the temporal contours of texts. Second, its conceptualization of language and context as reciprocally related provides a framework for considering the ways in which the temporal dimensions of rhetorical contexts are woven into the temporal landscape of texts and how that landscape, in turn, feeds back into the extra-textual contexts in which texts circulate.

The following analysis focuses on two texts: *Climate Change and Human Health,* and *The National Security Strategy of the United States,* each of which is significant in its own right. The CCHH was produced by the International Panel on Climate Change,[4] which represents the "gold standard" of climate science and is the first report to document the "human finger print" on global warming (Mooney 2005). Although the national security strategies of presidential administrations are generally considered to be routine documents, this is not the case with the Bush administration's policy. Indeed, it has been described as representing a "new paradigm for American policy on the same level as the Truman doctrine" because of its approach to the doctrine of preemptive war (Kirk 2003; also see Chomsky 2003).

Of particular analytic interest here, however, is that these two documents, which were produced in very different institutional contexts, demonstrate the complex role that representations of and claims about future "reality" play in legitimating particular policies and actions. In the following pages I present my analysis of the CCHH and NSS documents separately. My reasons are two-fold. First, the CCHH text concerns the domain of science and nature, while the NSS concerns the domain of economic and military policy. The functions the future serves, as well as the linguistic means by which it is manifested textually, differ for each document and its contextual domain. As such, each requires attention to different lexico-grammatical systems, processes, and features: my analysis of CCHH focuses on nominalization and modality, while my analysis of NSS focuses on tense and aspect. The different analytic foci enable me to demonstrate the unique linguistic representations and rhetorical functions of the future in each document. Briefly, to make its case for proximal future policies and actions, the CCHH text presents explicit arguments about distal future phenomena resulting from global warming. As such, representations and claims about the future feature prominently in the CCHH text. In contrast, the NSS policy argument is based primarily in claims regarding historical precedents and present circumstances and conditions, which

---

4.   The IPCC was awarded, along with Al Gore, the 2007 Nobel Peace prize.

project particular future realities and potentialities. Relative to the CCHH document, representations of the future are incorporated into the NSS in much more nuanced and covert, but equally potent, ways.

Secondly, as explained at the outset, these two documents map onto Aristotle's distinction between arhetorical and rhetorical futures. The CCHH focuses on natural phenomena and events in the world of nature and science, "things that occur naturally" and about which "it is useless to offer counsel"; the NSS is concerned with strategies and tactics within the human world of political policy and action, "matters about which people deliberate" (34–35). Although I do not accept Aristotle's distinction as absolute, I do not want to completely collapse it, either. This approach enables, indeed, requires me to elucidate the linguistic features and rhetorical strategies specific to each document, while also making connections between them at a more general level. Specifically, I demonstrate that an "inevitable" future does not derive solely from the natural world; rather, representations of the future are "naturalized" (Fairclough 1989, 2003) through linguistic and discursive devices in such a way as to legitimate the policies and strategies advocated in the CCHH and NSS documents. These naturalized, inevitable futures, however, are construed by different lexico-grammatical resources and serve different rhetorical ends in the their respective discursive and institutional contexts.

Analysis

Global warming and human health: From distal future realities to proximal future action

The data examined below comes from a section of *Climate Change and Human Health*, which explicates the impact that increases in sea levels, a major consequence of global warming, could have on human health and the ecosystem and recommends policies for preventing or mitigating that impact. As such, the text projects three interrelated future moments:

1. The occurrence of sea level rise by the year 2100 – "occurrence statements."
2. The impact of sea level rise on human health and the ecosystem – "impact statements."
3. Policies and actions for attending to sea level rise and its impact on human health – "policy statements."

The occurrence and impact statements project distal, epistemic futures; the future projected through the policy statements is a proximal, deontic future concerning what should be done in light of the epistemic futures.

The following analysis focuses on the rhetorical relationship among these three future moments, which are relationships of conditionality and contingency. Because future increases in sea levels is a condition upon which the occurrence of other future phenomena depend, the epistemic status of the future impact statements is contingent upon the epistemic status of the future occurrence statements. As such, this discussion follows an 'if/then' logic, "If sea levels rise/were to rise to X, what would the consequences be for human health and the ecosystem?" Similarly, the deontic future of policy and action is contingent upon the occurrence of an increase in sea levels and consequences of that increase for human health. Thus, the deontic force of the policy statements is dependent upon the epistemic status of the occurrence and impact statements.

My analysis of the CCHH text focuses on the construal of ideational meaning realized through the transformation process of nominalization and the construal of interpersonal meaning realized through the modal structure of the text. I am concerned here with the rhetorical relationship between three different future moments projected in the document: how is a distal future event represented and how does that representation function within claims concerning more proximal future events and actions? *Nominalization* is a process of transformation through which verbs, which construe ideational meaning in terms of temporally marked processes and actions, are transformed into nouns, which construe ideational meaning in terms of objects and entities, that is, as reified processes which lack a temporal component. Moreover, because nominalization transforms actions and processes, which receive temporal coloration when represented through verbs, into nouns, which do not have a temporal component, the use of nominalization has implications for the temporal and modal structure of the CCHH text.

My analysis of modality focuses on the relative security of the classification system used to represent future phenomena and actions associated with global warming. Modality, a linguistic system which construes interpersonal meaning, "describes the stance of participants in the semiosic process toward the state and status of the system of classification" (Hodge & Kress 1988:122) and provides the "direction toward which the readers" of particular statements and text are "invited" to go (Latour 1987:22). Statements represented as highly secure, that is, as "facts," point readers away from the conditions of production of the statement and toward questions concerning, for example, how best to respond to a given "fact" and the implications of that "fact." Statements represented as relatively insecure point the reader back toward the conditions of production to consider the integrity of particular claims (22).

I begin my analysis by explicating the structure and function of the future occurrence statements, focusing on the transformation process of nominalization and the surface markers of modality. I then show how the representations of the future projected through these statements function in the impact statements. This portion of my analysis focuses on the modal structure of conditional statements. Finally, I illustrate the rhetorical role these distal, epistemic futures play in the policy statements.

Constructing a future fact, projecting future reality

In its discussion of future sea level rise, or SLR, and its impact on human health, the CCHH makes 85 references to future SLR. Of interest here is that the vast majority of these references are constructed in nominalized forms. Specifically, nominalizations account for 91% of the references (e.g., "an increase in sea levels"), while the remaining 9% are constructed through verbal forms (e.g., "sea levels could rise in the next 50 years"). This highly nominalized structure has significant implications for how the future is represented within and through the CCHH text. While verbal constructions represent sea level rise as a yet-to-be-realized phenomenon, and thus, as inherently *irrealis*, nominal constructions do not. Rather, they suppress the irreality of future processes and events by rendering them as extant entities. Through nominalization, the temporal and modal qualifications normally encoded in verbal constructions are omitted from nominalized constructions. When lexicalized as verbs, processes and actions are located in specific temporal moments and are coded as to degree of likelihood, certainty, volition, and so forth. Nominalizations, however, do not receive explicit temporal or modal coding and, as such, they appear to reference existing, acontextual entities. Fleischman (1982) explains that such representations render future events as an assumed part of future reality rather than as a contingency. In sum, the extensive use of nominalization functions to suppress the contingency inherent in statements about the future, thereby rendering future SLR as an assumed future event – that is, as a "future fact." As my analysis will show, this nominalized structure functions as a rhetorically potent definition of the situation presented in the CCHH text. As van Dijk (2005) explains, such situational definitions serve as an "initial schematic category" that is sequentially relevant in discourses whose primary goals include recommending or legitimating specific actions or policies (71). In the CCHH text, the nominalized representation of sea level rise functions rhetorically to render policy proposals presented later in the text as "necessary," "logical," and "unavoidable" (71).

In this portion of my analysis I examine variations in the modal coding and character of the verbal and the nominal forms. Four of the eight verbal constructions come in the introductory section of the chapter. Two of the references present data about past SLR and the other two present data about future SLR:

(1)   During the past 18,000 years, global sea level has risen by *about 100 meters* in total (Warrick et al. 1996).

(2) During the past century, sea level has risen by *around 18 cm*, or an average of *1–2.5 mm/year* (Warrick et al. 1996).

(3) The "best" estimate of current ocean and climate models is that sea level will have risen by *around 1/2 a metre* by the year 2100 and will continue to rise thereafter, even if global green house gas emissions are stabilized (Wigley 1995).

Each statement receives modal qualification that hedges the amount of past and future sea level rise as approximations: "about 100 meters", "around 18 cm," "1–2.5 mm/year," and "around 1/2 a metre." The future statement is further hedged by being categorized explicitly as an estimate and through two uses of "will."[5] When looked at more closely, however, the modal qualification of the data about the future is a "complex, even contradictory package" (Hodge & Kress 1988:127). Although "estimate" clearly hedges the claim regarding the amount of future increases in sea levels, the emphatic modal "best" functions to shore up this estimate. This emphatic adjective, however, is potentially undermined by the use of scare quotes, which calls into the question the epistemological status of claiming a "best estimate" of a future phenomenon. Moreover, although "will" characterizes the data as inherently *irrealis*, it, nevertheless, conveys a relatively greater degree of certainty than would have been conveyed through "could" or "might."

Statements 1–3 above are further modalized through evidential coding that identifies the source of the data concerning past and future SLR. Of particular interest here is how the evidential qualification positions these statements relative to their original contexts of production. That is, each statement contains traces of where it came from and how it was produced: "(Warrick et al. 1996)", "(Wigley 1995)", and "current ocean and climate models." However, as the following analysis demonstrates, the evidential qualification of each statement functions, in varying degrees, to move them away from their condition of production and toward the status of "fact."

Rather than being directly incorporated into the statements, the original sources of the data regarding past and future sea levels are incorporated into the text parenthetically. In an alternative construction the citation information could have been incorporated directly into the statement and, relatedly, the data could have been presented through a projecting clause, as in this hypothetical construction:

---

5. Fleischman (1982) explains that because articulations of the future, through verbs such as "will", necessarily involve some element of prediction, the future is rarely a purely temporal category. As such, representations of the future inevitably receive nonfactive modal coloration (cf. also Close 1977 and Palmer 1986).

Wigley (1995) argues/claims/explains that the "best" estimate of current ocean and climate models is that sea level will have risen by around 1/2 a metre by the year 2100 and will continue to rise thereafter, even if global green house gas emissions are stabilized.

In this construction the data receive additional evidential qualification through the verbs of saying. This qualification, in turn, provides a direct link between the data and its original context of production. The use of parenthetical citation, however, eliminates the need for a verb of saying and its attendant evidential qualification. Rather, the preposition "of" establishes a relationship between the estimate and the data; this relationship, however is an ambiguous one of derivation or source rather than explicit epistemic status. That is, "of" merely provides information concerning the source of the "'best' estimate", "current ocean and climate models." Had the statement been written to include a verb of saying, additional information would have been provided: namely, the human agent behind the statement, Wigley, and that agent's assessment of the reliability of the statement. Moreover, in terms of Latour and Woolgar's (1986) hierarchy of modality, the parenthetical citation conveys a stronger degree of certainty because the data virtually stands on its own, whereas data projected through a verb of saying rank lower on the hierarchy of modality.

In addition to the surface markers of modality, the transformation process of nominalization underlying the statements of future SLR contributes to its modal structure and rhetorical function. Of particular interest here is the extensive use of nominalizations to represent the future phenomenon of SLR in both the introduction and body of the chapter. As mentioned earlier, over 90% of the references to future SLR are constructed as nominalizations. Eight of these occur in the introduction section. As can be seen in the following statements, these nominalizations position SLR from the outset as a presupposed future fact and, relatedly, focus the discussion on the amount, timing, and consequences of future SLR:

(4) *Sea level rise* and changes in the frequency and severity of extreme weather events *are likely to be* the most significant climate change phenomena to occur in these zones.

(5) But cities and coastal zones are currently experiencing difficulty in coping with *relative sea level rise, will be* especially vulnerable to *global sea level rise.*

The hedging expressed through "are likely to be" and "will be" qualifies the epistemic status of the information concerning the *character* of SLR; the *occurrence* of SLR is unqualified and presupposed.

I want to focus here on the statement that immediately follows the "best estimate" statement discussed above, which I include here for ease of reference:

> The "best" estimate of current ocean and climate models is that sea level will
> have risen by around 1/2 a metre by the year 2100 and will continue to rise
> thereafter, even if global green house gas emissions are stabilized. (Wigley
> 1995) The current best estimate thus predicts *a rate of sea level rise* for the
> period between now and 2100 that is 2–3 times greater than that of the past
> 100 years.

The process of nominalization is key to the modal structure of this statement. Specifically, the verbal clause "sea level will have risen by around ½ meter" has been transformed into the nominalization "a rate of sea level rise." Two dimensions of this transformation are important here. First, the expression of futurity and modal qualification conveyed by "will" are removed through the nominalization process. Second, not only has the process of sea level rise been transformed into a noun, but the dimensions of that process, which were originally modalized as approximations, have also been nominalized as "rate," which does not receive modal qualification. Consequently, in addition to establishing the phenomenon of future sea level rise as a fact, its features, which had previously been hedged, have been transformed into a feature of this fact.

Another important element of excerpt (6) is the variation in the surface markers of modality between the first and second sentences. Reference to the original source of the estimate of future SLR, "current ocean and climate models," has been omitted, thereby distancing the estimate from its original production context. However, now that it is extricated from that context, "best estimate" can function on its own as an impersonal agent that makes predictions about the future. By omitting the scare quotes that had originally marked "best" and also the concept of a "best estimate" of the future, this data is further distanced from its production context. As such, the "best estimate of future sea level rise" is no longer an epistemological puzzle to be reflected upon; it is data that is gradually becoming "solid enough to render its own consequences" (Latour 1987: 22).

Clearly, the modal structure of the future occurrence statements is a complex and, to an extent, contradictory package. Taken as a whole, however, the claims about future SLR evince a positive modal structure which points the discussion 'downstream', turning attention away from its original context of production and its status as an unrealized future phenomenon and toward its specific features and consequences. In the process, future SLR is gradually constructed and positioned as a future fact. As the following analysis shows, this downstream movement is sustained by the extensive use of nominalizations in the discussion of the future consequences of future sea level rise for human health and the ecosystem.

Consequences of the future: Suppressing conditionality and contingency

The introductory discussion of future SLR is followed by a discussion of the consequences of this assumed future event for the future status of human health and the
ecosystem. Of interest here is how references to future SLR are incorporated into
the future impact statements. Of the 73 references to future SLR presented in the
future impact statements, 95% are constructed as nominalizations. Of these 69,
19% are marked as to futurity and/or epistemic status. The remaining nominalizations are inserted into the discussion of future consequences without any modal
or temporal qualification. This extensive use of nominalized forms functions partially to suppress the contingent status of the future impact statements. In other
words, although these future consequences are contingent upon the occurrence of
another future event, this event is assumed unconditionally to be a part of future
reality.[6]

This suppression of contingency can be seen in the conditional statements
used to represent the future consequences of SLR. These statements are important
because of the central role conditional reasoning, and its linguistic manifestation,
plays in the CCHH project. The authors explain that unlike more conventional,
data-based research, their "forecasting" approach does not rely on direct empirical observation. Rather it "entails forecasting of future health implications and
employs an 'if/then' logic. It asks: 'If the climate changes to scenario X, then what
would be the likely health impacts?'" (McMichael, et al.: 3). The following analysis examines how this conditional reasoning manifests linguistically and functions
rhetorically within the CCHH text.

Conditionals are defined as statements that assert a logical relationship between two propositions, the protasis ("if" clause) and the apodosis ("then" clause),
in which the proposition in the apodosis is dependent upon the proposition in
the protasis (Fillmore 1986). The function of conditionals is not to assert that
an event has occurred, is occurring, or will occur; they merely assert the dependence of one proposition upon the truth of another (Dancygier 1998; Palmer 1986;
Sweetser 1990). In slightly different terms, the proposition in the "if" clause sets
up an imaginary world in which the proposition in the "then" clause is the case
(James 1982). Hodge & Kress (1988) explain that such hypothetical forms function modally to convey ontological, and hence, social distance, between the speaker
and the "reality" of the proposition (126).

The discussion of the future consequences of SLR contains 47 conditional
statements, which follow the general form "If sea levels rise to scenario p, (then)
the impact on human health and/or the ecosystem would be q." Of interest here

---

6.   I found this same phenomenon in my study of press coverage of the 1990 conflict between
Iraq and Kuwait (Dunmire 1997).

is that 75% of the conditional statements are constructed as what I term "elided" conditionals, rather than as full conditionals. Full conditionals take the form "If +noun phrase+verb phrase, (then) +noun phrase+verb phrase," as in "this would pose a direct hazard to the local population, or an indirect hazard if contamination entered the food chain." In this construction, both the condition presented in the protasis and the consequences presented in the apodosis are represented through verb phrases. Elided conditionals, in contrast, take the general form "Nominalization, (then) +noun phrase+verb phrase," in which the protasis is constructed as a nominalization of a verb phrase as in, "Increased erosion and reduced drainage would also increase the risk of flooding." In the elided form the unrealized future processes are rendered as unqualified, atemporal extant entities.

Of the elided conditionals, three quarters contain the SLR nominalization in the protasis, as in the following statements:

(6) *Sea level rise* could harm these ecosystems yet further.

(7) Over half of these [coastal wetlands] would be threatened by *a 1 metre rise in sea level* over the next 100 years.

(8) *Indirect effects of sea level rise* could include the loss of protective natural features such as mangroves.

(9) *Sea level rise* could impinge on local food production through its impact on the ecosystem.

In each of these statements the condition underlying the protasis, sea levels rising in the future, has been represented as the nominalization "sea level rise." By rendering the protasis in a nominalized form, these statements lose information that would have been conveyed through the full conditional form. Omitting "if" obscures the *irrealis* status of the future rise in sea levels, while omitting the verbal form removes the modal coding that verb forms convey, particularly in conditional statements. Fleischman (1989) explains that speakers signal the epistemic status of propositions through tense choices that locate events as relatively close to or distant from the moment of speaking (cf. also Chilton 2003). The closer an event is to the speaker's "now," the stronger its epistemic status; the more remote an event is from "now," the weaker its epistemic status. She further explains that in conditional statements speakers can represent an event as more or less likely to occur by using tense forms in the protasis that locate the event as close to or distant from the moment of speaking. Had these statements been constructed as full conditionals, the protasis would have been marked as a future condition that has yet to be realized: "If sea levels rise/were to rise, the ecosystem would be harmed yet further." The use of nominalization, however, transforms the event of rising sea levels as a future phenomenon into an entity that exists at the present moment.

As explained above, conditional statements function as speculations about states of affairs that are contingent upon the outcome of some other unrealized condition. As the preceding analysis shows, however, the speculative and contingent status of conditionals can be suppressed by transforming the protasis into a nominalization. This transformation is accompanied by a transformation in the representation of reality constructed through the conditional statement. The consequences of future SLR are no longer contingent upon a future event that might, could, or will take place; they are contingent upon an event that is unconditionally assumed to be a part of future reality, that is, a future fact. Indeed, the *realis* status of future rises in sea level is such that it necessitates "response" strategies.

Responding to the future: Transitioning from "will be" to "must"

The discussion of future SLR and its consequences concludes with a brief outline of what the CCHH text refers to as "Response Strategies." These strategies represent a deontic, proximal future as they concern what should be done "now" in order to "respond" to the more distal, epistemic futures. The use of "response" to categorize and characterize the future actions and policies being recommended is particularly telling of the extent to which future SLR has been established within the text as a future fact. According to the *Random House Dictionary* one of the two primary definitions of "response" is "any behavior that results from an external or internal cause." In the present context, the external cause prompting the response is a distal future event that has yet to occur. The epistemological paradox not withstanding, the use of "response" coheres with the logic of the future projected through the CCHH text: given the fact of a future rise in sea levels, strategies should be developed that would respond to that future fact and, similarly, mitigate or prevent its consequences. Moreover, "response" functions rhetorically to reinforce the assumed status of future SLR by presupposing its occurrence. Future SLR is explicitly mentioned in only 4 of the 19 response statements and only one of the references is modally qualified. In the rest of the response strategies, the occurrence of sea levels rising in the future is left unstated and, thus, presupposed. In the statements that outline particular response strategies, "response" is lexicalized as "prevent," "protect," "mitigate," "minimize," "retreat," and "adapt." As can be seen in the following examples, each of these statements presupposes the certain occurrence of future SLR by specifying ways to deal with its impacts:

(10)   In the meantime, therefore, *preventative action* should be planned, such as how to ensure effective flood warnings.

(11)   Coastal nations should implement comprehensive coastal zones management plans *to minimize the impacts of sea level rise.*

(12)   Additionally, national efforts should be made to identify particular services and resources at risk and to formulate *response strategies.*

As the preceding analysis in this section demonstrates, the temporal landscape of the CCHH text's discussion of the impact of global warming on sea levels is a rhetorically dynamic and potent one. It is a landscape in which the future is represented linguistically and discursively as a multi-faceted temporal domain comprising discrete future moments and phenomena that are juxtaposed in rhetorically consequential ways. Moreover, it is a landscape in which facts about the future serve as a primary means of persuasion as the CCHH makes its case for specific policies and actions. In the second part of my analysis I examine how representations of the past and present project images of a distal future that functions rhetorically to compel more proximal policies and actions.

National Security Strategy: Making the case for preemptive war

While the CCHH text uses explicit representations of the future in its arguments about the impact of global warming, the NSS text invokes images of the future less overtly by embedding them in representations of past and present security conditions and circumstances. The following analysis demonstrates how the NSS construes the post-9/11 security environment and how this construal legitimates the Bush administration's conception of preemptive war. Focusing on variations in tense and aspect, I explicate the subtle ways that representations of the future are latent within the document's representation of historical and contemporary security issues and in its representations of the actions of the "enemies" and "adversaries" facing the United States. These linguistic systems construe ideational meaning through their representation of the processes and actions comprising "reality." Tense has a further impact on interpersonal meaning through its modal function (Hodge & Kress 1988; Fleischman 1989).

Although tense and aspect are verbal categories concerned with time, they represent the temporality of situations and actions in different ways.[7] Tense functions deictically as it relates the time of a situation referred to in an utterance to some other moment, most often the moment of speaking. The present tense, for example, locates a situation as simultaneous to the moment of speaking. Aspect does not function deictically but rather represents the internal temporal constituency of a situation referred to in an utterance. Aspects are different ways of viewing and representing the internal character of a situation in terms of its completeness, progress, duration, etc. For example, the perfective aspect (e.g., Susan walked) presents a situation as a "single unanalysable whole, with beginning, middle, and

---

7.   This discussion is taken from Comrie (1976).

end rolled into one" (Comrie 1976:3). The imperfective aspect (e.g., Susan was walking when I saw her) represents a situation in terms of the internal dimensions of a situation with no reference to its beginning or end.

Throughout the NSS document, the temporal moments of past, present, and future, and the achievements, states, and processes comprising them, are juxtaposed in rhetorically significant ways. The following analysis reveals a dynamic temporal landscape in which representations of different temporal moments function rhetorically to advance the administration's conception of preemptive war. Variations in tense and aspect occur as the NSS moves from recounting the approach to national security in place during the Cold War of the twentieth century – deterrence and multilateralism – to declaring the need for a new approach for the twenty-first century War on Terrorism – prevention and unilateralism.[8] At the level of grammar, this movement is realized discursively through systematic contrasts in tense and through the aspectual profile of statements representing the actions and situations comprising the post-9/11 security environment. I begin by examining how variations in tense and aspect function to contrast the security environment of the Cold War with that of the War on Terrorism. I then consider how aspect functions rhetorically to characterize the present security environment so as to legitimate the Bush Administration's conception of preemptive war.

From the Cold War to the War on Terrorism: Construing the past, projecting the future

As part of the introduction to the NSS, the excerpts discussed below help define the post-9/11 security environment and create an intra-textual context in which subsequent, more focused arguments concerning preemptive war are made. The following analysis shows that arguments concerning the proximal deontic future of U.S. action and policy are not based on facts about the past but rather on representations of epistemic futures that project distal future "realities." Indeed, the text makes it clear that the future facing the country is not going to be "what the

---

8. It is important to point out that despite its rhetoric of "9/11 changed everything," the Bush Administration's doctrine of preemptive war has been under development since the end of the Cold War. As such, the terrorist attacks of September 11th did not, in fact, provide the impetus for the Bush Doctrine; rather, they merely represent a particular moment in "the fuller working out of this discourse logic" (Lazar & Lazar 2004:224; cf. also Burns & Ansin 2004; Dunmire 2005; Graham & Luke 2005; Kirk 2004). Moreover, while the doctrine of preemptive war represents a new discourse for publicly talking about U.S. military policy, it does not represent a new military practice (Foster 2006). The U.S. has justified military action on several occasions by making misleading or false statements concerning imminent threats facing the U.S. or its allies (e.g., The Gulf of Tonkin incident, Grenada, the sinking of the Maine during the Spanish-American War, the 1991 Gulf War).

past has been" as it makes a clean break from the past in order to set the stage for a future of a "preventative" national security strategy. This break from the past is realized through systematic contrasts in the simple past tense to recount remote events, the present perfect to draw particular elements of the past into the present, and, finally, complex verbal phrases that represent the present moment and project future actions and realities. These contrasts can be seen in the following excerpts:

(13)   a.   *Defending* our nation against its enemies *is* the first and fundamental commitment of the federal government.
       b.   *Today* that task *has changed* dramatically.
       c.   Enemies *in the past needed* great armies and great industrial capabilities *to endanger* America.
       d.   *Now* shadowy networks of individuals *can bring* great chaos and suffering to our shores for less than it *costs to purchase* a single tank (3a–d).

(14)   a.   *For the most part of the twentieth century*, the world *was divided* by a great struggle over ideas: destructive totalitarian visions versus freedom and equality.
       b.   That great struggle *is over*.
       c.   The militant visions of class, nation, and race which *promised* utopia and *delivered* misery *have been defeated and discredited*.
       d.   America *is now threatened* less by *conquering states* than by *failing ones*.
       e.   We *are menaced* less by fleets and armies than by catastrophic technologies in the hands of the embittered few.
       f.   We *must defeat* these threats to our nation, allies, and friends.

The first thing to note here is the contrastive use of the simple past tense for representing the security environment during the Cold War and the present perfect aspect for representing historical dimensions of the contemporary security environment. This variation demarcates the past into events that are entirely 'of the past' and, thus, not relevant to the present moment and those which are to be carried through to the present. In sentences (13c) and (14a), the simple past tense verbs "needed" and "was divided" are used to represent the struggles and enemies the U.S. faced during the twentieth century. Hopper (1995) explains that such verb forms render past events as remote and detached from both the speaker and the primary focus of the discourse. These events are marked with the perfective aspect and are, thereby, rendered as completed achievements of a prior temporal moment. The terminality and remoteness of twentieth-century struggles are reinforced through the declarative statement in (14b), "That struggle is over." Moreover, the temporal adverbs "in the past" and "for most of the twentieth century" further construct the "great struggles" of the twentieth century as discrete bounded events, the temporality of which does not overlap with the other temporal sequences and moments included in the excerpt. All of the references to

Table 1. Contrasts in tense and aspect in references to the Cold War

Simple past tense	Present perfect aspect
1. The great struggles *of the twentieth century* between liberty and totalitarianism *ended* with a decisive victory for the forces of freedom.	1. *Today*, that task [defending America] *has changed* dramatically.
2. Enemies *in the past needed* great armies and great industrial capabilities *to endanger* America.	2. *Throughout history*, freedom *has been threatened* by war and terror; *it has been challenged* by clashing tyrants; and *it has been tested* by widespread poverty and disease.
3. *For most of the twentieth century*, the world *was divided* by a great struggle over ideas: destructive totalitarian visions versus freedom and equality.	3. The militant visions of class, nation, and race which *promised* utopia and *delivered* misery *have been defeated and discredited*.
4. That struggle *is over*.	4. With the collapse of the Soviet Union, our security environment *has undergone* profound changes.
5. *The nature of the Cold War* threat *required* the United States ... *to emphasize* deterrence of the enemy's use of force, producing a grim strategy of mutually assured destruction.	5. But new deadly challenges *have emerged* from rogue states and terrorists.
6. None of these contemporary challenges reveal the sheer destructive power that *was arrayed* against us by the Soviet Union.	
7. *In the cold war*, especially following the Cuban Missile Crisis, we *faced* a generally status quo risk-adverse enemy.	
8. *In the Cold War*, weapons of mass destruction *were considered* weapons of last resort whose use risked the destruction of those who used them.	
9. For centuries, international law *recognized* that nations need not suffer an attack before they can lawfully take action to defend themselves against forces that present an imminent danger of attack.	

the Cold War, which are included in Table 1, are presented in simple past tense verbs.

While the simple past tense is used to recount specific components of the past, the present perfect is used in statements concerning abstract principles and phenomena (See Table 1). This variation relegates the specifics of the Cold War entirely to the past, while maintaining the present relevance of timeless principles and abstract phenomena. For example, in statements (13a) and (13b), the task of "defending our nation" is represented as a "commitment" that "has changed." The gerund "defending" and the present tense copula "is" renders this sentence as a statement of a timeless principle that is not unique to any particular temporal moment. As a nonfinite verb form, "defending" does not have the deictic function of finite forms, which locate actions or processes in the here and now (Halliday 1994). Similarly, the primary meaning of present tense forms such as "is" is timelessness (Fleischman 1989). The combination of the temporal adverb "today" and the present perfect "has changed" in the second sentence, however, functions deictically to locate the change in this principle within the present moment. Similarly, statement (14c) presents a contrast between the simple past tense verbs of "promised" and "delivered" and the present perfect "have been defeated." Within the logic of this sentence, this contrast situates the acts of "promise" and "deliver" at a moment in the past prior to their defeat. The use of the present perfect, however, also serves a broader discursive function: it enables a distinction between the militancy of the past and an "emerging" militancy that characterizes the present moment and projects an ominous future. The present perfect combines with the prepositional phrase "of class, nation, and race" to specify that a certain form of militancy has been defeated. As subsequent sentences reveal, however, militancy itself continues to be relevant to the contemporary security environment.[9]

In sum, the contrastive use of simple past tense verbs and present perfect aspect function rhetorically to make a clean break from specific dimensions of the past, while drawing others into the present. Although the specific enemies and strategies faced by the United States during the Cold War no longer exist, the nation, nevertheless, continues to face challenges and threats that it must defend against. Moreover, in excerpts (13) and (14) we see that statements concerning the past security environment are systematically juxtaposed with statements about the current environment. This rhetorical arrangement accentuates the distinction between the past and present by highlighting the progression of the discourse from recounting past achievements to describing the present state of the nation's security environment. The use of discrete, non-durative verbs renders the dimensions of the Cold War past as pointed and completed achievements, while the present

---

9. According to Lazar & Lazar (2004), such a discursive move is essential if the U.S. is to retain its super power status in the post-Cold War environment. That is, the fall of the Soviet Union left the U.S. without an "evil other" that could be used to legitimate its military policies and actions. What we see in the NSS text, a single text within what Lazar & Lazar term the "discourse of the New World Order," is the articulation of a new enemy. This new enemy not only legitimates U.S. global preeminence, but also enables the U.S. to define a new moral order for the post-Cold War security context (cf. also Graham et al. 2004; Graham & Luke 2005; Lakoff 2001; Leudar et al. 2004, van Dijk 2005).

moment is represented through verb forms that render it as a "more continuous state" (Kaufer & Butler 1996). That is, the present moment is encoded with durative aspect as a static situation that will "continue as before unless changed" (Comrie 1976:41). Lazar & Lazar (2004) similarly note that the president's post-9/11 discourse presents past ("raped, pillaged and plundered"), habitual ("to kill"), and projected ("would unleash blackmail and genocide and chaos") actions of the enemy. The temporal landscape of these statements covers a range of time frames, thereby "suggesting that the threat is an enduring one" (231). This sense of durativity is further conveyed through representations of the present moment. In the following analysis I illustrate how these representations describe the present while simultaneously projecting images of a distal future, a future that necessitates particular proximal actions and policies.

Sentences (13c) and (13d) above contrast the past "needs" of our twentieth-century enemies with the present capabilities of our twenty-first century enemies. Of interest here is that in describing the present moment, these statements also embed and project deontic and epistemic futures. The modalized verb phrase *can bring* describes the present state of contemporary enemies in terms of a capacity they possess. This phrase, however, also bears future coloration. Halliday (1994) characterizes the modal auxiliary *can* as a "potential form" which conveys a sense of "having the ability to," "readiness," and/or "inclination" (281). As such, *can bring* signifies a present moment in which our enemies have the ability and/or inclination to engage in some future act. In this context, then, *can* conveys prospective aspect as it "contains 'the already present seeds of some future situation,'" whose realization may be impeded by intervening factors" (Fleischman 1982:88). In slightly different terms, *can* retains a connection to the present, reinforced through "now," which is lacking in simple future forms such as *will*. Whereas *will* projects the future as a matter of course and as not explicitly tied to the present, *can* projects a future that has the potential to develop out of the present moment unless that development is impeded by intervening factors. As such, the use of *can* in this context is important in making the case for preventative war because it represents a future that can be "prevented" by U.S. action rather than a future that will develop as a matter of course, regardless of U.S. action.

A similar construction occurs in sentences (14d) and (14e), which describe the present state of the U.S. as one in which we "are now threatened" and "menaced" by a new type of enemy. As with "can bring," these verb phrases serve the dual function of describing the present and projecting potential future actions, consequences, and realities. That is, although a threat is made at a particular present moment, issuing a threat predicates an action that could or will be taken at some moment in the future. Chilton (2003) explains that as a speech act, threat has future action as one of its felicity conditions (100). Similarly, Kaufer and Butler (1996) explain that in making a threat "a speaker issues events that project negative [future] consequences" (248). Taken together, these statements about the present state of the nation's security environment illustrate the interplay between proximal and distal futures as the administration makes its case for preemptive war. The verb phrases "can bring", "are threatened", and "are menaced" describe a present dura- tive situation that projects distal future actions and realities that "may be impeded by intervening factors." The final statement in this excerpt reveals that it is these distal futures that necessitate the proximal future action by the U.S. as the NSS declares that "We must defeat these threats to our Nation, allies, and friends."[10]

Construing imminence: Conflating present character with future action

As mentioned earlier, the significance of the Bush Administration's national se- curity strategy derives from its redefinition of the conditions for U.S. military engagement. Known as the "Bush Doctrine," this redefinition sanctions the use of military force prior to any material, hostile actions being taken against the U.S. Central to this new doctrine of preemption is a new conception of "imminent threat" which serves as the impetus for preemptive action. The NSS points out that historically the international legal community has understood an imminent threat as "the visible mobilization of armies, navies, and airforces preparing to attack" (14). However, given the nature of the post-9/11 security environment, the administration declares that the U.S. "must adapt the concept of imminent threat to the capabilities and objectives of today's adversaries" (14). In place of the "visible mobilization" standard, the administration offers the concepts of "emerg- ing threats" and "looming dangers," threats and dangers which lack temporal and situational specificity:

(15)   And as a matter of commonsense and self defense, America will act against such *emerging threats before they are fully formed* . . . The U.S. has long main- tained the option of preemptive actions to counter a sufficient threat to our national security. The greater the threat, the greater the risk of inaction – and the more compelling the case for taking anticipatory action to defend our- selves, *even if uncertainty remains as to the time and place of an enemy's attack. To forestall or prevent such hostile acts by our adversaries, the United States will, if necessary, act preemptively.* (2, 14)

In previous work I have examined how the Bush Administration's conception of preemptive action endows it with the expertise to know the future (Dunmire 2005). Here I am interested in the actions, processes, and situations that com- prise this seemingly incongruous concept of emerging threat as imminent threat.

---

10.   See Dunmire (2007) for an analysis of how U.S. agency is construed as obligatory and necessary.

That is, by stipulating that the U.S. does not need such details as "the time and place of an enemy's attack" or for a threat to be "fully formed" in order to discern an imminent threat to the nation's security, the Bush Doctrine strips away the traditional, internationally accepted markers of an imminent threat: "the visible mobilization" of hostile militaries "preparing to attack." What, then, constitutes an "imminent threat" in the post-9/11 security environment? The following analysis addresses this question by examining how statements concerning the "capabilities and objectives of today's adversaries" manifest projections of a future "imminent threat" (14).

For this part of my analysis I noted all statements that represent actions and behaviors of enemies and adversaries and examined them in terms of their tense and aspectual profiles. The first thing to note is that, unlike the CCHH, the NSS does not use discrete, explicit projections of impending future realities to legitimate its policy prescriptions. More specifically, there are no statements in the NSS about actions the enemy is about to take in the immediate future. The document contains only two statements that explicitly project or predict the future actions of the enemy. One statement represents an action the enemy is likely to take and the other projects the consequences of such actions,

(16)   However, the nature and motivations of these new adversaries, their determination to obtain destructive powers . . . and *the greater the likelihood that they will use* weapons of mass destruction against us, makes today's security environment more complex and dangerous.

(17)   The inability to deter a potential attacker, the immediacy of today's threats, and the magnitude of potential harm that *could be caused by* our adversaries' choice of weapons do not permit that option.

In sum, the NSS does not represent the imminent threat posed by our enemies and adversaries in terms of impending future actions. Nor does it name specific individuals, groups, or countries that comprise the enemies and adversaries of the U.S. (Dunmire 2007). This paucity of specifically named enemies is, to some extent, an artifact of the genre. As a policy document, the NSS outlines general guidelines and principles and, as such, operates in a more abstract register than, say, a speech delivered to a particular audience which makes an argument for a specific military action. Interestingly, several studies of speeches and statements by Bush administration officials concerning the 9/11 terrorist attacks and the war in Iraq reveal a similar absence of specifically named enemies and adversaries (see, for example, Collins & Glover 2002; Graham et al. 2004).

The question arises, then, as to what comprises the type of imminent threat that has emerged within the post-9/11 security environment? The answer lies, I contend, in the use of the imperfective, nonprogressive aspect and the perfective aspect for representing enemy actions and capabilities. This aspectual profile renders the present security environment in such a way that it projects deontic and epistemic futures that compel the U.S. to take preemptive action. I begin by discussing statements within the imperfective aspect and then discuss those in the perfective aspect.

The NSS construes enemy actions primarily within the imperfective, nonprogressive aspects, as illustrated in the following excerpts:

(18)   In the 1990s we witnessed the emergence of a small number of rogue states that . . . *share* a number of common attributes. These states: *brutalize* and *squander, display* no regard, *threaten* their neighbors and callously *violate . . . sponsor* terrorism, *reject* basic human values and *hate* America.

(19)   Today, our enemies *see* weapons of mass destruction as weapons of choice.

(20)   Traditional conceptions of deterrence will not work against a terrorist enemy whose avowed tactics are wanton destruction and the targeting of innocents; whose so-called soldiers *seek* martyrdom in death and whose most potent protection is statelessness.

(21)   Yet in an age when the enemies of civilization openly and actively *seek* the world's most destructive technologies, the United States cannot remain idle while dangers *gather*.

Several aspectual features of the imperfective are of interest here. To begin with, the imperfective represents real, actual situations and actions (Halliday 1994) and references the internal temporal constituency of a situation or action by viewing them "from the inside" (Comrie 1976:4). Moreover, it renders actions and situations as "unbounded," "without endpoints," as "incomplete" (Bybee & Fleischman 1995). These characteristics of the imperfective are readily evident in the following excerpts:

(22)   Our enemies have openly declared that they *are seeking* weapons of mass destruction and evidence indicates that they *are doing so* with determination.

(23)   History will judge harshly those who saw this danger *coming* but failed to act.

What we get with these statements are representations of actions that our enemies are currently engaging in – "are seeking," "are doing" – and things that are happening – "danger coming" – which, at the moment of speech, are incomplete. Presumably, these actions and processes will continue until they are successfully completed or impeded.

Of interest here is that excerpts (22) and (23) are the only statements representing enemy actions that are coded within the *progressive* imperfective aspect; all the other statements, including those in excerpts (18)–(21), are coded within the *non-progressive* imperfective aspect.[11] As Comrie explains, the imperfective conveys a sense of "continuousness," which he presents as a subcategory of the imperfective aspect. He further divides continuous aspect into progressive and non-progressive. While the progressive aspect presents continuous actions and situations as occurring at the moment of speech – "are [at this moment] seeking" – the non-progressive does not. Rather the non-progressive construes actions as what an actor does *in general*, rather than what he/she does at a specific moment in time. This distinction can be seen by comparing the progressive statement "the enemy is threatening its neighbors" with the non-progressive statement "the enemy threatens its neighbors." Another important distinction between the progressive and non-progressive has to do with claims concerning the likelihood that an actor will engage in an action at other moments in time. The progressive does not make such claims; it merely represents an action as occurring contemporaneously with the speech moment and as continuing for some time (Comrie 1976). By representing a particular action as a generalized action, however, the non-progressive does make an implicit claim that the actor will engage in a particular action at some future moment. That is, the non-progressive represents an action as something an actor does in general and, thus, as something they have done and will do at other moments.

The implication of this aspectual profile is that it conflates action and character, thus construing the imminent threat facing the U.S. not in terms of what our enemies are doing but in terms of their inherent nature: in terms of who and what they are. In slightly different terms, the NSS does not represent the enemy in terms of actions located within and arising out of specific times and places. It represents them in terms of actions that transcend the specifics of context and that derive from their inherent nature.

The inherent potentiality of enemy action is represented more explicitly through the use of the perfective aspect, as in the following excerpts,

(24) Terrorists are organized *to penetrate* open societies and *to turn* the power of modern technologies against them.

(25) However, the nature and motivations of these new adversaries, their determination *to obtain* destructive powers hitherto only available to the world's strongest states, and the greater likelihood that they will use weapons of mass destruction against us, makes today's security environment much more complex and dangerous.

(26) These states are determined *to acquire* weapons of mass destruction, along with other advanced military technology, *to be used* as threats or offensively *to achieve* the aggressive designs of these regimes.

---

11. Two of the verbs, "hate" and "see," do not take the progressive form in this context.

(27) We must be prepared to stop rogue states and their terrorist clients before they are *able to threaten or use* weapons of mass destruction against the United States and our allies and friends.

(28) These weapons may also allow these states *to attempt to blackmail* the United States and our allies *to prevent* us from deterring or repelling the aggressive behavior of rogue states.

In these excerpts we see that enemy actions are represented through infinitive forms: "to penetrate," "to obtain," "to be used," and so on. When grammaticalized in the infinitive form, the perfective aspect renders actions and processes as *irrealis*: as potential, virtual, and, in some cases, as future (Halliday 1994). Thus, while the nonprogressive imperfective aspect construes enemy actions as generalized, actual actions, the perfective construes them as potential actions that the enemy is "organized" and "determined" to engage in at some point in the future. Moreover, through these excerpts we see that, indeed, post-9/11 imminent threats do not manifest as visible, physical actions occurring at identifiable times and places. Rather, today's imminent threats are virtual actions deriving from the more abstract physical and mental states of being "organized" and "determined" and, ultimately from the nature of the enemy. In short, the *imminent* threat facing the United State resides not in visible actions taking place at specific times and places; it resides in actions and potentialities *immanent* in the nature and character of "today's adversaries." Indeed, in his speech on December 14, 2005 concerning the progress of the Iraq War, President Bush noted that 9/11 "changed the way I viewed threats like Saddam Hussein" and declared, "In an age of terrorism and weapons of mass destruction" the U.S. cannot "wait for threats to fully materialize" (President 2005).

Conclusion

Working with texts from different discursive and disciplinary contexts, this chapter demonstrates the elaborate and nuanced ways in which representations of the future are linguistically constructed in deliberative discourse and how those representations function rhetorically. Representations of the future are explicitly incorporated into the CCHH text as the authors rely on a forecasting method to build their argument concerning climate change and human health. Through a systemic-functional analysis I illustrated how the linguistic process of nominalization and the linguistic system of modality construe the claims and evidence comprising this argument in rhetorically efficacious ways. By projecting a future "fact" about global warming, the text makes a compelling case for specific policy proposals, a policy that derives from the need to 'respond' to an impending future "reality." In the NSS text, representations of the future are not explicitly proclaimed and forecasted but rather take on a more nuanced and covert character. A particular vision of the future is latent yet discernible in the document's characterization of the Cold War and the War on Terrorism, which serve, respectively, as iconic representations of the past and present security environments. Focusing on variations in tense and aspect, I showed how these representations' construal of the future functions rhetorically to legitimate the Bush administration's conception of preemptive war. As in the CCHH text, this legitimation derives from the need to "respond" to a distal future reality that will come to fruition if preemptive, or, more accurately, preventative,[12] action is not taken in the more immediate future. In sum, what we see in these two texts is a "rhetorical evocation of a remote future time" that serves propositional and evidentiary functions in two deliberative arguments (Edelman 1988: 18).

As I argued in the introduction, this project is relevant to both rhetoricians and discourse analysts because both share an analytic and disciplinary interest in the linguistic representations and rhetorical function of the future in political discourse. Dick Hebdige (1993) articulates this mutuality of interests in his call for analyses of discursive representations of the future. For Hebdige, the future is a uniquely productive site for examining and understanding the "actively performative . . . functions of communication" (275). This understanding can come from exploring both the "particular discursive strategies" that "open up and close down lines of possibility" and the "prospectival figurative capacity . . . of particular metaphors and images: their deictic and performative functions, their literal relations to thinking possibility, to thinking possibilities" (275). In my mind, such an understanding is of interest to anyone concerned with the nature and function of language practices, be they "rhetoricians" or "discourse analysts."

References

Alessandrini, Anthony C. 2003. "Reading the Future". *Cultural Studies* 17: 211–29.
Aristotle. *The Rhetoric and Poetics of Aristotle*. (W. Rhys Roberts, Trans.). New York: Modern Library, 1954.
Bitzer, Loyd F. 1968. "The Rhetorical Situation". *Philosophy and Rhetoric* 1.1–14.
Burns, Michael & Ansin, Greg, producers. 2004. *Preventive Warriors*. Michael Burns Films.
Bybee Joan & Fleischman, Suzanne. 1995. *Modality in Grammar and Discourse*. Amsterdam: John Benjamins.

---

12. See Dunmire (2007) for an explanation of this distinction between "preemptive" and "preventative" war.

Chilton, Paul. 2003. "Deixis and Distance: President Clinton's Jusification of Intervention in Kosovo". In *At War with Words*, Mirjana N. Dedaic and Daniel N. Nelson (eds.), 95–126. Berlin: Mouton de Gruyter.

Chomsky, Noam. 2003, August 16. "Preventative War 'The Supreme Crime'". *Language in New Capitalism* [Online]. Available: www.zmag.org/content/showarticle.cfm?ItemID=4030

Close, R. A. 1977. "Some Observations on the Meaning and Function of Verb Phrases having Future Reference." In *Studies in English Usage: The Resources of Present Day English*, W. Bald & R. Olson (eds.) 125–156. Frankfurt: Lang.

Collins, John and Glover, Ross. 2002. *Collateral Language: A User's Guide to America's New War*. New York: New York University Press.

Comrie, Bernard. 1976. *Aspect*. Cambridge: Cambridge University Press.

Dancygier, Barbara. 1998. *Conditionals and Prediction: Time, Knowledge, and Causation in Conditional Constructions*. Cambridge: Cambridge University Press.

De Saint-Georges, Ingrid. 2003. *Anticipatory Discourses: Producing Futures of Action in Vocational Work Programs for Long-Term Unemployed*. Ph.D. dissertation, Georgetown University.

Dunmire, Patricia L. 1997. "Naturalizing the Future in Factual Discourse: A Critical Linguistic Analysis of a Projected Event". *Written Communication* 14 (2): 221–263.

_____. 2000. "Genre as Temporally Situated Social Action: A Study of Temporality and Genre Activity". *Written Communication* 17 (1): 93–138.

_____. 2005. "Preempting the Future: Rhetoric and Ideology of the Future in Political Discourse". *Discourse and Society* 16 (4): 481–514.

_____. 2007. "'Emerging Threats' and 'Coming Dangers': Claiming the Future for Preventive war". In *Discourse, War, and Terrorism*, Adam Hodges and Chad Nilep (eds.), 1–20. Amsterdam: John Benjamins.

Edelman, Murray. 1971. *Politics as Symbolic Action: Mass Arousal and Quiescence*. Chicago: Markham.

_____. 1988. *Constructing the Political Spectacle* Chicago: University of Chicago Press.

Fairclough, Norman. 1989. *Language and Power*. London: Longman.

Fairclough, Norman. 2003. *Analyzing Discourse: Textual Analysis for Social Research*. London: Routledge.

Fairclough, Norman. 2005. "Blair's Contribution to Elaborating a New 'Doctrine of International Community'". *Journal of Language and Politics* 4 (1): 41–63.

Fillmore, Charles. 1986. "Varieties of Conditional Sentences". *Proceedings of the 3rd Eastern States Conference on Linguistics*, 163–82. Pittsburgh: University of Pittsburgh Press,

Fleischman, Suzanne. 1982. *The Future in Thought and Language: Diachronic Evidence from Romance*. Cambridge: Cambridge University Press.

Fleischman, Suzanne. 1989. "Temporal Distance: A Basic Linguistic Metaphor". *Studies in Language* 13 (1): 1–50.

Foster, John Bellamy. 2006. *Naked Imperialism: The U.S. Pursuit of Global Domination*. New York: Monthly Review Press.

Graham, Phil and Luke, Allan. 2005. "The Language of Neofeudal Corporatism and the War on Iraq". *Journal of Language and Politics* 4 (1): 11–39.

Graham, Phil, Keenan, Thomas, and Dowd, Anne-Marie. 2004. "A Call to Arms at the End of History: A Discourse-Historical Analysis of George W. Bush's Declaration of War on Terror". *Discourse and Society* 15 (2–3): 199–221.

Grosz, Elizabeth. 1999. "Becoming . . .An Introduction". In *Becomings: Explorations in Time, Memory, and Futures*, E. Grosz (ed.). Ithaca: Cornell University Press.

Halliday, M. A. K. 1978. *Language as Social Semiotic*. London: Edward Arnold.

_____. 1985. *An Introduction to Functional Grammar*. London: Arnold.

_____. 1994. *An Introduction to Functional Grammar* (2nd edition). London: Arnold.

_____ and Martin, J. R. 1993. *Writing Science: Literacy and Discursive Power*. Pittsburgh: University of Pittsburgh Press.

Hebdige, Dick 1993. "Training Some Thoughts on the Future". In *Mapping the Futures: Local Cultures, Global Change*, J. Bird, B. Curtis, T. Putnam, G. Robertson (eds.), and L. Tickner, 270–279. London: Routledge.

Hopper, Paul. 1995. "The Category 'Event' in Natural Discourse and Logic". In *Discourse Grammar and Typology: Papers in honor of John W. M. Verhaar*, W. Abraham, T. Givon, & S. Thompson (eds), 139–150. Amsterdam: John Benjamins.

Hodge, Bob and Kress, Gunther. 1988. *Social Semiotics*. Ithaca: Cornell University Press.

James, Deborah. 1982. "Past Tense and the Hypothetical: A Cross Linguistic study." *Studies in Language* 3: 375–403.

Kaufer, David S. and Butler, Brian. 1996. *Rhetoric and the Arts of Design*. Mahwah, N.J.: Lawrence Erlbaum.

Kirk, Michael. 2003, producer. *The War Behind Closed Doors*. The WGBH Educational Foundation.

Kress, Gunther. 1995. "The Social Production of Language: History and Structures of Domination". In *Discourse in Society: Systemic Functional Perspectives*, P. H. Fries & M. Gregory (eds), 115–140. Norwood, NJ: Ablex.

Lakoff, George. 2001. "Metaphors of Terror." Available: <www.press.uchicago.edu/News/911lakoff.html.>

Latour, Bruno. 1987. *Science in Action: How to Follow Scientists and Engineers through Society*. Cambridge: Harvard University Press.

Latour, Bruno and Woolgar, Steve. 1986. *Laboratory Life: The Social Construction of Scientific Facts*. Princeton: Princeton University Press.

Lazar, Annita and Lazar, Michelle Michelle. 2004. "The Discourse of the New World Order: 'Out-casting' the Double Face of Threat". *Discourse and Society* 15 (2–3): 223–242.

Leudar, Ivan, Marsland, Victoria, and Nekvpil, Jiri. 2004. "On Membership Categorization: 'Us' and 'them' and 'doing violence' in Political Discourse. *Discourse and Society* 15 (2–3): 243–266.

Lazuka, Anna. 2006. "Communicative Intention in George W. Bush's Presidential Speeches and Statements From 11 September 2001 to 11 September 2003". *Discourse and Society* 17 (3): 299–330.

Levitas, Ruth. 1992. "The Future of Thinking about the Future". In *Mapping the Futures: Local Cultures, Global Change*, J. Bird, B. Curtis, T. Putnam, G. Robertson, and L. Tickner (eds.), 257–266. London: Routledge.

McMichael, A. J., A. Haines, R. Slooff, and S. Kovats, eds. 1996. *Climate Change and Human Health: An Assessment by a Task Group on Behalf of the World Health Organization, The World Meteorological Organization, and the United Nations Environmental Programme*. Geneva: The World Health Organization.

Miller, David and Thomas, Mark. 2004. *Tell Me Lies: Propaganda and Media Distortion in the Attack on Iraq*. London: Pluto Press.

Mooney, C. 2005, May/June. "Some Like it Hot." *Mother Jones*.

Morris, Meaghan. 1998. *Too Soon Too Late: History in Popular Culture*. Bloomington: Indiana University Press.

Palmer, F. R. 1986. *Mood and Modality*. Cambridge: Cambridge University Press.

Poulakos, John. 1983. "Toward a Sophistic Definition of Rhetoric." *Philosophy and Rhetoric* 16: 1. 35–48.

Poulakos, John. 1984. "Rhetoric, the Sophists, and the Possible." *Communication Monographs* 51. 215–226.

"President Discusses Iraqi Elections, Victory in the War on Terror. December 14, 2005. www.whitehouse.gov/news/releases/2005/12/20051214-1.html

"Response." 1987. *Random House Dictionary of the English Language* (2nd ed.). New York: Random House.

Scollon, Suzanne. 2001. "Habitus, Consciousness, Agency and the Problem of Intention: How We Carry and are Carried by Political Discourses." *Folio Linguistica* XXXV: 97–129.

Scollon, Suzanne and Scollon, Ron. 2000. "The Construction of Agency and Action in Anticipatory Discourse: Positioning Ourselves Against Neo-Liberalism." Available: www.gutenbergdump.net.

Scott, Robert. 1967. "On Viewing Rhetoric as Epistemic". *Central States Speech Journal,* 18: 9–17.

Sweetser, Eve E. 1990. *From Etymology to Pragmatics: Metaphorical and Cultural Aspects of Semantic Structure.* Cambridge: Cambridge University Press.

United States National Security Council 2002. *The National Security Strategy of the United States of America.* Available: www.whitehouse.gov/nsc/nss.html.

van Dijk, Teun A. 1998. *Ideology: A Multidisciplinary Approach.* London: Sage.

_____. 2005. "War Rhetoric of a Little Ally: Political Implicatures and Aznar's Legitimation of the War on Iraq." *Journal of Language and Politics* 4 (1): 65–91.

Weaver, Richard. 1994. "The Cultural Role of Rhetoric". In *Professing the New Rhetorics: A Source Book,* Teresa Enos and Steve Brown (eds.), 75–89. Englewood Cliffs, NJ: Blair Press.

CHAPTER 5

The intertextual forging of epideictic discourse

Construals of victims in the South Africa Truth and Reconciliation Commission Amnesty Hearings

Susan Lawrence
George Mason University

Introduction

On October 15, 1996, a former South African police officer named Brian Mitchell mounted a stand in a community hall in Pietermaritzburg, South Africa, and began to speak about his role in an infamous incident of 1988 known as the Trust Feed Massacre, in which eleven people gathered for a wake were killed in a rural community. The hearing was broadcast on radio and television and widely reported in the print media, for Mitchell was the first member of the former apartheid government's security forces to account for himself before the Truth and Reconciliation Commission in its public amnesty hearings. If Mitchell could persuade the Amnesty Committee Commissioners that he was telling the truth about his offense and that the offense had been politically motivated, he would become eligible to receive amnesty.[1]

The decision to exchange truth for amnesty was controversial, and the Truth and Reconciliation Commission justified it vigorously.[2] Against the weight of

---

1. Mitchell did receive amnesty from the Truth and Reconciliation Commission Amnesty Committee in December 1996. He had received a life sentence in 1992 for having ordered the massacre. In a 2003 commemorative address given at the site of the massacre, Deputy President Zuma acknowledged Mitchell as one who has attempted to help the community heal in the wake of the violence it sustained.

2. A pragmatic justification was the argument, advanced by Archbishop Tutu, the other architects of the TRC, and many TRC commentators (e.g. Graybill 2002) that had there been no amnesty, there would have been no negotiated and relatively peaceful transfer of power. Without the assurance of indemnification, the state's security forces would, as Tutu proposes in the Report, have "scuppered the negotiated settlement" (1:5). Another justification for the

releasing and indemnifying those who had committed murder and torture, against charges of sacrificing justice, encouraging impunity, and undermining the principles on which the new democracy would be grounded, it offered this counterbalance: the truth. The nation would learn what had happened under the apartheid regime. It would receive a publicly generated, authoritative account of who did what to whom, and why, from 1960, the year of the Sharpsburg massacre, to May 1994, the inauguration of Nelson Mandela as South Africa's first democratically elected president.

Why did the creation of such an account weigh so heavily against the objections to conferring amnesty on the perpetrators of gross human rights violations? The premise on which the Truth and Reconciliation Commission (TRC) was founded was that an understanding of the past would be crucial for unifying a formerly divided nation and effecting reconciliation among its citizens. Finding the truth would, for example, allow survivors to discover what had become of their friends and family members who had disappeared. It would, as the commission's final report says, "recover parts of the national memory that had hitherto been officially ignored" (1:113).

Yet the truth commission saw its commemorative function as going even beyond attempting to fill chasms in the national memory: it wanted to produce an account that would, specifically, promote social and political cohesion among people who had formerly been adversaries. While the commission did acknowledge that difficult truths might be initially divisive (*Report* 1:18), its approach endorsed public memory as a force that binds individuals into community, providing a shared understanding of the past and making available a set of ethical and political dispositions to guide future action.

To *account* for apartheid, of course, is also to assign responsibility, to help determine the "why" and the "how," a determination that was also part of the TRC's reconciliatory mandate. While this aspect of its mission is, in some sense, historical – the goal was to understand the antecedents and causes of this crime against humanity – it is also a deeply ethical project. The amnesty hearings were an acknowledgement that the nation deserved an explanation for the atrocities that had been committed, and that the new government would both demand and deliver that explanation, forecasting its commitment to accountability. On a more

---

amnesty was that the nation's judicial system would be overwhelmed should prosecutions be pursued (e.g. Hayner 2002:251). Jonathan Allen (1999) and David Crocker (1998) have pointed to problems with relying on the practical defense for the amnesty: Allen argues that relying on pragmatic justifications may lead us to reproduce old justifications for denying justice to individuals and to ignore the public amnesty's moral significance. He and others (Markel 1999; Villa-Vicencio 2000; Doxtader 2003), propose that the TRC's amnesty did produce significant forms of justice and deliberative activity.

local scale, an individual's – a perpetrator's – act of accounting for the human rights violations he had committed allowed him to perform an action with ethical implications for himself and for his audience.[3] The way that responsibility was talked about – accepted, deflected, or assigned – in these accounts has important consequences for uniting a divided society and fostering its transition to democracy.

And, indeed, the commission wanted its hearings to give rise to a renewed sense of responsibility. It wanted to counter the flawed apartheid-era sense of non-responsibility, indicted here in the report:

> individuals and the community as a whole must recognise that the abdication of responsibility, the unquestioning obeying of commands … moral indifference, the closing of one's eyes to events or permitting oneself to be intoxicated, seduced or bought with personal advantages are all essential parts of the many-layered spiral of responsibility which makes large-scale, systematic human rights violations possible in modern states.   (*Report* 1: 131–32)

What is needed, the report continues, is "an altered sense of responsibility" (1: 134), one that would supercede the indifference and thoughtlessness that characterized apartheid era, apartheid-*producing* constructions/abdications of responsibility. The hope was that the TRC accounts would, through their ascriptions of responsibility, have a transformative effect, giving rise to that altered sense.[4]

In this paper I address the question of how the TRC amnesty accounts might have that transformative effect and whether they were likely to do so. I examine how a particular feature of the historical and political context gave shape to some of the amnesty accounts and affected their capacity to accomplish what the commission hoped. Questions like this – about the reciprocal shaping of discourse and world – lie at the core of discourse analysis's disciplinary concerns. They are equally central to the concerns of rhetoric. It is not surprising that Weiss and Wodak (2003: 11) cite classical rhetoric as one of the disciplinary foundations of Critical Discourse Analysis. This paper shows how approaches and methods from rhetoric and discourse analysis may fruitfully address pressing contemporary questions about the mutually informing relationships between discourse and society.

---

3.   Most amnesty applicants were men: fewer than 30 were women.

4.   In this regard the commission focuses on the epideictic function of the discourse generated in the hearings. It is possible, of course, to approach the potential of this discourse from additional rhetorical lenses. Doxtader (2004), notably, has developed a theory of reconciliation that points to the deliberative capacity of the TRC accounts, proposing that reconciliation is always "a working faith in the works of words" to open up times and spaces in which adversaries can approach each other (284).

The discipline of rhetoric is grounded in concepts that have to do with how discourse is shaped, what its ends are, and how it in turn has effects in the world. These concepts are adequately robust to provide analytic leverage and adequately flexible for constantly changing social, political and historical situations. In this paper I use one rhetorical concept, *epideictic*, to clarify how the TRC accounts might effect social cohesion. I draw on another concept, that of *rhetorical figuration*, to interpret the relationships among a set of texts.

Like other disciplines, discourse analysis comprises both theoretical and methodological approaches. In addition to posing a question that comes from its core concerns, I adopt this discipline's attention to systematic, close analysis of specific uses of language, and I share its assumption that such uses of language give rise to social realities like responsibility, community, justice, and power. This paper does not, however, set out specifically to demystify power relations – that is, to show how power and discourse are mutually constitutive (although its line of inquiry is not irrelevant to that question). Recent work by scholars of Critical Discourse Analysis have addressed just this issue with respect to the TRC Human Rights Violations (or victims') hearings. Verdoolaege (2008), Blommaert, Bock & McCormick (2006) and Anthonissen (2006) have shown how victims' narratives evinced the traces of their former disempowerment, disempowering them in the present, and how such narratives were guided and mediated by commissioners. Other scholars of discourse studies have argued that the hearings, by omitting any testimony regarding apartheid's legalized abuses (forced removals, economic disenfranchisement), both expressed and reinforced the political settlement that allowed the ANC to take power (Mamdani 2001). This is an important body of work, especially as one of the commission's goals was, of course, to acknowledge and begin to reverse that disempowerment. This paper evaluates the TRC accounts according to the commission's goals as well, but it seeks to illuminate the reciprocal dynamic between the transitional situation and the discourse to which transitions give rise.

Epideictic discourse in transitional contexts

The rhetorical category *epideictic* can help elucidate how the hearings were to operate in this regard.[5] For Aristotle, epideictic was the species of rhetoric delivered on ceremonial occasions; its functions were praise and censure; its thematic

---

5.   I am indebted to Andreea Deciu Ritivoi – in conversations, working papers and published pieces – for my understanding of this line of inquiry *as* epideictic.

provinces were the noble or blameworthy deeds of the past[6] (*On Rhetoric* 1.3, p. 48 of the Kennedy edition). He specifies the end of the epideictic speaker as "the honorable [*kalon*] and the shameful, and these speakers bring up other considerations in reference to these qualities" (49, editor's parenthesis). After examining the scholarship that points to the limitations of Aristotle's treatment of epideictic, Duffy (1983) concludes that "Aristotle is mute on the social or philosophical function of the genre" (81). Desiring to invigorate Aristotle's interpretation of epideictic discourse, twentieth-century rhetorical scholars have theorized its capacity to unite an audience by engendering a commitment to common values. Perelman and Olbrechts-Tyteca (1969) propose that epideictic discourse "strengthens the disposition towards action by increasing adherence to the values it lauds" (50). Although this may have been a novel claim in the mid-twentieth century, the values-reinforcing capacity of epideictic is now accepted in rhetorical studies as one of the genre's defining characteristics: Oravec (1976), Duffy (1983), Loraux (1986), Sullivan (1993), and Ritivoi (2006) have, for example, used this quality as a point of departure for their own refinements and reinvigorations of the concept. Sullivan provides an exposition of the means by which discourse focused on praise and blame may increase an audience's adherence to values:

> A successful epideictic encounter is one in which the rhetor, as a mature member of the culture, creates an aesthetic vision of orthodox values, an example (*paradeigma*) of virtue intended to create feelings of emulation, leading to imitation. As such, epideictic instructs the auditors and invites them to participate in a celebration of the tradition, creating a sense of communion. (Sullivan 1993:118)

Epideictic oratory provides an example, a vision in language, which the audience desires to emulate; adhering to the same values, the audience coheres as a community. The TRC hearings, then, producing praise and blame, were to provide exemplars of responsibility that would inspire audiences to follow suit.

But twenty-first century contexts pose particular challenges even to recent reinterpretations of classical rhetorical concepts. In times of political transition, nations shifting from authoritarian to democratic forms of government attempt to chart courses between responsibility and amnesty, accountability and political expediency. Ritivoi (2006) has identified one problem that arises when we ask discourse to work epideictically in societies with violent pasts: how could such a discourse produce an exemplar from the past without resorting to expedient fiction? When to invoke the past is to invoke a history of atrocity, and to ignore it is to avoid responsibility, how can epideictic function?

---

6.   While Aristotle assigns the present as epideictic's main concern, he notes that epideictic finds it useful to recall the past; most of the examples given in the *Rhetoric* to illustrate epideictic draw on past actions.

Political transitions put rhetoric under pressure, and, as Teitel (2000) suggests, remind us that social realities such as history, justice, and responsibility are contingent and constructed in language (70). They also remind us that the binding of individuals into community is largely a rhetorical achievement; that is, it is accomplished through specific and situated uses of language. Events like the TRC hearings and the accounts that emerge from them offer the opportunity to study the linkages between transitional accounts of the past, their ethical resonances, and the rhetorical processes through which they emerge.

Contingency in the TRC amnesty accounts

The South Africa Truth and Reconciliation Commission hearings have been studied by theorists of transitional justice, including (and in addition to) historians, philosophers, political scientists, rhetoricians, and discourse analysts. Much of this scholarship has focused on the adequacy of the TRC's process and findings, published in its seven-volume report.[7] This body of work evidences the claim that transitions illuminate the contingency of truth. Collectively, this scholarship has generated a catalog of situational features said to have limited (or promoted) the completeness, impartiality and overall credibility of the account the TRC presented to the nation.

Participants in these debates identify such constraints from the entire span of the TRC's life and activities: severe limitations on staff and other material resources, its relatively brief life of two and half years,[8] a definition of *gross human rights violation* that excluded legalized crimes such as forced removals, the overjudicialization of the hearings, an emphasis on public hearings rather than behind-the-scenes investigation, attention to individual perpetrators rather than the apartheid system, a larger proportion of high-profile violations than those perpetrated against "ordinary" people, methods for taking and mediating victims' statements that encouraged particular kinds of narrative coherence over others, the inability of many victims to use prestigious forms of storytelling, witnesses'

---

7.   The first five volumes of the report were published in October 1998, before the Amnesty Committee had completed its work (hearings were held into 2001). Thus, the first five volumes did not take advantage of much of the material from the amnesty hearings. Volumes 6 and 7 were issued in March 2003.

8.   The TRC's lifetime was originally set at 18 months; when it became apparent that the commission could not accomplish its work within that period, it applied to Parliament for extensions. The bulk of the TRC's work was completed in 1998, when the first five volumes of the Final Report were issued. The Amnesty Committee conducted hearings into 2001; as noted above, the Justice Department issued volumes 6 and 7 of the final report in March of 2003.

loyalty to their allies and hostility to their opponents, and the partialness and partiality of the final report, with which no political party was satisfied and about
which one commissioner wrote a dissenting opinion.[9]

Critics of the amnesty hearing accounts have suggested that they are contrived,
pointing to their limitations in light of the TRC's goal of reconciliation.[10] In the
Minority Position of the final *Report*, Commissioner Malan mentions gingerly that
amnesty applicants are likely to have formulated their testimony to fit the language
of the criteria for establishing political motivation – criteria that are laid out in section 20 of the Promotion of National Unity and Reconciliation Act of 1995 (5: 441).
Indeed, it is to the political motivation requirement that many critics point when
discussing the potentially problematic inclusions and exclusions that characterize
the accounts. As Foster (2000) suggests, the applicants' need to argue that their
actions were politically motivated may preclude a fuller or more nuanced political
and psychological understanding of their actions. Similarly, Fullard and Rousseau
(2003: 210) argue that the political motivation requirement "involved privileging
the political and silencing a great deal of the social complexity that formed part
of a great deal of South Africa's political conflicts." Wilson (2001: 84–92) observes
specifically that the committee, having identified racism as belonging to the realm
of the personal rather than the political, ensured that in the Amnesty hearings,
racism would not be discussed as part of the context in which human rights violations were committed (84–92). Some critics (Jeffery 1999) find grounds for

---

9.   TRC commissioners and staff, and consultants who worked closely with the commission,
have noted in their memoirs and other publications that resources were limited and personnel
strained; see Boraine (2000), Buur (2001), Chapman and Ball (2002) Khoisan (2001), Orr
(2000), and Villa-Vicencio (2000). For discussions of how the commission's definition of
gross violation of human rights excluded apartheid's legalized crimes, see Mamdani (2001),
Bundy (2000), and Chapman and Ball. Krog (2003) and Fullard and Rousseau (2003) provide
discussions of the hearings' judicialization and its effects. Khoisan's memoir of working as TRC
investigative staff charges the commission with allocating most of its resources to public hearings
at the expense of investigations. Many commentators have noted the focus on individuals over
the apartheid system; among them are, again, Bundy and Mamdani, and Bell. Hamber and van
der Merwe (1998) have commented on the emphasis on high-profile perpetrators and offenses.
Blommaert et al. (2006), Burr, and Verdoolaege have analyzed victims' accounts for narrative
frameworks imposed on those accounts by the truth commission; Anthonissen (2006) also
shows how commissioners may frame witnesses' accounts. Cherry (2000) mentions the problem
of witnesses' loyalty to their allies. Among those who discuss the adequacy of the final report
are Bundy, Jeffery (1999), and Villa-Vicencio. The National Party, the ANC, and the Inkatha
Freedom Party all issued legal challenges to the publishing of the final report. Commissioner
Wynand Malan's minority position is included in volume 5 of the Report, 436–460.

10.   See, for instance, Pigou (2001), Foster (2000), and Slye (2000a, 2000b).

declining to engage with the testimony because it was strategically shaped. For others, it is the particular contours of the testimony that are problematic.

The idea that any use of language would not arise from its context sits oddly, of course, among rhetoricians and discourse analysts. And the TRC *Report* itself observed that truth "cannot be divorced from the way in which the information is acquired; nor can such information be separated from the purposes it is required to serve" (1:114). The key issue is not whether the accounts are contextually shaped; it is how they are shaped. These accounts had rhetorical goals that went far beyond their immediate function of helping determine whether human rights offenders would receive amnesty. They were to provide historical and memorial understandings of the past and guide action in the future. They were to provide the sense of responsibility that, as the final report said, had been largely absent from apartheid society. Thus the stakes were high when it came to the shaping of these accounts, as the vigorous debate about that shaping attests. These accounts, which were to improve social cohesion by orienting citizens to common values, became a compelling case for examining how an epideictic discourse is constituted in a transitional society. This chapter examines, specifically, how the need to establish whether amnesty applicants' offenses had been politically motivated gave the amnesty accounts their distinctive contours and affected their epideictic capacity.

Purpose as intertextual dynamic

The primary means by which participants in the hearings determined if offenses had been politically motivated was found in the legislation that established the Truth and Reconciliation Commission. The Promotion of National Unity and Reconciliation Act No. 34 of 1995 (the Act) lists the criteria by which Amnesty Committee members were to decide if applicants' offenses had been committed with a political objective. Section 20 (3) of the Act reads as follows:

3. Whether a particular act, omission or offence contemplated in subsection (2) is an act associated with a political objective, shall be decided with reference to the following criteria:

a. The motive of the person who committed the act, omission or offence;
b. the context in which the act, omission or offence took place, and in particular whether the act, omission or offence was committed in the course of or as part of a political uprising, disturbance or event, or in reaction thereto;
c. the legal and factual nature of the act, omission or offence, including the gravity of the act, omission or offence;

d. the object or objective of the act, omission or offence, and in particular whether the act, omission or offence was primarily directed at a political opponent or State property or personnel or against private property or individuals;

e. whether the act, omission or offence was committed in the execution of an order of, or on behalf of, or with the approval of, the organization, institution, liberation movement or body of which the person who committed the act was a member, an agent or a supporter; and

f. the relationship between the act, omission or offence and the political objective pursued, and in particular the directness and proximity of the relationship and the proportionality of the act, omission or offence to the objective pursued, but does not include any act, omission or offence committed by any person referred to in subsection (2) who acted

    i. for personal gain: Provided that an act, omission or offence by any person who acted and received money or anything of value as an informer of the State or a former state, political organisation or liberation movement, shall not be excluded only on the grounds of that person having received money or anything of value for his or her information; or

    ii. out of personal malice, ill-will or spite, directed against the victim of the acts committed.

(Promotion of National Unity and Reconciliation Act No. 34 of 1995)

These criteria dictated that participants consider the applicant's motive; the nature of the applicant's offense; whether that offense had been committed under orders or, on the other hand, if the applicant had the authority to order the offense; the identity and, in particular, the political affiliation of the victim; the political objective that the offense was meant to accomplish; the relationship between that objective and the offense (whether objective and offense could be seen to be directly related, and whether the offense was proportional to the objective); and whether the perpetrator had felt personal malice or received personal gain from the offense. When attempting to argue that or determine whether a given offense had been politically motivated, then, participants in the amnesty hearings considered these criteria.

To establish how the political motivation requirement shaped the amnesty accounts, I examine how the accounts invoke the criteria of the Act. Analyzing the relationship between the two texts, I both identify and characterize points of intersection between them, interpreting how the present text – an amnesty account – is related to a prior one – the criteria for establishing political motivation.

Introducing the concept of intertextuality to literary studies, Bakhtin/Volosinov (1986 [1929]) suggested that a central line of inquiry in studies of discourse might be the taking up of prior texts in present ones. In his study of reported speech,

Marxism and the Philosophy of Language, Bahktin/Volosinov provides a vivid analogy for how all uses of language might be approached, as he himself notes.[11] Examining how prior utterances are taken up in present ones, he argues that

> the true object of inquiry ought to be precisely the dynamic interrelationship of these two factors, the speech being reported (the other person's speech) and the speech doing the reporting (the author's speech). After all, the two actually do exist, function, and take shape only in their interrelation ... the reported speech and the reporting context are but the terms of a dynamic interrelationship.
> (Bakhtin/Volosinov 1986/1929:119)

Intertextual relationships are thus created and recreated in and among texts. As a field, discourse analysis has of course emphasized the need to examine this fundamental condition of discourse. Starting with the question of how discourse is shaped, Barbara Johnstone (2002) points to intertextuality as a primary avenue of inquiry. Critical Discourse Analysis in particular has made the analysis of intertextuality part of its program; such an analysis provides one means of interpreting how discourses change, and how they are constituted by, and constitute, ideology and power (Fairclough 1992; Wodak 1996).

Briggs and Bauman (1992) and Matoesian (1999) focus attention on the practices by which these relationships are fashioned. Revisiting Bakhtin/Volosinov's imperative, Matoesian infers that

> seen in this light, intertextuality includes the vast repertoire of metadiscursive practices for shaping the interrelationship between past and present discourses.
> (Matoesian 1999:77)

The practices in this repertoire have been surveyed by rhetoricians, discourse analysts, literary scholars and anthropologists. In an analysis of the intertextual dimensions of ethnography, Tyler (1987) writes that the means by which present texts may evoke prior texts and discourses

> range ... from overt citation of other texts to allusion by failure to mention what ought to be mentioned .... In between these two extremes are numerous means of implicating other texts and textual traditions, either by direct comparison or indirectly through presuppositions, genre conventions, common tropes, key concepts, and the set of commonplaces that constitute the so-called theory and method of a community of discourse.
> (Tyler 1987:90)

---

11.   In a move that anticipates the reversal and displacement of deconstruction, he writes "It is sometimes extremely important to expose some familiar and seemingly already well-studied phenomenon to fresh illumination.... In the course of such a reformulation of a problem, it may turn out that what had appeared to be a limited and secondary phenomenon actually has meaning of fundamental importance for the whole field of study.... We believe that one such highly productive, 'pivotal' phenomenon is that of so-called *reported speech*" (112–13, author's italics).

Fairclough (1992:119–123) lists possibilities such as discourse representation (speech or writing of another represented in one's own discourse), presupposition (propositions taken by the speaker/writer as given), negation (propositions invoked by the fact that they are argued against), and irony (echoing another's utterance to signify something entirely different). Leff (1997) has examined how historical figures may be invoked by direct mention, by adopting that figure's argumentative style, or by embodying the "spirit" of that figure. As Tyler's list suggests, this work tends to acknowledge that prior texts may be alluded to both explicitly and implicitly. For Fairclough (104), this difference is characterized as "manifest intertextuality" (explicit) and "constitutive intertextuality," or, more simply, "interdiscursivity" (implicit).

In order to describe points of intersection between the amnesty accounts and the criteria for establishing political motivation, and to delineate the conceptual distance between them, I draw on the concept of rhetorical figuration. *Figuration* provides a way to describe many of the practices noted in the literature on intertextuality. In classical manuals of rhetoric, the figures (metaphor, analogy, irony, hyperbole, onomatopoeia, repetition, and the like) were presented under the canon of style, after – and therefore outside of – invention and arrangement (e.g. Aristotle's *Rhetoric*, which gave the figures relatively short shrift, and, more extensively, the *Rhetorica Ad Herennium*). For traditionalists such as Vickers (1988), the figures are expressive devices that can give a discourse its emotional power. But other contemporary rhetoricians see figures as constitutive of discourse, rather than merely providing it with stylistic and emotional "value added," as Fahnestock (1999) puts it. Perelman's and Olbrechts-Tyteca's interpretation of the figures (1969) as functioning argumentatively reaches towards a notion of the figures as constitutive of argumentation rather than as increasing the persuasive power of an argument already composed. Fahnestock shows how the figures of series, opposites, reversal and repetition participate in scientific reasoning. And poststructuralism has elevated the trope to the fundamental condition of rhetoric; that is, like literature, discourse persuades tropologically through aesthetic pleasure rather than, like argumentation, by presenting theses for our conscious assent or dissent.

Use of the concept of figuration to examine patterns of intertextuality aligns well with some of the fundamental assumptions of discourse analysis, such as the assumption that any given use of language is one option selected from among alternative possibilities. But the selection is neither arbitrary nor determined by the nature of reality. A figurative use of language is ideological and driven by the rhetorical situation, which includes the rhetor's purpose, the institutional context, and history.

The figures used in this analysis are repetition (direct citation), synecdoche, metonymy, and metaphor.[12] This range of devices allows for interpreting both close and loose relationships among texts. Direct citation, or repetition, shows a very close relationship among texts; progressively looser ties may be interpreted through synecdoche, metonymy and metaphor. The language of a perpetrator's account may, for instance, *repeat* the language and categories of the Act; the relationship here would be one of direct citation or repetition. The language of the account may *provide specific instances* of the Act's general categories, putting that passage of the account in a synecdochal relationship to the Act. (Synecdoche may occur also in the reverse pattern, offering a more general category for a specific one, or it may interpret a part-for-whole relationship.) The language of the initial statement may *provide entities associated with, or attributes of,* categories cited in the Act; in this case the relationship is one of metonymy. Synecdochal or metonymical relationships may include components of either hyperbole or understatement, which afford additional nuances of interpretation. Finally, the language of the accounts may explicitly connect specific passages with the criteria, but the connection may ultimately be that of catachresis – a dubious application of the available resources to a context in which they don't work.[13] Thus, the language of the initial statements invokes that of the Act by repeating that language, and by providing specific instances and attributes of general categories cited in the Act. In this way, that language and those categories are given presence in the accounts.

In this essay, I argue that the intertextual dynamic between the Act and two perpetrators' initial statements in the Amnesty hearings shapes talk about victims of human rights violations in ways that trouble the accounts' epideictic potential. In what follows, I consider the segment of the hearings in which initial statements are delivered, narrate the two cases examined here, present the analysis of the intertextual dynamic between the criteria, on the one hand, and talk about victims in the initial statements, on the other, and discuss how that dynamic gives shape to responsibility as it emerges from the statements.

---

12. Synecdoche, metonymy and metaphor are three of the four tropes; irony, the fourth, was not identified as a dynamic that operated between the Act and the amnesty accounts examined here. It is probable that written transcripts do not afford the detail necessary to interpret ironic resonances in this analysis.

13. Perhaps the most authoritative interpretation of successful versus unsuccessful figuration is the amnesty committee, in its decisions.

Two amnesty applicants' initial statements

An applicant's initial statement is typically the first formal segment of an amnesty hearing. (Other main segments include an examination phase, in which applicants answer questions from attorneys and commissioners, and closing statements, in which attorneys make their recommendations for or against amnesty to the commissioners.) In some hearings the applicant's initial statement is drawn out through question and answer; in others the applicant delivers his own statement, often reading a prepared text, either partially or in its entirety. The two accounts here were prepared in advance and continuously delivered rather than elicited through question and answer.

Amnesty applicants' initial statements share some generic features, as they are likely to borrow wording from the amnesty application form or other guidelines. They generally begin, for instance, with a statement of current address and political affiliation. They then provide some background against which the offense is to be understood – the length of this background varies enormously – and then relate the details of the offense. They may or may not terminate with an apology or other statement suggesting change of heart or reform. The length of the statements varies; those examined here are relatively lengthy at just under 3000 words each.

A word about the authorship of the statements is in order. Applicants, depending on their level of notoriety and financial resources, received varying degrees of legal assistance. Some hired expensive attorneys; others did not consult with their assigned legal representatives until minutes before the hearing. Thus, some statements had considerable input from attorneys and others had little to none. It is also important to remember that the English language transcripts available to the public are, in many cases, translations of applicants' speech. This intricate web of human authorship is another expression of the accounts' intertextuality, of course, an indeterminate "collaboration" of the amnesty applicant, his attorney, a translator and a transcriber.

In the two cases examined here, the applicants are both enforcers or supporters of apartheid rather than its resisters.[14] The first case, number 0174/96, was

---

14. The majority of amnesty applicants were liberation movement activists from the ANC, a fact that tends to surprise international audiences. Members of the state's security forces were wary of the TRC, suspicious of its guarantees of even-handedness among perpetrators. The TRC did not conclude, of course, that the liberation movements were responsible for the majority of human rights violations committed between 1960–1994. Testimony from the Human Rights Violations hearings showed overwhelmingly that the apartheid state and its agents had committed the vast majority of violations. Whether those who had resisted apartheid would be required to apply for amnesty, and submit to having their actions called offenses and violations of human rights, was heatedly debated in the numerous talks and conferences leading up to the drafting of the legislation that created the TRC. Supporters of the liberation movements argued that they

heard on February 10, 1997, relatively early in the life of the Amnesty Committee hearings. It is that of William Harrington, a South African Police officer.[15] At the time of the hearing, he was in prison; he and his co-applicants had been convicted for their crime, which was murder, and Harrington was serving a sentence of 18 years. Harrington was not unusual among amnesty applicants in this respect: a large number applied from within prison.

The political backdrop for an amnesty case is typically complex. Resisting apartheid were multiple liberation movements, each of which may have been banned with its leaders in exile, may have operated a separate armed wing, and was likely to have established tighter or looser affiliations with various national, regional, or local political organizations. The apartheid state's security forces included the South African Police (SAP) with its various branches and squads and the army (SADF). The party in power was the National Party (NP); also active in the conflict were political parties and other groups from the (more) extreme right wing. Even the rudimentary background for any given amnesty case may, therefore, be somewhat intricate.

Harrington was stationed in an area rife with conflict between the ANC and the Inkatha Freedom Party (IFP), both of which were, at the time, characterized as liberation movements. The IFP and the South African police, however, tended to join forces in alliance against the ANC. In KwaZulu Natal, IFP sympathizers were recruited into the police force after an abbreviated training and were called "special constables," or more briefly "specials."

Harrington and his men abducted, assaulted and killed Mbongeni Jama, an 18-year old ANC activist, on February 24, 1991. Harrington's unit had been sent to keep watch over an ANC demonstration, legal since the recognition of the ANC

---

had fought for a just cause, and that to require them to apply for amnesty was to establish a perverse and wrong-minded moral equivalence between the enforcers of an unjust system and its resisters (see Mphahlele 2003 for a representative stance). Others, including those who prevailed, argued that it is possible to distinguish between "just ends" and "just means," and that requiring liberation movement activists to account for their actions before the commission was not necessarily to create a moral equivalence (this perspective is perhaps best articulated by Asmal, Asmal & Roberts 1997). More pragmatically, the TRC took the position that in order to address all sectors of society in its discourse and proceedings – that is, to include the entire nation in its reconciliatory efforts – it would have to include political violence directed against those who benefited from apartheid as well as against those who were its oppressed; the introduction to the *Report* points to the dangers of "remember[ing] in a partisan, selective way" (1:116). Thus, all instances of politically motivated killing, abduction, torture, and severe ill-treatment were to be considered gross violations of human rights, whether the perpetrator had been a member of the state's security forces or one of the liberation movements.

15.   Harrington appears also in Antjie Krog's (1999) memoir of the TRC hearings, but for a different offense.

a year earlier, and keeping the peace meant preventing ANC and IFP supporters from erupting against each other. The demonstration over, Harrington and the others departed in their van and encountered a small group of ANC supporters leaving on foot. For reasons that are disputed in the hearing, the policemen put Jama into their van, strangled and beat him, and for reasons that are again disputed, decided to kill him. This they did, after taking him to a remote area in the bush. They shot him and left his body there.

Harrington and his co-applicants claimed that when they first saw Jama, he had put his hand in his back pocket (presumably to hide something, or to check something that was hidden) and had then refused to be searched. One applicant claimed to have heard Jama utter a *sotto voce* comment to his compatriots, suggesting they kill the policemen. Once Jama was in the van, Harrington claims to have found on Jama a notebook ("pocketbook"), the contents of which, he said, implicated Jama in terrorist attacks in the area. For reasons they had difficulty explaining, the policemen threw the notebook from the van. When they were unable to get any information from Jama about his terrorist activities, they said, they decided to kill him.

The second case discussed here is that of James Wheeler (AM 2084/96), a supporter of the Afrikaner Weerstandsbeweging (AWB), a right wing organization devoted to Afrikaner political interests, and stridently opposed to non-Afrikaner governance, and especially to ANC rule. The AWB was particularly hostile to the ANC's ties to the Communist Party. In the time leading up to the elections, the AWB's leader Eugene Terr'blanche famously claimed on television that the AWB would take the country back by violence on the very night of the elections if need be, before it would allow the ANC to take power. On the evening of election day, April 27, 1994, Wheeler and a friend, Cornelius (Corrie) Pyper, hearing explosions, said they believed the AWB resistance had begun. They loaded Wheeler's shotgun and ammunition into his car and drove away, seeking "the opportunity to shoot black people." This they did: they drove up alongside a minivan, at which point Wheeler handed the gun to Pyper, who shot through the window at the van, killing the driver, Viyana Papiyana, and injuring his brother Godfrey. The police came for Wheeler and Pyper the next morning. They pled guilty to murder, attempted murder and illegal possession of weapons; fearful of the death penalty, they did not mention any political motivation during their trials. On October 17, 1994 each was sentenced to 15 years imprisonment. Their amnesty case was heard on March 25, 1998.

Intertextual shaping of talk about victims

My central argument is that construals of victims in these initial statements receive their shape from the political motivation requirement. One criterion for establishing political motivation concerns the victim's identity, and in particular whether the victim was the offender's political opponent: paragraph (d) of section 20 (3) suggests that that a politically motivated offense will be one that "was directed at a political opponent" rather than against "private property or individuals." As TRC observers expected, this requirement encouraged accounts that emphasized victims' and perpetrators' political affiliations and identities. Talk about victims invokes the "political opponent" criterion through repetition, hyperbole, synecdoche, metonymy and metaphor, and this criterion, in conjunction with the proportionality criterion, licensed construals of victims not only as political opponents but also as agents of violence, violence that called forth correspondingly violent responses.

The victim in Harrington's statement is named most frequently as "Jama" (24 mentions) or "Mr Jama" (19), appearing as "Jama" mainly in the part of the statement that narrates the events of the day he was killed, and as "Mr Jama" mainly in the parts of the statement that interpret those events. He figures also as "an ANC member" (twice), once as "a self-proclaimed ANC member," once as "a self-proclaimed communist," twice as "the ANC dog" (both times in reported speech), once as "my political opponent," once as "the enemy," and once as "your son." With only one exception, then, all direct invocations of the victim other than his name bear a strong relationship to the "political opponent" criterion.

The Act, in section 20 (2), focuses the definition of an apartheid-era policeman's political opponent on any "members or supporters" of "a publicly known political organization or liberation movement engaged in a political struggle against the State." To call the victim "my political opponent," then, is to repeat the language of the Act; to call him "the enemy" is to relate the two terms through hyperbole; the Act does not speak of enemies, but of opponents. To call the victim "an ANC member" is to offer a specific instance of a "publicly known liberation movement engaged in a political struggle against the State." Thus the relationship here is synecdochal, in which a specific term (species) is substituted for a general one (genus). To quote characters in the account as having spoken of "the ANC dog" is to relate the account and the Act through metaphor. When the victim becomes "a self-proclaimed communist" the figurative relationship becomes one of metonymy, in which something *associated* with the thing, or an attribute of the thing, is substituted for the thing itself (the pre-transition ANC had strong affiliations with the Communist Party). The figurative intertextual relationship, then, between this nomenclature and section 20 (3) of the Act is variously that of repetition, hyperbole, synecdoche, metonymy and metaphor. Repetition forges the closest ties between the two texts, with metonymy and metaphor creating looser ones; each provides one means by which the account invokes the "political opponent."

When we turn to the actions in which this political opponent/victim is embedded, the proportionality criterion of the amnesty hearings becomes salient. This criterion, expressed in paragraph (f) of section 20 (3), suggests that a politically motivated offense will be proportional to the political objective it was meant to achieve: "the proportionality of the . . . offence to the objective pursued" is one element of the situation that was to guide judgment here. This criterion was expected to assist amnesty applicants from the resistance movements, as their objective was imbued with a moral imperative absent from that of applicants who had enforced or supported apartheid. With a weightier and worthier objective, the more serious offenses of resistance-movement applicants would be more likely to be interpreted as proportional to that objective. It is probable, however, that the accounts of applicants from the state security apparatus also oriented to this criterion. According to it, the victim's death requires a political objective that could counterbalance an offense of this gravity. In the Harrington account, synecdochal relationships between the proportionality criterion and the initial statement license such an objective: they fashion a victim whose acts of terrorism had to be stopped.

The Harrington statement has the victim's captors finding a notebook in his pocket, a notebook that confirmed he was a member of the ANC and, specifically, "that he was involved in acts of terrorism with a[n ANC-related] combat group in the Richmond area." The account explicitly and repeatedly links these acts of terrorism to the reason for beating and killing him:

(1) Due to this information the specials [constables] and I started assaulting Jama for more information.

(2) Since we . . . were at war with the ANC, proof in his pocketbook was that he had participated in rallies in the Richmond area, in attacks against the IFP and the knowledge amongst us policemen was that Mr Jama had to be killed.

The initial statement orients most clearly to the proportionality requirement with the following two passages, which make the victim's purported actions the primary reason for killing him:

(3) Mainly to prohibit him from committing any further acts of terrorism, such as the one in the Richmond area, Mr Jama had to die.

(4) I could stop him from killing other people and burning more places as he had done in the Richmond area.

By this account, and by alluding synecdochally to paragraph (f) of the Act, the victim's own acts of terrorism elicit a proportional response from the offender.

In the Wheeler case, rendering the victims individually responsible for provoking an attack against themselves is out of the realm of the possible: Wheeler's victims were unknown to him, and he had hardly espied them before deciding to attack them. In this account the language that fashions the victims does not, then, bear a *direct* intertextual relationship to that of the Act; the victims do not figure as the applicants' political opponents or as agents of violence. They are, however, linked with the language of the act in an *indirect* relationship: the victims in the Wheeler statement figure synecdochally to other characters in the statement, characters who themselves bear a direct intertextual relationship to the Act. That is, the victims are linked *intra*textually to characters in the account who are construed as political opponents, enemies, and terrorists. The victims are named as "black people," and "black people" in this account also names those who murder civilian South Africans, threaten to overthrow the government, and establish a Communist state. Thus the victims of this offense become representative of the agents of violence.

The two victims are invoked in the account infrequently, four times in the recounting of the killing – its planning, execution and aftermath – and four times in a retrospective reflection on those events. Narrating the events that led up to and immediately followed the shooting, the victims are named twice as "black people," once as "the driver," and once as "a black person":

(5)   Corrie and I decided together to go and shoot black people....While we were driving I saw a mini-bus with black people inside in front of us in the road. I then took my shot gun from the back seat and gave it to Corrie ... Corrie fired a shot through the open front left door window of my vehicle at the driver ... From there we went to my brother's house in Krugersdorp where we ... said that we had shot at a black person in a mini-bus.

In the reflective passage that brings Wheeler's initial statement to a close, the victims are named as "a person ... and one more who were possibly not even ANC or SACP supporters or enemies of my people," once as "a young man ... and another," once as "Mr Godfrey Papyana ... and Mr Viyani Papyana," and once as "someone." While it is clear that the first set of references is racialized and the second individualized, the point I want to make now is that none of these construals of the victims meet the criteria for establishing political motivation. Indeed, to commit an offense against a person because of his or her race had specifically been ruled out as a political objective by the amnesty committee early in its hearings,[16] and it is unlikely that any participants in the hearings would have anticipated the

---

16.   This precedent was established, Wilson notes, in an amnesty case in which applicants claimed they killed a night watchman because he was black and held a job that would otherwise have gone to whites. Although the Amnesty Hearings suppressed talk about racism, the TRC

commissioners interpreting the shooting of black people, *tout court*, as a politically motivated offense.

An internal dynamic in this account, however, relates the phrase "black people" to political movements, organizations and opponents, an intratextual relationship that creates a looser intertextual link between the victims and the political opponent criterion, tying the victims' identity as "black people" to political activists, and, ultimately, to the political objective pursued by the applicants. In effect, the internal dynamic is one of repetition and part-for-whole synecdoche: "black people" names both the victims specifically and South Africa's non-white population more generally, and the victims through the use of this phrase stand, in a part for whole relationship, for black people as they are constructed in other parts of the account, and who are presented as political opponents.

The victims are targeted because they are black: the moment of decision is expressed as "Corrie and I decided together to go and shoot black people in order to try to obstruct the election," and the event immediately afterwards is cast as "we went to my brother's house … [and] said that we had shot at a black person in a mini-bus." Thus the account's primary identification of the victims is by their race.

Elsewhere in the account, black South Africans figure as political opponents. The statement's first mention of "the Black populations" presents them as political adversaries of the white Afrikaners. Speaking of his education, Wheeler says that

(6)   [Learning the history of the Afrikaner people] sharpened my awareness of the Afrikaners [sic] struggle for freedom and the onslaught against it by the Black populations as well as the English populations.

Shortly after, black South Africans are connected to the ANC which, in this account, figures always as "the ANC SACP [South Africa Communist Party] alliance."

(7)   The objective of the ANC SACP alliance was identified to us as the overthrowing of the White-controlled government and the establishment of a Black Communist government.

Additional passages in the statement evoke the ANC SACP alliance as promoting either the overthrow of the white government or the institution of a "Black Communist government." In another, the ANC is identified not only as a political adversary, but explicitly as an enemy: "During my military training … the ANC SACP alliance was identified as South Africa's most important enemy to me." As in the Harrington statement, these passages orient externally to the political opponent criterion through synecdoche, metonymy and hyperbole. They

---

Report did cite racism as a cause of apartheid and of the human rights violations that occurred under it. See, for example, 5:282.

also relate internally to the naming of the victims as black people; thus the victims are discursively related, at one remove, to the political motivation requirement.

The ANC is then associated with a terrorist campaign presented in vivid language:

> (8)   During that time there was a very strong terrorist campaign against the general population of the country with the assistance of the specially [sic] limpet mines while the so-called necklace methods of murder were used practically exclusively against Black people. Media reports and instructors in the South African Defence Force indicated practically without exception that it was the ANC SACP alliance which was responsible for this.

This passage invokes forms of violence visited against civilians and assigns responsibility for that violence to the ANC. The statement also alludes to well-known instances of resistance movement violence that include bombing a restaurant and a church, as well as episodes not claimed by organized movements. Attending meetings of the AWB, the organization to which he belonged, the applicant found that

> (9)   At a number of these meetings mention was made about our white farmers who were being murdered by black people and that it was their action to drive the white farmers from their land. Numerous times the Church Street bombing was mentioned as well as the Magoo's Bar bombing and the attack on an English church in the Cape. In these attacks innocent people were killed and others were injured.

Finally, "black people" are identified as the agents who killed the co-applicant's brother: "Early in 1994, Corrie's younger brother was murdered by black people."

Cumulatively, then, "black people" in this account figure primarily as political opponents, enemies, terrorists and murderers, providing a rationale for the applicant's claim that "I came to the conclusion...that it would not go well with the Afrikaners in South Africa if Black people or other populations would rule over them." Again, the victims of Wheeler's offense are intertextually related, at a remove, from the proportionality requirement: killing was more likely to be amnestied if its objective was not to protest an election but to prevent governance by terrorists.

Construals of victims and responsibility for human rights violations

As scholars of transitional justice have observed, the problem of attributing responsibility for state-sponsored human rights violations is not a simple one. Such attributions should acknowledge the complexity of contemporary authoritarian contexts, which give salience to issues of individual versus collective responsibility for atrocities, a problem raised by the TRC *Report* in its discussion of responsibility cited above. Another dimension of the problem is evidenced in the range of agents from political leaders to the "foot soldiers" of apartheid: how to distribute responsibility among those who made policy, gave orders, and carried them out? "At the century's end," Teitel (2000) observes, "there is a mounting sense that responsibility for modern persecution derives from individual agency against a background of systemic policy" (75). Accounts of responsibility might therefore acknowledge the agency (and lack of agency) of individual perpetrators, complicit beneficiaries, and political authorities. Moreover, they might incorporate social and historical realities such as racism and colonial conquest. As proposed earlier in this chapter, ignoring these complexities risks leading to the "morally objectionable options of whitewash or oblivion" (Crocker 1998:497).

A focus on individual perpetrators' accountability, however, was an important component of the truth commission's reconciliation process and its epideictic potential. The commission hoped that the hearings would, in effect, help rehabilitate perpetrators, a rehabilitation formulated by Philippe Salazar (2002) in terms of citizenship: having rendered their accounts at the amnesty hearings, "the agents of disruption and destruction [will] have reclaimed the right to attend the democratic banquet" (82). This re-entry into the life of the *polis* hinges, however, on individual acceptance of responsibility, an acceptance that would not only be personally transformative; it would be a public avowel of commitment to the new sense of responsibility, promising a more widespread commitment to that value and providing an exemplar to inspire emulation. Such accounts might also have provided the critical perspective on the past for which Ritivoi calls. Discourse could function epideictically, she suggests, if it found

> a vantage point from which to assess and process the past in order to learn from it, to critically evaluate individual accountability, and to understand how to rescue collective agency without shedding responsibility for specific actions.
>
> (Ritivoi 2006:121)

As critical perspective on the past and as exemplars, then, the accounts would be epideictically powered by perpetrators' acceptances of responsibility. This is not what occurred in the two accounts analyzed here.

Crucially, victims are not a valid locus of responsibility for state-sponsored atrocities. Accounts in which victims are responsible for the human rights violations committed against them obscure the oppression that called forth the resistance (as well as the history of peaceful resistance that preceded its criminalizing), and attribute responsibility to those who had the least political agency, diminishing the responsibility of those who wielded the greatest political agency. Blaming the victims also, and crucially, simply rehashes old authoritarian perspectives: from 1960 to 1990 (and perhaps beyond), the apartheid leadership justified its violence in just these terms. Calling for a new sense of responsibility, then, the TRC heard old stories. The epideictic shape of the Wheeler and Harrington accounts did not fulfill their epideictic potential.

Accounts of the past that arise during transitions are generated in one context to have meaning in others. The statements studied in this paper were formulated to win amnesty, but the hope was that they would also be suitable for constructing history, public memory, and collective values. Transitions ask rhetoric to do enormous work; even as they call on it to transform former adversaries into fellow citizens, they place constraints on its capacity to do so. This paper has examined how two accounts of who did what to whom, and why, were shaped by the need to determine whether perpetrators' offenses had been politically motivated. The construals of victims that arose from this constraint dampened the epideictic power of those accounts. This phenomenon may itself may be synecdochal to a broader problem: even as transitions depend on social realities such as history, memory, justice, responsibility and truth, they illuminate the contingency of these realities, their partialness and partiality, which undermine their capacity to transform division into unity. The next question might be how, having arrived at a rhetorical understanding of the problem, we might exert rhetorical agency in attempting to create the conditions under which more satisfactory accounts would arise.

Abbreviations

TRC   Truth and Reconciliation Commission of South Africa
Report   *Truth and Reconciliation Commission of South Africa Report*
Act   The Promotion of National Unity and Reconciliation Act No. 34 of 1995

References

Allen, Jonathan. 1999. "Balancing Justice and Social Unity: Political Theory and the Idea of a Truth and Reconciliation Commission". *University of Toronto Law Journal* 49: 315–353.

Anthonissen, Christine. 2006. "Critical Discourse Analysis as an Analytic Tool in Considering Selected, Prominent Features of TRC Testimonies". *Journal of Language and Politics* 5 (1): 71–96.

Asmal, Kader, Louise Asmal and Ronald Suresh Roberts. 1997. *Reconciliation Through Truth: A Reckoning of Apartheid's Criminal Governance*. Cape Town: David Philip.

Aristotle. 1991. *On Rhetoric*. Trans. George A. Kennedy. New York: Oxford University Press.

Bakhtin M. M. and Volosinov, V. N. 1986 [1929]. *Marxism and the Philosophy of Language*. Trans. Ladislav Matejka and I. R. Titunik. Cambridge: Harvard University Press.

Bell, Terry. 2001. *Unfinished Business: South Africa Apartheid and Truth.* Observatory, South Africa: Redworks.

Bizos, George. 2003. "Why Prosecutions are Necessary". In Villa-Vicencio and Doxtader 2003, 5–9.

Blommaert, Jan, Mary Bock and Kay McCormick. 2006. "Narrative Equality in the TRC Hearings: On the Hearability of Hidden Transcripts". *Journal of Language and Politics* 5 (1): 37–70.

Boraine, Alex. 2000. *A Country Unmasked: Inside South Africa's Truth and Reconciliation Commission.* Oxford: Oxford University Press.

Briggs, Charles L., and Richard Bauman. 1992. "Genre, Intertextuality, and Social Power". *Journal of Linguistic Anthropology* 2 (2): 131–72.

Bundy, Colin. 2000. "The Beast of the Past: History and the TRC". In Wilmot and van de Vijver 2000, 9–20.

Buur, Lars. 2001. "The South African Truth and Reconciliation Commission: A Technique of Nation-State Formation". In *States of Imagination: Ethnographic Explorations of the Postcolonial State,* Thomas Blom Hansen and Finn Stepputat (eds), 149–181. Durham: Duke University Press.

Chapman, Audrey R., and Patrick Ball. 2002. "The Truth of Truth Commissions: Comparative Lessons from Haiti, South Africa, and Guatemala". *Human Rights Quarterly* 23: 1–43.

Cherry, Janet. 2000. "Historical Truth: Something to Fight for". In *Looking Back/Reaching Forward: Reflections on the Truth and Reconciliation Commission of South Africa,* Charles Villa-Vicencio and Wilhelm Vervoerd (eds), 134–143. Cape Town: University of Cape Town Press.

[Cicero]. 1989. *Ad. C. Herennium: De Ratione Dicende (Rhetorica ad Herennium).* Trans. Harry Caplan. Cambridge: Harvard University Press.

Crocker, David A. 1998. "Transitional Justice and International Civil Society: Toward a Normative Framework". *Constellations* 5 (4): 492–517.

Doxtader, Erik. 2003. "Easy to Forget or Never (Again) Hard to Remember? History, Memory and the 'Publicity' of Amnesty". In Villa-Vicencio and Doxtader 2003, 121–155.

————. "Reconciliation – a Rhetorical Concept/ion". 2004. *Quarterly Journal of Speech* 89 (4): 267–92.

Duffy, Bernard K. 1983. "The Platonic Functions of Epideictic Rhetoric". *Philosophy and Rhetoric* 16 (2): 79–93.

Fahnestock, Jeanne. 1999. *Rhetorical Figures in Science.* New York: Oxford University Press.

Fairclough, Norman. 1992. *Discourse and Social Change.* Cambridge: Polity Press.

Foster, Don. 2000. "What Makes a Perpetrator? An Attempt to Understand". In Villa-Vicencio and Vervoerd, 219–229.

Fullard, Madeleine, and Nicky Rousseau. 2003. "Truth, Evidence and History: A Critical Review of Aspects of the Amnesty Process". In Villa-Vicencio and Doxtader 2003, 195–216.

Graybill, Lyn S. 2002. *Truth and Reconciliation in South Africa: Miracle or Model?* Boulder, Colo.: Lynne Rienner.

Hamber, Brian, Traggy Maepa, Tlhoki Mofokeng, and Hugo van der Merwe. 1998. "Survivors' Perceptions of the Truth and Reconciliation Commission and Suggestions for the Final Report". Johannesburg: Center for the Study of Violence and Reconciliation. http://www.csvr.org.za/papers/papkhul.htm.

Hayner, Priscilla B. 2002. *Unspeakable Truths: Facing the Challenge of Truth Commissions.* New York: Routledge.

Jeffery, Anthea. 1999. *The Truth About the Truth Commission*. Johannesburg: South Africa Institute of Race Relations.

Johnstone, Barbara. 2002. *Discourse Analysis*. Oxford: Blackwell.

Khoisan, Zenzile. 2001. *Jakaranda Time: An Investigator's View of South Africa's Truth and Reconciliation Commission*. Observatory, SA: Garib Communications.

Krog, Antjie. 2003. "The Choice for Amnesty: Did Political Necessity Trump Moral Duty?" In Villa-Vicencio and Doxtader 2003, 115–20.

_____. 1999. *Country of My Skull: Guilt, Sorrow, and the Limits of Forgiveness in the New South Africa*. New York: Three Rivers Press.

Leff, Michael C. 1997. "Lincoln Among the Nineteenth-Century Orators". In *Rhetoric and Political Culture in Nineteenth-Century America*, Thomas W. Benson (ed), 131–155. East Lansing, Michigan: Michigan State University Press.

Loraux, Nicole. 1986. *The Invention of Athens*. Trans. Alan Sheridan. Cambridge: Harvard University Press.

Maier, Charles S. 2000. "Doing History, Doing Justice: The Narrative of the Historian and of the Truth Commission". In *Truth v. Justice: The Morality of Truth Commissions*, Robert I. Rotberg and Dennis Thompson (eds), 261–278. Princeton: Princeton University Press.

Mamdani, Mahmood. 2001. "A Diminished Truth". In Wilmot & van de Vijver 2001, 58–61.

Markel, Dan. 1999. "The Justice of Amnesty? Towards a Theory of Retributivism in Recovering States". *University of Toronto Law Journal* 49: 390–445.

Matoesian, Greg. 1999. "Intertextuality, Affect, and Ideology in Legal Discourse". *Text* 19 (1): 73–109.

Mphahlele, Letlapa. 2003. "The Case for a General Amnesty". In Villa-Vicencio and Doxtader 2003, 9–12.

Norval, Aletta J. 2001. "Reconstructing National Identity and Renegotiating Memory: The Work of the TRC". In *States of Imagination: Ethnographic Explorations of the Postcolonial State*, Thomas Blom Hansen and Finn Stepputat (eds), 183–202. Durham: Duke University Press.

Oravec, Christine. 1976. "'Observation' in Aristotle's Theory of Epideictic". *Philosophy and Rhetoric* 9: 162–174.

Orr, Wendy. 2000. *From Biko to Basson: Wendy Orr's Search for the Soul of South Africa as a Commissioner of the TRC*. Saxonwold, South Africa: Contra Press.

Peacham, Henry. 1983 [1577]. *The Garden of Eloquence: A Rhetorical Bestiary*. Ed. Willard R. Espy. New York: Harper & Row.

Perelman, Chaïm, and L. Olbrechts-Tyteca. 1969. *The New Rhetoric: A Treatise on Argumentation*. Trans. John Wilkinson and Purcell Weaver. Notre Dame: University of Notre Dame Press.

Perelman, Chaïm. 1968. "Rhetoric and Philosophy". Trans. Henry W. Johnstone, Jr. *Philosophy and Rhetoric* 1 (1): 15–24.

Pigou, Piers. 2001. "False Promises and Wasted Opportunities: Inside South Africa's Truth and Reconciliation Commission". In *Commissioning the Past: Understanding South Africa's Truth and Reconciliation Commission*, Deborah Posel and Graeme Simpson (eds), 37–65. Johannesburg: Witwatersrand University.

Ritivoi, Andreea Deciu. 2006. *Paul Ricoeur: Tradition and Innovation in Rhetorical Theory*. Albany: State University of New York Press.

_____. 2003. "Interpreting Historical Legacies: The Ethos of Transition in Eastern Europe". *Interpretation and its Objects: Studies in the Philosophy of Michael Krausz*, Ritivoi (ed), 181–216. Amsterdam: Rodopi.

Salazar, Philippe-Joseph. 2002. *An African Athens: Rhetoric and the Shaping of Democracy in South Africa*. Mahwah, New Jersey: Erlbaum.

Slye, Ronald C. 2000a. "Amnesty, Truth, and Reconciliation: Reflections on the South African Amnesty Process". In *Truth v. Justice: The Morality of Truth Commissions,* Robert I. Rotberg and Dennis Thompson (eds), 170–188. Princeton: Princeton University Press.

_____. 2000b. "Justice and Amnesty". In Villa-Vicencio and Vervoerd 2000, 174–183. Cape Town: University of Cape Town Press.

_____. South Africa Promotion of National Unity and Reconciliation Act No. 34 of 1995. Act 95–34. 26 July 1995. http://www.fas.org/irp/world/rsa/act95_034.htm.

Sullivan, Dale L. 1993. "The Ethos of Epideictic Encounter". *Philosophy and Rhetoric* 26 (2): 113–133.

Teitel, Ruti G. 2000. *Transitional Justice*. Oxford: Oxford University Press.

Truth and Reconciliation Commission of South Africa. 1997. Amnesty Committee Hearing. Pietermaritzburg. 10 February 1997. Case AM 0173/96. William Basil Harrington, first applicant. http://www.doj.gov.za/trc/amntrans/am1997.htm.

Truth and Reconciliation Commission of South Africa. 1998. Amnesty Committee Hearing. Pretoria. 25 March 1998. Case AM 2084/96. James Wheeler, first applicant. http://www.doj.gov.za/trc/amntrans/am1998.htm.

Truth and Reconciliation Commission of South Africa. 1997. Amnesty Committee. *Decision* AC/97/0048, W. Harrington, F. Erasmus, and N. Madlala, applicants. 18 August 1997. http://www.doj.gov.za/trc/decisions/1997/970818_harrington%20etc.htm.

Truth and Reconciliation Commission of South Africa. 1998. Amnesty Committee. *Decision* AC/98/0032, James Wheeler and Cornelius Rudolph Pyper, applicants. 30 July 1998. http://www.doj.gov.za/trc/decisions/1998/980730_wheeler%20pyper.htm.

Truth and Reconciliation Commission of South Africa *Report*. Volumes 1–5. 1998. London: Macmillan Reference.

Truth and Reconciliation Commission of South Africa *Report*. Volumes 6–7. 2003. March 2003. http://www.doj.gov.za/trc/.

Tyler, Stephen A. 1987. "Ethnography, Intertextuality, and the End of Description". In *The Unspeakable: Discourse, Dialogue, and Rhetoric in the Postmodern World,* Tyler (ed), 89–102. Madison: University of Wisconsin Press.

Van der Merwe, Hugo. 2001. "National Narrative Versus Local Truths: The Truth and Recon-ciliation Commission's Engagement with Duduza". In *Commissioning the Past: Understan-ding South Africa's Truth and Reconciliation Commission,* Deborah Posel and Graeme Simpson (eds), 204–211. Johannesburg: Witswatersrand University Press.

Verdoolaege, Annelies. 2008. *Reconciliation Discourse: The Case of the Truth and Reconciliation Commission*. Amsterdam: John Benjamins.

_____. 2006. "The Debate on Truth and Reconciliation: A Survey of Literature on the South African Truth and Reconciliation Commission". *Journal of Language and Politics* 5 (1): 15–35.

_____. 2002. "The Human Rights Violations Hearings of the South African TRC: A Bridge Between Individual Narratives of Suffering and a Contextualizing Master-Story of Reconciliation". Publications in African Studies, Department of African Languages and Cultures, Ghent University, http://cas1.elis.rug.ac.be/avrug/trc/02_08.htm.

Vickers, Brian. 1988. *In Defense of Rhetoric*. Oxford: Clarendon Press.

Villa-Vicencio, Charles, and Erik Doxtader, eds. 2003. *The Provocations of Amnesty: Memory, Justice and Impunity*. Trenton, New Jersey: Africa World Press.

Villa-Vicencio, Charles, and Wilhelm Vervoerd, eds. 2000. *Looking Back/Reaching Forward: Reflections on the Truth and Reconciliation Commission of South Africa*. Cape Town: University of Cape Town Press.

Villa-Vicencio, Charles. 2000. "On the Limitations of Academic History: The Quest for Truth Demands Both More and Less". Wilmot and van de Vijver 2000, 21–31.

Weiss, Gilbert, and Ruth Wodak. 2003. "Introduction". *Critical Discourse Analysis: Theory and Interdisciplinarity,* Weiss and Wodak (eds), 1–32. New York: Palgrave Macmillan.

Wilmot, James, and Linda van de Vijver, eds. 2000. *After the TRC: Reflections on Truth and Reconciliation in South Africa*. Cape Town: David Philip.

Wilson, Richard A. 2001. *The Politics of Truth and Reconciliation in South Africa: Legitimizing the Post-Apartheid State*. Cambridge: Cambridge University Press.

Wodak, Ruth. 2006. "History in the Making/the Making of history: The 'German Wehrmacht' in Collective and Individual Memories in Austria". *Journal of Language and Politics* 5 (1): 125–154.

_____. 1996. *Disorders of Discourse*. London: Longman.

PART III

Identity and agency

Studying identity and agency

CDA, interactional sociolinguistics, narrative analysis, grounded theory

Barbara Johnstone

Carnegie Mellon University

Like the chapters in Section I, Zdenek's chapter in this section uses methods of **Critical Discourse Analysis**. Zdenek explores another area of sentence-level choice that can have powerful political effects: the representation of speech and ways of speaking. Zdenek asks how and how often deaf people are represented as rhetorical agents in newspaper reports about cochlear implantation (a technological treatment for deafness). To answer this question, he focuses on reported (or, more precisely, represented) speech and other kinds of metalinguistic discourse (talk about talk). He describes how often deaf people are quoted and how their words are represented when they are, who else is quoted as an authority on the subject, and how the signed languages of the deaf are represented.

As in the other chapters in this book that use CDA, Zdenek's objects of study are written texts, and the goal of the analysis is to show how the texts *could be* read as having a subtle ideological bias, pushed forward by the details of the language. Because its data is written monologue, most CDA research makes no direct claims about how texts *are actually* interpreted by the readers they are intended for.

The remaining chapters in this section, by contrast, illustrate methods of discourse analysis designed to highlight the interactional, dialogical nature of meaning-making, meant for the analysis of two-way or multi-way discourse and attentive to the ways in which meaning is shaped by audience's uptake. These are methods suited for some of the vernacular text-types and genres rhetoricians have recently become interested in, modes of discourse that include conversational and quasi-conversational discourse, sometimes in the "private sphere," that draws on and reinforces values.

Neeta Bhasin's analysis of a conversation among Indian students in the U.S. draws on **interactional sociolinguistics**, or IS. The origin of IS is in the work of

American anthropologist John J. Gumperz (1982). Gumperz' work on interethnic communication explored how interlocutors create intersubjective meaning as they interact, suggesting how their conversational contributions should be interpreted by means of "contextualization cues" ranging from prosody (intonation and loudness) to the way sentences are organized. When cultural expectations about the inferences that should be drawn from a particular way of talking differ among interlocutors, interactional problems may arise. For example, a well-known study of a holiday dinner conversation by one of Gumperz' students, Deborah Tannen (1981), explored why the New Yorkers at the table thought the Californians were uncooperative conversationalists, while the Californians thought the New Yorkers were being pushy and rude. Tannen showed that the problem was caused in large part by a tiny mismatch between the two groups' expectations about how long silence could last before someone had to fill it. The Californians were used to longer pauses between conversational "turns" than the New Yorkers were, so the New Yorkers tended to jump in first because they felt uncomfortable first, as a result dominating the conversation and making the Californians feel silenced.

The method of IS typically includes two steps. The first requires audiorecording and transcribing face-to-face conversation. Transcriptions in this tradition typically focus on the details the researcher is interested in rather than trying to capture every detail (an impossible task in any case). After identifying moments in the talk that seem to have been problematic or where new meaning seems to arise, the researcher plays bits of the recording to the speakers involved, asking them to talk about what they thought was happening at key points, what went wrong or right. This technique is known as "playback" or "feedback." Through playback, the researcher's hypotheses are tested with reference to a cultural insider's perceptions. This links Gumperz' technique with ethnography, the attempt to describe cultural knowledge as insiders understand it, which is a primary goal of cultural anthropology.

Many interactional sociolinguists continue to study the reasons for cross-cultural or interethnic miscommunication, but versions of IS's methods have also come to be widely used to study how personal and social identities arise and are deployed in talk. Bhasin's chapter exemplifies this use of methods from IS. Bhasin's primary focus is on a recorded conversation. Through a line-by-line analysis of how the interlocutors' contributions are responsively woven together, she shows how a joint cultural identity (Indianness) is mapped onto a supposedly shared set of cultural norms and practices ("Indian humor"), in opposition to another supposedly shared set of norms and practices ("American humor"). Most of the conversational work is done by one participant, Geeta, but Bhasin shows that Geeta can prevail only because others collaborate, agreeing with her, offering additional examples, giving supportive feedback in the form of *um-hmm*s and *right*s, and simply by continuing to listen. Although she did not use the playback technique, Bhasin did interview the people she recorded, asking them about the issues raised in the recorded conversation. This gives her two sources of evidence for the claims she makes about the rhetorically situated quality of national identity.

Narrative has been one of the major themes in humanistic and social scientific thought since the mid-twentieth century. The essence of humanness, long characterized as the tendency to make sense of the world through rationality, has come increasingly to be described as the tendency to tell stories, to make sense of the world through narrative. Martha S. Cheng's chapter illustrates one of a set of approaches to the study of discourse broadly referred to as **narrative analysis**. Narrative analysis begins with the observation that the stories that come up in casual conversation have a common structure, not unlike the structure that literary theorists and folklorists have identified in literary narrative and traditional tales. This observation is credited to sociolinguist William Labov and his student Joshua Waletzky (1997[1967]), who sketched the functions that clauses in "fully-formed" conversational narrative could serve. During the 1970s, scholars like Dell Hymes (1977) A. L. Becker (1979), and Wallace Chafe and his students (1980) began to describe how narrative in other cultural settings differed in structure from the Anglo-American stories Labov and Waletzky focused on.

Narrative analysis has flourished in the context of interest across the disciplines in the nature of history, memory, and personal identity, as scholars have come to see history as "commemoration," the result of negotiation and struggle, and personal identity as the coherent retrospective plotting of one's life story (see Johnstone 2001). It has become more and more apparent, however, that everyday conversational narratives are not always fully-developed "stories" with explicit plots and morals. Scholars like Carranza (1998) and Georgakopoulou (2006) have turned attention to "low-narrativity narratives" or "small stories," bits of talk that evoke the past, or even a hypothetical past, or a temporal sequence of events in the (hypothetical) future.

Cheng follows this line of work in her analysis of how narrative is related to rhetorical ethos in an online chatroom conversation, in which linguistic identity-work is at a premium in the absence of visual cues. She looks at how narratives – both more fully-formed stories and minimal references to actions – can position a speaker vis à vis other people, as one of a *we* or as an *I* versus a *them*; at whether and when participants in the chat represent themselves as agents of action; at how they evaluate the actions and events they recount; at how collaborative narratives as well as individual styles can serve to locate participants in the social worlds of their shared profession and of the online course they are participating in; and at what social actions are performed by means of the narratives.

Amanda Young's exploration of how teenage girls talk about agency for contraceptive choice is more eclectic in method. As do many interactional sociolinguists, Young analyzes data from conversations and subsequent interviews with the people involved. To identify moments when the girls are speaking as agents, she looks at grammatical choices, the typical focus of CDA. In addition, though, Young draws on **grounded theory (GT)** to identify recurring features of the content of her texts. Unlike the methods we have touched on so far, GT originated in sociology rather than in linguistics, among scholars who mistrusted the ways in which pre-chosen, top-down theories about human behavior could determine what researchers saw and how they explained it (Glaser & Strauss 1967). The central claim of GT is that explanatory models should emerge from data via a repeated process of analysis, theory-building, and further analysis leading to refinement of the theory. "Theory evolves during actual research," as one overview puts it, "and it does this through continuous interplay between analysis and data collection" (Strauss & Corbin 1994: 273). Like all the methods of discourse analysis discussed so far, GT acknowledges that it is fundamentally interpretive. However, the recognition that there is no single correct analysis of a body of discourse does not vitiate the need for systematicity. With GT as with any other approach to discourse analysis, some interpretations are better than others. This is not because some theories are more fashionable than others, but because some analyses are more rigorous others, more responsive to alternatives and "outliers" (cases that don't work the way the average one does), more careful to account for every aspect of the text, not just ones that illustrate the researcher's point, more conscientious about searching for cases that might provide counter-evidence. Like IS and ethnography (see the introduction to Section III), GT searches for explanations that reflect insiders' understandings of what is going on: "Interpretations must include the perspectives and voices of the people whom we study" (Strauss & Corbin 1994: 274).

Methods of GT are useful when the focus is on what people say rather than, as in research using CDA, the details of how they say it. Young started by identifying places in her data where her research participants were using grammatical signals of agency such as first-person sentence subjects (*I* or *we* rather than *they*, for example) and active verbs. She found, as she expected, that "in addition to those textual markers, expressions of agency emerged in more complex constructions." To identify these, she returned to the segments that had been picked out on the basis of structural criteria and looked more carefully at each one, asking if a source of agency was identified and if so where it was located (was the girl represented as the agent of choice, for example, or was her boyfriend?). Young's close reading was guided by increasingly specific questions suggested by her texts; from asking whether they represented agency at all, she moved to questions about the contexts in which they did, realizing through repeated rereadings that the girls tended to represent themselves as agents when analyzing how they made decisions and when talking about and thus manipulating what they knew. The process continued in this way until Young had developed a robust, reliable way of identifying and categorizing talk about agency in her data.

References

Becker, A. L. 1979. "Text-Building, Epistemology, and Aesthetics in Javanese Shadow Theater". in *The Imagination of Reality: Essays in Southeast Asian Coherence Systems*, A. L. Becker and A. Yengoyan (Eds), 211–44. Norwood, NJ: Ablex.

Carranza, Isolda. 1998. "Low-Narrativity Narratives and Argumentation". *Narrative Inquiry* 8: 287–317.

Chafe, Wallace (Ed). 1980. *The Pear Stories: Cognitive, Cultural and Linguistic Aspects of Narrative Production*. Norwood, NJ: Ablex.

Georgakopoulou, Alexandra. 2006. "Thinking Big with Small Stories in Narrative and Identity Analysis". *Narrative Inquiry* 16: 122–30.

Gumperz, John J. 1982. *Discourse Strategies*. Cambridge: Cambridge University Press.

Hymes, Dell. 1977. "Discovering Oral Performance and Measured Verse in American Indian Narrative". *New Literary History* 7: 431–57.

Johnstone, Barbara. 2001. "Discourse Analysis and Narrative". in *The Handbook of Discourse Analysis*, D. Schiffrin, D. Tannen, and H. Hamilton (Eds), 635–49. Malden, MA; Oxford, UK: Blackwell.

Labov, William, and Joshua Waletzky. 1997 [1967]. "Narrative Analysis: Oral Versions of Personal Experience". *Journal of Narrative and Life History* 7 [Special Issue on *Oral Versions of Personal Experience: Three Decades of Narrative Analysis*]: 3–38.

Strauss, Anselm, and Juliet Corbin. 1994. "Grounded Theory Methodology: An Overview". In *Handbook of Qualitative Research*, N. K. Denin and Y. S. Lincoln (Eds), 273–86. Thousand Oaks, CA: Sage.

Tannen, Deborah. 1981. "New York Jewish Conversational Style". *International Journal of the Sociology of Language* 30: 133–49.

CHAPTER 6

Muted voices

Cochlear implants, news discourse, and the public fascination with curing deafness

Sean Zdenek
Texas Tech University

Introduction

The debate over cochlear implants brings to the fore questions of agency, power, and ideology, questions of particular interest to rhetorical critics and critical discourse analysts. A small device surgically implanted in the ear and connected to an external speech processor, the cochlear implant is designed to bypass non-functioning or damaged hair cells in the inner ear by stimulating the auditory nerve directly with bursts of electrical impulses. Depending on how the debate is framed, the implant promises either to restore hearing to deaf and hard-of-hearing children and adults, or to undermine the rights and viability of a linguistic minority with its own unique culture (Deaf Culture). Are deaf people tragically afflicted with an impairment that requires the mainstream (hearing) culture to care for, monitor, and educate those deemed "impaired" in order to make them more normal (i.e. more like hearing people)? Or is Deafness "a different way of being" (Sparrow 2005: 138) that is rooted in a unique culture and language (in this case, sign language)? These questions coalesce into a basic distinction between two views of deafness: the mainstream view of the medical establishment that being deaf constitutes a disability; and the Deaf Culture view that Deafness is the identity and culture of a linguistic minority. These views are both reflected and shaped discursively. In this chapter, I suggest how the resources of Critical Discourse Analysis (CDA) can be brought to bear on the question of rhetorical agency. Who has the right to speak for deaf people? To what extent are deaf voices spoken for by the mainstream news media? My sample is a collection of news articles about cochlear implants in major papers around the world over a recent three-year period. As rhetorical critics and theorists seek to reformulate agency after postmodernism, CDA offers a means to enrich our understanding of a concept that is central to rhetoric.

In this chapter I follow the Deaf Studies convention of making a conceptual and orthographic distinction between deafness as a physical condition and Deafness as a cultural identity. Baynton (2006, p. 45) explains the distinction: "The use of 'deaf' (with a lower case *d*) to refer primarily to an audiological condition of hearing loss, and 'Deaf' (with an upper case *D*) to refer to a cultural identity (deaf people, that is, who use American Sign Language, share certain attitudes and beliefs about themselves and their relation to the hearing world, and self-consciously think of themselves as part of a separate Deaf culture) has become standard in the literature on Deaf Culture."

Rhetorical agency and critical discourse analysis

The concept of agency is tied to our very understanding of rhetoric. The classical rhetorical tradition is grounded in an ideology of individualism and agency: individual speakers (agents) seek to persuade specific audiences in specific situations. This conception of agency continues to influence our modern understanding of rhetoric. Lloyd Bitzer's (1968) notion of the rhetorical situation, for example, posits a controlling exigence that "can be completely or partially removed if discourse introduced into the situation can so constrain human decision or action as to bring about the significant modification of the exigence" (quoted in Farrell & Young 2004:33). In this framework, the speaker is autonomous, removed from the components of the situation (exigence, audience, and constraints) as she considers the most appropriate response. The response (discourse) is also treated as removed from the speaker. While Bitzer's original formulation has been criticized for objectifying the situation (e.g., see Vatz 1973), it has had a profound effect on rhetorical studies. It is part of a larger focus in modern rhetorical studies on oratory and great orators, as inaugurated in Herbert Wichelns' founding text (1993 [1925]; see also Gaonkar 1990).

The postmodern critique of rhetorical agency, often linked to the work of Dilip Gaonkar (1997), charges that despite efforts to "thicken" the classical lexicon, rhetoric is problematically rooted in the classical notion of the citizen:

> A view of speaker as the seat of origin rather than a point of articulation, a view of strategy as identifiable under an intentional description, a view of discourse as constitutive of character and community, a view of audience positioned simultaneously as "spectator" and "participant," and finally, a view of "ends" that binds speaker, strategy, discourse, and audience in a web of purposive actions.
>
> (Gaonkar 1997:32)

In contrast to an "intentionalist," agent-centered view of discourse and criticism, Gaonkar (1997) offers an "intertextual" view. Whereas the former defers the textual object by turning it into an effect of the writer's strategic design (p. 332), the latter takes into account what Campbell calls the "cultural grammar" through which textual object, author, and critic are situated (p. 53–4). For Gaonkar, an intentionalist strategy "cannot unlock the grammar of massive social formations such as 'modern science' that are propelled by 'system imperatives'" (p. 337–8), nor can it show how discourse "is produced and populated with significations within a matrix of technologies – literary, social, and material – that elude the reach and the imprint of the subject" (p. 337). To see Darwin, for example, "as a Super Rhetor, bestriding history like a strategic colossus" (p. 128), is to fail to account, as Gaonkar argues, for *The Origin of Species* as discourse articulated at the intersection of a number of competing, institutional frameworks.

The postmodern critique has led to a reformulation of the concept of rhetorical agency. While stopping short of characterizing agency as an illusion (see Geisler 2004: 12), rhetoricians are exploring how human agency is articulated within institutions: "its radical contingency, its fragmentary qualities, and/or its dependence on generative systems beyond the seat of an insular individual consciousness" (Lundberg & Gunn 2005: 86). For example, William Kinsella (2005: 303) explores how, in the context of the rhetoric of science and technology, "the locus of agency has shifted increasingly from the individual to larger systems of power/knowledge" in the face of "unprecedented degrees of institutionalization." In this way, organizations are treated as "primary social actors" (p. 305) within institutions that are seen as "reified, sedimented," and "increasingly recalcitrant" (p. 304).

Rather than characterize human agents as simply or only overwhelmed, oppressed, or constituted by institutions and discourses, some rhetorical critics have pursued a "reconciliation" of contingency and agency that "allows agency to remain with the agent and yet acknowledge[s] its embedding in the externals of communicative interaction" (Geisler 2004: 13). In such cases, *resistance* is key to rhetorical theory: "how rhetors without taken-for-granted access do, nevertheless, manage to exercise agency" (p. 11). For example, in her study of mothers who manage to resist the "disciplinary grid" of breastfeeding discourse, Amy Koerber (2006: 100) argues for a negotiation of the extremes of transcendent agency and overbearing structure. Koerber (2006: 88) writes, "We must account for rhetorical agency without reducing such agency either to the occupation of preexisting subject positions or to strategic, subject-centered language use that enables transcendence of such predefined positions." Human agency and disciplinary power are viewed in this study as "inextricably linked," a view that fits with the wider interest among rhetoricians in reconciling what Gaonkar refers to as intentional vs. intertextual perspectives. Indeed, a number of respondents to Gaonkar's critique of agency in *Rhetorical Hermeneutics* (Gross & Keith 1997: see esp. chapters by Leff,

Miller, and Campbell) argue for more fluid interaction between the rhetorical and structural traditions. In Campbell's words, "We can recognize that from different perspectives the speaker can be described accurately one way or the other or as a tensional fusion of both" (p. 123)

What discourse analysis can bring to the ongoing effort to reformulate rhetorical agency is a detailed, linguistic-oriented, micro-level account of how agency circulates in texts. Because proponents of critical discourse analysis (CDA) – an increasingly popular and mature approach to doing DA – are interested in questions of resistance and power at the intersection of discourse and social theory, CDA is an especially appropriate choice. Moreover, given the trend in rhetorical studies, according to a recent report on rhetorical agency (Geisler 2004: 14), towards "opening up" the "essential mechanisms" – and especially the conditions and limitations – for agency and action, CDA's focus on the *mechanisms* of language can provide ways to enrich our understanding of rhetorical agency.

The specific linguistic features identified in the textual artifact vary, but "actor analyses" (Meyer 2001: 16) are common in CDA, which is not surprising given its advocacy role. Key questions include: Who or what are the actors in the text? In what ways are they linguistically inscribed with agency and power? How does agency in the text link up with conventions and institutions of power in society? Critics often pay special attention to the use of pronouns, deixis, time and tense (p. 16), strategies of nomination and labeling, strategies of predication (see p. 27), modality, and number and type of agents in text (Fairclough 2005: 63) – especially the attribution of agency to nonhuman actors (such as "the economy"). I turn now to an example of how this perspective can be productively applied to a social problem – the rhetoric of cochlear implants – with the goal of exploring some of the ways in which agency is linguistically achieved, contested, and muted in written texts.

Case study: The debate over cochlear implants

The cochlear implant is a small electronic device that can help to provide a sense of sound to a person who is profoundly deaf or severely hard of hearing. Whereas hearing aids amplify sounds, the cochlear implant bypasses the tiny hair cells in the cochlea (which may be damaged, absent, or not present in great enough numbers) and stimulates the auditory nerve directly with rapid-fire electrical impulses (Chorost 2005: 81).

The cochlear implant has been hailed as a miracle. Cochlear Ltd., one of the largest implant producers, calls the implant on its website "a technological triumph. It's the only medical device designed to restore a human sense." Their motto – "Hear Now. And Always" – crystallizes a view that resonates in popular accounts: namely, that implants provide immediate access to a full range of sound for recipients of all ages. Indeed, outcomes have been promising, even cause for celebration, especially for post-lingually deafened adults who were accustomed to processing sounds before the onset of deafness. In the case of implanted children, younger recipients tend to do better: "The earlier the baby's brain wakes up and says, 'Hey, this is audio data, I'm going to be an audio brain,'" then the less habilitation that baby needs" ("The Death" 2000: 38; see also Gonsoulin 2001: 553). But the National Association of the Deaf (NAD) cautions against generalizing these outcomes to all pre-lingually deafened children. The parent of a deaf child puts it this way:

> Having the implant doesn't make you hearing. It makes you hearing if you do all the work, I guess. But it doesn't make you hearing – just boom. A lot of parents are misinformed and they don't work with their children. [The numbers of children in regional day school programs] has not diminished at all, even with the influx of cochlear implants.   ("The Death" 2000: 37)

The "just boom" view that is reflected, for example, in the "Hear Now" rhetoric of Cochlear Ltd. does not account for – and to some extent clashes with – a different view, one that aims to temper the excitement about implants with the reality that each patient's results will differ.

While the surgery is expensive (between $40,000 and $60,000), it is covered by some health insurance providers ("Cochlear implants FAQ"). The FDA has gradually relaxed the age requirement on the implant, which was originally approved for adults only. Now, American children as young as 12 months may qualify for surgery ("Cochlear implants" 2000). As of 2005, the FDA reports that "nearly 100,000 people worldwide have received implants. In the United States, nearly 22,000 adults and 15,000 children have received them" ("Cochlear Implants" 2000). The risk of complications from surgery are very low. The technology continues to improve as well. Since the speech processor is worn outside the body, its software can be updated ("re-mapped") easily.

But the cochlear implant is not just a technology. A full account of the implant must include how it reflects and shapes our cultural attitudes about deafness. Michael Chorost's (2005: 189) preference for a processor worn on the body, despite the better performance of the Behind the Ear (BTE) model, begins to suggest the shape of these attitudes:

> [The version that looks like a hearing aid] is a lot easier to put on, and it works just as well. Better, in fact, because it has a clever microphone design that uses the outer ear as a funnel to collect sound. But I usually choose to wear the box on my hip. The reason? *It doesn't look like a hearing aid.* Few people know *what* the heck it is, and I find that wonderfully liberating. It frees me from all the cultural baggage that hearing aids carry.

For Chorost, the performance of the technology is, surprisingly, only one criterion for choosing between the two options. Other issues seem to play a deciding role for him – even when he is confronted with a seemingly easy choice. Chorost implies that deafness is not just a physical condition that the deaf person alone experiences and negotiates (e.g., with implants, hearing aids, sign languages, interpreters, Deaf communities), but also a perspective imposed from without by a majority hearing culture that not only subjects hearing aid wearers to discrimination but has historically made decisions about what to do with deaf people (e.g., see Baynton 1996).

The dominant ideology of deafness in American culture defines deafness as a disability to be corrected or, at the very least, ameliorated. The medical community tends to subscribe to this view, which has also been called the "infirmity model" (Lane 1999:18) and the "pathological view" (Brueggemann 1999:13) by Deaf activists and Deaf studies scholars.[1] In an article written for head and neck surgeons, Thomas Gonsoulin (2001:553) describes the medical community's perspective: "a nonhearing person operates from a deficit position" that significantly and negatively affects her "neural development." As a result, implant specialists and audiologists are driven by a desire to find a remedy for a physical condition that prevents nonhearing persons from participating in the wider (hearing) culture, acquiring (spoken) language, and developing both intellectually and socially. Gonsoulin (2005:554) suggests that what motivates the medical profession is "beneficence":

> The very reason for being a physician is to help others. This is our calling and often the validation of who we are in society. Almost by definition, deaf persons, from the profoundly to the mildly deaf, have a disability. It is part of our nature, part of our mission in life, to attempt to ameliorate that disability. We feel called to push the edge of increasing success for a promising scientific otologic intervention.

Starting from a "deficit" or "disability" perspective, Gonsoulin (2001:554) suggests that it is difficult not to find "absurd" the argument that "deafness is not a disability."

According to Deaf studies scholars, the disability perspective makes a number of problematic assumptions because it starts from the perspective that only hearing people have access to a necessary precondition for humanness. When deafness

---

1. Brueggemann (1999:13) makes a distinction among three views of deafness: disability, pathology, and culture. The first two she distinguishes on the basis of the "institutions behind them: literacy education finds itself most intertwined with attitudes and assessments of disability, while science – particularly biomedicine and its technologies – paves a way to pathology." Most scholars, however, make one basic distinction between disability and culture (e.g., Lane 1999; Sparrow 2005; Gonsoulin 2001), and I follow their lead here, although I acknowledge the usefulness of Brueggemann's tripartite distinction.

is reduced to a physical deficit, its potential to catalyze a vibrant and unique culture is missed or, even worse, considered absurd. Rather than starting from a set of values that "are largely negative" (Lane 1999: 18), the cultural model typically starts with the claim that because Deaf people have their own language (e.g., American Sign Language), they are a linguistic minority, akin to any other linguistic minority and deserving of the same respect and protection.

The Deaf Culture or Deaf World perspective (now written with capital letters) starts from a different set of questions than the deafness-as-defect perspective. For example: "What are the interdependent values, mores, art forms, traditions, organizations, and language that characterize this culture? How is it influenced by the physical and social environment in which it is embedded?" (Lane 1999: 19). The Deaf Culture perspective, moreover, defines Deaf identity (or "Deafhood") in relation to each member's participation in the traditions of the Deaf community, the social ties that bind Deaf people, the educational experiences they share in schools for the Deaf, the stories they tell and pass on, the Deaf clubs that have historically played an important role in the lives of Deaf adults, and so on – in short, each member's enculturation and embeddedness within a Deaf community and Deaf worldview. Rather than starting from the perspective that deaf people are a problem for a "beneficent" society, the Deaf Culture perspective calls attention to the ways in which deaf bodies have been managed historically and continue to be controlled through educational philosophies (e.g., "oralism"), the popular media, and technologies such as cochlear implants (e.g., see Baynton 1996; Branson & Miller 2002; Brueggemann 1999; Lane 1999; Padden & Humphries 2005).

The cochlear implant debate brings questions of agency to the fore. Who has the right to speak for deaf people? Do cochlear implants release deaf people from the burden of being deaf by giving them the means to join the mainstream culture? How do social structure, deafness, and (lack of) agency interact? Do the "'disadvantages' faced by people who are deaf . . . have social and institutional causes" that require "changes in the way society is organized" (Sparrow 2005: 137)? In short, to what extent do deaf people have a right to self-determination when their values clash harshly with the values of the mainstream culture?

Agency in news articles about cochlear implants

How does the implant controversy play out in the news media? To what extent do deaf people have agency in news accounts? In what follows, I report on one finding from a study of cochlear implants in major newspapers around the world for the period 2002–2004. Articles were collected using the LexisNexis database (search term "cochlear," with results restricted to major papers around the world). Articles wholly concerned with the business of cochlear implants (e.g., a financial or stock report on Cochlear Ltd.) were eliminated from the corpus. All other articles were included, for a total of 136 news articles in the sample, spread out evenly over three years (46 in 2002, 44 in 2003, 46 in 2004). I followed Bazerman's (2004: 327) "rule of thumb" for defining a corpus: "diminishing returns plus a couple more. That is, the sample size should be large enough that adding additional samples will be unlikely to give you major new news or variations."

Overall, my analysis points to a lack of d/Deaf voices in the news, an over-reliance on implant advocates (doctors, audiologists, hearing parents of deaf children) to represent and speak for Deaf Culture, and a need for more balanced, more informed, and more culturally sensitive treatment of the ethics and implications of implant surgery. In what follows, I explore 1) the cochlear implant news genre from the perspective of technological agency, 2) the macro-level discourse practice of "sandwiching" as it pertains to Deaf Culture, 3) the reliance on implant advocates to speak for Deaf Culture and Deaf people, 4) the depiction of sign language as inferior and in conflict with common sense, and 5) the possibility for resistance within the confines of the cochlear implant news genre.

Technological agency and the miracle cure

In the mainstream news media, the most common way of writing about and explaining cochlear implants is through the trope of the miracle cure. Whether or not the implant is explicitly referred to as a miracle, it is often described as a catalyst for sudden and dramatic changes. These changes are the result of a single event in the implant cycle that is reported on religiously and obsessively: the switch-on event, which occurs about four to six weeks following surgery. By this time, the patient has had time to recover from surgery (the incision has healed) and the implant can now be activated. The switch-on event crystallizes in one single and joyous moment all of the hopes and dreams that have been leveraged on the implant. As such, the meaning of cochlear implant technology is determined in advance of surgery, activation, and speech therapy sessions. As the catalyst for seemingly miraculous changes, the technology is ascribed a high degree of agency: implant recipient, families, and even audiologists submit to its power in the sometimes hushed and always awe-inspiring activation rooms. The technology bends people and institutions to its will. Even something as ambiguous as a toddler's cry in the moments following his implant's activation – e.g., Is he crying because the electrical stimulation is painful? What does activation mean in terms of success if he is still too young to tell us what he hears? – is interpreted as a sign of another successful cure.

Indeed, success stories drive the discourse, even when articles report on future implant recipients and future switch-on events. For example, a patient scheduled to have her implant switched-on tomorrow may already be guaranteed of success today (according to the news story), even though she is deaf today and will usually need to make a "long-term, and likely, life-long commitment to auditory train-ing, rehabilitation, acquisition of spoken and visual language skills, follow-up, and possibly additional surgeries" (NAD position statement 2000). In the news, the switch-on event is both the climax and the end of the story, not the beginning of a long and often arduous process. The news articles very rarely acknowledge the in-tensive therapy that awaits an implant recipient or the impact the surgery will have on her family. Finally, because the switch-on event is offered as the triumphant end of the story, the implant is characterized as a transporter device that mediates two and only two "worlds" – deaf and hearing. World-thinking is prevalent in news articles about implants, because the assumption is that every person is either deaf or hearing. The rich tapestry of deaf and hard-of-hearing individuals is obscured and reduced to a simple and misleading opposition: you either hear or you do not.

There is hardly room in this discourse for people who are neither deaf nor hearing. A deaf/hearing binary informs news articles about cochlear implants. Be-cause the implant is characterized as a miracle cure, each implant user can logically inhabit only one or two possible subject positions: hearing or deaf. No wonder, then, that the switch-on event ushers implant recipients into a "new world" of hearing. The hearing world is linked to life ("hearing life around her" ["Hers is resounding joy"]); the deaf world is a death sentence ("doomed to be deaf forever" ["Deaf to oppression"]).

Sandwiching: Muting Deaf voices at the macro level

Deaf people, particularly those who identify with Deaf Culture, are rarely given the opportunity to voice their views in news articles about cochlear implants. In-stead, the articles in the corpus reduce Deaf Culture to a simple, and at times irrational, opposition to implants. While a small number of articles in my sam-ple discuss Deaf Culture at length and on its own terms, most pay only lip service. A common macro-level technique, one employed across the majority of articles, is "sandwiching," in which Deaf Culture is tightly sandwiched between large slices of pro-implant discourse. Sandwiching creates the appearance of balance and fair-mindedness, but often reduces Deaf Culture to an aside. According to Jim Kuypers (2002:210):

> The practice [of sandwiching] refers to the placement of something between two other things of very different character. The press maintains that it is fair since it reports "both sides" of an issue. Although it is true that the "other side" is often presented . . . the manner in which it is presented can detract from its potential impact. Generally speaking, the press places whatever side of the issue it does not support in between complimentary points of view, which invariably agree with the position espoused by the press.

In the case of cochlear implant discourse, sandwiching provides a way for the press to satisfy the ethical obligation to be fair while at the same time subtly identifying with the preferred view. The other view (in italics below) is almost an afterthought thrown in to give the appearance of balance:

(1) Besides the 22,000 Americans who have them, several hundred thousand more are considered good candidates for from [sic] the implants. *But there is great debate among* **deaf people** *about the implants, with* **some questioning** *their effectiveness and arguing that the use of sign language is preferable because it produces a sense of community.*

Two American doctors – Dr. Thomas J. Balkany, a surgeon and chairman of otolaryngology at the University of Miama, and Dr. Noel Cohen of New York University Medical Center – recently completed a survey of surgeons ("Drug agency is studying").

(2) **Wheeler** (head of Right to Hear, an advocacy group for oral training) argues that investing $50,000 to fit each child with an implant would pay for itself ten times over through savings from avoiding special schooling and other support services for deaf and hard-of-hearing children.

This is a sensitive issue. **Few** *dare raise it because* **many deaf people are hostile** *to implants. There has to be a way to respect* **their choices** *while offering alternatives to parents and children who seek other options. I hope Heather* [i.e. **Heather Whitestone McCallum**, a former Miss America who is "hearing sound again" after being implanted] *continues to use her personal experience and celebrity to try to persuade lawmakers to give cochlear implants a fair hearing* ("An ideal voice").

(3) [Article opens with an implant success story: *four-year-old Kennedy and her mother*. Then touches briefly on the Deaf community:] *Different opinions on the treatment exist within the deaf community,* **Sharon Emery** *wrote in an Oct. 15 article in* Deaf Today. **Some** *see deafness as a positive aspect of their lives that provides them with a distinct culture and identity based on relating to the world visually. That culture includes its own traditions and language – American Sign Language.*

Some individuals see implants as a denial of that identity, while **others** "would pursue everything possible to hear and participate in the speaking culture," Emery wrote.

[Article then returns to the main subject: **Kennedy, her mother Dawn Allen,** and the preferred pro-implant view.] **Allen** believes that parents and patients should research cochlear implants and make their own decisions ("Toddler joins 'hearing' world").

Without including the full text of news articles here, it is difficult to convey the large degree to which Deaf Culture is reduced to an aside and the extent to which the surrounding large slices of pro-implant discourse are so thoroughly determined and enthusiastic. In example (1), the "great debate among deaf people" is not connected to the larger discussion of potential risks for meningitis in people with implants. The article thus misses an opportunity to link concerns in the Deaf community to the subject of the article. The result is that the "great debate" seems detached from the real concerns of the experts. In all three examples, the larger pro-implant discussion that frames the opposing view gains credibility from being grounded in the opinions of specific people (not "some people") who are socially authorized to speak about hearing (two named doctors, Wheeler [the head of Right to Hear], the editorial author ["I"], Heather Whitestone McCallum, Dawn Allen and her daughter Kennedy). While example (2), an editorial, shows sensitivity to the values of "many deaf people" (notwithstanding the vagueness of such a term), it also characterizes the other side as "hostile." Their presumed hostility is contrasted with a glowing account of the "sheer joy of hearing" that Heather Whitestone McCallum and others have experienced. Example (0) is taken from a typical article about implants – i.e., a miracle story – one that, apparently, is based on information gathered primarily through two personal interviews: one with the mother of the implant recipient and another with the director of an oralist school in Houston that stresses speech therapy and strongly discourages the use of sign language. The article quotes the director of the school at length, identifies with and valorizes her perspective throughout, and ends with the center's contact information. Information about the Deaf community is gathered, it appears, from an article in *Deaf Today*.[2]

---

2. Baynton's (1996, 2006) history of sign language, and in particular the nineteenth-century debate between manualism and oralism, offers a framework for understanding the dramatic shift at the end of the nineteenth century from a philosophy for deaf education dominated by sign language to one dominated by speech and "quite hostile to sign language" (2006, p. 39). The triumph of oralism was the result of associating deaf people who sign with a growing fear of foreigners and immigrants. This fear thrives today in so-called "English only" initiatives. In the nineteenth century, oralism provided the means to integrate deaf people into a national community by teaching them to speak English (2006, p. 39). Even though the debate between oralism and manualism "still exists" today (1996, p. 168), oralism is "widely rejected" (1996, p. 6). I would argue, however, that despite the public school system's focus on multiple methods for teaching deaf children, oralism continues to hold sway as the dominant method for teaching implanted children. In news articles, for example, implant advocates (audiologists, surgeons, reps from speech schools for the deaf, and hearing parents), regularly dismiss sign language. If children with implants are going to learn to speak, the pro-implant argument goes, they must not be permitted to use sign language as a crutch. In this way, the argument against sign language thrives today in pro-implant discourse, despite the inroads sign language has made, for

The CDA critic might thus note the contrast between the real people who support and represent implants and the way in which the opposition – with the possible exception of Sharon Emery – is ill-defined, unreal, and objectified ("deaf people," "some questioning," "many deaf people," "their choices," etc.). At the same time, both sides are comparable grammatically; the opponents are as likely to occupy the subject position as the proponents, which gives, like sandwiching, the appearance of balance. This appearance is belied, on close reading, both by the lexical differences between the names given for each side and by the macro-level strategy of sandwiching.

Speaking for the Deaf community

As example (3) shows, information about the Deaf community may be filtered through written texts, as opposed to gathered directly from interviews with Deaf people or people who sign. There is nothing inherently problematic with this approach, of course, and in fact an article in *Deaf Today* may provide more comprehensive and more credible information than an interview with a single member of the Deaf community. Still, example (3) raises questions about who gets to speak for the Deaf community and why the criteria of fair-mindedness and balance do not extend to a journalist's sources. Why is the interview with the director of the oralist school in Houston not balanced with an interview with the director of a residential school for the Deaf?

Unlike example (3), information about the Deaf community is sometimes not attributed to anyone in particular but instead results from vague generalizations or stereotypes. The Deaf community perspective is thus reduced to a straw opponent. As the following examples suggest, the opposing perspective is also tightly sandwiched between direct quotes from implant advocates:

(4)   [Quote from Gerald **O'Donoghue**, Professor of Otology:] "It is critical to catch them [infants who qualify for an implant] early. They must be identified within the first three years because this is when the brain is most responsive. If this window of opportunity is missed, their **language skills** will be severely impaired. There is a lot of evidence from the States to support early intervention."

*However, **not everyone** approves of such intervention. In the UK, apart from the 50,000 registered deaf, there are a further 145,000 registered as hard of hearing. A **small section of the deaf community views their disability** as a cultural issue. They interpret attempts to treat it as cultural intolerance or medical arrogance.*

example, among hearing parents of pre-lingual hearing infants (Beyer 2006; Acredolo, Goodwyn & Abrams 2002).

O'Donoghue rejects this concern, saying that 90 percent of deaf children are born to hearing parents. "These parents don't see deafness as a positive thing – they are desperate to communicate with their child. Their joy when the implant is switched on is fantastic to watch" ("A sound case for experts").

(5)   **Wasser** [the father of the 10-year-old implant recipient named Luke] believes that the implant will make his son's life easier, especially as he gets older and "conversation gets more complicated ... the social interactions are broader. He'll hear better – that's the sole reason for doing it."

What about teaching **Luke** *sign language and reading lips – was that ever an alternative to the cochlear implant, which carries some controversy in* **the deaf community**? It's an issue that draws an emotional response from **Quest** [Luke's mother], who has to stop for a moment, because the tears come to her eyes as she considers it. She explains that **Luke** was not taught sign language or to read lips (although he has naturally picked up lip-reading skills over the years) because "we're a hearing family...we chose speech and hearing because we're a speaking and hearing family" ("He'll hear better").

(6)   **Doctors** say that deaf children with implants or hearing aids should attempt only one language, and since Singapore's national schools use English, that's what they must learn.

The most passionate detractors of cochlear implants, ironically, tend to be in **the deaf community.**

Dennis Tan's mother was stricken with measles while she was pregnant with him and he was born deaf. **Tan** *does not use a hearing aid and* **has trouble speaking clearly.**

He says the Singapore Government should spend more money on sign-language classes and closed captioning for television, which he says would improve the quality of life of all of Singapore's deaf people, not just a few.

But **Koh Ang Hong** is grateful for her daughter **Naomi's** bionic ear, saying Naomi can expect to live a "normal life" [End of story] ("Ear that cuts").

In examples (4) and (5), the objections from the Deaf community are raised in the form of generalizations that cannot be attributed to anyone, and certainly not to anyone with authority to speak for the Deaf community. The objections are framed by and sandwiched between the direct responses of implant advocates: a professor who specializes in implants and the parents of an implanted boy. In example (4), the source for the opposing view might as well be the source for the dominant view (i.e., Professor O'Donoghue), because the opposing view in the article starts from an assumption that many in the Deaf community reject – that deafness is a disability (Sparrow 2005: 136). Similarly, in example (5) the views of

Luke's parents (heavy with pathos as Luke's mother holds back tears) almost literally drown out the Deaf community. Example (6) breaks ranks by including an indirect quote from one of those "passionate detractors" in the Deaf community. But the detractor (Dennis Tan) only seems to bolster the implant proponent's argument that people who refuse implants will have "trouble speaking" (and thus fitting in). Furthermore, Tan's concerns do not directly address the issue at hand, opposition to implants. The last word is a mother's response, which invokes the "normal life" that Tan, by implication, will never have.

In addition to sandwiching and, especially in the case of example (4) representing the opposing view as relatively unpopular ("not everyone," "a small section"), the representatives for the pro-implant view are represented linguistically as controlling the systems of value in which deaf people, particularly children, circulate. In example (4), deaf infants are grammatically positioned as objects of the otologist's actions ("catch them"); when they are grammatical subjects in the next sentence ("They must be identified"), they are semantic patients in a passive construction. This both reflects and helps to naturalize their lack of agency in the face of the dominant ideology. That they are too young to speak is only one part of the larger story about controlling deaf bodies and voices: O'Donoghue speaks for that "small section of the deaf community"; Wasser speaks for 10-year-old Luke in example (5) ("Wasser believes the implant will make his son's life easier"); the journalist positions Luke as object ("What about teaching Luke…?"); the doctors speak for deaf children in example (6) ("Doctors say deaf children"); and Koh Ang Hong speaks for her daughter Naomi ("is grateful for her daughter Naomi's bionic ear"). In these examples, deaf people – infants, children, and adults – are silent and passive (with the exception of Tan, who is represented as having "trouble speaking clearly." Ideological passivity shapes and is shaped by grammatical passivity.

Representing sign language and reaffirming "common sense"

The opposing view (that of the Deaf community) is at times no more than a vague generalization, because it is represented as lacking the commonsensical authority of the dominant view. In my sample, it is repeatedly assumed that speech (and only speech) is the source of language, communication, and thought. Only speech (never sign language) is linked to language development, which is linked to intellectual development. Before we ever get to read about Tan's view in example (6), we confront his inability to speak clearly and, perhaps, draw a negative conclusion about his ability to think clearly. Despite playing a prominent role as an official foreign language on college campuses, and despite being recognized by linguists as a real language, sign language is often ignored or denigrated in the articles in the corpus:

(7)   **Hearing is vital for language acquisition**, so if a decision is not made early enough, a child's ability to speak could be impaired, noted Hagan [a science writer] ("From the science magazines").

(8)   Restoring deaf children's **ability to hear** as early as possible is crucial for their **intellectual development**. Children who would have encountered developmental problems because of their **inability to communicate** now have the chance to develop alongside those with perfect hearing, and can attend mainstream schools ("A sound case for experts").

(9)   After that crucial period ["within the first 24 months of life"], **language comprehension and speech** begin irreversible degeneration, says John Wheeler, head of Right to Hear advocacy group ("An ideal voice").

(10) "Children can **learn sign language at any age**, but they have a very narrow window of opportunity for learning to listen." [Quote is from director of oralist school in Brisbane, Australia] ("Deaf get a fair hearing").

(11) "Cochlear ear implants are helping deaf children to lead more normal lives," he [politician Dean Brown] said.

Mr. Brown said the students would be **restricted to learning by sign language** in the public education system [if funding for the oralist center dries up, as it nearly did] ("Cora Barclay funds rescue").

In these examples, hearing is linked to language development, intellectual development, and communication (examples (7), (8), and (9)). Sign language is considered neither a real language nor a form of communication. In fact, sign language is treated as something to be accepted grudgingly – e.g., a restriction placed on intellectual development (example (11)) – or deferred indefinitely – e.g., something to be acquired "at any age," but preferably after the more pressing issue of "curing" deafness is addressed (example (10)).

The distinction between sign language and hearing/speaking is also shaped in these examples by the ticking clock: the need for parents to make a quick decision to implant before it is too late ("if a decision is not taken early enough," "as early as possible," "after that crucial period," "they have a very narrow window"). Speech and "intellectual development" are positioned against the "inability to communicate" and the total absence of language.

Thinking of deafness as anything other than a physical defect to be fixed at any cost is represented as flying in the face of common sense. What parent wouldn't want their child to hear? Who wouldn't want to live in the "real world"? In the news articles, the answers to these questions go without saying. But more importantly, the questions assume a hearing readership that cannot associate being deaf with being happy, successful, well-adjusted, popular, and so on.

(12)   Why would a deaf person not want to hear? ("The Sounds of Silence").

(13)   "And if there is the least chance of your child being able to hear, what do you do?" ("Breaking the Sound Barrier").

(14)   We never hear arguments … [against] restoring eyesight or repairing spinal-cord damage, so **why the negative attitude towards helping** those who can't hear? ("Cochlear Marvel").

(15)   "I have always felt I was part of the hearing world," she [former Miss America Heather Whitestone McCallum] says. "It's not just the hearing world, it's the **real world**" ("Hearing Repaired").

(16)   "I don't think sign language is wrong," says Alvarez [the mother of a young implant recipient]. "It has its place. [But] the majority of deaf kids are born to hearing parents. **I have to believe these parents want their kids to be hearing, and we have the technology**" ("Deaf Center Helps Children").

(17)   "We really didn't understand their [the Deaf community's] reaction. **We thought we were trying to provide the best future for her [our daughter]**" ("Tackling Sounds of Silence").

(18)   But I cannot say I am glad he is deaf. A hearing life, in a hearing world, is so much easier, and what parent wants to see a child **struggle**? ("Deaf to Reason").

(19)   Trisha Kemp, of the Cochlear Implanted Children's Support Group (CICS), says that while she sympathizes with deaf parents unwilling for their children to have cochlear implants, **the fact of the matter is that it's a hearing world**" ("Breaking the Sound Barrier").

It is hard to take issue with appeals to common sense (the "fact of the matter" in example (19)). These appeals are epistemologically rooted in "nature" and "reality" – in a seemingly obvious and universal understanding of how the world is. They are also rooted in the "ethical principle of beneficence" (Gonsoulin 2001:554), as examples (14), (17) and (18) suggest. But beneficence – the seemingly innocent act of wanting to help those who are perceived to need it – may mask the paternalistic desire to control the other (Lane 1999).

To summarize, the mainstream, "audist" view of deafness as a disease to be cured is represented and perpetuated through the use of the interrogative form to promote a point of view that goes without saying, the construction of false dichotomies that leave little to no room for anything but implantation, the incredulous tone from parents and others who can not fathom deafness as anything but a death sentence, the framing and narrowing of meaning around key terms (e.g., "language," "communication," "intellectual development") so that they become identified with speaking but not signing, and the discursive context of developmental pressures which further naturalize the pro-implant argument.

Representing the Deaf community as the oppressor

Deaf Culture is portrayed in the news as radically "other, " often synonymous with a radical, irrational agenda. For example, in "Deaf to Reason," a long editorial written by Fiona Leney, a mother who chose to implant her son, Deaf Culture is held up for ridicule. The "world of Deaf Rights" is described as a "topsy-turvy" one in which "smug" activists hold the ridiculous belief that implanting a child is "the equivalent of rape." The Deaf community is described as a "small minority" and a "bullying minority" of radicals – "hijackers" who impose their beliefs on well-meaning, rational parents like Leney who only want to "help our son to hear significantly better." The "Deaf community ideologues," when faced with such a seemingly innocuous proposition, are "horrified that I could put my child through such torture." In sum, the writer of this editorial reduces Deaf Culture to an absurd refusal to listen to common sense: "they have no right to tell us that it is best for our son not to hear." But because she views deafness as an "impair[ment]" only, she finds no common ground with them. In terms of agency, then, rational common sense confronts the irrational actions of misinformed and dangerous ideologues.

In another editorial, "Deaf to Oppression," author Andrew Bolt asks incredulously, "How mad can multiculturalism get?" His answer: "Mad enough, it turns out, to insist that more than a dozen Australian children stay deaf." His writing drips with sarcasm and disdain for what he calls the Deaf Culture argument:

(20)   All this fashionable identity politics means, of course, that to give deaf children hearing would be to steal them from their culture, just as those who rescued Aboriginal children from gross neglect and abuse are now accused of "stealing" a "generation" and committing "cultural genocide" ("Deaf to Oppression").

Bolt finds it "absurd" that the Deaf Culture position is given any credence at all. He dismisses the "shoddy arguments" put forth "by the cleverest of academics" (Bolt cites Lane 1999, and Branson & Miller 2002 as examples) who argue that disabilities are socially constructed. As far as Bolt is concerned, the meaning of "disabled" is clear and stable: it "means simply that someone can't hear." For Bolt, it is tragic that intellectuals and Deaf radicals argue about the value of being Deaf while "six-year-olds who just want to hear are being sentenced to deafness." The real culprit, then, is not the history of discrimination against people who are deaf (Branson & Miller 2002), or the attempt by social institutions to control deaf bodies and minds (Lane 1999). It is Deaf Culture itself. Its radical "ideology" is responsible for making children "suffer."

Bolt's discursive sleight of hand inverts the traditional relationship between oppressor and oppressed. In Bolt's reformulation, Deaf radicals have become the oppressors. The history of discrimination against deaf people is erased. In its place are put well-meaning, benevolent people like Bolt who only want to help deaf children, yet find their way repeatedly blocked by irrational bullies. At times, Deaf radicals evoke fear:

(21) It finally came to **D-Day** for the decision. Were we going to go ahead with a Cochlear or just going to take her to lip reading or sign language. There was an **absolute barrage** we copped when we made the decision for the Cochlear. **We were called vampires** ... in some of the letters," he [the father] says, shaking his head ("Tackling Sounds of Silence").

(22) While cochlear implants have been growing in popularity, particularly for children under three who are in their primary speech-learning stage, deaf activists have compared the procedure to **Nazi medical experiments. Tensions have run so high that some parents have allowed their children to be interviewed for positive stories on cochlear implants only on the condition of anonymity** ("Deaf like Me?").

(23) From Congress to newborn wards, parents and policymakers face Deaf activists who extol the virtues of living Deaf. Meanwhile, implant surgeons are labeled "profiteers" and anti-Deaf "bigots," and accused of **genocide. Some are so besieged they dare not even offer patients the option of an implant.** Meanwhile, we swallow the myth that keeping a baby deaf is morally and medically equivalent to letting the baby hear ("Bringing Sound to Life").

In these examples, well-meaning, hearing parents of deaf children run for cover from crazed deaf activists who are characterized as terrorists in a war zone ("D-Day," "absolute barrage," "Nazi medical experiments," tensions running high, "so besieged," "genocide"). The tables are turned as oppressor and oppressed swap places.

Resisting from the margins

Letters to the editor do provide an outlet for responses to perceived inaccuracies about implants and Deaf Culture, although such letters to the editor are extremely rare. The letters published in response to Bolt's piece about multiculturalism gone mad (example (20)) include one from the president of the Australian Association of the Deaf (AAD), another from the president of the Victorian Council of Deaf People, and a third from a deaf-and-blind writer. The letters make the following points:

- Bolt "seems to have a simplistic faith that hearing can be fixed easily. However, a cochlear implant is not a cure for deafness."
- Bolt has not taken into account the "considerable support" that children require after being implanted.

- Bolt needs some lessons in Deaf culture, which the AAD will be happy to provide.
- Bolt "has failed to get the facts from deaf people themselves."
- Implants "are not a quick-fix operation."
- "No one, not even a loving parent, should be allowed to make this decision for their child."
- Not all deaf people want to be cured ("Implants for Deaf Misunderstood").

The letters offer a potentially persuasive response, especially in their often over-looked caveat that the implant is not a "quick-fix" or a "cure." Yet these, the views of leaders in the Deaf community, are cut off from the main discussion in both time and space, relegated to the back pages (or to unique URLs) of a small number of newspapers as short rebuttals to a long editorial.

There are two other cases in my sample of letter writers taking issue with mis-informed views about Deaf Culture. In one case ("Implants No Cure"), two deaf authors who have written a children's book about cochlear implants take issue with an article by John Wheeler, the chairman of Right to Hear (an implant advocacy group), for making a series of questionable claims: that implants are a cure for deafness, that implanted babies will hear normally, and that the Deaf community is adamantly opposed to implants. The second author calls Wheeler's arguments "out of date," and wonders whether Wheeler is familiar with the NAD's more bal-anced position on cochlear implants. (The NAD position statement, which was revised in 2000, recognizes the rights of parents to make informed decisions for their children, even if parents ultimately choose an implant for their child.) In the other case, two writers respond to Fiona Leney's article, "Deaf to Reason" (see above). One letter ("Beat the Bullies"), written by Jessica Rees, praises Leney for "standing up to the bullies who impose their inflexible deaf agenda," and encour-ages Leney to "teach her son to shrug off these deaf propagandists and enjoy the freedom of speech the real world affords." The second letter ("A Word to the Hear-ing"), published a week after the first, takes issue with Rees' suggestion that deaf people don't live in the "real world." According to the second writer,

(24)   I can understand that, as a cochlear implant user with 20 years' experience, Ms. Rees has strong views, but to imply that the world in which implantless deaf people live is somehow unreal is to show why the activists have ended up in the position they now adopt. British Sign is a real language, Deaf culture is a real culture, and there is nothing inferior, or unreal, about either the deaf or hearing worlds ("A Word to the Hearing").

In sum, leaders and others in the Deaf community are virtually absent from the main discussion and relegated to playing a minor, virtually inaudible defense in the back pages of newspapers, while implant supporters (hearing parents, speech and listening therapists, and implant specialists) not only dominate the discussion but speak for d/Deaf people and respond to journalists' overly simplified views of the Deaf community.

Conclusion

This sample analysis of a social problem suggests how "power is signaled not only by grammatical forms within a text, but also by a person's control of a social occasion by means of the genre of a text" (Wodak 2001: 11). Because the Deaf community has seemingly little control over the social occasion of writing a mainstream news article about implants (compared to the implant specialists, oralist school representatives, and audiologists), they are locked out of the debate. Rather than speaking for themselves, they are spoken for by those whose values are compatible with the values of the mainstream culture (and hence with the mass media).

This sample analysis also suggests how, in the context of news discourse, the Deaf community is not merely weaker politically. They lack rhetorical agency. Because they are not typically consulted during the interviewing and research phases of news story production, they are left with the unenviable position of playing defense after the fact in the editorial sections of the same newspapers that promote the views of implant advocates. Rhetorical agency is conventional. To take efficacious action, one must negotiate the conventional constraints of genre and form (see Geisler 2004: 14). In news discourse about implants, generic conventions seem to keep Deaf people (and those who represent Deaf Culture) from the table. They are rarely consulted, perhaps because they are inaudible to hearing journalists with mainstream values. Moreover, they lack the authority of the medical establishment. When culturally Deaf people are consulted, their views may simply be left on the cutting room floor (e.g., see "Myths and Facts"). Nan Johnson (2003) suggests that rhetorical critics need to "document the extent to which rhetorical agency has been denied along racial and class lines in the United States." To race and class we might add deafness, insofar as Deaf people "are not perceived to speak for conventional values and aims." Indeed, they may not "speak" at all. While this sample analysis shows again how rhetorical agency is a "requisite performance of conventionality," it also sets out to disrupt the conventions that maintain the status quo of mainstream values.

The seeds of an alternative discourse about implants are being scattered, albeit rarely and almost invisibly, in the pages of the same news media that reinforce conventional values. This alternative discourse is skeptical of quick fixes, presents Deaf Culture on its own terms as a linguistic minority, provides a more balanced account of the debate over implants, and includes voices from leaders in the Deaf community. Ideally, this imagined discourse about implants would adhere to what the NAD calls a "wellness model":

> The general public needs information about the lives of the vast majority of deaf and hard of hearing individuals who have achieved optimal adjustments in all phases of life, have well-integrated and healthy personalities, and have attained self-actualizing levels of functioning, all with or without the benefits of hearing aids, cochlear implants, and other assistive devices.
>
> (NAD position statement 2000)

An alternative news discourse about cochlear implants – one based on a wellness model – would start from the perspective that the current discourse has been dominated by a narrative of inevitable triumph over tragedy and a simplistic faith in the implant as a miracle, a quick fix. It would be committed to making room in the discourse for other stories, so that the range of views in the news media more accurately reflects the range of views in the general population – not just the views of hearing people. A more balanced and ethical discourse about cochlear implants would allow the Deaf community a voice, to offset the common sense view (i.e., hearing at any cost, deafness as defect only) with the views of those whose voices are too often muted or absent.

Finally, what can we learn about rhetorical agency by applying a CDA lens? First, CDA provides a set of tools for "opening up" the "essential mechanisms" of rhetorical agency (Geisler 2004: 14). CDA explores how agency is mediated at a linguistic level. Second, CDA offers an orientation for doing critical research in rhetorical studies. In the case of rhetorical agency, a critical approach complements CDA by asking how rhetorical agency intersects with (and is sometimes denied along the lines of) race, class, gender, access, ability, and so on (see Johnson 2003). And third, CDA is built on a significant body of linguistic and social theory, which no doubt has implications for our current understanding of rhetorical agency, and especially for the relationship between rhetoric and action.

References

Acredolo, L., Goodwyn, S., and Abrams, D. 2002. *Baby Signs: How to Talk with Your Baby Before Your Baby Can Talk*. New York: McGraw-Hill.

Bauman, H-Dirksen L. 2004. "Audism: Exploring the Metaphysics of Oppression". *Journal of Deaf Studies and Deaf Education* 9 (2): 239–246.

Baynton, D. 2006. "'A Silent Exile on this Earth': The Metaphorical Construction of Deafness in the Nineteenth Century". In *The Disability Studies Reader*, L. J. Davis (ed.), 33–48. 2nd Ed. New York, NY: Routledge.

Baynton, Douglas. 1996. *Forbidden Signs: American Culture and the Campaign Against Sign Language*. Chicago and London: The University of Chicago Press.

Bazerman, Charles (2004) "Speech Acts, Genres, and Activity Systems: How Texts Organize Activity and People". In *What Writing Does and How It Does It: An Introduction to Analyzing Texts and Textual Practices*, C. Bazerman and P. Prior (eds), 309–339. Mahweh, NJ: Lawrence Erlbaum.

Bitzer, Lloyd. 1968. "The Rhetorical Situation". *Philosophy & Rhetoric* 1: 1–14.

Blommaert, Jan and Chris Bulcaen. 2000. "Critical Discourse Analysis". *Annual Review of Anthropology* 29: 447–466.

Branson, Jan and Don Miller. 2002. *Damned for Their Difference: The Cultural Construction of Deaf People as Disabled*. Washington, D.C.: Gallaudet University Press.

Brueggemann, Brenda Jo. 1999. *Lend Me Your Ear: Rhetorical Constructions of Deafness*. Washington, D.C.: Gallaudet University Press.

Campbell, John Angus. 1997. "Strategic Reading: Rhetoric, Intention, and Interpretation". In *Rhetorical Hermeneutics: Invention and Interpretation in the Age of Science*, A. Gross and W. Keith (eds), 113–137. Albany, NY: SUNY Press.

Chorost, Michael. 2005. *Rebuilt: How Becoming Part Computer Made Me More Human*. Boston, MA: Houghton Mifflin.

Chouliaraki, L. and Norman Fairclough. 1999. *Discourse in Late Modernity: Rethinking Critical Discourse Analysis*. Edinburgh, UK: Edinburgh University Press.

"Cochlear implants". 2000. Official website of National Institute on Deafness and Other Communication Disorders (NIDCD). NIH Publication No. 00-4798. Retrieved 18 May 2005. http://www.nidcd.nih.gov/health/hearing/coch.asp.

"Cochlear Implants FAQ". Official website of The National Association of the Deaf (NAD). Retrieved 25 November 2005. http://www.nad.org/site/pp.asp?c=foINKQMBF&b=399061.

Cochlear, Ltd. Official website. Retrieved 15 September 2006. http://www.cochlear.com/.

Condit, Celeste Michelle. 2003. "Why Rhetorical Training Can Expand Agency". *The Alliance of Rhetoric Societies Conference on the Status and Future of Rhetorical Studies*. Northwestern University. Sept. 11–14. Retrieved 17 Sept. 2006. http://www.comm.umn.edu/ARS/Agency/Condit,%20agency.htm.

Fairclough, Norman. 2001. "Critical Discourse Analysis as a Method in Social Scientific Research". In *Methods of Critical Discourse Analysis*, R. Wodak and M. Meyer (eds), 121–138. London, UK: Sage.

_____. 2005. "Critical Discourse Analysis in Transdisciplinary Research". In *A New Agenda in (Critical) Discourse Analysis*, R. Wodak and P. Chilton (eds), 53–70. Amsterdam and Philadelphia: John Benjamins.

Farrell, Kathleen and Marilyn Young. 2005. "The Situational Perspective." In *The Art of Rhetorical Criticism*, Jim Kuypers (ed.), 33–55. Boston, MA: Pearson.

"FDA Public Health Notification: Continued Risk of Bacterial Meningitis in Children with Cochlear Implants with a Positioner Beyond Twenty-four Months Post-implantation". 2006. Official website of U.S. Food and Drug Administration. Retrieved 16 September 2006. http://www.fda.gov/cdrh/safety/020606-cochlear.html.

Gaonkar, Dilip. 1990. "Object and Method in Rhetorical Criticism: From Wichelns to Leff and McGee". *Western Journal of Speech Communication* 54: 290–316.

_____. 1997. "The Idea of Rhetoric in the Rhetoric of Science". In *Rhetorical Hermeneutics: Invention and Interpretation in the Age of Science*, A. Gross and W. Keith (eds), 25–85. Albany, NY: SUNY Press.

Geisler, Cherly. 2004. "How Ought We to Understand the Concept of Rhetorical Agency? A Report from ARS". *Rhetoric Society Quarterly* 34 (3): 9–17.

Gonsoulin, Thomas P. 2001. "Cochlear Implant/Deaf World Dispute: Different Bottom Elephants". *Otolaryngology – Head and Neck Surgery* 125 (5): 552–556.

Gross, Alan and William Keith, eds. 1997. *Rhetorical Hermeneutics: Invention and Interpretation in the Age of Science*. Albany, NY: SUNY Press.

Jäger, Siegfried. 2001. "Discourse and Knowledge: Theoretical and Methodological Aspects of a Critical Discourse and Dispositive Analysis". In *Methods of Critical Discourse Analysis*, R. Wodak and M. Meyer (eds), 32–62. London, UK: Sage.

Johnson, Nan. 2003. Working Group Paper on "Rhetorical Agency". *The Alliance of Rhetoric Societies Conference on the Status and Future of Rhetorical Studies*. Northwestern University. Sept. 11–14. Retrieved 17 Sept. 2006. http://www.comm.umn.edu/ARS/Agency/Nan%20Johnson,%20agency.htm.

Kinsella, William. 2005. "Rhetoric, Action, and Agency in Institutionalized Science and Technology". *Technical Communication Quarterly*. 14 (3): 303–310.

Koerber, Amy. 2006. "Rhetorical Agency, Resistance, and the Disciplinary Rhetorics of Breastfeeding". *Technical Communication Quarterly* 15 (1): 87–101.

Kryzanowski, Michał. 2005. "'European Identity Wanted!' On Discursive and Communicative Dimensions of the European Convention". In *A New Agenda in (Critical) Discourse Analysis*, R. Wodak and P. Chilton (eds), 137–163. Amsterdam and Philadelphia: John Benjamins.

Kuypers, Jim A. 2002. *Press Bias and Politics: How the Media Frame Controversial Issues*. Westport, CT: Praeger.

Lane, Harlan. 1999. *The Mask of Benevolence: Disabling the Deaf Community*. 2nd ed. San Diego, CA: DawnSignPress.

Lundberg, Christian and Joshua Gunn. 2005. "'Ouija Board, are there any Communications?' Agency, Ontotheology, and the Death of the Humanist Subject, or, Continuing the ARS Conversation". *Rhetoric Society Quarterly* 35 (4): 83–105.

Meyer, Michael. 2001. "Between Theory, Method, and Politics: Positioning of the Approaches to CDA". In *Methods of Critical Discourse Analysis*, R. Wodak and M. Meyer (eds), 14–31. London, UK: Sage.

"Myths and facts". Cochlear War website. Retrieved 20 September 2006. http://cochlearwar.com/myths_and_facts.html#mf02.

NAD Position Statement on Cochlear Implants. 2000. Official website of The National Association of the Deaf (NAD). Retrieved 25 November 2005. http://www.nad.org/site/pp.asp?c=foINKQMBF&b=138140.

Oberhuber, Florian. 2005. "Deliberation or 'Mainstreaming'? Empirically Researching the European Convention". In *A New Agenda in (Critical) Discourse Analysis*, R. Wodak and P. Chilton (eds), 165–187. Amsterdam and Philadelphia: John Benjamins.

Padden, Carol and Tom Humphries. 2005. *Inside Deaf Culture*. Cambridge, MA: Harvard University Press.

Smith, Cheri, Ella Mae Lentz and Ken Mikos. 1993. *Signing Naturally: Student Workbook Level 1*. San Diego, CA: Dawn Sign Press.

Sparrow, Robert. 2005. "Defending Deaf Culture: The Case for Cochlear Implants". *The Journal of Political Philosophy* 13 (2): 135–152.

"The Death of Deafness". 2000, Mar/Apr. Part 1. *Hearing Health* 25–39.

Turnbull. Nick. 2004. "Rhetorical Agency as a Property of Questioning". *Philosophy & Rhetoric* 37 (3): 207–222.

Van Dijk, Teun. 1986. *Racism in the Press*. London, UK: Arnold.

Van Noppen, John-Pierre. 2004. "CDA: A Discipline Come of Age?". *Journal of Sociolinguistics* 8 (1): 107.126.

Vatz, Richard. 1973. "The Myth of the Rhetorical Situation". *Philosophy & Rhetoric* 6: 154–161.

Wichelns, Herbert. 1993 [1925]. "The Literary Criticism of Oratory". In *Landmark Essays on Rhetorical Criticism*, T. Benson (ed.), 1–32. Davis, CA: Hermagoras Press.

Wodak, Ruth. 2001. "What CDA is About – A Summary of its History, Important Concepts and its Developments". In *Methods of Critical Discourse Analysis*, R. Wodak and M. Meyer (eds), 1–13. London, UK: Sage.

_____ and Gilbert Weiss. 2005. "Analyzing European Union Discourses: Theories and Applications". In *A New Agenda in (Critical) Discourse Analysis*, R. Wodak and P. Chilton (eds), 121–135. Amsterdam and Philadelphia: John Benjamins.

News articles cited (listed by title)

"An ideal voice for those who want to hear again". 2002, October 7. Robert Joiner. Editorial. *St. Louis Post-Dispatch*. B7.

"A sound case for experts". 2002, February 13. Anjana Ahuja. *The Times* (London). No page number.

"A word to the hearing". 2004, February 15. Letter to the editor. *Sunday Telegraph* (London). Features, 24.

"Beat the bullies and let the deaf speak". 2004, Februrary 8. Letter to the editor. *Sunday Telegraph* (London). Features, 22.

"Breaking the sound barrier". 2002, July 23. Justine Hancock. *The Times* (London). Features, 14.

"Bringing sound to life". 2002, April 30. John Wheeler. *The Washington Post*. A19.

"Cochlear implants found to raise meningitis risk". 2003, August 4. Kawanza Griffin. *Milwaukee Journal Sentinel*. 04G.

"Cochlear marvel". 2002, April 18. Megan Blackley. *Herald Sun* (Melbourne, Australia). Opinion, 17.

"Cora Barclay funds rescue at 11th hour". 2003, June 19. Catherine Hockley. *The Advertiser* (Australia). News, 2.

"Deaf center helps children 'maximize listening'". 2002, May 17. Vickie Beck. *Tampa Tribune*. Baylife, 1.

"Deaf get a fair hearing with early diagnosis". 2003, September 20. Adrian McGregor. *The Weekend Australian*. C15.

"Deaf like me?". 2002, April 15. Cathy Young. *Boston Globe*. A17.

"Deaf to oppression". 2002, March 25. Andrew Bolt. *Herald Sun* (Melbourne, Australia). Opinion, 19.

"Deaf to reason". 2004, February 1. Fiona Leney. *Sunday Telegraph* (London). Review, 01.

"Drug agency is studying ear implants' links to meningitis". 2002, August 3. Philip J. Hilts. *The New York Times*. A9.

"Ear that cuts education bills". 2002, October 12. No author listed. *Herald Sun* (Melbourne, Australia). Careers, 50.

"From the science magazines: Do deaf children have a right to the sound of silence?". 2004, September 1. Jenny Kleeman. *The Guardian* (London). Guardian Leader, 22.

"He'll hear better – that's the sole reason for doing it". 2002, May 30. Valerie Hauch. *Toronto Star*. G22.

"Hearing repaired". 2002, August 8. Svetlana Kolchik. *USA Today*. Life, 9D.

"Hers is resounding joy; 'Miracle' cochlear implant operation has opened world for 7-year-old girl". 2004, August 11. Vincent T. Davis. *San Antonio Express-News*. Metro, 1B.

"Implants for deaf misunderstood". 2002, April 1. Letters to the editor. *Herald Sun* (Melbourne, Australia). News, 16.

"Implants no cure". 2002, May 6. Letters to the editor. *The Washington Post*. A20.

"Tackling sounds of silence". 2004, September 15. Mike O'Connor. *Courier Mail* (Queensland, Australia). Features, 21.

"The sounds of silence". 2002, April 21. Dr. Gifford-Jones. *The Toronto Sun*. Lifestyle, 38.

"Toddler joins 'hearing' world; Katy youngster gains with cochlear implant". 2003, January 30. Sandra Meineke. *The Houston Chronicle*. This Week, 01.

CHAPTER 7

"American humor" versus "Indian humor"

Identity, ethos, and rhetorical situation

Neeta Bhasin
Hobart and William Smith Colleges

Introduction

This study argues for a rhetorical approach to the processes of identity construction. I articulate concepts from rhetoric with ideas from interactional sociolinguistics to explore the relationship between language and social identity. I examine particular rhetorical situations and contexts of production in which Indian students on a college campus form, establish, and negotiate individual and group identities. Contexts of production can encompass not only the local context of interaction, but also the macro-social conditions in which discourses are produced and circulated; however, I focus largely on the former in this study. I illustrate how identity and language mutually construct each other and how the cultural meaning of both is achieved in social interaction. I show in detail how identity emerges in interaction as a situated achievement, the outcome of a rhetorical process in which people draw from socially constituted repertoires of resources and hone them into claims about self and others for presentation to particular interlocutors. In particular, I bring to bear insights of rhetoricians regarding ethos and rhetorical exigency in exploring the imaginative possibilities of discursive practices in creating identity and community in a group of international students from India at an American university. I show how these students interactively create a relational "imagined community" of Indians, in opposition to Americans, through the discursive use of linguistic and ideological resources as they talk about an Indian film as a group. Then, to explore how rhetorical situation can shape identity, I contrast how they portray themselves vis à vis Americans in this conversation with how they talk about American and Indian ethos in individual interviews.

The study of immigrants and other kinds of communities that emerge out of transnational flows of people, discourse, commodities, and power has been a rather neglected site in the discipline of rhetoric. Emergent forms of migration, labor, and the flow of capital are giving rise to new ways of organizing and orienting to new structures of the relations between processes of globalization and the construction of multiple levels of locality, which both hinder and enhance these flows. Discourses of individuals and groups caught, willingly or otherwise, in these shifts and changes can be understood in terms of what Foucault refers to as "polyvalent mobility" (1985). In other words, they derive force from the multiple and overlapping social and cultural spaces they inhabit, and from the subjugated knowledges (Foucault 1980) and their sedimented forms they bring into play. Rhetoric, I believe, can provide conceptual tools to understand these particular forms of internationalization and globalization and the attendant discourses, because the discipline, as Maurice Charland, among others, has claimed, "signals a commitment to the idea of agency in discourse" (Charland 2003: 119). If we take rhetoric to be a method of inquiry, as I do in this study, then the focus of the inquiry ought to be on those identifiable human agents who exercise their power to bring about effects and to reconstitute and change the situation. Thus, agency in this rhetorical view is not formulated *a priori* to the context but arises out of the situated dynamics of a specific place and time (Ahearn 2001). This is the major advantage a rhetorical approach has over other theories and methods employed in identity studies, immigration studies, and globalization studies, which while delineating large institutional, economic, and cultural shifts, often fail to identify agents and to locate the specific local site of agency. Rhetorical concepts, on the other hand, can be instrumental in understanding how local actors themselves connect to the global, the national, the ethnic and other forms of identification by re-imagining them or rejecting the notions that are presented to them.

Furthermore, I hope to show that concepts such as "identity politics," "multiculturalism," and "globalization" are locatable at the micro-level, in the quotidian and mundane lives of people. These constructs are creatively used as performative resources, and indexically invoked under conditions derived from the interactions themselves. Thus, the characteristics of "culture'" and "identity" are not inherent, but presupposed cultural categories mapped onto, or transformed into, features of culture and situated identity that become interactionally relevant.

Background

With its less restrictive entry requirements, the Immigration and Naturalization Act of 1965 opened the gates of the United States of America to Third-World immigrants. Whether the new migrants come with the intention or desire to settle down in the host country or not, all of them have to negotiate their daily life amidst prodigious social and cultural change. They have to grapple with the unfamiliar and often disorienting socio-cultural and political realities that confront them in the new place. This study focuses on a particular *contact zone* (Pratt 1991) in the United States that gives rise to new exigencies for imagining and talking about identity, as well as new uses and new creations of rhetorical resources to adapt to, and sometimes change, the situations that rhetors find themselves in, paying particular attention to their will, initiative, and creativity.

The way the new migrants experience the new surroundings and the speed of their adjustment depends, to a large extent, on their ability to speak English. As a consequence of colonialism, middle-class migrants from India, unlike many other Asian migrants, have the advantage of knowing the dominant host language, which probably buffers the impact of culture shock. However, for these newcomers, English becomes much more than a tool for communication; it plays a key role in establishing and advertising their social identities. John Gumperz (1982) has shown that outsiders who enter a new cultural and linguistic setting may learn a language well in terms of grammar, and this knowledge might be adequate for the "instrumental contacts" that constitute much of the working day. Those explicitly rhetorical situations, however, where speakers are evaluated on their ability to explain or describe something that is not shared knowledge, or to produce intricate narratives, often prove to be difficult for newcomers to handle. Lack of fluency in such discourse practices can lead to breakdowns in communication that can result in stereotypical or pejorative evaluations, and may perpetuate social divisions.

Lloyd Bitzer (1968) defines a rhetorical situation as a situation in which a rhetor sees the need to change reality and realizes that change may be brought about through rhetorical discourse. In other words, a rhetorical situation is a complex interaction of persons, objects, events and relations "presenting an actual or potential exigence which can be completely or partially removed if discourse, introduced into the situation, can so constrain human decision or action as to bring about the significant modification of the exigence" (Bitzer 1968:6). Indian students in America come to experience a set of disjunctions between place, culture and identity that needs to be addressed and adjusted if they are to "fit in" and "belong." Their lives qualify, I argue, as rhetorical situations that call for negotiating life amid cultural, social, and political change through discursively mediated self and group representations. Thus, I investigate the linguistic construction of ethnic and national identity among Indian students in the United States. In particular, I explore how one group of Indian students makes sense of and creates cultural meanings around the differences between American English and Indian English, as they collaboratively mount a critique of "American" humor to forge "us" and "them" categories, and also as each talks to the researcher individually.

In his path-breaking work, sociologist Benedict Anderson presented the argument that nations are "imagined communities" (Anderson 1983). Anderson argues that the confluence of print technology and the development of capitalism gave rise to national consciousness. At this juncture, Latin began to lose its monopoly on print, leading to the decline of religion and religiously imagined communities. And more importantly, newspapers, books, and novels in vernacular languages give their readers an awareness of larger citizenry beyond their localities and create what Anderson calls a "horizontal comradeship," thus making it possible to imagine the nation. The originality of this idea lies in the claim that nations were not just the products of sociological conditions, such as language or race or religion, but that they had to be imagined into existence. While his revisionist notion went a long way in exposing the misplaced concreteness of nation, Anderson did not explain the strategies through which "the imagined" becomes second nature or an identity. He had much less to say about how people imagine the nation in their daily life and the various ways they negotiate and put on display the social meaning and value of national community in their everyday social life.

Along with "nation," the term "ethnicity" has become an increasingly important label in discussions of identity. Like nationality, ethnicity is increasingly viewed as a strategic choice which is dynamic, shifting, and based on complex politics of representation. In her discussion of the linkages between language and ethnicity, Nancy Dorian (1999) claims that while ethnicity can feel very primal or primordial, its underpinnings are social, not biological. Etienne Balibar and Immanuel Wallerstein (1991) talk about "fictive ethnicity," which people use to create a community based on "an identity of origins, culture and interests which transcends individuals and social conditions." For Balibar (1991), the fictiveness of this kind of community lies less in its artificial or illusory nature than in the way it is put together by people, in its constructedness, which he labels "fabrication." Positions such as those of Balibar and Anderson, while theoretically insightful, do not account for exactly how ethnicity and nationality are constructed in the course of cultural, political, and economic actions and with what consequences. They do, however, oblige us to proffer more nuanced descriptions of not only ethnicity, but also of the notion of construction itself.

Drawing on the insights of John Gumperz, Joshua Fishman, Charles Antaki and Sue Widdicombe, this chapter takes the position that ethnicity and language mutually construct each other and that the cultural meaning of both is located in social interactions (Gumperz 1982; Fishman 1999; Antaki & Widdicombe 1999). Since ethnicity is socially constructed, it is also apt to change as and when people adapt their identity to the rhetorical exigencies of the interactive situations they are in. People create and deploy national and ethnic identities in the context of small-scale cultural, economic, and political interactions through particular and micro-rhetorical strategies. As Sue Widdicombe has argued, what is crucial in exploring the link between identity and language is not whether people can be labeled or described in a particular way, but how individuals and groups make identity relevant or ascribe identity to self and others. Identity, thus, is not what people "are" but what they "do" (Antaki & Widdicombe 1999).

Richard Buttny's work on the use of reported speech in narratives is also relevant to the framework of this study. Buttny highlights the evaluative nature of reported speech, pointing out that the speaker does not merely "report" speech, but also assesses the "problematic character of the actions performed through other's words" (Buttny 1997:477). Furthermore, the critical appraisal of another's speech discloses the reporting speaker's attitude and stance on reported speech. Since Buttny's research concerns the discourse of race on a university campus, where in-groups and out-groups are racially marked, his findings are particularly pertinent to my study, where in-group and out-group are culturally (and not just nationally) marked. Reported speech, in such cases, works as a category of evidence, which in the guise of objectively "constructing a portrait" can hold the other culpable (Buttny 1997:479–480). The notion of "culture," as the conversational practices of the participants of this study will illustrate, is a complex socio-historical and political palimpsest of ethnic and national designations, and therefore, a rich site for understanding discursive constructions.

Methods

To elucidate these points, I turn to one specific group of Indian migrants – Indian students at Carnegie Mellon University, who form the largest group of international students on campus.[1] Since the majority of these students are recent migrants (they have been in the U.S. for five years or less), one can safely assume that they are in the early stages of developing linguistic strategies to deal with new experiences in a radically different setting. The fact of their newness is reinforced both inside and outside the academic institution, foregrounding their identities as foreigners and Indians. From the time of their arrival in the U.S., to the international student orientation, to working out the details of their accommodations, food, dress, transportation, technology and the like, almost every facet of daily life has marked them as foreigners and underscored how they are different from American and other students and what they have in common with their fellow Indians. As we will see, these Indians, who are linguistically, regionally and culturally heterogeneous at home, are led to construct themselves as a more homogeneous group in the U.S. Thus both the target population of the study and the circumstances in which it finds itself are conducive to exploring the issue of linguistic construction

---

1.   For instance, in 2000, out of 8,514 students at Carnegie Mellon University, 2,021 were non-U.S. citizens. And, out of 2,021 international students, 341 were from India. (*Carnegie Mellon Factbook* 2001, Volume 15.)

of social identities. Moreover, as a graduate student at the university, I had access to this population.

In analyzing the data, I took the approach provided by interactional sociolinguistics, particularly influenced by the analytical frameworks and techniques of John Gumperz (1982). This approach includes a close analysis of transcribed talk, in the context of ethnographic participant observation. I focus on the particular linguistic devices, the conversational competencies such as alignment, footing, and "membership categorization," and the rhetorical strategies, such as ascription of group characteristics through representations of the words and behavior of its prototypical members, that the participants deploy in the service of mobilizing their "Indianness" against an equally co-constructed "American" identity, in the process submerging their regional identities. I decided to act as a participant-observer in the group discussion with the intention of putting the participants at ease, thus eliciting casual and unconscious speech and behavior. I believe that my being Indian, like the participants of my study, helped me to achieve this, reducing the interviewer effect.

The participants and the setting

I recruited five Indian students for this study, two females and three males. All were graduate students who had been in the United States for less than five years. The two female participants, Geeta and Shilpa, had been in the U.S. for eight months; Hacker for three years; Paul for four; and Mike for a little over a year. (All the names are pseudonyms chosen by the participants themselves. It is interesting to note that the two women chose Indian names while the three male participants opted for Western names). They had very different attributed identities in India. They were from different regions of the country. Three of the students were from two southern Indian states, two from two different eastern states, and one from the north. They did not even share a common native language. They spoke Hindi, the national language of India, and English with varying degrees of proficiency. In short, at home, these students had quite diverse demographic ethnic and linguistic profiles.

In order to encourage talk about linguistic, ethnic, and national ideologies, I showed an Indian film to the participants and audio- and video-taped their talk during and after the film. I thought that screening the film would trigger a spontaneous discussion and perhaps, heighten sociolinguistic saliency in the setting. The movie, *Hyedrabad Blues*, is about an Indian student in America who returns to his hometown in southern India after four years and the problems he faces due to the changes in his attitudes and expectations. The film sets up the protagonist to be perceived as an "Americanized" version of his former self. As I had hoped, this film prompted a spontaneous discussion of the kinds of situations Indians students encounter when they come to the United States.

In addition to being a participant-observer in the group interaction, I also conducted one-on-one conversations with each of the five participants. In each interview, I attempted to elicit information about their family backgrounds, their reasons for coming to the U.S., and their experiences with and perspectives on American speech and behavior. The one-on-one conversations took place over the course of three days, and they were conducted almost two weeks after the group conversation.

The group conversation

In the group conversation, the students interactively constructed a homogenous Indian ethnic/national identity in the U.S., in part by typifying and critiquing "American humor" in a conversation about fellow students. The five participants (six, including me, "Neeta") achieve in-group cohesion or "ethnic bonding" through a set of moves in the conversation which claim the exclusionary and inclusionary stance of the participants as a group (of Indians) vis-à-vis Americans, displaying, "performing," and negotiating a largely "imagined" (Anderson 1983) ethnic identity through a collaborative process that unfolds in the course of the interaction. The conversation shows clearly that there is an emergent quality to the construction of identity that manifests itself not in one utterance, but unravels in the dynamic trajectory of the interaction. We see this, for example, in this segment of the conversation, which I will discuss in detail below.

1   **Geeta:** Yeah. Some – the – American humor I – find very difficult to understand,
2   you know. Some of the slapstick lines [
3   **Neeta:** [what kind? Like?
4   **Geeta:** I don't know, I don't see- maybe – maybe they understand them, but I
5   don't see the humor in them.
6   *(general laughter and a collective "Yeah.")*
7   **Geeta:** Like you hear – you hear Clair speaking, right? *(to Neeta).* And you
8   hear a lot of – I don't know. she has her own set of witticisms that she sort of hands
9   out at random and she finds – she finds it very funny herself, but I just – don't.
10 And I'm telling you because you've heard her speak and maybe you can
11 pinpoint what exactly...
12 **Neeta:** Yes, I've been here ten years, so I'm probably a little more used to-you
13 know, I mean.....
14 **Geeta:** Her regular line would be – suppose I tell her that I missed a class, she'll

15   be – and suppose I tell her that "Oh this professor is very disorganized," I say. "Oh
16   **Geeta**: he's not disorganized, he's just trying to psych you out. Ha, ha, ha."
17   (*laughter*)
18   **Geeta**: I don't see the humor in that, you know. I'm, you know, giving
19   her these blank stares and she probably thinks, "oh this poor girl, I probably got
20   her very nervous" and in a way to lessen the blow, she said, "oh Geeta, don't
21   worry, you'll get it next time, you're too hard on yourself." And then she goes –
22   **Shilpa**: Nobody tells me that.
23   **Geeta**: Basically – but- I mean – yeah, these are the standard lines that 'he's trying
24   to psyche you out" and things like that which is supposed to be funny . . .
25   ostensibly, but I don't get the humor.
26   **Paul**: There are two things that I want to comment on, one is that I've always – if
27   you had . . . uh . . . European humor is very, very interesting. These guys, like, have
28   a very good sense of humor.
29   **Neeta**: Who are these guys?
30   **Paul**: I mean..like, I hang out with a few Europeans still. So their sense of humor
31   is absolutely amazing. Germans, Swiss, uh . . . and uh . . . Spanish . . . one Spanish.
32   So –
33   **Neeta**: From Spain or from Latin America?
34   **Paul**: Spain, Spain. Yeah. So it's very different crowd I interact with and . . . the
35   other point I forgot.
36   (*laughter*)
37   **Hacker**: Yeah, that was good humor . . .
38   (*more laughter*)
39   **Geeta**: I think I like the Indian brand of humor the best.
40   **Neeta**: May be because we're used to it, you know.
41   **Hacker**: It's all a cultural thing because previously when I was working my
42   manager some- I mean, once a while he'll forward me these jokes and all . . . I
43   mean out of the 15 or 16 jokes, it'll have a small joke-I'll hardly find one or two,
44   ok, that I'll be able to understand. Rest of them=
45   **Neeta**: Tell me-
46   **Mike**: This is a very- Humor is a very cultural thing=
47   **Hacker**: Very cultural thing.
48   **Mike**: because it's very- it's related to language a lot.
49   **Paul** (*laughing*): Now I remembered.
50   **Geeta**: Like this guy, William Safire's columns, he writes on language. I find
51   that . . . funnier. He's an- he's an all-American . . . but he's good.

Reported speech, summary quotes, and the construction of a prototypical group member

Geeta is the driving force behind this interaction. Right from the start (line 1–2) she constructs the unitary notion of "American humor" and puts forth the idea of the "difficulty in understanding American humor" that propels the conversation forward. Her construction of "American humor" as "difficult to understand" yet labeled by her as "slapstick" marks an exclusionary stance and provides the image on which the rest of the interaction turns. This utterance also signals Geeta's resistance to being put in the same group as Americans. When I ask her to specify, she further sets up a direct contrast between "they" and "I" (line 4–5), "they" meaning Americans who "maybe understand" slapstick lines whereas Geeta doesn't "see the humor in them"(line 4–5). The response to this membership categorization move is approved by others, as is indicated by their laughter and affirmation (line 6). The bonding created by the general ratification of her opinion about American humor is further strengthened by Geeta's use of the pronoun "you"(line 7, "like *you* hear Clair speaking, right?"), which functions as a collective pronoun, generalizing what is basically her own particular perception of how Clair, the American graduate student in her department, talks. However, the use of the pronoun "you" shifts from its collective reference to refer to me in particular (lines 10–11. "I'm telling you because you've heard her speak and may be you can pinpoint exactly" …). This move on Geeta's part is an attempt to extract validation for her evaluative comment about the American graduate student. It is quite possible that Geeta could have asked the question because I know the student in question, or because I have been in the United States longer than she has and presumably know something about American humor or the lack of it. It seems, however, that there is an implicit assumption in Geeta's explanation ("I'm telling you because you've heard her speak") that I, as a compatriot, would concur with her evaluation of her colleague's "American" sense of humor. The three possibilities are not, of course, mutually exclusive.

Geeta also reconstructs a conversation in which she parodies Clair's response to her comment (lines 14–16). "Yeah. Her regular line would be – suppose I tell her that I missed a class, she'll be – and suppose I tell her that 'Oh, this professor is very disorganized,' I say. 'Oh, Geeta, he's not disorganized, he's just trying to psych you out. Ha, ha, ha.'" The direct contrast that Geeta creates between her comment, "Oh this professor is very disorganized" to Clair's response, "Oh Geeta, he's not disorganized" via repetition and parallelism has the effect of making her colleague seem condescending while at the same time not funny at all. The deliberate caricature of Clair's laugh, "ha ha ha," by Geeta underscores the difference between her and Clair's senses of humor. In lines 18–21 she parodies another conversation with Clair in which while positioning herself as the misplaced target of Clair's condescension and undeserving of her pity, she presents the other woman's sense of humor as impoverished. Through her performance, she constructs the phrase "psych you out" (lines 16, 24) as a prototypical example of Clair's humor and – by extension – American humor. This supposed typicality of American humor is also insinuated by Geeta's use of "regular line" (line 14) and "standard lines"(line 23). Her use of the word "ostensibly" (line 24) stands out in contrast with the slang "psych you out" and evokes the contrast between formal English and American English, thus marking yet another move to differentiate herself from Americans. This is not to say that Geeta might not be narrating her actual experiences, but her linguistic and rhetorical choices construct the American woman as patronizing and lacking in humor. As Geeta makes the insinuation that Clair is lacking in humor, she suggests that Clair's humor is unintelligible not only to her, but to the whole group.

Noteworthy about Geeta's role in the group interaction is the way she uses reported speech, both direct (lines 15–16, 20–21) and indirect (lines 19–20, 23–24) attributed to Clair to construct an image of prototypical American speech. Buttny describes direct speech as that in which the words of the original source are reproduced, and indirect speech is where the propositional content but not the words are reproduced (Buttny 1997:479). Reported speech, Buttny contends, is not merely a report, but also an evaluation that reflects the reporting speaker's positioning toward what was said. As Bauman points out (1986), direct quotes can enable the reporting speaker to duplicate performative aspects of the original speech – in other words not just the language but also the stylistic and prosodic aspects of the words (Bauman 1986). Geeta uses the previous words of Clair, originally uttered in a very different context, and reconstructs them for the purposes of the present context of the group conversation – a context that has a different audience with a different kind of involvement in the rhetorical situation. The assessment and evaluation of her reported speech is indicated through Geeta's parody of Clair's laughter and her exaggerated voice quality (line 16). It is relevant to apply Buttny's term "summary quotes" to the reported speech by Geeta when she constructs a portrait of Clair as a prototypical member of her group. As the reporting speaker, Geeta quotes Clair (lines 15–16, 19–21), herself (line 15), and a dialogue between the two (lines 15–16, 18–21). Her reported speech not only makes a claim about what was actually said, but also insinuates what could have been said or will be said by Clair to Geeta in these kinds of exchanges between the two. By blurring the line between what was said and what was purported to be said or thought, and by interspersing reported speech and her own commentary, Geeta is able to summarize Americans by using the words of a prototypical member, Clair, using the ascription of characteristics to an individual to achieve group level ascription.

Keith Basso's *Portraits of "The White Man"* (1979), which deals with the complex forms of joking and other linguistic play in which the Western Apache imitate and make fun of the behavior of Anglo-Americans, makes a similar point. Distorted quotation, argues Basso, works as a commentary on how to hear what is said, and very explicitly to mock, to deride, to parody and thereby to subvert the content of what is being said and its prototypical speaker (Basso 1979:45). Just as in the portraits of Anglo-Americans by the Western Apache, Geeta uses a humorous style of delivery to ridicule and mock not merely the propositional content of Clair's utterances, but also Clair herself, the source of the stereotype. Reported speech functions here as evidence which, when interspersed with Geeta's own commentary, presents her (Geeta's) own interpretation as objective. Reported speech also lets Geeta distance herself from the message while holding Clair, the American, responsible.

As Buttny points out, "portraits of the other are inherently relational" (1997:502). While constructing (and assessing) the portrait of Clair and her sense of humor as prototypically American, Geeta also implicitly creates a contrasting portrait of Indians and their humor. In the following section, I illustrate how the initiative taken by Geeta contributed to the development of in-group cohesion and a critique of out-group speech and behavior as the group conversation proceeded.

Sense of humor, culture, and the crystallization of in-group allegiance and out-group distinction

Paul then joins the conversation by putting forth "European sense of humor" as a contrast to American humor (line 26–28) and attributing superiority to the former. This preference for European humor is not presented as his particular preference, but rather as a general and universal opinion (his utterance is not preceded by "I think" or "I feel."). The other participants respond positively to his assertion through laughter. He further reinforces his identification with and affinity for Europeans (line 34. "So, it's a very different crowd I interact with ") by insisting that he interacts with a "different" crowd and thus, by implication and unlike Geeta, is not subjected to the poor sense of humor of the Americans. It's also worth noting that Paul's assertion about European humor remains uncontested in the group, which makes it possible to argue that in-group cohesion has already begun to congeal and the rest of the interaction is an unfolding of this agglutination. Paul's self-deprecating "the other point I forgot" (line 34–35), mocking his own forgetfulness and flakiness, provokes laughter from the group and a comment from Hacker, "that was good humor" (line 37). One can conclude that the adjective "good" is used by Hacker not to indicate the quality of the joke *per se*, but to show that everyone in the group understood the humor of the situation. In this sense it also presented as a contrast to "American humor," which is "difficult to

understand" (line 1). The exclusionary stance of the interaction and the solidifi-
cation of national identity become all the more clear when Geeta (line 39) takes
an overt and unambiguous position by stating that she likes "the Indian brand of
humor the best."

Lines 41–48 illustrate the joint construction of the meaning of humor by
Hacker and Mike. The first reference to humor as a "cultural thing" by Hacker (line
41) is taken up by Mike (line 46) and later again by Hacker (line 47). The indeter-
minacy of the statement "humor is a cultural thing" makes several interpretations
possible. Hacker uses the phrase to point out the differences between American
and Indian humor by bringing up the anecdote about the jokes which his manager
forwards to him (line 41–44), and which he doesn't understand and/or doesn't
find funny. Mike's use of the phrase, on the other hand, is more hesitant and less
derisive. He relates humor to American culture and culture to language (line 48).
One plausible reading of these connections that Mike makes could be that American humor is difficult to understand because of the way Americans use English
or Americanisms (which all participants had admitted at different points during
discussions that they had problems understanding) and not because they were not
funny. Mike's conciliatory move sets the tone for the following comment by Geeta
(line 51, "he's an all-American … *but*, he's good"), who clearly views William
Safire as an exception to the rule of bad American humor. However, this concession
on her part is used to further reiterate her negative evaluation of American humor.

In this latter half of the interaction (lines 26–51), one can see an advance-
ment of in-group cohesion through group-level ascriptions. In their seemingly
unexceptional conversational practices, such as Paul's personal endorsement of
European sense of humor as superior to the American one because he "hangs
out" with Europeans (lines 30–32) and Hacker's personal anecdote about his manager's difficult-to-understand jokes (lines 41–46), these participants build alliances
and counter-alliances. Such personal experiences and narratives within reported
speech can also work to validate the claim that American sense of humor is flawed
because it is difficult to understand. There are, however, utterances in the group
conversation that attempt to mitigate the negative assessment of out-group by presenting a slightly more complex portrayal of Americans and their sense of humor.
After my comment that our enjoyment of the Indian brand of humor might be
because we are used to it (in response to Geeta's comment in line 39), Hacker,
interestingly, suggests that understanding humor is a "cultural thing" (line 41) to
contextualize his subsequent comment about his own difficulty in understanding
his manager's "American jokes." The designation of humor as a cultural category
is an effort by Hacker to relativize, which is echoed by Mike (line 46). However, these extenuating utterances are sidelined by Geeta's sardonic comment that
serves to highlight William Safire's good sense of humor as an anomaly, and thus,
emphasizes the negative evaluation of American humor.

My participation throughout this group interaction is revealing of someone struggling to maintain some critical distance and objectivity. I was very conscious of my role as a researcher in the group interaction and therefore, through my questions (lines 3, 29, 33, "what kind? Like?"; "Who are these guys?"; "From Spain or from Latin America?"), I tried to elicit clarifications and elaborations on the comments made by the participants. This stance also reflects my resistance to the in-group cohesion based on the critique of American humor.

What do the findings suggest?

The dynamics of the group interaction indicate clearly that ethnicity is contextually constructed. The participants in the conversation negotiate an ethnic/national identity through the use of language in a co-operative process that unfolds in the course of the group interaction. Geeta takes the initiative in the collaborative construction via membership categorization of "us" and "them" divisions based on a pejorative evaluation of American humor. Other participants, in a display of agreement and solidarity, join in as the conversation progresses. None of the participants advertised their ethnic/national identity at the outset. Yet throughout the conversation their "Indian identity" is mutually defined, redefined, and honed as they react to the exigencies of the conversation. Thus, in the course of the interaction, one can see the emergent quality of identity formation. The participants in the conversation craft their "Indian" identity interactively via the discursive use of linguistic resources, and each individual presents his/her identity claims to others for ratification.

On the larger sociopolitical stage and in this interaction itself, "Indian" is a designation that collapses a number of idioms, ethnic origins, and regional cultures. After they started coming to the U.S. in large numbers after 1965, the U.S. census assigned Indian immigrants to the generalized categories of "Asian American" or "Asian." But these descriptors were not the ones embraced by Indians in everyday life. This is true even today, when many official and non-official discourses of "Indian" and "Indianness" clearly distinguish between Indians and Asians. Sandhya Shukla points out that because of the specific historical conditions under which India developed as a nation-state, "being Indian" has come to index a set of meanings. Thus, Indian subjects are "read" as Indians by others (marked by India, the nation) and "experience the world through that sensibility," thus, often "mobilizing ethnicity by adopting 'Indian' as a primary self-descriptor" (Shukla 2003). The group's adoption of the label "Indian" can also be explained by using Einar Haugen's notion of "internal cohesion and external distinction." Haugen maintains that nation is not only a political unit, but also a social one and "like any unit, it minimizes internal differences and maximizes external ones. On the individual's personal and local identity it superimposes a national one by identifying his ego with that of all others within the nation and separating it from that of others outside the nation" (Haugen 1966:927–928). At home, these students would not necessarily think of themselves as sharing anything except a national identity. The way they enact a shared identity in the conversation is clearly a response to the way Indians are categorized in the U.S. as a cultural and not just a national group. For these students, "being Indian" becomes significant in a new and different and way when they are in the U.S. In the following section, I discuss how in the one-on-one conversations, like the group conversation, "being Indian" becomes a resource in interactions for these students in the U.S. in a way it might not be elsewhere.

The one-on-one conversations

The one-on-one conversations with the five participants were conducted, not just to collect background and demographic information, but with a view to amplify my understanding about how they represent themselves, how they make sense of the new sociolinguistic setting, and how they frame the negotiation of their identities in this new setting. These individual conversations were also interactional sites where identity was negotiated, albeit of a different kind than in the group conversation. These one-on-one interactions with me were particularly likely to be the loci of identity construction because I, too, was a member of this Indian community on campus.

In addition to asking the participants questions about their age, education level, the place/region they hailed from, and what language(s) they spoke at home and work, I tried to elicit talk about their reasons for and the circumstances of coming to the U.S. and about their first few years in the U.S. and at the university. Among other things, I asked the participants if they experienced anything like "culture shock" when they first came to this country. The one-on-one conversations were semi-structured in nature. Although I had some questions that I asked of each of the participants, my role was not particularly directive.

My questions about the differences between Indian and American English yielded particularly useful insights into the speakers' feelings about linguistic and cultural differences between Americans and Indians. All five participants commented on the "formality" of Indian English. All of them had used a more formal variety of English, mostly in academic settings, and admitted to having some difficulty in speaking and understanding colloquial English. Hacker was the only participant who had had no formal education in English. He claimed that he had learned to speak English before he came to the U.S.

All of the participants believed that there were clear differences between American and Indian English. This acknowledgement, however, was often accompanied by the qualification that Indian English was more like "British English." They gave several examples of various lexical, phonological, and grammatical differences, such as "taking the exam" versus "giving the exam" (the latter is a commonly used expression in spoken Indian English). Other examples included the use of "first floor" to refer to what is called "ground floor" in India and many such confusing differences that can divide the speakers of a common language. All five participants suggested that understanding these linguistic differences and then changing to American expressions was a process that began soon after they came to the U.S. Hacker claimed that he was not even aware of when he started speaking "the American way." He explained his experience thus:

> I do not think I use that, but a couple of times, like people say that I changed couple of things, like initially I used to say "shedool" [schedule]. Now, ok (laughs) I don't know when I switched to "skejool" ... and couple of days ago somebody called up looking for Keith [his housemate] and Keith was taking bath. So I mean, probably this is a U.S. change or I mean – had in – had it been in India, probably I would have said that he is taking bath or something like that. This time I said, "He's in shower." When I said that then I realized that "Oh, ok, this is a change in me."

All participants except Geeta admitted to using Americanisms and American slang. This could be because Geeta had been in the U.S. less than a year and was struggling to adjust to the new surroundings. Her classroom, where she taught freshmen English and experienced serious communicative difficulties, became one of the sites where she fought her linguistic and cultural battles. She talked about the changes she made in her English in the following terms:

> I've been told, uh ... probably even by some of my classmates as well as ... no, not teachers, but maybe more classmates that I should speak more slowly, take time to enunciate properly and I, I guess things that general- well just uh-get used to spacing out my phrases or sentences, uh, because that's the way Americans are used to talking as well as hearing things. And ... so I have to be very conscious of-, well, most of the times I do forget, but sometimes I'm conscious about speed at which I speak and I try to regulate that and also – well, also I try to sort of uh ... provincialize my language, that is, I tend to use a very formal way of speaking and I try to sort of work on that, you know, that is, be more accessible as far as my vocabulary and my articulation goes ... Make sure that the other person understands me, otherwise it stands to no purpose that I'm teaching a class and nobody understands me.

As she did in the group interaction, Geeta uses the strategy of setting up a contrast between an American way of speaking and her way of speaking. Her assessment of out-group members and their speech is distinctly censorious and

disparaging. Her use of the word "provincialize" frames her attempt to colloquial-
ize her speech as a lowering of standards. Later in the interview, she brings up
the idea that American English requires a "dumbing down of the expression."
Here is an excerpt from the interview that illustrates how, while her choice of
words to describe American English can be positive, the sense underlying them
is derogatory:

> Yeah, definitely in the U.S. here I have learned that one can be very straightfor-
> ward, very fast, very forward, very sparse, very bold or indulgent or you know
> hand out very bold expressions and still make a lot of sense. And that's what I've
> discovered in the classrooms that people get their point across in ways that ...
> take very little effort and it can also make a lot of sense. Uh ... I think American
> speaking is ...(laughs)... the best example of American speaking can be found in
> Hemingway's books, you know. I think people in America speak or write as they
> speak or ... uh ... in the ... I mean – well, the best American novels, I don't think
> they use words that are more than five or six letters. That will be the average size
> or whatever.

Geeta also felt that while she was making steady progress toward adapting to American English in school, it was her day-to-day, quotidian interactions outside the
academy that were the hardest for her to tackle. She found Americans to be "im-
patient", "brusque" and dismissive" while she, on the other hand, "struggled to
articulate the simplest questions." Geeta equated "the American way of talking"
with "the American way of being," but her labels such as "fast" and "indulgent"
had less positive connotations than adjectives used by other participants. She also
characterized American speech as a lower form of English.

All the participants made a direct correspondence between language and an
(imagined) collective ethos of Americans. Adjectives such as "bold" and "straightforward" were not merely descriptors of American English, but also reflected the
students' view of the American character and American worldview. For instance,
Paul claimed that Indians are "hypocritical" whereas Americans are more "hon-
est" and "define everything correctly" so that if "somebody says something you
can take by the face value." He narrated this anecdote to illustrate the way Indians
and Americans differ culturally:

> A friend of mine quoted this, a very good example, a very good way of portray-
> ing things. In India you first have to build a trust, so if somebody – a person A
> comes to me, I just don't trust him straight off. He has to build a trust over a
> period of time. Whereas in U.S. what happens is that a person A comes, I trust
> him unless he screws it up. The method and the way in which things work are
> completely different and I'm more into what's American ...way of thinking with
> regard to those.

Mike and Shilpa echoed Paul's admiration for American "bluntness" in their personal interviews with me. Mike felt that one has to be more "frank" in the U.S. :

> It's easy to hide things and you can get away with them, but it's- people generally-
> there's more- their society is more honest, more, more open so. . .. it's uh – I think
> it's people-it's better to be – it's good to be open, that's what I like. That's one of
> the good things which is not – which is lacking in India.

Shilpa expressed the same sentiment thus:

> It's like you have to use very simple English in Indian terms when you are talking
> to people and – uh when you are talking to...say, you are presenting your ideas
> to a faculty or something in India, you generally have to be very formal and put it
> down in a very formal way. Here you can just mail the person- you just give the
> ideas as points. You can't – I have never done it India. So that was a very major
> difference and then ...it's a lot of words – I mean – words, basically the way we use
> it is different.

On the topic of cultural differences, three of the participants alluded to the
"identity crisis" of American-born Indians, who were referred to as "ABCDs,"
an abbreviated form of American-Born Confused *Desis. Desi* means "native"
or "compatriot" in Hindi, and it is often used with derogatory connotations.
American-born Indians were said to have "split personalities" and to be "lacking in
values," and "wanting to be something they are not." These evaluative designations
clearly reflect the derogatory attitude of the participants towards American-born
compatriots and their supposed mixed-identities.

Group conversation and one-on-one conversations:
Identity and rhetorical situation

Just as in the group conversation, identity is also performed, ascribed, and negotiated in one-on-one conversations. Moreover, just as in the group discussion, where
the participants constructed a collective ethos for themselves and ascribed one to
Americans, in their conversations with me the participants did the same. In other
words, taking into account the inherent relationality of portraits, in constructing
an image of Americans, Indians, the in-group members, implicitly created a representation of themselves as well in both group and one-on-one conversations. The
group conversation illustrated how, for these participants, "being Indian" is used
as a joint resource in interactions to mark their difference from Americans; similarly, the one-on-one conversations show how "being Indian" becomes significant
on an American campus and in American society. However, despite these broad
similarities, the divergences are striking. The differences reveal the extent to which
identity arises in the context of particular rhetorical situations.

While both the group conversation and the one-on-one conversations were
sites where identity work was done, the strategies the participants used and the

resources available to them were different. The one-on-one conversations did not have the dynamism of the group interaction and were, therefore, not particularly favorable to charting the emergent quality of identity construction. Also, with only two interactants, they were more constrained than the group conversation, particularly in terms of providing the scope for collaborative constructions of identity. The participants were more self-conscious and more formal during their one-on-one conversations. Group discussion, on the other hand, was more conducive to casual and unself-conscious speech.

However, in their one-on-one conversations with me, all the participants, except Geeta, painted a more favorable and a more complex portrait of Americans, as opposed to demonstrating the in-group loyalty that marked the group conversation. Furthermore, in the one-on-one conversations, the participants' portrayals and assessments of Indians were more critical than their evaluation of American speech and attitudes, which is the reverse of the findings of the group conversation. Whereas in the group discussion American humor and linguistic attitudes were talked about negatively, the participants formulated American ethos more favorably when they conversed with me individually. This variance between the findings of group conversation and the one-on-one conversations gives credence to the argument that the way people form their opinions, the way they express them, and what those opinions are, depends on the rhetorical exigencies of the situation. During their personal conversations, when they were alone with me, the participants showed less hesitation in proposing and projecting alignments with Americans. In the group interaction, however, the participants worked together to construct a negative view of American humor by putting forth a set of self and other identity attributes. It is through these exclusionary and inclusionary alignments in the interaction that the participants created their "imagined community" of Indians in opposition to an equally co-constructed "Americanness."

It is also noteworthy that humor does not emerge as a marker of cultural difference between Indians and Americans in any of the one-on-one conversations, not even Geeta's. It is not even mentioned. As Goffman points out, humor can facilitate the reframing of an interaction or the aligning of interactants (Goffman 1974), and it can also aid in the introduction of awkward topics. Embedded in humor, serious messages can be communicated, responsibility can be apportioned, and evaluations can be made in a seemingly light-hearted way rather than with an accusatory tone and content. Talking about humor, if not always "humorously," allowed the students to dissect and assess the complex and problematic nature of their adjustment to a different environment and people, while at the same time displaying and performing their own brand of "humor" to an audience that is implicitly constructed as more congenial and receptive as the group interaction progresses. Keith Basso's study of the Western Apache (Basso 1979), which draws on Goffman's dramaturgical model of human communication study, is highly relevant here. According to him, the Western Apache tell jokes about, perform, and parody "sounding American" to deride, mock and thus resist Anglo-American speech and behavior. Through their linguistic play and cultural symbols, the Western Apache illustrate that American is what Apache is not. Since my role in one-on-one conversation was limited to asking questions and at times seeking clarifications or elaborations of certain points, an interaction with markedly different constraints and exigencies than the group conversation, humor did not emerge as a resource for individual participants to do identity work.

There were some other notable issues that came up during the group discussion which deserve deeper consideration. For example, one is the assertion made by Paul during the group discussion that it is more difficult to understand "black Americans" than "other Americans." His comment that he "never understands black Americans, especially in the movies," did not elicit any argument or even a discussion from other members. The lack of any discussion regarding the comment could mean that the other participants agreed with Paul because they had similar experiences. It could also indicate recognition on their part of the mismatch between reality and its representation (on film, in this case). It could also stem from a refusal to acknowledge that the concept of "black speech" contradicts the unitary notion of American speech that they had conveniently constructed for themselves.

The other issue was the considerable "teasing" the participants faced from friends and family in India about their use of American slang, other Americanisms, and the noticeable changes in their pronunciation of certain English words. When I questioned them about why they think they were being mocked or teased, their answers were revealing. It seems to me that they saw "Americanization" in terms of language as losing one's authentic identity and acquiring one that is foreign. This anxiety regarding the supposed loss of authentic identity and denigration of mixed identities might help explain some of the boundary maintenance moves in the group discussion. While the instances of being made fun of by family and friends were not presented as being traumatic by any of the participants, they all admitted to being embarrassed about the real or imagined changes in their speech and attitude. Here the connection between speech and character or individual ethos emerges with much clarity. It is quite possible that the unease felt by the participants was due to the similarity between their situation and that of the American-born Indians. Like the ABCDs, they too had started showing the signs of being "confused" and having "split personalities," and perhaps more problematically, of being edged into a liminal zone where they are perceived to be neither here nor there.

In this chapter, I set out to explore the ways in which "cultural politics" is played out in face-to-face interaction. My research on the Carnegie Mellon campus sheds light on how Indian students make sense of the cultural and linguistic differences between Americans and Indians, and how they construct their identity and that of Americans through a series of linguistic strategies. Specifically, I explored how a co-constructed, emergent ethnic identity can be mapped, for specific interactional purposes, onto an attributed national identity. These five students, who have very different attributed identities and would be seen as belonging to different ethnic groups in India, together fashion an "imagined" Indian national identity. By providing evidence for the interactional achievement of ethnic/national identity, this paper attempts to fill the gap left by those who have long asserted the notion of "imagination" without showing what rhetorical and discursive resources people draw on to give shape and meaning to their imagined communities.

References

Ahearn, Laura M. 2001. "Why Agency Now?" *Annual Review of Anthropology*. 30. 109–137.

Anderson, Benedict. 1983. *Imagined Communities: Reflection on the Origin and Spread of Nationalism*. New York: Verso.

Antaki, Charles and Widdicombe, Sue, Eds. 1999. *Identities in Talk*. Thousand Oaks: Sage Publications.

Balibar, Etienne and Immanuel Wallerstein. 1991. *Race, Nation, Class: Ambiguous Identities*. London:Verso Press.

Balibar, Etienne. 1991. "The Nation Form: History and Ideology". Balibar and Wallerstein 1991. 86–106.

Basso, Keith H. 1979. *Portraits of "the Whiteman": Linguistic play and cultural symbols among the Western Apache*. Cambridge: Cambridge University Press.

Bauman, Richard. 1986. *Story, Performance, and Event: Contextual Studies of Oral Narrative*. Cambridge: Cambridge University Press.

_____. 2000. "Language, Identity, Performance." *Pragmatics* 10.1: 1–5.

Bitzer, Lloyd. 1968. "The Rhetorical Situation." *Philosophy and Rhetoric*. 1. 1–14.

Buttny, Richard. 1997. "Reported Speech in Talking Race on Campus." *Human Communication Research*. 23. 477–506.

Charland, Maurice. 1987. "Constitutive Rhetoric: The Case of the *Peuple Quebecois*." *Quarterly Journal of Speech* 73. 133–50.

_____. 2003. "The Constitution of Rhetoric's Tradition." *Philosophy and Rhetoric* 36:2. 119–134.

Dorian, Nancy C. 1999. "Linguistic and Ethnographic Fieldwork." *Handbook of Language and Ethnicity* ed. by Joshua A. Fishman. New York: Oxford University Press.

Foucault, Michel. 1980. *Power/Knowledge: Selected Interviews and Other Writings 1972–1977*, trans. Colin Gordon et al., ed. by Colin Gordon. New York: Pantheon.

_____. 1985. *History of Sexuality*. New York: Vintage.

Fishman, Joshua A. Ed. 1999. *Handbook of Language and Ethnicity*. New York: Oxford University Press.

_____. 1999. "Concluding Comments." *Handbook of Language and Ethnicity* ed. by Joshua A. Fishman. New York: Oxford University Press.

Goffman, E. 1974. *Frame Analysis*. New York: Harper and Row.

Gumperz, John. 1982. Discourse Strategies. Cambridge: Cambridge University Press.

Haugen, Einar. 1966. "Dialect, Language, Nation." *American Anthropologist. 68.* 922–935.

Kachru, Braj B. 1986. *The Alchemy of English: The Spread, Functions and Models of Non-Native Englishes.* Oxford: Pergamon Institute.

_____. 1992. *The Other Tongue: English Across Cultures.* Urbana: University of Illinois Press.

Lo, Adrienne. 1999. "Codeswitching, Speech Community Membership, and the Construction of Ethnic Identity." *Journal of Sociolinguistics* 3/4: 461–79.

Pratt, Mary Louise. 1991. "Arts of the Contact Zone." *Profession* 91. 33–40.

Reyes, Angela. 2002. ""Are you losing your culture?": Poetics, Indexicality and Asian American Identity." *Discourse Studies* 4(2). 183–199.

Shukla, Sandhya. 2003. *India Abroad: Diasporic Cultures of Postwar America and England.* Princeton: Princeton University Press.

CHAPTER 8

Ethos and narrative in online educational chat

Martha S. Cheng
Rollins College

Introduction

The concept of ethos, traditionally taken from Aristotle's *Rhetoric* and referring to the role of the rhetor's character in a speech, has typically been deployed in studies of planned, formal texts. However, modern investigations of ethos emphasize the interactive nature of ethos formation – interaction among the rhetor's social roles and prior reputation, the discourse, and the audience's expectations. This chapter presents a study of ethos formation in an online educational chat in which discourse among participants is informal and unplanned. In this conversational context, the factors shaping ethos are more explicit, due to the immediate responses from conversation partners.

Some modern developments in theories of ethos correspond with major areas of narrative theory, specifically discussions of identity and practical wisdom. Thus, although the analysis presented here looks at general discourse patterns, most of it focuses on the use of narratives in ethos formation. The chat narratives fulfilled certain functions, such as providing evidence for a claim or building common ground, that demonstrated two qualities cited by Aristotle as necessary for ethos: practical wisdom, and good will. The narratives also demonstrated specific linguistic strategies of identity construction that have been well studied in other fields, but not yet associated with ethos by rhetoricians. The discussion explores how these findings affirm and expand our understanding of ethos when applied to unplanned, informal conversation.

Rhetoricians and rhetors have grappled with the concept and practice of ethos since the beginning of rhetoric's recorded history. Aristotle was the first to explicitly define ethos as the character of the speaker as perceived through the speech (1991:37). Together with logos and pathos, ethos was one of the three artistic *pisteis* available to rhetors. Over the years, many theorists have been uncomfortable with Aristotle's explanation of ethos, since he did not acknowledge the speaker's "real" character outside of the speech. He seemed to overlook prior reputations, social roles, and actual moral character, leading scholars to suggest that he endorsed deception or did not care about the speaker's actual morality. However, other scholars endorsed Aristotle's purely artistic view of ethos, and took it even farther, claiming that character (real or otherwise) cannot exist outside of discourse.[1]

Amossy (2001) describes the debate between actual and perceived ethos as stemming from conflicting sociological and pragmatic perspectives. The sociological perspective recognizes social roles and institutional powers in ethos construction, while the pragmatic view holds that ethos is only constructed within and by the utterance. Amossy's article, "Ethos at the crossroads of disciplines: Rhetoric, pragmatics, sociology," offers a middle ground on which these two perspectives complement one another. She illustrates through her analysis of literary and political texts that speakers, aware of stereotypes associated with their persons, either build upon or work against those preconceived notions to achieve their desired ethos. Thus, Amossy claims, ethos results from the interaction between prior social roles or institutional powers and the discourse of the speech.

Other modern studies of ethos focus more closely on specific qualities needed to establish ethos. Aristotle listed three such qualities: virtue, practical wisdom, and good will (1991:120–121). He described good will as wanting the good of one's audience. To be trustworthy, the rhetor must appear to have the audience's interests in mind. Burke presents a similar idea in his concept of "identification." In the *Rhetoric of Motives* he describes person A as being identified with person B when they share the same interests (1950:20). Also, identification requires similarity between speaker and audience. He goes so far as to say, "You persuade a man only insofar as you can talk his language by speech, gesture, tonality, order, image, attitude, idea, *identifying* your ways with his" (1950:55).[2] Aristotle also encouraged speakers to adapt their characters to the character of the audience (1991:163–172). But unlike Aristotle, Burke does not rely on the orator's speech alone in order to display similarities with the audience. In fact, he encourages us to think more broadly of rhetoric, beyond one particular address to a "general body of identifications that owe their convincingness much more to trivial repetition and dull daily reinforcement than to exceptional rhetorical skill" (1950:26). Over time, the rhetor would have to consistently display the appropriate signs of character in various social roles and contexts, indicating similarities and shared interests with the audience.

---

1.   See Baumlin (1994) and Jasinski (2001) for discussions of the debate regarding actual vs. displayed ethos.

2.   Emphasis in original.

In addition to identification, the quality of practical wisdom (*phronesis*) also has found new prominence in contemporary theories of ethos. Aristotle's distinction between *phronesis* and scientific deliberation is well known. Rather than seeking invariable universal truths like the philosopher or scientist, a person with *phronesis* "deliberate[s] well about what is good and advantageous for himself"(1953:209) in particular situations. *Phronesis* is concerned with the variable decisions, or opinions, people make to achieve a good life. Nussbaum describes it as "the ability to recognize, acknowledge, respond to, pick out salient features of a complex situation...gained only through a long process of living and choosing that develops the agent's resourcefulness and responsiveness" (1986:305). The need for a 'long process of living and choosing,' of life experience in order to achieve practical wisdom was emphasized by Aristotle. In fact, according to Nussbaum, Aristotle carefully avoided laying out any procedure or method when describing practical wisdom. One cannot use a formula or follow a set of rules when faced with particular, contingent matters. Instead, one needs perception, flexibility, and responsiveness. Thus, the young cannot possess this intellectual virtue, even if they possess other virtues, simply because they have not lived and experienced enough (1953:214–215).

Garver's study of Aristotle's *Rhetoric* focuses on practical wisdom and character (1994, 2004). He uses practical wisdom to argue that the separation of logos and ethos is superficial, not substantive. He claims that the reasoning in rhetoric, which is always concerned with contingent matters, only persuades when it is also a sign of practical wisdom. And, at times, reasoning does not persuade when it is not also a sign of character. When an audience witnesses a rhetor's reasoning and judges it to be good reasoning, they are also judging the character of the speaker – that the ends and values guiding that reasoning are signs of practical wisdom. Thus, ethos derives from logos via practical wisdom. Like Aristotle's, Garver's ethos develops only within the speech; no prior information impacts the speaker's ethos. However, the centrality of practical wisdom in Garver's theory requires us to look beyond the immediate speech context, to a wider social context. Practical wisdom, as contingent knowledge rather than universal, depends upon *doxa*, the commonly held beliefs of the audience. Such beliefs can change over time in reaction to various social and cultural circumstances. In order to understand and evaluate any use of practical wisdom, we must take into account how broader social beliefs interact with a specific rhetorical situation.

Many contemporary scholars have rediscovered practical wisdom in their explorations of narrative rationality. Within rhetoric, Walter Fisher (1987, 2003) has been the primary advocate for a narrative paradigm of rationality, which he describes as similar to Aristotle's concept of practical wisdom. He argues that the fundamental way humans make meaning is through placing specific events, people, and objects into narratives, rather than processing information through analytical logical models. Thus, "narration is the foundational, conceptual configuration of ideas for our species" (1987: 193).

In other fields, scholars such as Ricoeur (1991), MacIntyre (1984), and Bruner (1987, 1990) make similar claims about narrative, particularly in regard to identity formation and self-understanding. A long-standing question for those interested in identity is how people are able to manage the many changes and social/cultural forces in their lives while maintaining a consistent self with agency. Many claim that it is through narrative that people manage the various aspects of their lives to achieve their identities. In *Life in Quest of Narrative* (1991) Ricoeur states:

> It is therefore by means of the imaginative variations of our own ego that we attempt to obtain a narrative understanding of ourselves, the only kind that escapes the apparent choice between sheer change and absolute identity. Between the two lies narrative identity. (33)

Thus, it is through the narrative of our lives that we maintain a sense of continuity or stability but also negotiate the events of our lives and social and cultural influences. Narrative is the nexus of identity.[3] Sociolinguists offer empirical support for this theory through their analyses of narratives used in everyday conversations. They have been able to point out specific narrative strategies that contribute to identity formation (Linde 1993; Schiffrin 1996; Johnstone 1996; Dyer & Keller-Cohen 2000).

Although narrative's well-established relationships with identity and practical wisdom suggest that it could also play a significant role in developing these qualities during ethos construction, narrative usually has been seen by rhetoricians as a tool for logos. In Book 3 of the *Rhetoric*, Aristotle briefly discussed narrative as a way to present facts in a judicial case or as a way to exhibit someone's virtues in epideictic rhetoric. In contemporary theory there is much work on narrative as a type of argument or proof within an argument (Fisher 1984, 1987; Perelman & Olbrechts-Tyteca 1969). Also, Booth's (1961, 1988) well-known work shows us how narratives can bring an audience to accept certain worldviews or ideologies.

This theoretical focus correlates with the tendency of rhetoricians to study planned, formal texts such as political speeches, in which the rhetor uses an implied audience when planning her persuasive strategies and then delivers the set message either in a face-to-face situation or through written texts. The implied audience may or may not correspond with the actual audience, and the rhetor is often uncertain of the reception of the message. The study of unplanned informal

---

3.   This type of identity formation, referring to a sense of selfhood, differs from the identification discussed by Burke, which refers to similarities of characteristics and interests between speaker and audience. However, these ideas are closely related in that the audience tries to perceive the speaker's identity when judging whether or not they identify with her.

discourse, in which interaction with the audience is more immediate, and from which much work on narrative and identity originates, has remained largely the realm of anthropologists, sociolinguists, and discourse analysts.

Thus, convinced that our understanding of ethos can be enriched by narrative theories of identity and self, I offer in this chapter an analysis of discourse that lends itself to studying verbal means of self-presentation – online chat, a form of computer-mediated communication (CMC). Early in its existence, CMC, which usually refers to exchanges between individuals via technologies such as email, instant messaging, and synchronous chat, was recognized as an important new medium, significantly different from spoken, face-to-face interaction or traditional print.[4] Unlike face-to-face conversation, CMC lacks visual cues such as gestures, facial expressions, and appearance that can affect communication. And unlike traditional print, CMC can involve real time interaction. Studies of CMC have grown so that the field now boasts several interdisciplinary peer-reviewed journals and conferences.[5] Rhetoricians and communication scholars see CMC as involving new communication forms in which traditional ideas about rhetoric may need to be revised. And as the internet has become ubiquitous in modern culture, CMC has been studied as part of larger web and networking sites that build virtual communities and constitute new public spheres (Holt 2004; Warnick 2007). In *Rhetoric Online*, Barbara Warnick describes the broad research agenda facing rhetoricians:

> What assumptions about the nature of textual production and the reception of traditional speech and print texts do not hold for texts that are "born digital?" How can existing rhetorical theories be modified and reshaped for the analysis of new media? (2007:26)

The traditional rhetorical concept of ethos especially merits attention in CMC. From the first days of CMC research to the present, identity and self-presentation has been a consistent area of investigation (Geise 1998; Sherman 2001; Walther 1993). Although many of these studies do not use the term "ethos," much of what they study overlaps with what rhetoricians consider ethos. Online identity formation (or ethos) is especially interesting since in certain forms of CMC participants lack prior knowledge of each other and it is likely they will never meet face-to-face. Thus, individuals have the opportunity to create their online personas, distinct from their personas in other forms of interaction. While the research in

---

4. Psychologists performed most of the early studies of CMC, using empirical studies to compare face-to-face and CMC. For an overview of the early studies see Bordia (1997). For an overview of early work within discourse studies see Herring (2002).

5. See *Journal of Computer-Mediated Communication, Human Communication Research, Human-computer Interaction, Computers in Human Behavior.*

this area is rich and informed by different disciplinary perpectives, generally it suggests that online ethos is more negotiated and interactionally developed than rhetoricians' traditional notion of ethos as planned and performed by a speaker. Context, determining social roles and evoking schemas and stereotypes, heavily influences initial impressions. Then, more personal, individual identities are developed through participants' responsiveness, cooperation on tasks, problem solving, and revealing more individualized information in response to the ongoing dialogue (Sherman 2001).

Rhetoricians have also reexamined ethos in online contexts when there is no individual author or source, as with as corporate websites (Warnick 2007) or when one's conversation partner is not human, as in the case of artificial intelligence (Miller 2004). These studies also highlight the inadequacy of our traditional notion of ethos and emphasize the contextual, negotiated nature of online ethos.

In addition to self-presentation and identity, another theme in CMC studies is its use as an educational tool. It is not an overstatement to say that educational institutions everywhere are incorporating more and more technology, including CMC, into pedagogical practice. The spread of CMC in education has been accompanied by an increase in research on its effects. A recent review of educational CMC research found that synchronous CMC, usually chats, helped to build a sense of community and promote interactive learning over asynchronous CMC (Hrastinkski & Keller 2007; also see Hlapanis et al. 2006). The immediate interactivity of synchronous chat encourages the development of interpersonal connections, which naturally build upon perceived individual identities.

Thus, by choosing educational chatroom interaction as the data for this study, we have a discourse in which ethos building is central, but limited to written text. By narrowing the factors contributing to ethos formation to the verbal, we can focus on the relationship between narrative and ethos more clearly. The data also differs significantly from traditional objects of rhetorical study so that we can reconsider traditional ethos in new media. The data analyzed in this study comes from an early (1996 and 1997) use of synchronous chat in a distance education course; at the time, it was truly a "new" medium. Unlike today, when chats are common in various online environments, participants then had little prior synchronous chat experience to draw on in order to negotiate their online ethos. In these chats, we have a relatively unpracticed, spontaneous use of narrative, which can provide a point of reference for studies of later chat interaction.

By analyzing the relationship between narrative and ethos in these educational synchronous chats, this study contributes to understanding identity formation online, narrative strategies in educational chat, and the general relationship between ethos and narrative. Specifically, the study addresses two questions: 1) what kind of ethos do participants of the online chat develop and 2) how does their use of narrative contribute to their ethos?

Dataset

The chat transcripts examined in this study are from four different classes from 1996 and 1997 of a Managing Software Development (MSD) course at Carnegie Mellon University (CMU). This course was part of CMU's core curriculum for the Masters in Software Engineering degree and the Certificate in Software Engineering program. Usually it was one of the first core courses that the students took. Its goal was to give students the skills and knowledge necessary to manage the resources and development of large-scale software products. The class material was broken down into content modules or sections. The students were supposed to go through each module by first doing the reading, then the assignments, watching the videotaped lecture, and finally participating in the chat. Participation in the chat was optional (it did not affect the grade) but all students joined in regularly, although some missed chats occasionally.

The students were professionals in the software engineering field with either advanced degrees or over ten years' professional experience in software development. The prerequisites of the course stated that the students "must have had industrial software engineering experience with a large project, or a comprehensive undergraduate course in software engineering." Some students were local (in Pittsburgh), but the majority of students were spread throughout the United States. None had taken a distance education class before. And finally, the students and instructors never met face-to-face.

The following excerpt from the *Course Companion Guide* introduces the students to the chatroom:

> As a distance education student, you reap the benefits of recent advances in chatroom technology – a technology that offers you a way to communicate in real time through your keyboard and computer with others throughout the world. Imagine-you will be involved in "classroom" discussions with men and women who live thousands of miles away, but who share common interests and concerns about the software development industry. In distance education, the chatroom replaces your professor's office hours, that time before and after class when you clarify a point or ask a question about the class lecture. Additionally, [the instructor] will facilitate discussion on topics requiring your analysis and synthesis of key concepts found in your readings and the videotaped lectures.

The guide clearly set up the social context for the participants; the chat was supposed to function as both office hours and class discussion that they would normally have if they were meeting in a typical face-to-face class. The synchronous, online group interaction provides the students with an opportunity to ask the teacher questions and clarify class points. We can expect that the students participating in the chats would most likely be seeking practical help with understanding course material.

Table 1. Courses, instructors and number of chats analyzed

Course	Instructor	# of chat sessions
October 1996	Teach	21
January 1997	Teach	26
September 1997	Karl	28
May 1997	Karl	19
TOTAL		104

The data of the study consists of the chat transcripts of 4 courses, shown in the Table 1.[6]

General discourse patterns

The initial analysis looked at who spoke and about what. The analysis found that the instructor, "Teach", took 30–79% of the conversation turns (Sacks et al. 1974) in his chats with an average of 47%. Karl, the other instructor, ranged from 28-74.8%, with an average of 44%. No consistent reason was found for why in some chats the instructors spoke often and in others they spoke less frequently. At times they spoke more extendedly to explain concepts or tell stories, while in other chats they did not need to explain anything in detail, only guide discussion. But in either case, *both instructors consistently participated more than any individual student.* Some students tended to participate more than other students (Anne in the 1/97–7/97 course and Chris 1/97–5/98 course) but rates of student participation did not change over time. That is, students did not tend to participate more or less as the course progressed.

Another part of the analysis looked at the topics of discussion. A preliminary study of the chats established four categories of discussion topics: course logistics (such as, "What is due when?" or "What are we doing next?"), chat logistics ("I'm having trouble logging in."), class topic, and small talk. When the entire corpus was studied, class topic consistently dominated each chat session, followed by chat logistics, then course logistics, and least of all, small talk (see Table 2).

Interestingly, the instructors dominated in each topic area, including small talk, not only in the course-related topics. As Table 3 shows, Teach made 43% of the contributions to the total amount of small talk that occurred in his classes while Karl made 35% of those in his classes.

Overall, the quantitative analysis shows that the chats are focused on class topics, indicating that the conversation is task-driven. It also shows that the instruc-

---

6.   The screen names of the instructors and students have been replaced by pseudonyms.

Table 2. Average percentage of topic occurrence in chats

Topic	Average %
Class Topic	71.0%
Chat Logistics	13.5%
Course Logistics	6.5%
Small Talk	9.0%

Table 3. Percentage of total turns by each instructor in each topic area during their courses

Topic	Teach	Karl
Course Logistics	50%	50%
Small Talk	43%	35%
Chat Logistics	56%	48%
Class Topic	46%	44%

tors dominate the conversations overall and in each topic area. The participants seemed to work within the social context set up by the *Course Guide*, suggesting that one aspect of the ethos of the participants will be related to their social roles as teacher and student within a classroom setting.

Other general discourse patterns were found through looking at two particular chat sessions: the April 14, 1997 and December 22, 1997 chats. Each of these occurred about halfway through their respective semesters. In general, the analysis of these two chats supports interpreting the chat interaction as being guided by typical classroom behavior. The participants' behavior corresponded with what would be expected in a classroom in how much they spoke, about what, and in what order.[7] Also, the informal register (Finegan 1994: 365–398; Johnstone 2002: 147–151) suggests they saw each other as peers.

It seems from the general discourse patterns that the participants were quite aware of what they are doing – classroom discussion, and with whom – a teacher and professional peers. Their behavior was appropriate to the context and their audience. The linguistic behavior discussed here is far from a complete picture of the interaction in these chats. However, this analysis shows clearly that the participants follow shared social norms regarding classroom behavior and politeness.

---

7. Turn-taking patterns reflected classroom interaction identified by Sinclair and Brazil (1982) and Heap (1988). Overall topic organization followed lesson themes, as discussed in Green and Wallat (1981).

Narratives

As discussed earlier, sociolinguists, philosophers, and literary theorists have identified narrative as a primary means for the development and expression of identity,
particularly in unplanned discourse.[8] In the analysis of the chats, narratives were
investigated at two levels: micro and macro. At the micro level, I looked at how
the construction of the individual narratives might affect ethos. That is, how the
way the stories are told might influence the speaker's image. Second, at the macro
level, I asked how each narrative functioned in the overall conversation; what
illocutionary force did they have?

Sociolinguists describe narratives as stories in the everyday sense of the word.
William Labov laid out a structure of narrative, which has become foundational
in discourse studies of narrative.[9] He defines "narrative as one method of recapit-
ulating past experience by matching a verbal sequence of clauses to the sequence
of events which (it is inferred) actually occurred" (1972: 359–360). He identified
six features of fully formed narratives: abstract, orientation, complicating action,
evaluations, resolution, and coda. (1972: 363).

Although Labov requires these features to define a full narrative, he acknowledges that there can be narratives that do not express all of these characteristics. He
defines a minimal narrative as a set of clauses containing a single temporal juncture. Carranza (1998) uses a broader definition of a minimal narrative in her study
of narrative and argumentation in conversation. Drawing from the work of narratology, specifically that of Gerald Prince, she argues that narrativity is a "question
of degree." An utterance may be more or less narrative depending upon how fully
it meets the criteria of stories. She lists the conditions, taken from Prince, that
determine a text's narrativity:

1.   represents non-trivial, discrete, specific and positive events occurring at dif-
     ferent times and having a meaning in terms of a human project,
2.   depicts a conflict between two opposites,
3.   constitutes a structure with a beginning, a middle, and an end, and
4.   its audience recognizes a narrative quality in it thus contributing to the inter-
     pretation and development of the text. (1998: 288)

The degree to which a narrative fulfills these conditions determines its narrativity.
Carranza's study looks at narratives whose time frames do not fully meet the first

---

8.   In sociolinguistics, see Schiffrin (1996), Linde (1993), in psychology, Bruner (1986), in
philosophy, Taylor (1989), MacIntyre (1984), and Ricouer (1991).

9.   For review and criticism of his work see the special issue of *Journal of Narrative and Life
History* 1997. 7: 1–4.

criterion listed above. In her analysis, hypothetical or future events also count as narratives, although with a low degree of narrativity.

Similar to Carranza's minimal narratives are "small stories" that involve discourse with narrative elements or a narrative orientation. These are bits of narrative told in passing during everyday talk, such as condensed references to shared experiences, hypothetical stories, and even refusals to tell. Bamberg (2004) and Georgakopoulou (2006) have argued for the relevance of small stories for narrative research, especially in relation to issues of self and identity. Recognizing small narratives in everyday talk opens the way to understanding how people manage their sense of self in interactive discourse. Also, according to Georgakopoulou, valuing small stories marks a "new narrative turn" moving from traditional studies of full life stories that implied a unified, coherent self to highlighting changing, contingent, negotiated selves (2006:128). This study of chatroom discourse looks for Labov's full narratives, minimal narratives[10] and small stories.

For example,[11] in the November 24, 1997 chat, the first comment by Elton is a narrative. He is complaining about the lack of knowledge on the part of a manager.

(1)

1.	Elton:	*The SA manager asked the other day what C/S stands for ?*
2.	Nelson:	I am sure there must be a "Dilbert" for that
3.	Karl:	Well, I can think of several things it could stand for...
4.	Jake:	Elton: C/S usually stands for Client/Server?
5.	Elton:	Thanks Karl?
6.	Elton:	I know Jake. that's my very point. She did not know that. Yet is responsible for testing my C/S apps.
7.	Nelson:	Ask to see here test plan
8.	Karl:	Horror stories from the trenches... anyone want to try to top this one? :)
9.	Elton:	Should I get another job? (ops sorry this is not a consoling session!)
10.	Jake:	Yes, Her's

Table 4 indicates the number of narratives found in the chats of each course.

---

10. An event in a minimal narrative will be understood as an occurrence of some phenomenon interpreted and given meaning by the speaker. The event may have a historical foundation or it may refer to hypothetical or habitual events (Prince 1982; Carranza 1998).

11. All excerpts from transcripts appear as it did to the participants with two exceptions. The names of the students and teachers have been changed to protect privacy. Also, narratives discussed in the analysis are italicized, bolded or underlined.

Table 4. Number of narratives in each course[12]

Course	# of chats	# of narratives
October 1996	21	7
January 1997	26	43
September 1997	28	34
May 1997	19	10

Narrative micro-level strategies

The micro analysis, which looked at the internal structure of the chat narratives, revealed several rhetorical strategies that contributed to the ethos of participants. These strategies, including positioning, display of agentive and epistemic selves, and individual style, are drawn from the work of psychologists, sociologists, and sociolinguists interested in identity construction. This section will describe each of these strategies as found in the chats and how they contribute to ethos.

Positioning

Positioning refers to how speakers express the relationships among characters in stories. Davies and Harré (1990) define it as "the discursive process whereby selves are located in conversations as observably and subjectively coherent participants in jointly produced story lines" (1990: 2). Speakers can position themselves in relation to events and others. For example, they can be the agent or victim of some event. Such positioning contributes to the overall character they portray in their discourse.

In the chats, participants used various positioning strategies. The most obvious strategy was to refer to themselves as "we," indicating they were members of the same class or as software engineers. Other times "we" referred to the speaker and his/her company. Participants consistently did not identify themselves with "users," "managers," and "clients." Another common strategy was taking on responsibility for actions that would be viewed positively by the others. Example (2) is a sample from the February 10, 1997 chat session that highlights one student's positioning of himself in a narrative–a positioning which supports a positive, professional ethos.

---

12.   Of note in Table 4 is the high number of narratives in the January and September 1997 chats. Each of those courses had one student (Anne and Chris, respectively) who was particularly chatty. They participated often and for long turns, telling more narratives than other participants. In the other two courses, October 1996 and May 1997, no students stood out as more vocal than the others.

(2)

1. Teach: how are most requirements represented in your organizations?
2. Elton: *At West Publishing, as a technical writer, I received a large packet that described the application functions*
3. Teach: described" in what form?
4. Tim: They are documented in what we call a requirements document.
5. Teach: and "documented" in what form?
6. Elton: *It included proposed screen shots. The form was, this is the blah screen. The foo button does goo.*
7. Elton: *The document usually formed the starting point to a round-about method of development*
8. Teach: what made it round-about?
9. Elton: *The people that wrote it were somewhat high level. It was unclear where the input came from to form their document.*
10. Teach: Jade, you did DoD 2167 stuff, right?
11. Elton: *Working on it, we had other ideas and shaped the program to be a mix of what they initially thought would work and what we later learned would work.*
12. Jade: missed that one – I was a chemE in that life
13. Teach: how did you learn, from the development process itself, or in some other way?
14. Elton: DoD 2167? We were a private commercial company tailoring to the legal community.
15. Tim: I am somewhat familar with DoD 2167.
16. Elton: *The process was through spheres of influence. I affected change cause I played basketball with the lead programmer. I brought him interface suggestions, and if he liked them, they went in.*

In this part of the chat the instructor, Teach, has asked the students how requirements are represented in the students' companies. A student's response could have been purely descriptive, a report on company practice. In this case, Elton responds with a personal narrative beginning with how he experiences representations of requirements; "I received a large packet." He goes on to describe a typical process in which requirements are represented and makes a critical evaluation: "the document usually formed the starting point to a round-about method." He follows the evaluation with a description of the process and presents it as problematic. Finally, he tells how he helps resolve the problem: "I affected change cause I played basketball with the lead programmer." This narrative follows the typical pattern of narratives as described by Labov (1972): abstract (the question), orientation (description of the document), complicating action (why it was round-about), evaluation, and resolution (Elton affects change through basketball).

With regard to ethos, Elton's positioning of himself in the story is notable. Initially he is passive in the story: "I received a large packet" and he distances himself from the document: "*The people* that wrote it"; "*it was unclear* where the input came from to form *their* document." When there is a move toward a solution Elton suddenly has agency and authority as part of a group: "*we* had other ideas ...what *we* later learned would work." Finally, in the resolution of the conflict Elton is the solitary agent in solving the problem: "*I* affected change cause *I* played basketball." Through this narrative, Elton distances himself from persons and things that are problematic and identifies himself with the solution, showing himself to be a competent and effective professional. Such positioning would not be possible in a simple description or report. Throughout the chats the participants find opportunities through narrative, as Elton has here, to show themselves as performing well professionally and judging principles of their discipline correctly.

Evaluation
Another characteristic of individual narratives that contributes to ethos is evaluation. Speakers can make implicit or explicit comments that express how they feel about others in the story or about the point of the story – is it a good thing, bad, puzzling? What value does the speaker give to the story? Labov offers this definition of evaluation: "Evaluation of a narrative event is information on the consequences of the event for human needs and desires" (1997:403).

Speakers can implicitly make evaluations through some action in the stories. For example, I can tell my colleagues a story of a student who has been habitually irresponsible begging for a better grade and then I refuse, without much discussion, to improve his grade. I show through my action that I do not think the student deserves a better grade due to his irresponsibility. Bruner (1986) calls this a display of the "agentive self." In this case, my agentive self is one that does not have much sympathy for students whom I consider irresponsible. I might, on the other hand simply state that I think the student doesn't deserve a better grade. Bruner calls an explicitly stated evaluation a display of "epistemic self." In example (3) Amy tells a short story and then evaluates it.

(3)

1. Teach: any personal experiences as examples?
2. Elton: Where I worked, we tried to establish standards to new hires could fit in quickly.
3. Amy: *We're currently writing and adopting a new process. Looking at the IEEE Standards shows us how little process we were actually engaging in.*
4. Arnold: I once spent weeks developing development standards which were never used
5. Arnold: they were only requested to satisfy an auditor.

6. Elton: The standards we created were too specific and changed from project to project
7. Amy: *The training issue is really important, in my experience.*
8. Amy: *I'm tasked with both writing standards and applying them to a pilot project. It's very painful!*

Amy ends with the comment "It's very painful!" This comment acts as an evaluation of her story that she both writes and applies standards. Her point is that doing both is difficult or too much work.

As evaluation demonstrates how a person feels toward an event, others can interpret what value the speaker is drawing on to make the evaluation; it demonstrates a judgment. Depending upon how acceptable the value is to the audience, such an evaluation will strengthen or weaken the speaker's ethos. If someone listening to Amy habitually writes and applies standards (what she is complaining about) without much difficulty, her evaluation, "It's very painful!" might elicit a negative reaction from that person. On the other hand, if the audience agrees that it is a difficult task, her evaluation would probably elicit a positive response.

On another level evaluation can contribute to ethos by expressing individual commitment to a point or strength of feeling. Daiute and Nelson (1997) studied stories by children and found that evaluations help children have ownership of their stories. As children adapt cultural scripts to express their own experience they often use evaluation to particularize their stories and give them "their" stamp. Through their study, Daiute and Nelson came to the conclusion that "evaluation serves as a context for development of self through the interpretive force of explicitly stated evaluation"(1997: 210). Evaluations allow for the expression of speakers' values and also show their level of personal involvement or ownership of the story. In other words, evaluations give the audience another means by which to judge the ethos of speakers through showing the strength of their beliefs and commitments.

In the story below, example (4), Joanne tells about her experience as the new configuration manager for a project. Throughout the telling of the story she makes evaluative comments.

(4)

1. Joanne: II am the NEW configuration Manager for this project.
2. Joanne: *I am always getting, what do you mean I have to wait a week!!!*
3. Todd: I am the only change management process where i work
4. Joanne: *I gave you the file and I know it works.*
5. Teach: great, two gatekeepers
6. Joanne: *I could go on forever, but I won't*
7. Teach: what do they wait the week for?
8. Todd: The only CM we do is small Scope documents that bullet point items that will be included in a release and those that may be defered

9. Dan: requirements tracebility
10. Joanne: *For me to rebuild the code in CM, test it and write up the release notes.*
11. Joanne: *Also create the installation package.*
12. Joanne: *Yes I MUST MUST MUST test the code again.*
13. Joanne: *Having it work in the developers space means NOTHING!*
14. Teach: so we have Todd doing some version control and some data storage of potential changes,
15. Teach: and we have Joanne doing some release prep and final QA
16. Todd: If you call my white board and a flip chart data storage, {it is a process, though}
17. Teach: yes, Todd, I do – how does Joanne's testing fit in with the CM process?
18. Joanne: *I also have to decide what changes get added to which release.*
19. Joanne: *I do not give it a systems test, just a quick does it work test.*
20. Joanne: *After the change is put a testing area for the real testers.*
21. Teach: like a use would
22. Teach: user
23. Joanne: *Basically, if I know it doesn't work, there is no sense sending it to the tester.*

Joanne is emphatic about the need for testing. She shows this through what she says and how she manipulates type, "Yes I MUST MUST MUST test the code again...Having it work in the developers space means NOTHING." By this kind of evaluation Joanne demonstrates her deep personal conviction about the point being made. She is not simply stating a general professional guideline, but rather a principle she holds very dearly. She shows individual belief, a professional authoritativeness, and personal experience, all of which can contribute to her ethos as an experienced professional who is serious and conscientious about her work.

Collaborative narratives

Recognizing stories that are collaboratively constructed highlights the interactional nature of discourse (Schegloff 2001). When the participants weave a story together they are working cooperatively, being responsive to each other and taking up each other's contributions to the conversation. This kind of behavior contributes to ethos in a less direct way than strategies such as positioning and evaluation. Cooperatively working together implies a mutual respect and regard for each other's thoughts and opinions, showing goodwill. Usually, working cooperatively strengthens group ties. In contrast, breaking from the methods of group work distances speakers from their audience. For example, in her study of a dinner party conversation, Tannen (1984) found that when speakers used like methods in their story rounds, rapport developed; when participants broke from the established norm for rounds, others distanced themselves from the speaker.

Neal Norrick's work (1997) looks at the function of collaborative storytelling of stories well known by speaker and audience. For example, he examines retellings of the story of a family gathering by those who were at that gathering. He focuses on the retelling of shared experiences, noting that there is little referential reason to tell the story (everyone already knows what happened), but rather the story is told explicitly to build group rapport. In addition to seeing collaborative storytelling as strengthening group ties, he notes that collaboration strengthens the feeling of belonging among all the participants. They verify and strengthen each other's group membership by recognizing their right to and value in participating in building the story. Thus, collaboration can support ethos by showing that one is respectful of others and by strengthening in-group bonds through agreed-upon methods of interaction.

In addition to building good will through working successfully together, collaboratively building a story draws upon and develops shared values. As seen in the chat examples, at times the point of a story is not initially clear or agreed-upon by everyone. But as the story gets negotiated, participants come to agree on the theme. Through this process they create shared values or reveal already shared common ground. Thus, collaboration serves ethos in two ways: good will through working successfully together and by building stronger agreed-upon social standards from their profession.

In example (5) below, initially there are two participants, Teach and George. They are discussing QFD (Quality Function Deployment), a technique to translate customer needs into technical specifications. Teach isn't sure about when to use it. In the first part of the exchange Teach presents a hypothetical narrative in order to explain why he is not comfortable with using it: "…you are sort of forcing yourself to look for implementation functions early on…." He then presents further narratives, ("two things came up recently") to show that he is not decided on QFD's value.

(5)

1.	Teach:	I wanted to see what people thought about it as a requirements refinement tool
2.	Teach:	do you know where it is used the most?
3.	George:	I have no experience with it and don't know where it is used most
4.	Teach:	near as I can tell, the two most frequent uses are right after architectural design
5.	Teach:	and also sometimes as a specification tool
6.	Teach:	*the thing that bothered me, even as I was talking about it,*
7.	Teach:	*is that you are sort of forcing yourself to look for implementation functions early on*
8.	Teach:	*and these may accidentally be confused with a real design, even though the thought processes were nil*

9.   George: I can see the value of the matrix, but agree with the premature design features id

10. Teach: *two things came up recently that might change the way I talk/think about this*

11. George: If the customer need is agreed to, it is helpful

12. Teach: *yes, it is easier for the average customer.*

13. Teach: *one thing is that COCOMO 2.0 is coming out with a three- phase estimation process*

14. George: whch three?

15. Teach: *first phase: object points, second phase : function points, third phase: LOC*

16. Teach: *but the object points thing is what got my attention*

17. Teach: *it is not "objects" in the OOA/OOD sense*

18. Teach: *unless, of course, you are using those*

19. George: ok. the three phase approach makes sense and may help resolve some of the conflicts some of our business customers have with LOC and function point estimates

20. Teach: *right...especially relating LOC and FP*

Teach describes the new process. He begins tentatively and allows George (underlined) to state the main point of how it will be a better process. George assists Teach in building this story and determining the theme. The exchange continues with Elton joining in:

21. Elton: Can you clarify what he means by object points as compared to function points

22. Teach: *near as I can tell from the early papers, object points are counted*

23. Teach: *when you have some logical object, like "user interface object"*

24. Teach: *so, if there is a single page/screen/window of UI with buttons and fileds, etc. That one thing is the object and the number of points relates to how much functionality*

25. Teach: *make sense?*

26. Elton: So object points is a way to more accurately determine function points?s

27. Teach: *nope, still different*

28. Amy: **Or are the three phases increasingly less abstract and finer granularity?**

29. Elton: So the object c\gets a count seperate from the function points.

30. Teach: *Amy has nailed it....that was the idea*

Again, Teach presents the process in an exploratory manner with a hypothetical story, ("so if there is a single page/screen/window...") and allows a student to interpret the main point (Amy, in bold). Teach is thinking aloud in a sense, trying to figure something out. The students try to find the point of his narratives in order to understand what he is getting at. Teach could have just said, "two things bother me...1)...2)..." Instead, he takes his students through his thought processes and they help elicit the points of the narratives.

In the classroom chats, the collaborative narratives sometimes have a main storyteller whose story evolves according to the questions asked by the others. At other times Teach will lead students to construct a story that demonstrates a class point, even though the student may not see the point initially. Finally, stories can be offered as a way to figure something out and participants interpret events to help the main storyteller come to a conclusion and understand the point.

Individual style
Finally of note are the individual stylistic differences in language use that can contribute to ethos (Johnstone 1996). In the following example, example (6), both Liz and Amy tell stories, but in very different ways.

(6)

1. Edith: What has been your experience in planning? To what level of detail do you go?
2. Amy: *In my jobs, I planned to the granularity of about 1 person-week's worth of work.*
3. Amy: *Sometimes finer, sometimes coarser. parts of the project.*
4. Edith: How fine is fine? Did this cause you any troubles?
5. Liz: We generally look at the contract deliverable list, and estimate by person-weeks, like Amy does.
6. Amy: Sometimes I'll plan even a couple-hour task, if it results in a deliverable.
7. Edith: Tausworth shows the math to prove that about one week chunks are right. Any more & you get lost in updating the plan
8. Amy: *I'm in an FDA-controlled industry, and so we have to put lots of documents in special files.*
9. Amy: *I often put them in a schedule so I don't forgot to do them, even though they may take a couple of hours!*
10. Liz: Often run into problems with scheduling programs like MS Project, trying to control partial assignment of resources. For example, if a person has to work 2 tasks simultaneously, and may have to stop and restart.
11. Edith: The really small tasks can be tracked on checklists...but it's important too have a deliverable fo r everyone every week.
12. Amy: *I really dislike that about MS Project. How do you represent working on several tasks part time?*
13. Liz: Agreed that anything more granular than a week generates more updates for the person managing the schedule.
14. Edith: There's a hack to do it–will write you if no one remembers off the top of her head.

15. Amy: That would be great, Edith. I'd really appreciate it.
16. Liz: <u>Usually have to specify percentage of the resource applied to a task, but it easily degenerates into very detailed manipulations on a large project.</u>
17. Edith: Even more than the updates is keeping the plan up to date when things slip.
18. Liz: <u>Since MS Project can view the information from different perspectives, i.e., use of a resource, you can (and must) always check to ensure you are not overtasking someone.</u>
19. Amy: *Or when people just ignore the schedule. That is my biggest problem!*
20. Liz: :-) Don't we all
21. Amy: *Oh, I mean the people working for me ignore the schedule. I don't ignore it, I just watch it slip and get tense!*
22. Amy: :)
23. Liz: <u>We had an inexperienced person in charge of the schedule, and when she was told to add some milestones and deliverables, she simply added 2 days for writing a paper, ignoring the fact that the person was already tasked somewhere else.</u>
24. Edith: I find i have to discuss it with every one each week –but it seems pretty overwhelming if it's too detailed.
25. Liz: <u>When you look at the resource allocation, the person ended up working over 24 hours a day, during certain periods!</u>
26. Amy: *My problem is I have responsibility without power. But I'm sure that's a topic for another day!*

Amy and Liz tell stories in response to the same question, "What has been your experience in planning?" But their narrative styles are quite different. Amy's is much more personal than Liz's. A simple indication of this is their positioning, seen through their use of personal pronouns. In this exchange Amy uses "I" ten times and "my" twice. Liz, on the other hand, never uses "I" or "my." Instead, Liz uses "we" twice. Amy places herself as the protagonist in her story, making it a personal story. Liz's "we" refers to her company, which distances her from the actions she describes. And often, Liz does not use any agent in her narrative, even though there is an implied subject. For example, "Usually have to specify percentage of the resource applied to the task..." When she makes her thematic point she uses the universal "you": "When you look at the resource allocation, the person ended up working over 24 hours a day, during certain periods!" Even though this event is one particular to her experience – it is not a common phenomenon in her field, but rather a result of her particular circumstances – she does not make herself an actor in the narrative, but implies a generalized experience. Compare Liz's thematic point with Amy's: "My problem is I have responsibility without power." The point of her story is a personal one. Also, Amy makes four evaluations in this exchange while Liz makes one. Although their topics are the same, how they plan their work, Amy's story is very much *her* story, about her experience and how she feels about it. Liz's story is less personal, more generalized and objective.

Individual stylistic choices in narrative indicate careful rhetorical strategies for projecting oneself (Johnstone 1996, 2002). Even though we may view Amy as portraying a stronger self than Liz in this exchange, both participants' style can contribute to their respective ethos by giving us a sense of their individual personalities. Individual style demonstrates in part, the uniqueness and humanness of the speakers. The positive connection between individual style and ethos has to do with the importance of individuality (in Western cultures) for a sense of selfhood and "moral and epistemic authority" (Johnstone 2002: 26). In the chats, individual style contributes to the professional, collegial ethos of the participants by contributing to their more general ethos as individuals.

Overall, the participants used several strategies at the micro level to develop ethos. Through positioning themselves and others in the narratives, speakers set up relationships among the characters and themselves. These relationships usually aligned the speakers with positive characters and values and distanced them from negative ones. Another method of ethos building was through collaboratively building the narratives. By working together to tell a story with a common theme, the participants demonstrated and developed common values and built rapport. Also, through evaluation, speakers emphasized their feeling or commitment to the point of the stories they told. Finally, speakers had individual story telling styles, which revealed some of their individual personality.

Narrative macro-level strategies

The macro level analysis took each narrative as a whole and asked what function it served in the overall conversation. The focus here was on the action performed by the narratives rather than on their content. In the classroom chats, narratives functioned in the following ways:

1. sharing a personal story
2. establishing common ground or pointing to a shared ideological outlook
3. providing evidence for a claim
4. illustrating a class point from one's own experience
5. presenting a problem case for analysis

Sharing a personal story
"Personal stories" were identified as those that were non-class related and which revealed some personal information that would not be known otherwise. Usually these were volunteered, rather than being solicited. In example (7) from the April 7, 1997 chat two personal stories are offered. The participants in this exchange are

Teach, the teacher of the course, and two students, Laurie and Arnold. It occurs in the first few minutes of the chat session, after Teach welcomes Laurie back from a trip. He begins the exchange by suggesting that they should have tried getting her connected to the chatroom while she was in-flight:

(7)

1.	Teach:	I was sorry we could have tried you with a laptop and an in-flight phone just to see if it works
2.	Laurie:	*Teach – I was on such a tiny airplane – it had no modern conveniences. The pilot told us to sit in the back in order to distribute the weight!!*
3.	Laurie:	*Also – alarms kept going off – very nerve-wracking*
4.	Teach:	what was the airline?
5.	Teach:	Horizon?
6.	Laurie:	United Express
7.	Laurie:	Horizon is much better.
8.	Teach:	definitely
9.	Teach:	actually, the little commuter jobs have lots of automated warning stuff
10.	Laurie:	It is good to have automated warnings but your passengers should not be able to hear them !
11.	Teach:	<u>I was up in Pgh International Tower last Thursday morning when a commuter aborted his takeoff because he had an alarm</u>
12.	Teach:	<u>didn't even know what the alarm was until he pulled over onto a taxiway</u>
13.	Teach:	very true, there is only a stall alarm in the planes I fly the most,
14.	Laurie:	Now I would really hate to hear a stall alarm.
15.	Teach:	<u>and if you make a near-perfect landing, it ought to squeak just as you touch down</u>
16.	Teach:	<u>the passengers panic even though by that time our wheels are rolling on the runway</u>
17.	Arnold:	Teach how long have you been Flying?
18.	Teach:	<u>it's only been since WWII that the stall warnings got really installed....before that your first wanring was when it changed from sky to ground out the front windshield</u>
19.	Teach:	I finally got enough money together in 1990

Laurie responds to Teach's initial suggestion by explaining why it would not have worked, "…it [the plane] had no modern conveniences" (Line 3). She then goes into detail about her flight experience and makes an evaluation of that experience (Lines 3–4). In this short narrative Laurie shares a personal experience with Teach. She could have simply written that she would not have been able to get online while on such a small plane. Instead she elaborates on the tinniness and lack of modern conveniences by telling how they were asked to distribute the weight and how alarms kept going off. For her, the alarms were especially disturbing ("…very nerve-wracking). Her follow-up comments reiterate her dislike for alarms (11, 15). Teach shares a story related to Laurie's (12–13) but then continues with a narrative about flying in general (14, 16–18, 20), sharing an insight into his hobby. In both these personal narratives we learn something about the speakers that we would not have known otherwise. Laurie had a nerve-wracking experience on a small plane and does not like plane alarms. Teach flies planes as a hobby.

In personal stories one can demonstrate certain admirable qualities or display specific knowledge. In Teach's narrative he reveals himself as a pilot and demonstrates knowledge of flying when he discusses how landing *should* sound and when he refers to the history of plane alarms. While this might not contribute directly to his ethos as teacher of the course, it does give the impression of someone who has an interesting hobby and who knows what he is talking about when he discusses planes. In a sense he is displaying some 'expert' knowledge in a field outside of software development, which can contribute to his overall ethos.

Laurie's story supports ethos in a less direct way. She tells us that she had a bad experience on a plane and especially dislikes plane alarms. This seems like an instance of pure "autobiographical impulse"(Rosen 1988) – Laurie needing to tell her story. But what does this story do for her conversation partners in terms of their impression of her? At the very least it adds practical knowledge about Laurie. On another level, by sharing her story with others she invites them into her world, sharing her experience and impressions of that world with her. Such an act can help build rapport among people since it indicates an openness to be known rather than someone who wants to be personally distant. Also, offering a story of one's experience is often interpreted as an invitation to receive a story, as can be seen by Teach's follow-up story. (Swapping stories will be discussed in the next section.) This openness to sharing and interaction is a sign of good will, one of the qualities Aristotle required for ethos.[13]

Establishing common ground

We can interpret the previous example not only as Laurie and Teach offering personal stories, but also as Teach responding to Laurie's story in an effort to establish common ground. Teach acknowledges Laurie's story, and its theme, by telling his own story with a similar theme. By affirming each other's themes, story swapping explicitly points to shared values and ideas, allowing speakers to identify with one another. Chat participants commonly used narratives in this way, thereby establishing good will with their conversation partners.

---

13.   Of course story-telling could backfire. One might talk too much about oneself or tell a story which gives a negative impression (Tannen 1984:99). In my study of these chatrooms, stories did not seem to elicit negative responses. The common practice was of some follow-up or affirmation of the story theme by others.

In example (8) from the November 10, 1997 chat, Marian is trying to figure out a specific process (1). Karl, the instructor explains it to her (2).

(8)

1. Marian: actually, I can't seem to understand how lines of code written in the languages cocomo was designed for relate to the GUI/case products programmers use today

2. Karl: So, Marian, what you need to figure out is what relative amount of complexity each table, form, report, etc., adds to the system, then calibrate the schedule/effort equations from there

3. Marian: wouldn't your coefficients and powers change

4. Karl: yes

5. Marian: thanks :)

6. Karl: *Marian: trust me, I know what you're going through... I'm trying to re-do FP to be based on Rumbaugh OMT artifacts rather than EI, EO, etc...*

7. Marian: gotta love it!!

After Karl's explanation he then adds a short narrative in (6). In this instance he is not only sharing common ground, but also expressing a good intention toward her in an effort to help her feel understood, "I know what you are going through."

In example (9) from the December 1, 1997 chat, Karl and Nelson swap stories that have a common theme. Karl is talking about the plans for his upcoming wedding:

(9)

1. Karl: We plan on doing without some frills to make sure we have extra for the photographer

2. Nelson: Good idea

3. Karl: The scary thing... so far, we have the same ideas and priorities.

4. Nelson: I know, what that is like. I'm on my second time around and its such a difference

5. Karl: *Going back to risk analysis – the first thing that ran through my mind when she outdoor wedding wasn't "oh, that sounds nice" but "won't it be too hot?"*

6. Nelson: I have a military background. Once we went on a picnic and I did not loke the spote becase there were no exit routes and the killing zones were poor

7. Karl: :)

8. Karl: so contingency planning should be a reflex reaction for you now, right?

9. Nelson: Yeah right!!!! ;-)

In Line 5 Karl relates the discussion of his wedding plans back to a class topic–risk analysis. He gives a short narrative of what went through his mind (actually quoting himself) when his fiancé mentioned an outdoor wedding. The point of the story seems to be that he automatically does risk analysis, a process in software development, even in those areas of his life far removed from software development. Nelson responds to Karl's story with his own (6), demonstrating the same point about using a professional process in a personal situation. Karl indicates that he appreciates the point of the story and its humor by using a smiley face emoticon, and then explicitly stating the point of the story (8). Nelson then affirms that they understand each other with his emphatic, "Yeah right!!! ;-)".

This exchange of stories does not serve to further discussion of a class topic even though the themes are related to risk analysis. What it does do is build rapport and common ground between Karl and Nelson. Through their stories they show that they have an experience in common. They can identify with each other's tendency to export professional process to personal life, a tendency, which is not negative, but rather humorous.

Another function of narratives was to exchange "horror stories". These were usually stories from the participants' professional lives recounting some difficulty or bad practice – something that frustrated them. In example 1 from November 24, 1997, which we saw earlier, Elton complains about the lack of knowledge on the part of the manager.

(1)

1. Elton: *The SA manager asked the other day what C/S stands for?*
2. Nelson: I am sure there must be a "Dilbert" for that
3. Karl: Well, I can think of several things it could stand for...
4. Jake: Elton: C/S usually stands for Client/Server ?
5. Elton: Thanks Karl?
6. Elton: I know Jake. that's my very point. She did not know that. Yet is responsible for testing my C/S apps.
7. Nelson: Ask to see here test plan
8. Karl: Horror stories from the trenches... anyone want to try to top this one? :)
9. Elton: Should I get another job? (ops sorry this is not a consoling session!)

The actual narrative here is only in line 1. Elton simply recounts a question by the SA manager, not elaborating or being explicit about the point of the story. Regardless, Nelson gets the point right away, expressing his understanding in his comment that "there must be a Dilbert for that" (2). One of the primary themes of the Dilbert comic strip is the ignorance and incompetence of managers. In Elton's story, the manager's question is demonstrating a lack of knowledge that is considered ridiculous. Nelson's and Karl's responses confirm the point of the story and affirm a shared perspective.

In the May 4, 1997 chat, frustration with management is again the theme of a story:

(10)

1. Karl: *I won't name the company... but once upon a time, there was a manager*
            on a project located near ours...
2. Karl: *... he'd go in late at night and change everyone's files*
3. Chris: Psycho
4. Karl: pretty much

Again this is a short, simple narrative, which recounts an action by a manager. Karl's situating of the story (1) in keeping the company anonymous and beginning with "once upon a time" indicate that what he is about to tell should be interpreted as a story of some note, particularly negative. Chris immediately understands the point of the story (3) – interpreting the actions of the manager as Karl meant them to be interpreted (4).

Sharing these horror stories highlights a shared ideological outlook. In these cases, the ineptitude or misconduct of managers, which is a common difficulty faced by the students of the Managing Software development course. These stories show the speakers "identify[ing] with the audience...sharing and affirming their [other participants'] prejudices" (Kinneavy & Warshaurer 1994:176), which contributes to ethos through an expression of good will.

The last three functions I will discuss, providing evidence for a claim, illustrating a class point, and presenting a problem case for analysis, all rely on the participants' personal experience to make a contribution to the class discussion.

Providing evidence
At times narratives served as evidence to support claims. Class discussion often dealt with good practices for managing software development – which processes were most efficient and accurate. Students and teachers often used their own work experience as evidence for some claim regarding a good or bad practice. In the October 20, 1997 chat, example 11, they discussed a method of how to plan a system. Some suggest that they use a "User Manual" method, that is, have the manual written first and then build the system, using the manual as the guideline. Jake offers his opinion of this suggestion:

(11)

1. Jake: *Regarding the User Manual as an easy-to-read requirements doc (the*
            comic book approach?) I have designed and built systems where I hadn't
            the foggiest idea of what it was going to look like or ...
2. Karl: The user's manual approach works in the case where a system is described by its features/user tasks. Control systems or other automated systems may not work as well...

3. Chris: That thinking will inevidibly change when the function is difficult to implent or is impractical.
4. Jake: *what the breakdown of user functionality was going to be until I was well into the design phase. I just don't see it (User Manual) working for new systems. It is a romantic idea, though.*

In lines 1 and 4 Jakes tells a narrative about how he designed systems. His experience was that at times user functionality (the necessary information to write a user manual) could not be known until he was well into the design phase. He offers this experience as evidence for the claim "I just don't see it (User Manual) working for new systems" (4).

Illustrating a class point from one's own experience
A common use of narrative in these chats was to illustrate some class topic from one's own experience. Often the teacher introduces a topic and then asks what experience people have had with it. In the following example from November 3, 1997, the teacher brings up a topic and the students offer their experiences unsolicited. The topic, "maximum parallelization" and "over-optimistic analysis," refers to a method of scheduling work for a software development project.

(12)

1. Karl: there are some other causes... the idea of maximum parallelization and over-optimistic analysis
2. Jake: *I once had a totally successful project (on time, on budget, no bugs). How I did it was spending a lot of time structuring architecture & tasks down to the very lowest level.*
3. Rich: over estimation is big, people like to be heros
4. Jake: *Not many projects you have the time to do that again.*
5. elton: I belive in "buffers". Build the plus/minus into each task.
6. Karl: Maximum parallelization: the idea that there is a minimum project duration no matter how much parallel development you do
7. Warren: I am in the midst of a pretty good workplan and the key was minimizing sequential constraints, and getting estimates from the analysts, and adding contingency for risk
8. Karl: Warren: I'd love to live in that world more often...
9. Martin: How can you possibly estimate accurately without having done a similar project for comparison?
10. elton: In a project I am managing I am using the "component" concept. Build the project frame work based on component. and let each component owner estimate duration...
11. elton: ... for each component...

12. Warren: Seems like a good approach Elton, do you add anything to their estimates?

13. Karl: Over-optimism: estimates are LOW much more often than they're HIGH – people naturally tend to assume that everything WILL take no longer than what it SHOULD take if all goes "right"

14. Martin: That's what we're doing, but each component estimation is an educated guess.

15. Nelson: You don't have to have a similar project. If you re estimating at the task level, you only need to have a similar task and then build the dependencies

16. Martin: That's true.

17. Karl: Martin: staying within a somewhat similar domain is generally an inherent assumption in estimation processes

In Line 1 Karl introduces the topic and later defines the concepts of "maximum parallelization"(6) and "over-optimism" (13). Jake offers a "success story" from his personal experience (2) and comments on its rarity (4). Warren then tells about his current situation (7), offering it as a positive example of good scheduling, which Karl acknowledges (8). Elton also tells about a current project (10) in which he uses a specific scheduling method, "component concept," and explains what it is.

Presenting a problem case for analysis
Finally, participants also used narratives to present problem cases for discussion or to introduce questions. The class topic being discussed when the following exchange occurs is creating plans. Victor brings up a common problem he has.

(13)

1. Victor: One of the common problems I face when creating plans is...

2. Victor: to show an assignment with gaps in time..

3. Victor: *For example, resource A wants to work on an assignment few hours a week and takes up another assignment and comes back to the original assignment for some more weeks.*

4. Warren: Can you schedule the task for three weeks and the resource at 20%?

5. Karl: That shouldn't be a problem – schedule the resource for only when (s)he is available.

6. Karl: The task itself (in PERT terms) will have a start and end date corresponding to the actual calendar time, but the amount of effort allocated should be pro-rated.

7. Victor: But In MS Project, (Version 4.1) we can't show broken gantt bar for an assignment...can we?

Victor presents a problem he often experiences (1)–(2) and uses a narrative to give an example (3).

Throughout the chats participants used narratives of their professional experience to provide evidence, illustrate a class point, or present a problem case. The narratives were a *means of reasoning* about class topics. Such reasoning reflects practical wisdom, in which "the content of rational choice must be supplied by nothing less messy than experience and stories of experience" (Nussbaum 1990:74) so as to achieve the good life. In the chats, participants actively contributed to the goals of the discussion by quickly applying their experience to the problems being discussed. In this case, logos and ethos are inseparable. Stories of experience also contribute to ethos by showing expertise and authority. In a study of electronic support groups, Galegher et al. found that members groups "draw authority from their ability to connect their own experiences with the problem presented by other people in the group" (1998:501). Thus, by effectively using stories of their experience to work through class topics, the participants demonstrated practical wisdom, expertise, and authority.

Discussion

This study investigated ethos formation in an unplanned, informal, text-based context, an online classroom chat. The analysis found that part of the participants' ethos related to their roles as instructor and students. Participants relied on the social context, a classroom discussion, and the corresponding social roles to guide their general behavior. Discourse patterns followed those of face-to-face classroom discussion with the instructors guiding the discussion and students responding to their prompts.

Within the general patterns of classroom behavior, participants used narratives to demonstrate more specific qualities of character. Through strategic positioning, evaluations, and stylistic choices, speakers portrayed their positive behavior, revealed personal values, and demonstrated individuality. This kind of narrative identity formation has been well established in sociolinguistics but rarely tied to ethos by rhetoricians. Yet the narratives clearly helped participants strengthen their ethos by demonstrating qualities such as knowledge, competence, and authority appropriate to their profession.

These qualities, reflective of practical wisdom, are also established by the functions the narratives served within the chats. Participants spontaneously applied stories of their personal experiences to the topics and questions brought up by others. These narratives often helped them work toward the goals of the chats to understand class topics more thoroughly. In addition to showing practical wisdom, the narratives also helped participants identify with one another, building good will. By story swapping and collaboratively building stories, participants worked with each other to build common ground and establish rapport.

Thus, my analysis of the chats illustrates specific ways people negotiate ethos during their online interaction. As argued by Amossy (2001), we see both social/institutional forces (the classroom context and teacher/student roles) and discourse moves (narratives) influencing ethos formation. Also, like previous studies of CMC, we find that identities become personalized as as online conversation develops and participants learn more about each other and work together toward mutual goals. In these chats it is clear that being *responsive* to others and *actively contributing* to the conversational goals plays a large part in establishing ethos because such behavior reflects good will and practical wisdom. Given that scholars have long associated narrative with identity and practical wisdom, these findings are no surprise. But the analysis of these chats lets us see exactly how the narratives operate in an unplanned context to contribute to the two qualities deemed essential for ethos.

References

Amossy, Ruth 2001. "Ethos at the Crossroads of Disciplines: Rhetoric, Pragmatics, Sociology". *Poetics Today* 22 (1): 1–23.

Aristotle. 1953. *Ethics.* (J.A.K. Thomson, Trans.) New York: Penguin Books.

_____. 1991 *On Rhetoric: A Theory of Civic Discourse* (G. A. Kennedy, Trans.). New York: Oxford University Press.

Bamberg, Michael. 2004. "Talk, Small Stories, and Adolescent Identities". *Human Development* 47 (6): 366–369.

Baumlin, James S., and Baumlin, Tita F. (Eds.). 1994. *Ethos: New essays in rhetorical and critical theory.* Dallas: Southern Methodist University Press.

Booth, Wayne C. 1961. *The Rhetoric of Fiction.* Chicago: University of Chicago Press.

_____. 1988. *The Company We Keep: An Ethics of Fiction.* Berkeley: University of California Press.

Bordia, Prashant. 1997. "Face-to-Face versus Computer-Mediated Communication: A Synthesis of the Experimental Literature". *The Journal of Business Communication* 34 (1): 99–120.

Bruner, Jerome. 1986. *Actual Minds, Possible Worlds.* Cambridge: Harvard University Press.

_____. 1987. "Life as Narrative". *Social Research* 54: 11–32.

_____. 1990. *Acts of Meaning.* Cambridge: Harvard University Press.

Burke, Kenneth. 1950. *A Rhetoric of Motives.* New York: Prentice Hall.

Carranza, Isolda. E. 1998. "Low-Narrativity Narratives and Argumentation". *Narrative Inquiry* 8 (2): 287–317.

Daiute, Colette and Nelson, Katherine. 1997. "Making Sense of the Sense-Making Function of Narrative Evaluation". *Journal of Narrative and Life History* 7 (1–4): 207–215.

Davies, Bronwyn and Harré, Rom. 1990. "Positioning: Conversation and the Production of Selves". *Journal for the Theory of Social Behavior* 20: 43–63.

Dyer, Judy and Keller-Cohen, Deborah. 2000. "The Discursive Construction of Professional Self through Narratives of Personal Experience". *Discourse Studies* 2 (3): 283–304.

Finegan, Edward. 1994. *Language: Its Structure and Use.* New York: Harcourt Brace College Publishers.

Fisher, Walter. 1984. "Narration as a Human Communication Paradigm: The Case of Public Moral Argument". *Communication Monographs* 52: 1–22.

_____. 1987. *Human Communication as Narration: Toward a Philosophy of Reason, Value and Action*. Columbia: University of South Carolina Press.

_____. 2003 "Reconfiguring Practical Wisdom". In *The Fifth Conference of the International Society for the Study of Argumentation*, F. H. van Eemeren, J. A. Blair, C. Willar & F. A. Snoeck Henkemans (eds), 319–323. Amsterdam: Sic Sat.

Galegher, Jolene, Sproull, Lee and Kiesler, Sara. 1998. "Legitimacy, Authority, and Community in Electronic Support Groups". *Written Communication* 14 (4): 493–530.

Garver, Eugene. 1994. *Aristotle's Rhetoric: An Art of Character*. Chicago: University of Chicago Press.

_____. 2004. *For the Sake of Argument: Practical Reasoning, Character, and the Ethics of Belief*. Chicago: University of Chicago Press.

Giese, Mark. 1998. "Self Without Body: Textual Self-Representation in an Electronic Community". *First Monday* 3(4).

Georgakopoulou, Alexandra. 2006. "Thinking Big with Small Stories in Narrative and Identity Analysis". *Narrative Inquiry* 16 (1): 122–130.

Green, Judith L., and Wallat, Cynthia (Eds.). 1981. *Ethnography and language in educational settings*. Norwood, NJ: Ablex.

Heap, James L. 1988. On task in classroom discourse. *Linguistics and Education*, 1: 177–198.

Herring, Susan. C. 2001. "Computer-mediated Discourse". In *Handbook of Discourse Analysis*. D. Schiffrin, D. Tannen & H. E. Hamilton (eds), 612–634. Malden: Blackwell.

Hlapanis, Giorgos, Kordaki, Maria, and Dimitrakopoulou, Angelique. 2006. "Successful Courses: The Role of Synchronous Communication and E-Moderation Via Chat". *Campus-Wide Information Systems* 23(3): 171–181.

Holt, Richard. 2004. *Dialogue on the Internet: Language, Civic Identity,and Computer-Mediated Communication*. Westport: Praeger.

Hrastinkski, Stefan, & Keller, Christina. 2007. "Computer-mediated Communication in Education: A Review of Recent Research". *Educational Media International*, 44 (1), 61–77.

Hyde, Michael J. 2004. "Introduction: Rhetorically We Dwell". In *The Ethos of Rhetoric*, Michael. J. Hyde (ed), xiii–xxviii. Columbia: University of South Carolina Press.

Jasinski, James. 2001. *Sourcebook on Rhetoric: Key Concepts in Contemporary Rhetorical Studies*. Thousand Oaks: Sage Publications.

Johnstone, Barbara. 1996. *The Linguistic Individual: Self-Expression in Language and Linguistics*. New York: Oxford University Press.

_____. 2002. *Discourse Analysis*. Malden, MA: Blackwell Publishers.

Kinneavy, James L. and Warshauer, Susan C. 1994. "From Aristotle to Madison Avenue: Ethos and the Ethics of Argument". In *Ethos: New essays in Rhetorical and Critical Theory*, J. S. Baumlin and T. F. Baumlin (eds), 171–190. Dallas: Southern Methodist University Press.

Labov, William. 1972. *Language in the Inner City: Studies inBlack English Vernacular*. Philadelphia: University of Pennsylvania Press.

_____. 1997. "Some Further Steps in Narrative Analysis." *Journal of Narrative and Life History* 7 (1–4): 395–415.

Linde, Charlotte. 1993. *Life Stories: The Creation of Coherence*. Oxford: Oxford University Press.

MacIntyre, Alasdair. 1984. *After Virtue: A Study in Moral Theory* (2nd. ed.). Notre Dame: University of Notre Dame Press.

Miller, Carolyn R. 2004. "Expertise and Agency: Tranformations of Ethos in Human-Computer Interaction". In *The Ethos of Rhetoric* M. J. Hyde (ed), 197–218. Columbia: University of South Carolina Press.

Norrick, Neal. 1997. "Twice-told tales: Collaborative Narration of Familiar Stories". *Language in Society* 26:199–220.

Nussbaum, Martha C. 1986. *The Fragility of Goodness: Luck, Ethics in Greek Tragedy and Philosophy.* Cambridge: Cambridge University Press.

————. 1990. *Love's Knowlege: Essays on Philosophy and Literature.* New York: Oxford University Press.

Perelman, Chaim and Olbrechts-Tyteca, Lucie.1969. *The New Rhetoric.* Notre Dame: University of Notre Dame Press.

Prince, Gerald. 1982. *Narratology: The Form and Function of Narrative.* New York: Mouton Publishers.

Ricoeur, Paul. 1991. "Life in Quest of Narrative". In *On Paul Ricoeur: Narrative and Interpretation,* David Wood (ed), 20–33. New York: Routledge.

Rosen, Harold. 1988. "The Autobiographical Impulse". In *Linguistics in Context: Connecting Observation and Understanding.* Deborah Tannen (ed), 69–88. Norwood: Ablex Publishing Corporation.

Sacks, Harvey, Schegloff, Emanuel A. and Jefferson, Gail A. 1974. "A Simplest Systematics for the Organization of Turn-Taking for Conversation". *Language* 50: 696–735.

Schiffrin, Deborah. 1996. "Narrative as Self-Portrait: Sociolinguistic Constructions of Identity". *Language in Society* 25: 167–203.

Schegloff, Emanuel A. 2001. "Discourse as an Interactional Achievement III: The Omnirelevance of Action". In *The Handbook of Discourse Analysis,* D. Schiffrin, D. Tannen and H. E. Hamilton (eds), 229–249. Malden, Mass.: Blackwell Publishers.

Sherman, Richard C. 2001. "The Mind's Eye in Cyberspace: Online Perceptions of Self and Others". In *Toward CyberPsychology: Mind, Cognition and Society in the Internet Age,* G. Riva & C. Galimberti (eds), 53–72. Amsterdam: IOS Press.

Sinclair, John M., and Brazil, David. 1982. *Teacher Talk.* Oxford: Oxford Univeristy Press.

Tannen, Deborah. 1984. *Conversational Style: Analyzing Talk among Friends.* Norwood, NJ: Ablex.

Walther, Joseph B. 1993. "Impression Development in Computer-Mediated Interaction" *Western Journal of Communication* 57: 381–398.

Warnick, Barbara. 2007. *Rhetoric Online: Persuasion and Politics on the World Wide Web.* New York: Peter Lang.

CHAPTER 9

Disciplinary rhetorics, rhetorical agency, and the construction of voice

Amanda Young
University of Memphis

Introduction

While it is clear that rhetorical agency is key to rhetorical inquiry, its definition is slippery and fluid (Ahern 2001; Geisler 2004; O'Hair, Villgran, Wittenberg, Brown, Gerguson et al. 2003; Turnbull 2004; Campbell 2005; Koerber 2006). As Geisler (2004) points out, there is a tension between the traditional rhetorical approach to agency, which focuses on the rhetor's capacity to act, and the postmodern approach, which claims that individual agency is socially constructed and illusory. Scholars in rhetoric continue to struggle to define rhetorical agency in a way that takes into account how it is constructed in texts and how it can result in action (Young & Flower 2001; Flower 2003; Geisler 2004, O'Hair et al. 2003; Campbell 2005).

Amy Koerber argues for a theory of rhetorical agency that accounts for the "negotiation among competing alternative discourses" (2006:94). In studying what she calls the disciplinary rhetorics of breastfeeding, Koerber cites the tension between how rhetorical agency is traditionally defined, and "what, in value, it ought to be" (94). She describes a disciplinary rhetoric as the discourse of a particular normative culture, such as medical discourse, where agency is assumed to lie in the rhetorical acts of the speaker or writer. She argues, however, that such an assumption limits our understanding of rhetorical agency. Through her interviews with nurses and midwives, she found that the disciplinary rhetoric of breastfeeding, i.e., discourse intended to reflect the accepted norm of practice, is full of conflicting messages and is based on a cultural norm that individuals may or may not be able to access. In spite of their ambiguities, however, disciplinary rhetorics are, by definition, difficult to resist. Koerber found that in spite of this difficulty, breast-feeding advocates and their clients were able to become agents in their own narratives and to support one another in practices that defied the norm.[1]

The challenge, then, is not to simply define rhetorical agency but rather to recognize it in context. Geisler (2004: 13) cites John Lucaites' argument that "every rhetorical performance enacts and contains a theory of its own agency – of its own possibilities – as it structures and enacts the relationships between speaker and audience, self and other, action and structure." In this chapter, I explore the discourse of teenage girls who are interacting with a computer program and adult mentors about abstinence and contraceptive use. In examining both their adherence to and their resistance to the disciplinary rhetoric of "safe sex," as prescribed by Planned Parenthood, I show how they create their own rhetorical agency. Their discourse demonstrates some of the fundamental properties of rhetorical agency: questioning (Turnbull 2004), negotiation (Young & Flower 2001; Flower 2003; Koerber 2006), choice (O'Hair et al. 2003), and evaluation (Campbell 2005).

Identifying rhetorical agency

Within disciplinary rhetorics, and the discourse of those whose agency is traditionally uncontested, the identification of rhetorical agency can appear uncomplicated. A physician may say, for example, "We will run some tests." The first person "we" could suggest that the doctor, along with other providers who answer to him, will conduct the tests. Or it could imply a shared decision between the physician and the patient. Regardless, the judgment about the need to run the tests and the decision about which tests to run seemingly belong to the physician. Within the reality of medical practice, however, "we" could include the established medical protocols used to respond to specific symptoms. It could include the restrictions of the insurance company or the situated practices of a particular medical setting. Agency can also be mitigated by specific discursive moves such as discourse markers, grammatical limiters, and question tags (Rymes 1995). Ultimately, however, agency resides in the patient, who agrees or refuses to be tested, regardless of the first person construction in the discourse of the physician.

Rhetorical agency, then, resides not just in language, but in the context of the discourse, in narratives that are constructed by speakers, and in the stances that are created or reflected within the discourse. Locating rhetorical agency requires more than recognizing a vocabulary; discourse that reflects or creates rhetorical agency must be localized and operationalized within a particular rhetorical situ-

---

1. Examples included breastfeeding twins, which doctors often advise against, and resisting the introduction of bottle-feeding in the hospital nursery, in spite of a woman's choice to breast feed.

ation (Bitzer 1968; Young, Becker, & Pike 1970). Thus we can enrich our understanding of rhetorical agency by examining the ways in which situated discourse
reflects the forethought of the speakers and structures his or her intentionality,
self-reflectiveness, and self-efficacy beliefs.

The discourse of the seven teenage girls described in this chapter demonstrates
their negotiation with the disciplinary rhetoric of Planned Parenthood in order to
establish their own agency in decisions about abstinence and contraceptive use. We
see them subscribing to the disciplinary rhetoric of "safe sex" – but only until the
reality of their lives conflicts with the norms that are imposed on them. They then
begin to establish their own rhetorical agency by mitigating the stance of authority
with their own values, goals, and experiences.

Context of the study

What's Your Plan? (*WYP*) (Young 1999) is an interactive, multimedia program
that engages teens in multi-leveled activities of interpretation, decision-making,
and planning. (See the appendix for an outline of the program.) In an observational, discourse analytic study at an urban high school, seven girls and their adult
mentors worked through each section of the program. The girls were all enrolled
in the Peer Helpers Program of Planned Parenthood, an in-school program that
trains teens to counsel their peers in abstinence and safe sex practices. Data for
the study include the textual responses that the girls typed into the program when
prompted, as well as transcripts from conversations with their mentors, and post-
interviews that I conducted with each girl. Because of their experience with Peer
Helpers, the girls were comfortable with the disciplinary rhetoric of Planned Parenthood, and we see them using it to negotiate with themselves (Nienkamp 2001),
hypothetical others defined by the program (including boyfriends, parents, and
healthcare providers), and their mentors. But we also see some of the girls resisting
the disciplinary rhetoric as they begin to define problems based on their own experience and then evaluating risks and consequences using a "toolkit" of rhetorical
strategies and socially constructed knowledge that is unique to their situation.

WYP is designed to elicit a detailed picture of a young woman's interests in and
perceived barriers to abstinence or contraceptive use, as well as her expectations
in relationships, her beliefs about abstinence and sexual activity, her perceived
self-efficacy in communicating with important others in her life, and her ability to make concrete plans that build on her existing knowledge. The program
is designed for a variety of settings, including a teen and mentor working one-
on-one, or teens working together in small groups in a classroom or community
organization.

Methodology

Data collection

Seven girls, ages 15–18, from the school's Peer Helpers Program, participated in the study. During a day-long session (with multiple breaks and lunch), they worked one on one with adult mentors whom I had previously trained using the *Mentor's Guidebook for What's Your Plan?*[2] In the two weeks following the sessions, I interviewed each girl about her experience and asked her to expand on various parts of the texts she had entered while using the program. All of these interviews were audio-taped, as were the entire sessions with the mentors, most of which lasted three to four hours. Additional data included the texts that each girl entered into the computer. The names of all participants referred to in this chapter are pseudonyms. Each girl's participation generated about 30 pages of data.

Coding

In transcribing the mentoring sessions, I counted a text unit as all of the data corresponding to one section of the program, or to one specific question within a section. This method allowed me to identify the most important attribute of the discourse about each section and code it accordingly. In analyzing the data, I asked three questions:

1. How is rhetorical agency influenced in this discourse by the disciplinary rhetoric of Planned Parenthood?
2. Where does each girl begin to resist the disciplinary rhetoric?
3. How does this resistance help each girl to create her own representation of agency?

To begin development of the coding scheme, I first identified specific sentence-level linguistic structures that might signal rhetorical agency, such as first-person subjects, active verbs, and purpose statements. I then looked for text in which knowledge building, conflict, or planning was the topic. I found, however, that expressions of agency also emerged in more complex constructions. To identify

---

2. Based on concepts developed at the Community Literacy Center of Pittsburgh (Peck, Flower & Higgins 1995), the guidebook stresses a mentoring relationship that supports students in identifying multiple options and their likely outcomes, trying to decipher the "story behind the story," and taking a rival stance that will enable decision makers to look at a problem from a new perspective. I also was very careful to alert mentors to sections of the program that could evoke stories of sexual abuse and trauma, and the Planned Parenthood representatives gave us suggestions about responding to any concerns about abuse. However, no suggestions or hints of abuse arose.

those constructions, I used the initial coding scheme as a launching point to guide multiple close, careful readings of the coded data.

The second step in developing a comprehensive coding scheme for agency was to ask what source of agency was suggested by the overriding flavor of the text unit. The question that guided this phase was: What matters most to the writer/speaker in this particular text unit, her decisions or the decisions of someone else? Using grounded theory methods (Glaser & Strauss 1967), I found that three categories emerged: personal or "self-agency," other agency, and no agency. In the first category, "self-agency," is text that shows the teen assuming control of her relationship, her decision-making process, her accrual of knowledge, or some other specific aspect of her life. The second category, "other agency," describes text which shows the teen allowing some other person to control some aspect of her life. The third category includes text that does not attribute power or control to any specific individual, or "no agency." Text units that coded for self-agency manifested at least one the following characteristics:

(1) They showed that a girl's goals, feelings, or needs were driving her decision:
     "She'll still maintain respect for herself. And that'll make her stronger because she didn't succumb to that peer pressure." (typed into the computer program)

(2) They foregrounded her actions:
     "Just tell him straight, you're not going to have sex til you're married and that this was a decision that you made for yourself. HE'S JUST GOING TO HAVE TO DEAL WITH THE FACT." (*sic*, typed into the computer program)

(3) They showed that she had a plan to acquire knowledge:
     "Because maybe me telling myself isn't enough and by hearing it from my best friend she might make me think more." (typed into the computer program)

(4) They foregrounded her decisions:
     "I'm not going to lose my virginity to someone who has other chicks on the side. I have so much more respect for myself. I want someone to treasure me." (interview)

(5) They narrated a story in which the girl (or a character standing in for her) precipitated an event involving sex:
     "Well, um, I just now broke up with my boyfriend and I'm glad personally that I didn't have sex with him because, I mean, it was really becoming, um, an internal conflict ..." (interview)

After the coding scheme was finalized, two independent coders and I reached 84 percent agreement on 20 percent of the data, and I then coded the rest of the data. Table 1 shows the pseudonym for each girl, the number of sections she completed, and her scores for self-agency.

Table 1. Number of text units for each participant and percentages for text units coded for personal agency

Pseudonym	Number of Sections Completed	Positive for Self-Agency	
		N	%
Bria	31	18	58
Chrissy	24	9	38
Dana	19	12	63
Keri	19	13	68
Monique	32	22	69
Renee	29	17	59
Serena	32	8	25

Rhetorical agency, problem analysis, and decision-making

In further analysis of the *WYP* segments that were coded as self-agentive, I began to see two major themes developing. The first is decision analysis, which corresponds to the first and fourth of the agency criteria listed above (goals, feelings and needs driving her decision; and foregrounding her decisions). The second is knowledge manipulation, which corresponds to the second and third criteria (her actions are foregrounded; and she has a plan to acquire knowledge). For example, Criterion #3, "text that shows the girl has a plan to acquire knowledge" shows up in statements about making a doctor's appointment, talking to a friend, or looking for printed material. But I also found that these girls have much more complex ideas about what to do with the knowledge they already possess. In other words, they are much more interested in knowledge evaluation than in knowledge seeking.

Agency in analyzing decisions

WYP is designed to support girls in their decision-making, so it is not surprising that a large portion of the text units were coded positive for either the first or fourth criterion: text that shows the writer's goals, feelings, or needs driving her decisions, or text that shows the writer foregrounding her decisions. The text units that code positive for these attributes, however, also demonstrate a more complex, multi-dimensional view of the decision making process. The three most salient views of the decision making process that I identified are constructing the self, analyzing the decision-making process, and discussing the consequences of a decision. (see Figure 1)

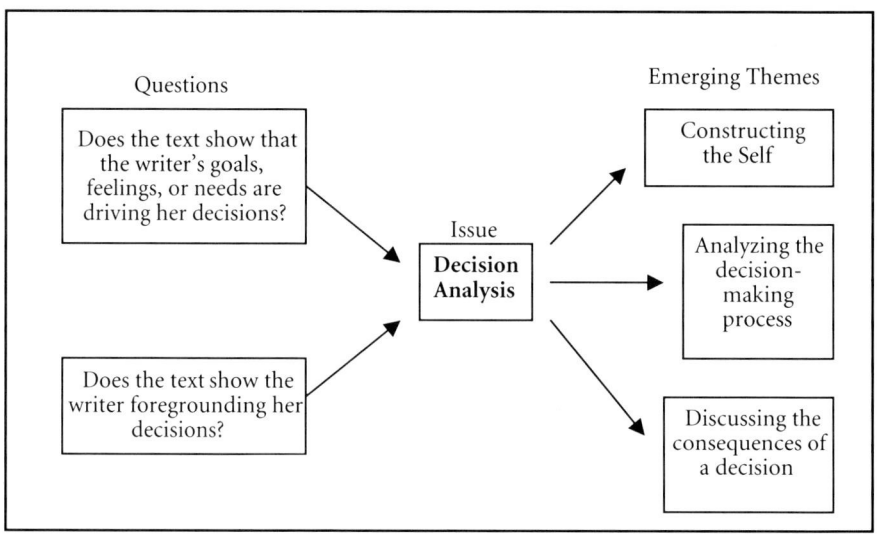

Figure 1. Coding for agency, criteria 1 and 4

Constructing the self through decision analysis
Nienkamp (2001) describes an internal rhetoric that lies between the traditional view of rhetoric as an act of persuasion before an audience and the concept of "rhetoricality," or the way that "language pervades and conditions our existence" (26). This concept of the rhetorical construction of self is evident in the texts as the girls used the scenarios and prompts in *WYP* to construct a reality about themselves. Austin's (1975) idea that words can perform an action, such as create a marriage bond or impose a sentence, can be extended, according to Greenblatt (1980), to more complex processes such as the creation or destruction of self concepts or belief systems. In the case under study, the performance is the construction of self, in the sense that the girls who seem to have the strongest sense of agency are able to connect the scenarios in the program to their own lives, whether or not they are sexually active. They can then interject themselves into that scenario and discuss plans and decisions in ways that reflect the disciplinary rhetoric of Planned Parenthood that they have chosen to embrace. In doing so, they are writing and talking about themselves, not just about the fictional characters in the *WYP* scenarios, and, they are actively engaging in planning and decision making, not just responding to a story.[3]

The first four sections of the *WYP* program ask the girls to respond to the scenario of Tyrone pressuring Brandy to have sex. They are asked to describe the

---

3.   Brandy and Tyrone are the characters in the program who are negotiating their sexual relationship.

"good things that could happen" if they do have sex, the "bad things that could happen" if they do have sex, the good things if they do not have sex, and the bad things if they do not have sex. Many of their responses showed features of a rhetorical construction of self, the most salient being the tendency in one of the seven girls, Bria, to put her emotional welfare ahead of any other aspect of her health. Specifically, she continually presented herself in self-constructive, rather than self-destructive, language. For example, when the program challenges the girls to respond to the statement "You'd do it if you loved me," Bria writes:

(6)   Don't ever let anyone brainwash you with that lame old stuff. It's not about you loving him. It's about you loving yourself and obviously the feeling isn't mutual.

All seven girls scored positive for agency in the third section (the good things that could happen if Brandy and Tyrone do not have sex), again reflecting their training in the Peer Helpers Program. But only Bria goes beyond the prescribed answer of avoiding pregnancy and STDs. She writes:

(7)   She'll still maintain respect for herself. That'll make her stronger because she didn't succumb to that peer pressure.

Throughout these four sections, Bria moves back and forth between first and second person in the text that she types into the program. But in her conversation with her mentor, she continually expounds on her answers with long, personal stories (told in the first person) about her own experiences with her boyfriend. In her discussion about virginity, it is clear that her decision not to be sexually active has as much to do with her emotional and mental self as with her physical self:

(8)   I'm attracted to him but not on that level and I don't think he's worthy of my virginity cause that's something very special and you can only give that away once. You never get it back. And they were also saying that, you know, he is one of those people, he's always the first person, ya, then after that, you know, it wasn't special to him. It was something so special to me that wasn't special to him. It turned out that way. And there's a whole bunch of other things that go along with it ...

Then two conversational turns later:

(9)   Ya, um, if he doesn't happen to be the right person, then if he turns out to be a jerk, then afterwards, you know, you gave him something special that was a part of you. You gave him a part of you and after that's done, you could lose respect for yourself and then you just kind of turn into a little ho and you could just start doing it with everyone, you know, cause, you feel used and it's like I don't care. If someone already took advantage of me so why don't I just go wild and I know people who have let that happen to them. You know, that's pretty weak but, I mean, what can you say?

Bria speaks at length in these excerpts about her conflicting emotions surrounding her decision to remain a virgin. Her concept of "losing her virginity" goes beyond having not been sexually active. In an earlier excerpt she talks about being "a virgin, a sexual virgin," indicating that there is more than one type of virginity and suggesting that virginity has as much to do with her own personhood as it does with whether or not she has experienced sex. She establishes that who she is as a person will be greatly affected by whether or not she has sex, especially if it is with the wrong person. While she admits that it is "weak" to allow a mistake to be the reason for going "wild," she illustrates a consciousness in this dialogue that she, as well as any girl, is defined by a multiplicity of factors, including her relationships, her self-image, her choices, and her vulnerabilities.

But while she speaks so strongly about remaining a virgin, Bria is also aware of self conflict and sees it as another facet of her self:

(10)   I'm glad personally that I didn't have sex with him because, I mean, it was really becoming, um, an internal conflict in myself, I was fighting with myself every day, and saying you should just go ahead. I was so afraid of compromising myself that all I said about it was, look, wait til I got married, but, then, I don't know.

The next several sections of the program, which I call the conversation pages, ask the girls to respond to simulated conversations with important people in their lives: mother, father, best friend, boyfriend, sister or cousin, and then self. In the text generated in these sections, the girls demonstrate another facet of self by identifying their limitations in problem solving. Bria admits that:

(11)   I know I can't know everything.

while Serena sees that her limitations include her status in life:

(12)   Because no matter what I say, I'm the child, he's the adult.

In Section 5, the conversation with the best friend, Dana explains why she chooses a friend who will support her:

(13)   My telling myself isn't enough.

But Dana also sees herself as ultimately responsible for her decisions:

(14)   Follow your heart, not your mind. Because people can get in your mind but no one can enter your heart.

In Section 6, the conversation with an older sister or cousin, Dana makes it clear that her welfare must be the central focus of her decision:

(15)   This is true and ask myself who am I doing it for, me or him, because if I'm doing it for him then that is wrong. You never go out of your way just to make someone happy if it definitely might hurt you.

Bria and Dana, the two girls who most often demonstrate this self-constructing facet of agency, assume agency by interjecting themselves into Brandy and Tyrone's dilemma, by discussing their emotional and psychological needs in specific ways, by recognizing their limitations, by establishing support systems for the future, and by identifying their plans for responsible decision making.

Analyzing the decision-making process

The ability to understand and talk about the decision making process is a second facet of agency that *WYP* encourages. Some of the comments that indicate a young woman is "foregrounding her decision" are straightforward:

(16)   My reasons for saying this are … (unprompted explanation)

(17)   I'm glad that I made the decision not to.

(18)   She should make her decision and explain to him why she feels this way.

But these excerpts and others also represent a more complex awareness of how and why the girls are making the decisions that they are. An analysis of these texts reveals a number of rhetorical moves that the girls are making which, while not sequential or uniform, are clearly identifiable as decision analysis. Some of these moves take place while the girl is in the process of making a decision asked for by the program. Others are in response to the program asking for an explanation of her decision. Still others are unprompted, emerging in conversation between the girl and her mentor. These moves, which include defining and comparing context, identifying conflict, and exploring and inferring risk, help us to understand how these girls frame their experiences and problems and how they calculate and mitigate risk. Figure 2 illustrates these categories in relation to the overall coding scheme.

"Defining and comparing contexts" occurs early in the program and appears throughout, both prompted and unprompted. In the first section of the program, which asks for the good things that could happen if Brandy and Tyrone *do* have sex, Dana answers:

(19)   I don't think that there would be anything good. My reason for saying this is because they have been only talking for 2 months and that is not enough time to make a decision like that.

In another section, the conversation with the boyfriend, Bria makes a similar statement, but she offers an alternative:

(20)   After just two months? It's rushing it a bit. I could understand if maybe after six months and you're not a virgin.

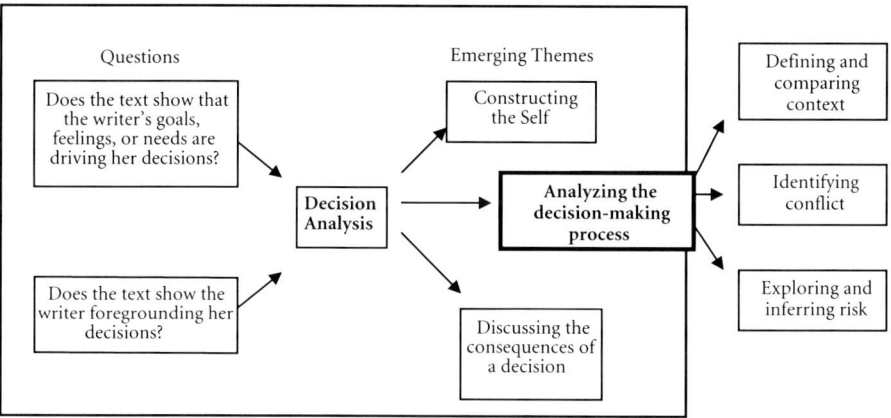

Figure 2. The three components of decision analysis found in the data

Bria, however, is also aware that others can use context to pressure her to accept their point of view. When discussing how guys talk to girls about sex, she writes:

(21)   You get a lot of people that say if you loved me, you'd do it and how, you know, take the time span in the relationship, like when you expect something to change and how long you been talking for. You know, x amount of months, so don't you think it's time or do you ever think about having sex? You know, you always hear stuff like that.

Both Bria and Dana are conscious of their use of context to explain their decisions, moving beyond a simple description of the context and explaining some mitigating factor or adding some alternative. Later in the program, all of the girls are asked to specifically consider context when they choose the levels of intimacy that are appropriate in the kind of relationship that they've chosen to think about. (At the beginning of the program they choose from "dating around," "a first date," "going steady," or "a committed relationship.") Dana, for example, says that it's not okay to allow a guy to touch her breast:

(22)   Not if I'm just starting to go steady with somebody.

In the process of defining and comparing context, many of the girls also move into the second feature of the decision making progress, which is "identifying conflict." Bria speaks at length about her internal conflict in the context of breaking up with her boyfriend:

(23)   I was fighting with myself every day …. I was so afraid of compromising myself.

Bria is talking about a conflict that is settled, at least for the time being. Serena, however, illustrates how individuals often bring competing belief systems into play when contemplating a decision (Cicourel 1993). In the conversation with an older sister or cousin, she has selected the sister who asks her to think about the negative possibilities and to ask herself whether she would be doing this for herself or for the boyfriend. Serena's response suggests that she is beginning to resist the disciplinary rhetoric of Planned Parenthood as she articulates her unresolved conflict of wanting both the freedom of making her own decisions and the comfort of having someone else make them for her:

(24)   Every time she would tell me something, I would tell her, you're not telling me nothing. Because I don't know if I want to or if I don't want to. She's making it my decision and I want to hear yes, but then I want to hear no. That's why I keep going back and forth.

Interestingly, Serena had already said that she doesn't have an older sister or cousin to talk to, so this conversation is hypothetical. Still, she is aware of her conflicting desire to want to make her own decisions but at the same time to have someone tell her what she should do. Monique offers a similar frustration after choosing the same sister to respond to:

(25)   I don't know. That's why I'm coming to you for help. Because when you ask someone a question and they answer it with a question you get frustrated.

One purpose of Planned Parenthood's disciplinary rhetoric is to structure girls' ability to identify and deal with the risk of unplanned pregnancies and sexually transmitted diseases (STDs). The texts from *WYP* demonstrate the ability of these girls to "explore and infer risk," the third category under "analyzing the decision making process." The program gives them the opportunity to identify particular risks and talk about them. All of the girls are cognizant of the risks of unprotected sex, and they are quick to list them at various points in the program, demonstrating their experience with Planned Parenthood. More interesting, however, is their ability to move beyond those immediate risks to their physical health and to consider risk to their emotional health and to their relationships (including friends, relatives, and parents – not just boyfriends). When asked about the good things that could happen if the characters Brandy and Tyrone *do* have sex, Dana and Keri both explicitly mention the risk of a sexual relationship. Keri speaks in general terms:

(26)   Nothing good ever comes out when you have sex at a young age.

Dana, however, is more specific. She is concerned about the relationship between Brandy and Tyrone and about Brandy's reputation:

(27) It can change everything. It can make things worse because he might think she's easy or that he doesn't have to work at all for it.

The second section, which asks about the bad things that could happen if Brandy and Tyrone have sex, elicits many more comments about both the physical and emotional risks of having sex at an early age. All of the girls mention pregnancy and STDs. But they also discuss the relationship and their concern that boys just want sex.

(28) If she decides to stop having sex with him he might get mad and leave her or get it from someone else. She could even get pregnant unexpectanly [sic]. He could tell his friends and they might think she's easy too. It also will ruin her reputation. (Dana)

(29) Also most guys use girls. So if he's like that he probably won't want anything to do with her after they have sex. (Keri)

Another interesting aspect of the girls' treatment of risk is their ability to infer a specific risk when neither the program nor the mentor mention it. This move, which Bereiter and Scardamalia (1987) call live knowledge, is an important facet of rhetorical agency that the girls are constructing: the ability to combine expert knowledge from two realms – outside expertise and their own experience – to create new knowledge and then to apply it to their own decision making. Renee makes this move in Section 6, the conversation with a best friend. When asked which person would help her to make a good decision, she chooses the friend who says, "Only two months, are you sure? It's a lot of responsibility, you know." The hypothetical friend doesn't identify the "it" she is referring to, but all of the other six girls assumed "it" was a sexual relationship. Renee takes it a step further and infers the risk of having a child:

(30) The first one cause she's asking about my responsibilities and about having a kid. That would make me think. That's a lot of responsibilities.

Serena makes a similar move in the same section. Like Renee, she chooses the first friend as the one who would help her make a good decision. But in explaining why, she refers to the third friend, who says: "Hello! Does AIDS mean anything to you":

(31) Cause I already know #3. That's already in my mind. I should wait longer. Because I haven't known him long enough to know his background, who he's been with and who the people he's been with, who they've been with, and etc.

Discussing the consequences of a decision
It is in text units where girls are discussing the consequences of a decision that we see the disciplinary rhetoric of Planned Parenthood begin to falter. While a coding scheme can give the same scores to many statements of agency, a close, contextu-

What someone else will do	Negative consequences avoided	Positive consequences encountered	Positive consequences engaged and built upon
He'll just have more respect for her.	She don't have to worry about if she's pregnant.	She could save her virginity.	She'll still maintain respect for herself. And that'll make her stronger because she didn't succumb to that peer pressure.

Weak Agency ←--→ Strong Agency

Figure 3. Range of responses showing weak to strong agency

alized reading shows a continuum of agency, ranging from weak agency to strong agency. Girls who analyze their decisions, usually in response to "what if" questions, demonstrate this range of agency as they discuss consequences in terms of either themselves or some other person and in terms of either positive or negative consequences. Text units that reflected weak agency showed girls shrinking away from the self-confident tone of Planned Parenthood and moving toward a concern about what others think of them or how others will react to them. The range of answers in this section is illustrated in Figure 3.

Weak agency takes on an avoidance tone, while strong agency takes on a tone of "value added." Section 3 of the program, the good things that could happen if Brandy and Tyrone don't have sex, illustrates this point. All of the girls talk about the negative consequences that will be avoided by abstaining, but only Bria and Dana address the positive, maintaining respect. Bria's response illustrates an even stronger sense of agency than does Dana's. Bria is concerned about Brandy actively maintaining her own morals and sense of self respect. Dana, however, refers to what Tyrone might do: "He might respect her more." Bria is concerned about what Brandy can do for herself. Dana is concerned about what Tyrone will do in response to Brandy's decision.

This continuum of agency can work when the result is negative, as well. Consider Bria's answer to the bad things that could happen if Brandy and Tyrone don't have sex:

(32)   She'll never know that pleasure

compared to other responses that describe what Tyrone might do *to* Brandy: bad mouth her, leave her, or get sex somewhere else.

Strong agency, then, involves the ability to build multiple representations of problems, to identify conflicts, to articulate values, and to establish goals, all of which are intended outcomes of the Peer Helpers Program. Weak agency, even though it is foregrounding a decision-maker's goals and values, gives much of the agency back to the "other" and actually undermines the goals of Peer Helpers. In the responses garnered from Section 3, each girl states her values and goals. But those on the weaker end of the continuum are leaving it up to the "other" to help her reach them.

Agency in manipulating knowledge

In this context, "manipulate" encompasses a variety of cognitive and rhetorical moves, including identifying sources of knowledge, evaluating those sources, drawing on sources of self knowledge, combining knowledge from different sources, and parsing knowledge. These moves are demonstrated by the girls using *WYP* as they interpret various conversations and scenarios and develop action plans. Manipulation of knowledge corresponds to the second and third coding criteria (her actions are foregrounded; and she has a plan to acquire knowledge). (See Figure 4).

The girls' texts that offer the clearest demonstration of knowledge manipulation tend to be coded as showing both that they are foregrounding their actions and that they have a plan to acquire knowledge. Contrary to my expectation that foregrounded actions would entail more concrete, physical actions and that acquiring knowledge would pertain to plans to see a doctor, talk with a friend or parent, watch a certain television show, or access a Web site, the actions the girls foregrounded were often cognitive or rhetorical moves intended to identify or

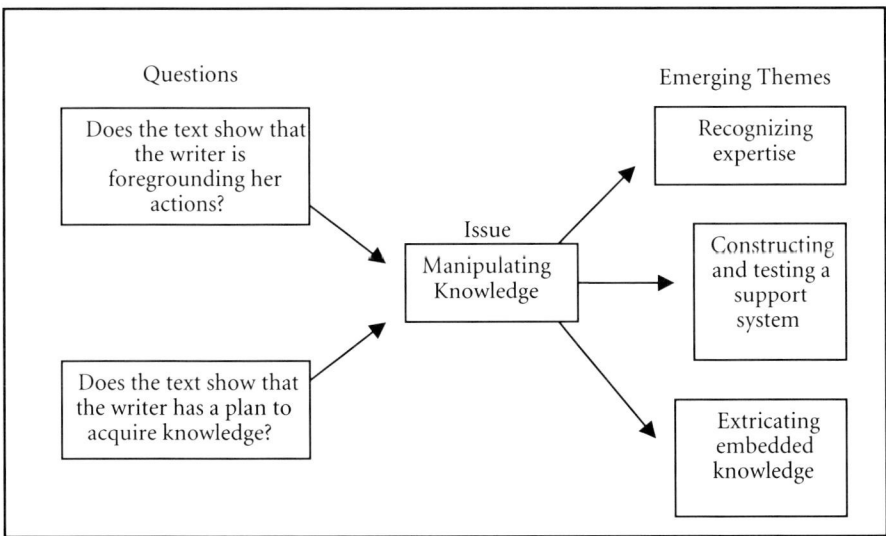

Figure 4. Manipulation of knowledge

evaluate knowledge. I also found that these moves are more salient, and probably more important to agency, than simply stating a plan to acquire more knowledge. The interesting questions then became, What do these girls see as valuable sources of knowledge?, and what do the girls represent themselves as doing with knowledge?

Texts from the sections of the program that ask for a specific plan show the girls making an effort to combine medical knowledge and life-world knowledge and to identify decisional support. In Section 6, for example, Bria discusses a conversation she had with two of her friends:

> (33)   I talked to one of my friends about it and she gave me a big pep talk or something like I was a football player about to go into a game. She was saying that "You're so intelligent and such a beautiful person" and that "this guy is not right for you and he doesn't deserve your virginity" and "to wait because the right person will come along." And another friend was telling me like " Hello, STDS." I was like "ya, that's true." That would be terrible for your first time to get something.

Recognizing expertise

Included in this coding category are moves that illustrate a girl's confidence in her own expertise, her acknowledgment of someone else's expertise, and her ability to evaluate sources of knowledge. All of these are expressions of agency because, in Wertsch's (1991) terms, they are specific items in a tool kit that the girls are using to negotiate safe, healthy decisions for themselves.

In Section 5, where Renee creates her model of the "mature guy," she expresses confidence in her ability to recognize maturity:

> (34)   I'd know if he was immature

And in the same section, Monique expresses her confidence in understanding how a guy would approach a girl:

> (35)   You don't just sit there and ask someone.

Throughout the conversation pages, the girls recognize the expertise of others. In talking about the father, they make comments like these:

> (36)   He knows how guys are cause he's one himself and he was once a teenager.

> (37)   Because I know that my dad ... knows what's going on. I believe you a little because you were a young boy once so you know how they think, because he's experienced and I know my dad wouldn't steer me wrong.

When asked about an older sister or cousin to talk to, Chrissy, surprisingly, refers to her brother:

(38)   Yes, my brother, because he listens to me and he can tell me from a male's point of view.

Also under the rubric of recognizing expertise is the girls' ability to explicitly evaluate the advice they receive, or to articulate what counts as knowledge. Bria, for example, says:

(39)   Because it's sound evidence. If you hear about someone else's past experience, something that someone else has already gone through, then that helps you not to make the same mistake.

Others actively evaluate the source of knowledge or advice:

(40)   Because I know that my dad did make wrong decisions at one time so he knows what's going on.

Constructing and testing a support system

Integrated within the girls' moves to evaluate expertise are comments about constructing and testing a support system. Dana explains clearly why she needs support, both in evaluating information and in making decisions:

(41)   Because maybe me telling myself isn't enough and by hearing it from my best friend she might make me think more. You are right and I should definitely think this through more. Because she is and I need to have a support person who helps me regardless if it's right or wrong. I need someone to tell me the truth even if I don't like what she has to say.

Serena says that she doesn't have a support system, but she describes how she would construct one:

(42)   I don't have somebody to talk to. But like when I'm talking, I'll ask this person, what would they do if this happens to them. And if they say something that I would say, then I may be comfortable talking to them.

Bria talks at length about a web of support she has created that gives her both positive and negative examples to learn from and how she evaluates their input:

(43)   Ya, because I don't think she would be a true friend if she said "oh okay if it's something you really want to do, then go ahead." No, I want you to tell me if there are drawbacks whether I'm going to get angry or not. That's still showing that you're a true friend. Like my one friend, she was really putting him down and I got really angry with her. Everything that she said about him was so true. Sometimes you don't want to hear it, especially if it's true. I got an attitude with her then. I was like why, she's just trying to help me, she's just telling the truth.

Extricating embedded knowledge

Some of the girls demonstrate an ability to work through layers of knowledge, both in making plans and in evaluating information. In the section on relationships, Renee builds a series of qualifying statements when she is talking about goals in a relationship:

(44)   I think love is important in a relationship because love is the base of any relationship. If you don't have love then you don't have respect for each other and if you don't have respect then your communication signals are going to be down you won't be able to communicate.

Serena, in her analysis of risk, is drawing on embedded knowledge to calculate her likelihood of acquiring an STD from a partner. In the imaginary conversation with a friend, she says that she would need to know:

(45)   his background, who he's been with, and who the people he's been with, who they've been with and etc.

Here Serena is drawing on her mental representation of men's sexual practices, her knowledge of STDs, and her coaching (probably from Planned Parenthood).

Conclusions

Agency entails planning and decision-making. It also requires self-evaluation and the recognition of internal and external expertise. Agency is constructed and expressed in how people manage conflicts and design plans for change that acknowledge people's beliefs and readiness to change behaviors if warranted. All of these moves are evident in the discourse of these seven girls, suggesting that they have assimilated, at least to some degree, the disciplinary rhetoric of Planned Parenthood, and have moved beyond it to develop their own rhetorical agency. Their texts show them experimenting with agency in a variety of ways, including:

–   critically analyzing their decision making processes,
–   expressing their resolve to remain virginal,
–   looking at a problem from someone else's perspective,
–   recognizing new sources of expertise, both within themselves and in others,
–   planning ahead to ensure the kind of relationship that they want, and
–   talking more openly about difficult issues that are easily misunderstood.

WYP is built on the metaphor of conversation. For example, students "visit" the Conversation Pages to interact with hypothetical people in hypothetical relationships. But the program is much more than a metaphor. The students who used *WYP* found themselves in very real conversation with themselves, with each other, with their mentors, and, as revealed in post interviews, with the people in their lives who are most important to them. Each of the seven illustrated a degree of sophistication in using the disciplinary rhetoric of Planned Parenthood. Each of them demonstrated success in developing their own rhetorical agency. And each of them showed evidence of their need to continue developing that agency to make the decisions that support their own values and goals.

Appendix

Outline of *What's Your Plan?*

1. Welcome Screen
2. Demographics
3. Choosing a level of relationship to consider later in the program
   a. First date
   b. Dating around
   c. Going steady
   d. Committed Relationship
4. Sections 1–4: Responding to scenario of Tyrone pressuring Brandy to have sex
   a. Good things that could happen if they *do* have sex
   b. Bad things that could happen if they *do* have sex
   c. Good things that could happen if they *do not* have sex
   d. Bad things that could happen if they *do not* have sex
5. Section 5–10: Conversation Page. Each character provides three versions. Users are asked to listen to each and then decide which one would be most helpful to them.
   a. Best friend
   b. Older sister or cousin
   c. Mother
   d. Father
   e. Boyfriend
   f. Self (Brandy)
6. Section 11–15: Teen Scene (not discussed in this chapter)
7. Section 16: Planning for Tomorrow

References

Ahern, Laura. 2001. "Language and Agency". *Annual Review of Anthropology* 30. 109–137.
Austin, J. L. 1976. *How To Do Things with Words*. ed by J. O. Urmson & Marina Sbisa. Cambridge, Mass: Harvard UP.

Bandura, Albert. 1997. "Self-Efficacy: Toward A Unifying Theory Of Behavior Change". *Psychological Review* 84. 191–215.

_____ 2002. "Growing Primacy Of Human Agency In Adaptation And Change In The Electronic Era". *European Psychologist* 7. 2–16.

Bereiter, Carl, & Scardamalia, Marlene. 1987. *The Psychology of Written Communication*. Hillsdale, New Jersey: Erlbaum.

Bitzer, Lloyd. 1968. "The Rhetorical Situation". *Philosophy and Rhetoric* 1. 1–14.

Campbell, Karlyn Kohrs. 2005. "Agency: Promiscuous and Protean". *Communication and Critical/Cultural Studies* 2. 1–19.

Cicourel, Aaron. 1993. "Hearing is not Believing: Language and the Structure of Belief in Medical Communication". *The Social Organization of Doctor-Patient Communication,* 2nd edition ed. by Alexander Dundras Todd and Sue Fisher, 46–49. Norwood, New Jersey: Ablex.

Flower, Linda. 2003. "Talking Across Difference: Intercultural Rhetoric and the Search for Situated Knowledge". *College Composition and Communication* 55. 38–68.

Geisler, Cheryl. 2004. "How Ought We to Understand the Concept of Rhetorical Agency? Report from the ARS". *Rhetoric Society Quarterly* 34. 9–17.

Glaser, Barney G., & Strauss, Anselm L. 1967. *The Discovery of Grounded Theory: Strategies for Qualitative Research*. Hawthorne, NY: Aldine.

Greenblatt, Stephen. J. 1980. *Renaissance Self-Fashioning: From More to Shakespeare*. Chicago, Ill: Chicago UP.

Koerber, Amy. 2006. "Rhetorical Agency, Resistance, and the Disciplinary Rhetorics of Breastfeeding". *Technical Communications Quarterly* 15. 87–101.

Nienkamp, Jean. 2001. *Internal Rhetorics: Toward a History and Theory of Self-Persuasion*. Carbondale, Ill: Southern Illinois UP.

O'Hair, Dan, Villagran, Melinda M, Wittenberg, Elaine, Brown, Kenneth, Ferguson, Monica, Hall, Harry T, & Doty, Timothy. 2003. "Cancer Survivorship and Agency Model: Implications for Patient Choice, Decision Making, and Influence". *Health Communication* 15. 193–202.

Peck, Wayne, Flower, Linda, & Higgins, Lorraine. 1995. "Community Literacy". *College Composition and Communication* 46. 199–222.

Rymes, Betsy. 1995. "The Construction Of Moral Agency in the Narratives of High-School Drop-Outs". *Discourse & Society* 6. 495–516.

Turnbull, Nick. 2004. "Rhetorical Agency as a Property of Questioning". *Philosophy and Rhetoric* 37 (3), 207–222.

Wertsch, James V. 1991. *Voices of the Mind*: *A Sociocultural Approach to Mediated Action*. Cambridge, Mass: Harvard UP.

Young, Amanda. 1999. "What's Your Plan?" Carnegie Mellon University.

_____. 2000. "Patients as Problem Solvers: Toward a Rhetoric of Agency in Healthcare." Ph.D. dissertation, Carnegie Mellon University.

_____ and Flower, Linda. 2001. "Patients as Partners, Patients as Problem Solvers". *Health Communication* 14. 69–97.

Young, Richard E., Becker, Alton. L. & Pike, Kenneth. L. 1970. *Rhetoric: Discovery and Change*. New York, New York: Harcourt.

PART IV

Entextualizing controversy

Studying entextualization and controversy

CDA, participant observation, computer-aided corpus analysis

Barbara Johnstone
Carnegie Mellon University

Like Chris Eisenhart's and Susan Lawrence's chapters in Section I, Craig Stewart's chapter in this section enriches traditional sentence-grammar analysis in the **Critical Discourse Analysis** mode by adding rhetorical categories and concepts to the mix. Collectively, Eisenhart's, Lawrence's, and Stewart's chapters make the point that the processes and categories linguists think of when they think about language – transitivity, modality, lexical choice, and the like – are not the only areas of choice in which subtle ideological work can occur. Eisenhart illustrates the ideological effects of genre; Lawrence uses patterns of figuration to drill into the details of the effects of naming and wording.

Stewart introduces two larger-scale variables: framing and argumentation style. The idea that human cognition is organized by means of structured sets of expectations, or frames, originated in the work of cognitive scientists like Schank and Abelson (1977). At the same time, sociologist Erving Goffman (1974) was suggesting that social interaction was organized and interpreted in terms of frames. The idea was taken up in linguistics in work by Deborah Tannen (1979, 1993) and others and in communication studies by scholars like Pan and Kosicki (1993).

Argumentation has long been a concern of philosophers and rhetoricians. Classical rhetoric offers Aristotle's distinction between dialectic, in which arguments are based on shared sets of rules for arriving at truth, and rhetoric, the art of using arguments based on probability. In contemporary rhetoric and argumentation studies, vernacular modes of argumentation have been added to scholars' purview, in addition to the formal, disciplinary modes that were traditionally the focus. At the intersection of rhetoric and linguistic pragmatics, "pragma-dialectics" (van Eemeren & Grootendorst 1994, 2004; Jacobs & Jackson 1989) explores how arguments arise in conversation and describes the inferential processes people use (or should use) in everyday disputes. Stewart uses Stephen Toulmin's (1958) model of argument to describe one of the ways that scientific discourse about a controversial psychiatric study reflects popular-media discourse about it, despite the bright-line boundary scientists attempt to maintain between the scientific and the popular.

Susan Gilpin's chapter exemplifies some of the methods of **participant observation**. Participant observation is the primary research technique of ethnography, or the description of cultures. It was developed by cultural anthropologists interested in finding out from the perspective of natives what foreign cultures were like, particularly the small, isolated, traditional societies that have been the focus of anthropological research until fairly recently. Stocking (1983:7) describes the main features of traditional participant observation research this way: "Entering as a stranger into a small and culturally alien community, the investigator becomes for a time and in a way part of its system of face-to-face relationships, so that the data collected in some sense reflect the native's own point of view." The experience of participant observation fieldwork is a key element of anthropology's disciplinary self-image, in which such fieldwork is valued as an important formative experience for new scholars as well as because it reflects and encourages a holistic approach to describing culture and an egalitarian, relativistic ethic with respect to evaluating societies (Stocking 1983:8).

Beginning in the 1960s, anthropologists began to question the assumptions underlying participant observation, in part because worldwide decolonization began to make it clearer how deeply the approach was influenced by imperialistic attitudes about the relationships between "natives" and Western scholars. As a result, ethnographers began increasingly to talk about fieldwork and try out new ways of imagining whether and how participant observation can lead to knowledge. At the same time, scholars in other fields began to adopt participant observation research methods and join in the discussion about how to use the results.

What differentiates participant observation from casual looking around has to do with the nature of the researcher's participation in the group being studied and the care and systematicity with which records are made and analysis undertaken. Participant observers spend time developing roles for themselves in the groups they are interested in, and then more time as group members, filling one or more roles as insiders and simultaneously making systematic efforts to come to understand what is going on in the group from the perspective of other group members. Participant observers try to uncover and record the unspoken common sense of the group they are studying, the "*immediate and local meanings*" (Erikson 1986:119) in terms of which the local world hangs together for local people. Thus, as Spradley points out (1980:13–20), ethnography is a corrective to social theory that assumes that everyone's beliefs and behaviors can be explained in the same terms, showing instead how social theory has to be "grounded" (Glaser & Strauss 1967; see the Introduction to Section II) in particular situations.

Every analysis of discourse starts with a corpus – a body of texts or transcripts which includes either everything the analyst wants to make claims about (all the letters Constantin Visoianu wrote to the U.S. authorities, all the government reports about the Waco incidents) or a systematic subset of it. Developing a corpus is thus an essential step in any study; any discourse analysis is in this sense a corpus analysis. However, the term **corpus analysis** has come to have a more specialized use both in linguistics and in rhetoric as a label for an analysis that is based on a large set of texts or transcripts (Sinclair 1991; Stubbs 1996; Biber 1988; Hart 1994; Collins, Kaufer, & Vlachos 2004). What "large" means in this context is highly variable. Among the most widely used corpora of text or talk in English are the Brown corpus of just over a million words of edited American English, the London-Lund corpus, which contains 435,000 words of spoken British English, the Lancaster-Oslo-Bergen corpus of one million words of British English, and the Cobuild corpus of written and spoken English, which contains over 200 million words (Stubbs 1996:xvii–xviii). Most studies are based on a selection from one or more corpora.

Corpora like these began to be assembled at the same time computers began to be available to academic researchers. The Brown corpus, for example, was first published in 1964 "for use with digital computers," according to its manual (Francis & Kucera 1964). In principle, one could ask the same questions of a large corpus of texts as one asks of a smaller one; the patterning of linguistic elements across time or context that can be seen in a large corpus of materials could, in principle, be seen by a human or a team of humans. But analyses of large corpora are practical only with the help of computers. Thus most corpus analysis, in this specialized sense, is assisted by computers, which can find repeated words and – if the words in the corpus are appropriately labeled, or "tagged" – structures many times faster than humans can.

The output of a computer-aided corpus analysis varies according to the computer's instructions for searching and for displaying its findings. "Concordance" software finds all the occurrences of a word and displays them with their surrounding text. Other programs produce lists of words arranged by the frequency of their occurrence (the most frequent are sometimes identified as "key words") or find repeated collocations (words that are used together). "Factor analysis" sorts word-classes into groups based on whether they co-vary. (A very influential study using this technique is Biber 1988.) These results are commonly (although not always) submitted to statistical tests to discover which are robust and which are probably accidental.

Peter Cramer's chapter describes a computer-aided corpus analysis. Cramer shares with all the other authors in this volume the assumption that linguistic choice at all levels is rhetorical. Unlike the others, Cramer explores not a set of choices, but one choice: the print news media's choice of a word to use as the cover term for what went on with respect to a museum exhibit in New York that included a painting that some people, among them the city's mayor, found objectionable. Focusing on a single instance of word choice, Cramer was able to track this choice in 273 texts, totaling 204,203 words. Cramer started by using a computer search tool to locate all the articles in three New York newspapers that talked about these events. He then read all of them "manually" (or, perhaps better, humanly) locating words commonly used to categorize the events, words such as *battle, outcry, flap, fuss,* and *controversy.* Then he used another electronic tool – concordance software – to locate and pull out every instance of each of these words in all the newspaper articles that constituted the corpus.

Cramer then focused on the most common of these terms (*controversy* was at the top of the list), exploring how they worked in the sentences they were in. Because, "in contrast to this sort of CDA study design, [Cramer's] study examined a single feature over many instances, and across large corpus of texts," he developed a way of coding each instance using a four-item list of possibilities as to what kind of event each term could be used to represent.

Cramer's methods are in some ways the inverse of Gilpin's. Gilpin examines a very small number of interactions in great detail, getting at them through her own detailed, minute-by-minute observations and through interviews with the people involved and subsequent conversations with them. Her aim is to see how the kind of proto-political discourse she calls heuretic engagement is shaped by constraints and affordances of all kinds; to answer this question, she looks at a single instance under multiple lenses. Cramer examines a very large number of texts, but focuses on a single thing about them, the word that is chosen for one set of events. Cramer looks at his data through one lens, asking how the meaning of a word is shaped by co-text, by the surrounding words. He uses his findings to illustrate the contingency and discursive constructedness of an event category, "controversy," that rhetoricians have commonly taken for granted.

References

Biber, Douglas. 1988. *Variation across Speech and Writing.* Cambridge: Cambridge University Press.

Collins, Jeff, Kaufer, David, and Vlachos, Pantelis. 2004. "Detecting Collaborations in Text". *Computers and the Humanities* 38: 15–36.

Erikson, Frederick. 1986. "Qualitative Methods in Research on Teaching". In *Handbook of Research on Teaching,* M. C. Wittock (Ed.), 119–161. New York: Macmillian.

Francis, W. N., and Kucera, H. 1964. *Brown Corpus Manual.* Department of Linguistics, Brown University. Accessed 14 Feb. 2008 <http://icame.uib.no/Brown/bcm.html>.

Hart, Roderick P. 1994. *Verbal Style and the Presidency: A Computer-Based Analysis*. New York: Academic Press.

Jacobs, Scott, and Sally Jackson. 1989. "Building a Model of Conversational Argument". In *Rethinking Communication*, B. Dervin, L. Grossberg, B. J. O'Keefe and E. Wartella (Eds.), 153–71. Newbury Park, CA: Sage.

Goffman, Erving. 1986[1974]. *Frame Analysis: An Essay on the Organization of Experience*. Boston: Northwestern University Press.

Pan, Z., & Kosicki, G. M. 1993. "Framing Analysis: An Approach to News Discourse". *Political Communication* 10: 55–75.

Schank, Roger C., and Robert P. Abelson. 1977. *Scripts, Plans, Goals, and Understanding: An Inquiry into Human Knowledge Structures*. Hillsdale, NJ: Lawrence Erlbaum.

Sinclair, J. M. 1991. *Corpus, Concordance, Collocation*. Oxford: Oxford University Press.

Spradley, James P. 1980. *Participant Observation*. New York: Holt, Rinehart, and Winston.

Stocking, George W., Jr. 1983. *Observers Observed: Essays on Ethnographic Fieldwork*. Madison: University of Wisconsin Press.

Stubbs, Michael. 1996. *Text and Corpus Analysis: Computer-Assisted Studies of Language and Culture*. Oxford: Blackwell.

Tannen, Deborah. 1979. "What's in a Frame? Surface Evidence for Underlying Expectations". In *New Directions in Discourse Processing*, R. Freedle (Ed), 137–81. Norwood, NJ: Ablex.

_____ (Ed). 1993. *Framing in Discourse*. New York, Oxford: Oxford University Press.

Toulmin, S. 1958. *The Uses of Argument*. New York: Cambridge University Press.

Van Eemeren, F. H., and R. Grootendorst. 1994. *Studies in Pragma-Dialectics*. Amsterdam: International Centre for the Study of Argumentation.

_____. 2004. *A Systematic Theory of Argumentation: The Pragma-Dialectical Approach*. New York: Cambridge University Press.

CHAPTER 10

How a media controversy can influence a scientific publication

The case of Robert L. Spitzer's "reparative therapy" study

Craig O. Stewart
Old Dominion University

In this chapter I use rhetorical theory and critical discourse analysis to investigate how non-technical discourse – specifically, a media controversy – influenced subsequent technical discourse about a controversial study of a putative treatment for homosexuality called "reparative therapy." Paul (2004) notes that, although the traditional model of popularization has been questioned, most studies do not consider the influence of non-technical discourse about science on technical discourse of science. Paul's study finds that popularizations of chaos theory played a significant role in the diffusion of that concept in scientific discourse. Here, I illustrate how discourse about science emerging from a media controversy – drawing on technical and non-technical discourses – may influence subsequent technical discourse about scientific research. My approach integrates Goodnight's (1982) top-down, normative framework of argument spheres with Fairclough's (1992) bottom-up, descriptive framework of orders of discourse. My analysis of the publication of psychiatrist Robert L. Spitzer's reparative therapy study shows how media controversy over this contested scientific study influenced subsequent technical discourse about the study, at both macro-levels (e.g. framing, argumentation strategies) and micro-levels (e.g. grammar). The discursive boundaries between science and non-science were policed by the journal's editor and by Spitzer, who were largely successful. However, some critics were able to challenge these discursive boundaries, even within a scientific order of discourse.

I begin by situating Spitzer's journal publication in relation to ongoing debates over reparative therapy and the pre-existing controversy surrounding his conference presentation. I then describe how ideas about spheres or orders of discourse from rhetoric and discourse studies articulate with one another, and how this theoretical synthesis can be employed in the study of social controversies that draw on discourses of and about science. I then apply this model in an analysis of the publication of Spitzer's reparative therapy study.

Reparative therapy and the Spitzer study

Broadly speaking, reparative therapy is a controversial psychoanalytic treatment for homosexuality. Its proponents argue that homosexuality is a psychosexual disorder that originates in a failure to identify with the same-sex parent in early childhood. In adulthood, they argue, gay men and lesbians attempt to symbolically repair this 'broken' gender development through same-sex sexual activity. Reparative therapy attempts to repair the failure to identify with the same-sex parent by such methods as 'transferring' onto the therapist aspects of the problematic early childhood family dynamics and initiating the client into non-sexual same-sex relationships (e.g., Nicolosi 1992). Very few mental-health professionals, many of whom are members of the National Association for Research and Therapy of Homosexuality (NARTH), practice reparative therapy or other 'conversion' therapies for homosexuality. Such attempts to convert homosexuals into heterosexuals run counter to the official positions of the American Psychiatric Association (APA), which removed homosexuality as a category of mental illness in 1973, as well as other professional mental health organizations. In 2000, the APA reaffirmed its position that homosexuality is not a mental illness, challenged the scientific legitimacy of the theories and research supporting reparative therapy, and recommended "that ethical practitioners refrain from attempts to change individuals' sexual orientation, keeping in mind the medical dictum to 'First, do no harm'" (American Psychiatric Association 2000:2).

Despite the professional and scientific position that reparative therapy is neither scientifically nor ethically valid, conservative Christian organizations began to put reparative therapy and "ex-gay" ministries at the center of their public advocacy on gay and lesbian issues, beginning with a 1998 advertising campaign that portrayed self-identified ex-gays as "living proof" that homosexuality can be changed through therapeutic and religious interventions (Fetner 2005). In May, 2001, Robert L. Spitzer presented a study at the APA's annual convention in which he concluded that "highly motivated" gay men and lesbians can change their sexual orientation through reparative therapy. Spitzer's controversial findings spurred a minor media controversy, wherein discourse of and about the study was recontextualized in a number of sources, with each recontextualization varying "depending on the goals, values and priorities of the communication" (Fairclough 1995b:41). Mainstream news sources such as the Associated Press reported Spitzer's study within a conflict frame, presenting a clash between

Spitzer and mainstream psychiatric science. News media for conservative Christian audiences utilized a responsibility frame, presenting Spitzer as responsible for "agitating" gay rights activists, whereas news media for lesbian, gay, bisexual, transgender (LGBT) audiences, like mainstream media, reported the study in the context of a conflict frame. Political organizations representing both LGBT rights groups and ex-gay organizations produced press releases which attempted to define their positions as scientific and their opponents' positions as non-scientific (Stewart 2005).

This media discourse about Spitzer's study in 2001 complicates traditional notions about the popularization of science. As Myers (2003) argues, the boundaries between scientific and public discourse are more fluid than is often assumed in studies of scientific popularization. Popularization is no longer seen exclusively as a linear, one-way transaction, in which an originating scientific text is translated and simplified for lay audiences in popular science magazines or news media. When Spitzer's study was reported in the media in 2001, it was not simply a matter of importing discourse from the scientific sphere into the public sphere for the lay audience's education or edification. Rather, the reporting was situated within, and drew from, a variety of textual sources and discursive practices (cf. Beacco et al. 2002; Myers 2003). Thus, the controversy over Spitzer's study constituted not a single communicative event, but a "chain of communicative events" (Fairclough 1995b) – including the conference paper, press releases, interviews, and news reports. This chain did not end with news media discourse, however, but extends to include subsequent technical discourse about this study. After the 2001 convention paper, Spitzer submitted his research for journal publication, and in October, 2003, an article based on his research was published in the *Archives of Sexual Behavior* (hereafter referred to as *ASB*) , together with an introduction by the journal's editor, K. L. Zucker, 26 peer commentaries, and a response to these commentaries from Spitzer.

Articulating the rhetoric of science with Critical Discourse Analysis

In an influential essay, Goodnight (1982) proposes three spheres of argument: the personal, the public, and the technical. These spheres are "branches of activity – the grounds upon which arguments are built and the authorities to which arguers appeal" (216). Similarly, Fairclough (1995a) describes orders of discourse as "relatively stabilized configurations of discourse practices" (2). Unlike argument spheres, though, orders of discourse are not strictly bounded, and can be used to describe a variety of discourse practices, rather than a dichotomous (e.g., public vs. technical) or a tripartite system (public vs. technical vs. personal). As Fairclough (1995a) states, "Boundaries between and within orders of discourse are constantly shifting, and change in orders of discourse is part of sociocultural change" (13). In contrast, while Goodnight (1982) acknowledges "that the spheres of argument are not entirely constant over time, and are subject to revision by argument" (217), he does assume that the three spheres that he identifies are always the relevant ones, and it is not clear to what extent either new spheres could be created, or whether practices within those spheres can be significantly transformed (e.g., Kang 2004). For Goodnight, boundary shifts between these spheres do not represent changes in discourse practices, but rather "attempts to expand one sphere of argument at the expense of another" (Goodnight 1982:217).

Approaching Goodnight's (1982) spheres as high-level, "societal," orders of discourse allows us to investigate intertextual and interdiscursive influences among these orders of discourse, without making normative assumptions about what is 'appropriate' or 'inappropriate' discourse in one sphere or another.[1] Intertextuality refers to the "property texts have of being full of snatches of other texts, which may be explicitly demarcated or merged in, and which the text may assimilate, contradict, ironically echo, and so forth" (Fairclough 1992:84). Interdiscursivity refers to "the heterogeneous constitution of texts out of elements . . . of orders of discourse" (85). Both intertextuality and interdiscursivity figure prominently in the context of controversial science. For example, at the level of intertextuality, Beacco et al. (2002) show how "snatches of text" from scientists, members of the public, advocates, and others come together in media texts about controversial science issues, and how non-experts draw on scientific sources to create their own arguments with respect to those issues. In the case of media discourse about controversial science, "journalists . . . represent the discourse of many speakers *in their different social roles* . . . where scientific knowledge is essentially sought as justification, in an argumentative mode" (Beacco et al. 2002:283, emphasis added).

Data and method

The data for this study are Spitzer's (2003) article, Zucker's (2003) editorial introduction, 26 peer commentaries, and a response to these commentaries from Spitzer. The remainder of this issue of *ASB* contained book reviews, many of which were, perhaps coincidentally, on gay and lesbian issues. Thus, Spitzer's article was the only original research report in this issue of the journal. It is worth noting that *ASB* makes a regular practice of publishing letters to the editor, and in the

---

1. "Societal" orders of discourse subsume more "local" orders of discourse. So, the societal-level scientific order of discourse includes the more local scientific orders of discourse of, for instance, physical versus social sciences, and within each, the orders of discourse of *Science* or the *Archives of Sexual Behavior*.

issues comprising Volumes 30–34 (2001–2005), the journal published a discussion on a category of mental illness called Dyspareunia (Vol. 34, No. 1, February 2005), and a similar section of peer commentaries on two articles on pedophilia (Vol. 31, No. 3, December 2002). But although it is not unusual for the *Archives* to publish discussion and commentaries, it is not the journal's regular practice to pair research reports with peer commentaries, or to devote entire issues to a single research report. Thus, the decision to publish with peer commentaries suggests a response on the editor's part to the controversy that preceded, as does the sheer amount of commentary – 50 journal pages, including references, compared to 25 pages of peer commentary on two articles about pedophilia.

Spitzer's 15-page article, entitled "Can some gay men and lesbians change their sexual orientation? 200 participants reporting a change from homosexual to heterosexual orientation," includes an approximately 200-word abstract, approximately 2 pages of introduction and literature review, 2 pages of Methods, approximately 5 pages reporting results, including 4 graphs and 2 tables, approximately 3 pages of discussion, a half-page appendix reporting the "interview questions for the 10 change measures," and just over a page of references. Spitzer interviewed 200 participants, 143 men and 57 women, who

> satisfy two criteria: (1) predominantly homosexual attraction for many years, and in the year before starting therapy, at least 60 on a scale of sexual attraction (where 0 = *exclusively heterosexual* and 100 = *exclusively homosexual*); (2) after therapy, a change of at least 10 points, lasting at least 5 years, toward the heterosexual end of the scale of sexual attraction. (Spitzer 2003:405)

Spitzer reports that 12% of the men and 28% of the women in his sample reported being in the 60–79 range, with the rest in the 80–100 range. The participants were 96% Christian, and religion was "extremely" or "very" important for 93%. Over three quarters of them "had publicly spoken in favor of efforts to change homosexual orientation, often at their church" (406). Spitzer notes in his conference paper, but not in his journal article, that "the primary motivation for participating in the study for almost all subjects was their interest in providing evidence, from their own experience, that homosexuality can be changed and to offer hope to others" (Spitzer 2001: 15).

The first two figures are bar graphs representing the percentage of subjects in 20-point intervals on the 100-point "Sexual Attraction Scale" and "Sexual Orientation Self-Identity Scale" (in which 0 indicates completely heterosexual and 100 completely homosexual) for "pre" and "post" therapy (408–409). The third figure reports percentage of subjects in five categories of frequency of homosexual sex, "Never," "Few times a year," "Few times a month," "Few times a week," and "Nearly every day" for "pre-" and "post-therapy" (409). The fourth figure reports percentages reporting being bothered "not at all," "slightly," "moderately," "markedly," or "extremely," by "homosexual feelings" for "pre-" and "post-therapy" (410). Males and females are represented separately in each figure. Table 1 reports percentages for males and females at "pre" and "post" on "10 dichotomized homosexual measures," such as "20 or higher on the sexual attraction scale," or "opposite sex fantasies (without trying) on 20% or more of masturbatory occasions among participants who masturbated" (411). Table 2 reported the overall percentage of participants who reported for "pre" and "post" whether they had "heterosexual sex at least a few times a month," "emotional satisfaction with heterosexual relationship at least 8 on a 1–10 scale," and "physical satisfaction with heterosexual sex at least 8 on a 1–10 scale" (411).

An important part of Spitzer's argument hinges on whether the participants in his study achieved what he called "good heterosexual functioning," for which he set the following criteria: "(1) during the past year, the participant was in a heterosexual relationship and regarded it as 'loving'; (2) overall satisfaction in the emotional relationship with their partner (at least 7 on a 1–10 scale); (3) heterosexual sex with partner at least a few times a month; (4) physical satisfaction from heterosexual sex at least 7 (the same 1–10 scale); (5) during no more than 15% of heterosexual sex occasions thinks of homosexual sex" (406–407). Spitzer argues that 66% of men and 44% of women in his study met these criteria. More broadly, as Spitzer argues in the discussion section:

> This study indicates that some gay men and lesbians, following reparative therapy, report that they have made major changes from a predominantly homosexual to a predominantly heterosexual orientation. The changes following reparative therapy were not limited to sexual behavior and sexual orientation self-identity. The changes encompassed sexual attraction, arousal, fantasy, yearning, and being bothered by homosexual feelings. The changes encompassed the core aspects of sexual orientation. Even participants who only made a limited change nevertheless regarded the therapy as extremely beneficial. Participants reported benefit from nonsexual changes, such as decreased depression, a greater sense of masculinity in males, and femininity in females, and developing intimate nonsexual relationships with members of the same sex (413).

The 26 peer commentaries were written by researchers and practitioners in psychiatry, psychology, counseling, social work and related fields. The commentaries were solicited through a call broadcast on four listservs: "SEXNET, an Internet research discussion group ..., the International Academy of Sex Research ..., the Society for Sex Therapy and Research ...,, and Division 44 [The Society for the Psychological Study of Gay, Lesbian and Bisexual Issues] ... of the American Psychological Association" (Zucker 2003:400). Overall, of the 26 commentaries, 17 were generally critical of Spitzer's research, eight were generally positive, and one was mixed. Most of the commentaries ran from two to three pages.

As Fairclough argues, boundaries between orders of discourse can become contested sites of socio-cultural change. Control over what gets counted as scientific discourse, and who gets to control such determinations, is particularly ripe for struggle. Scientists' authority to speak on controversial social issues is obtained by rhetorically constructing strict discursive boundaries between science and non-science (e.g., Condit 1996; Gieryn 1999; Taylor 1996). Spitzer, the editor of *ASB*, and most of the peer commentators rhetorically demarcated the boundaries of 'science' to include Spitzer and his research, and to exclude the media discourse that had preceded it in May, 2001. However, despite both excluding discourse from the 2001 media controversy and arguing explicitly for the need to exclude politics from the discussion of reparative therapy, this scientific publication was indeed influenced by the preceding media controversy.

I demonstrate this influence in the following ways. First, following from a previous analysis of the 2001 media controversy (Stewart 2005), I show how a specific element of news media discourse practice, the conflict frame, is reproduced by both the journal editor and Spitzer in ASB. Second, I show how the published research report responds argumentatively to criticisms that were publicized in the 2001 controversy. These argumentative responses are evident both in micro-rhetorical (i.e., grammatical) shifts from the 2001 conference paper to the 2003 journal articles and in macro-rhetorical argumentative strategies – specifically, the use of explicitly stated Warrants (Toulmin 1958) to flesh out particular counter-arguments to criticisms of the study. Finally, despite the journal's stated goal of excluding non-scientific discourse from its purview, I show how a few of the peer commentators attempted to construct different rhetorical boundaries, either to position Spitzer and his study as non-scientific, or to consider how different kinds of discourse might be included in the scientific discussion of reparative therapy and its effects.

Interdiscursive influences in framing Spitzer's study in a scientific order of discourse

Framing is a concept used by news media scholars to investigate how headlines, lead paragraphs, and other syntactic and lexical choices in news texts help to create particular perceptions about events and stories (e.g., Pan & Kosicki 1993; see also Goffman 1986; Tannen 1993). The discourse practices of the news media order comprise a set of available frames, many of which favor dramatic narratives (Bennett 2003). Dramatic framing can be instantiated by a conflict frame pitting two or more interlocutors or positions in opposition to one another. News discourse tends to recontextualize science on sexual orientation through a "biological determinism vs. chosen behavior" conflict frame (Wilcox 2003). In Wilcox's analysis, the position that homosexuality is a "chosen behavior" is presented as a "disembodied, taken-for-granted backdrop," for which no source or attribution was given, and "against which the self-interested claims of gay communities stand to be validated or rejected by science" (241). As shown in Stewart (2005), the 2001 recontextualizations of Spitzer's study by the news media were also framed in terms of conflict; however, this conflict was specifically defined as "Spitzer vs. the American Psychiatric Association" in much of this discourse. Although this frame made present the source of claims that homosexuality can be changed, it also constructed this source, Spitzer, as politically disinterested, and his arguments as relying on objective evidence. Conversely, criticisms of Spitzer's claims were often attributed to politically interested "gay rights activists," and the APA's arguments were represented without supporting evidence.

In the 2003 recontextualization in *ASB*, both the editorial introduction to the special section and Spitzer's introduction/literature review in the research report situate this study within a conflict frame, very similar to those found in the news media order of discourse, pitting reparative therapists against the APA and other mental health professional organizations. Further, these interlocutors are framed such that reparative therapists are constructed as (relatively) disinterested, whereas the professional mental health organizations are portrayed as politically interested. Further, these groups' arguments are represented as underdetermined by objective criteria, whereas reparative therapy is accepted as a default position, until disconfirmed by scientific research. Thus, the framing of this dispute in this scientific order of discourse mirrors the ideological framing of the news media order of discourse, in which the notion that homosexuality can or should be changed is taken for granted, whereas contrary claims are represented as politically interested and requiring empirical validation.

Editorial introduction

Spitzer's study had already been reported in the media and had been criticized as "unscientific" by psychiatrists and psychologists as well as by gay and lesbian rights advocates. At the same time, it was touted as a major scientific advance by advocates of reparative therapy and by ex-gay ministries and other political conservatives. Zucker, the journal editor, acknowledges the political nature of the debate over sexual orientation change in the title of his editorial ("The politics and science of reparative therapy"), and the ideological commitments of some of the interlocutors in the debate.[2] However, he does not directly mention the previ-

---

2. Zucker describes "reparativists" as "both politically and ideologically conservative and 'rightist'" and "constructionists" as "both politically and ideologically liberal and 'leftist'" (399).

ous media controversy over Spitzer's study, except to allude to it at the end of his introduction:

(1)   It is the Editor's view that a scholarly journal is a legitimate forum to address controversial scientific and ethical issues rather than leaving the complexity of the attendant discourse to 'the street' (Zucker 2003:400).

Zucker characterizes "reparative therapists" politically, as a "movement of … dissenters" vis-à-vis the mental health profession. However, the discourse of this group is represented neutrally, as "arguing" for the existence of a clinical population whose "desire [to change their sexual orientation] should not only be respected, but treated," and as "describ[ing] a technique" for this "treatment." Additionally, "reparative therapist" Charles Socarides is represented as having "disagreed with the decision to remove homosexuality from the DSM." Otherwise, the positions of reparative therapists are not represented in the editorial. That is, what specifically reparative therapists argue with respect to the psychological aspects of homosexuality, or the mechanisms by which sexual orientation change occurs, is not presented.

Within the conflict frame that Zucker constructs between "NARTH and its critics," discourse about "reparative therapy" from "the street" is delegitimized. Zucker makes repeated appeals to (the lack of) empirical data about the "outcomes" of reparative therapy. Additionally, Zucker discounts "ethics" or "sexual politics" as legitimate sources of evidence for "reasoned and nuanced conclusions" about reparative therapy. With this demarcation between the discourses of science and of "the street," only "professional organizations," and not reparative therapists, are accused of making street-level statements "contaminated by rhetorical fervor," because of their lack of empirical support. Although Zucker states that "*any* decisive claim [about reparative therapy] … really must be taken with a rather substantial grain of salt," only professional organizations are represented in the editorial as making such claims ("formal resolutions" and "clear statements"). In sum, reparative therapy is represented as a "technique" or "treatment," which reparative therapists have "described." In contrast, the mainstream position of the mental health field is described as "contaminated by rhetorical fervor," and as a "decisive claim" made without appropriate empirical backing. In other words, the burden of proof lies with critics of reparative therapy, who must empirically disconfirm the claims of reparative therapists.

Spitzer's literature review

Like Zucker's editorial, Spitzer's introduction and literature review establish a conflict frame between reparative therapists and mainstream mental health organizations. In Spitzer's representation of the dispute, the discourse of reparative therapists is represented neutrally, with verbs such as "believe," "say," or "estimate," whereas the professional organizations' statements are represented with potentially loaded verbs such as "assert" and "warn." The positions of reparative therapists are offered without citations or attribution, except for an estimate of outcomes.[3] In contrast, the positions of the mental health field are attributed to the statements of various professional organizations, which are cited. Further, lengthy quotes from the American Psychiatric Association's statements are offered.

Unlike the claims of the "reparative therapists," both the authority and veracity of the APA's position are directly questioned: "Is this *seemingly authoritative position statement true?*" (emphasis added). Spitzer's literature review answers this question, citing evidence that there are as many as "84 articles or books having some relevance to the possibility of sexual orientation change," of which 19 "provide enough data to evaluate the effect of the treatment" (404). Spitzer discusses in detail three of these previous studies, only one of which is in the latter 19. Although there is published data, Spitzer states that "all of these 19 studies have one or more serious methodological shortcomings," thus creating an exigency for Spitzer's intervention.

The recontextualization of Spitzer's study within a scientific order of discourse echoes the conflict frame used in news media orders of discourse to represent science on sexual orientation in general (Wilcox 2003), as well as the controversy over Spitzer's study in particular (Stewart 2005). This frame is established more narrowly in Spitzer's published article, as being specifically between "reparative therapists" and "professional organizations" in mental health fields, thus excluding discourse from non-scientific sources. However, in both orders of discourse, the position that homosexuality can or should be changed is privileged; in the news media, this is by way of presenting this position as a background assumption, without sourcing or attribution. In the scientific order of discourse, this privilege is instantiated by representing the mental health field's position on reparative therapy as politically interested and unsupported by data, while eliding the political positions of reparative therapists and glossing their theoretical positions without discussing the (lack of) empirical backing of these positions. While this technical discourse excluded direct intertextual influences from media orders of discourse (that is, there were no direct representations of non-scientific discourse), interdiscursive influences of those orders of discourse were present in the framing of the study and the ideological impact of that framing.

---

3.   In the first paragraph of the article, Spitzer does provide some parenthetical citations for "reparative therapists," but to support the statement, "In the past, [attempting to alter sexual orientation] was considered both desirable and possible." The only contemporary citation of a "reparative therapist" in the article is to a submitted manuscript. More recent theoretical works, such as Nicolosi's (1992) volume, are not cited.

Argumentative responses to the 2001 media controversy

In this section, I investigate the influence of news media discourse on the technical discourse of Spitzer's study at the level of textual shifts between Spitzer's 2001 conference paper and 2003 article.[4] I show how mentions of Spitzer's personal role in the historical context of the APA's 1973 removal of homosexuality from the DSM and of potential political misuses were deleted in 2003, although these were important parts of how Spitzer, and the media, framed the study in 2001. These deletions contribute to the demarcation that excludes "non-scientific" discourse from the 2003 recontextualization of Spitzer's study. Additionally, micro-rhetorical shifts in the language that Spitzer uses to represent his subjects and how he recruited them suggests that, despite the lack of explicit reference to the 2001 controversy, Spitzer was responsive to criticisms of his sampling procedure that were made in that controversy. Finally, I show how Spitzer uses explicit argumentative warrants to justify his methodology in light of criticisms by other scientists as well as political activists that his study lacked scientific rigor.[5]

Deletions

At the time of his 2001 conference presentation, Spitzer situated his work in a broader political and historical context, especially in the context of his own role in removing homosexuality from the DSM in 1973. Referencing himself frequently, both in the third-person and with first-person pronouns, while critiquing the methods of previous researchers, Spitzer positioned himself as personally skeptical:[6]

> (2) *I* certainly shared this viewpoint [that homosexual orientation cannot be changed], so how did *Bob Spitzer*, who *played a central role* in eliminating homosexuality as a mental disorder from DSM-II in 1973 come to have doubts

---

4.   References to Spitzer's 2001 conference paper come from his PowerPoint slides and notes, which he graciously shared with me.

5.   Before presenting his hypothesis, Spitzer states, "This study attempts to contribute to that research [on reparative therapy's risks or benefits] by studying whether some individuals receiving reparative therapy do, in fact, change their sexual orientation from homosexual to heterosexual" (405). However, the hypothesis suggests that the most likely outcome is that people do change their sexual orientation, rather than presenting two possible outcomes as equally likely.

6.   Although Spitzer does not mention the 1973 decision of the APA in the article, he does mention the 1973 DSM decision and his role in it in the response to the peer commentaries ("the anger that has been directed at me for doing this study reminds me of a similar reaction to me during my involvement in the removal of the diagnosis of homosexuality from DSM-II in 1973" [472].)

about this consensus. The answer is that at the 1999 APA annual meeting in Washington *I* talked to several people who were picketing the meeting and claiming that, contrary to a recent APA position statement, change of sexual orientation was possible and should not be discouraged and that they, personally had changed from homosexual to heterosexual. *I* started to wonder, could it be that some homosexuals could actually change their sexual orientation? After much thought, and realizing that previous studies claiming that such change was possible had all kinds of methodological flaws, *I* concluded that my curiosity would only be satisfied if *I* conducted a study of *my own* (Spitzer 2001:4).

Spitzer argues that his interest in this topic began with his interactions with political picketers at the APA convention (a story which parallels that of his involvement in the 1973 removal of homosexuality from the DSM, wherein he spoke with gay and lesbian activists about their position).[7]

Besides situating himself and his study within both the historical and contemporary political debates about homosexuality, Spitzer concluded his 2001 presentation by thinking ahead to potential public and scientific "misuse of study results":

(3)   We are concerned that about [sic] the misuse of our study results.
       The first is to assume that homosexual orientation is changeable for most highly motivated individuals.
       The second is to dismiss the value to some conflicted homosexuals of a shift in sexual identity and unwanted sexual behavior, even when sexual orientation is not substantially changed.
       The third is that the study results could be used to justify coercive treatment and the denial of civil rights to homosexuals.
       The fourth is to imply that homosexuals should try to change
       (Spitzer 2001:39–40).

The first, third, and fourth of these potential misuses anticipate the arguments that some political conservatives might make using Spitzer's study as evidence, thus recognizing that this study's reach extends into social and political orders of discourse. The second anticipates objections that gay- and lesbian-affirmative

---

7.   The following account is from Bayer (1981), based on interviews with Spitzer: "Robert Spitzer ... came into contact for the first time with homosexuals demanding a revision of psychiatry's attitude toward homosexuality. Impressed by both their passion and their arguments, he agreed to arrange for a formal presentation of their views before a full meeting of his committee and to sponsor a panel at the APA's 1973 convention on the question of whether homosexuality ought to be included in the Association's official listing of psychiatric disorders" (116).

therapists might make, based on concerns about harm caused to those who try but cannot shift their sexual orientation. In the 2003 journal article, on the other hand, only the second misuse is discussed in detail, while considerations of other potential political misuses of the study are not discussed.[8] In sum, in his 2001 conference paper, Spitzer explicitly addresses the historical context (in personal terms) as well as potential political consequences for his study; in 2003, Spitzer is largely silent on both of these considerations which played significant roles in the 2001 controversy.

Micro-rhetorical shifts

The recruitment of subjects from ex-gay ministries and NARTH was a major source of the public criticism of Spitzer's study in 2001 (Stewart 2005). Although these criticisms are not mentioned in the text, linguistic, or micro-rhetorical, shifts in the description of Spitzer's recruitment of subjects (including a shift to describing them as "participants" rather than "subjects") suggest that these criticisms influenced how this portion of the methodology is represented in the 2003 article. The following excerpts are from the 2001 conference paper and 2003 journal article, respectively.

(4) 2001 Conference Paper
Our 200 subjects were primarily recruited from ExGay religious ministries that offer a variety of programs to help homosexuals who want to overcome their homosexual feelings.
And from NARTH, the National Association for Research and Therapy of Homosexuality, a group of mental health clinicians and lay people who by and large regard homosexuality as a treatable developmental disorder.
The 'Other' was largely other subjects [in the study], therapists who do sexual reorientation Rx, as well as responses to notices of the study on the radio and in newspaper advertisements.
The referral source, by various means, *got in contact* with potential subjects who then called my office to arrange for an interview (Spitzer 2001. 12).

(5) 2003 Journal Article
Forty-three percent of the 200 participants *learned* about the study from ex-gay religious ministries and 23% from the National Association for Research and Therapy of Homosexuality, a group of mental health professionals and lay people who *defend the right* of gay men and lesbians to received sexual

---

8. Spitzer does acknowledge in his discussion that his difficulty recruiting subjects may indicate that the change he describes is rare, but offers that the difficulty may have been due to "reluctance of ex-gays to be interviewed and reluctance of therapists to contact former clients" (413).

reorientation therapy. In all but a few cases, these individuals were not chosen by these organizations; the *individuals decided on their own* to participate
after reading repeated notices of the study that these two organizations had
sent to their members. Nine percent of the participants were recruited from
their former therapists who had heard about the study. The remaining 25% of
the participants were largely referred by therapists who provide sexual reorientation therapy or by other individuals that were participating in the study.
All of *the participants, not the referral source, called the author* to arrange for
an interview (Spitzer 2003:406).

The first shift is between the passive and active voice for "subjects" (or "participants"). In the conference presentation, the subjects "were recruited" from "ExGay
religious ministries" and NARTH, whereas in the subsequent article, the subjects
have become agentive "participants", who "learned about" the study from these
organizations. In the conference presentation, NARTH is described as "a group of
mental health clinicians and lay people who by and large regard homosexuality
as a treatable developmental disorder," a formulation which makes present their
opposition to mainstream psychiatric science. In the subsequent journal article,
the description becomes, "a group of mental health professionals and lay people
who defend the right of gay men and lesbians to received sexual reorientation therapy," which places the group in a seemingly positive political position with respect
to patients. Finally, in the 2001 conference paper, when describing the immediate
contact between subjects and Spitzer, the "subjects" are agents ("subjects who then
called my office"), but in an embedded clause; the topical focus of the sentence is
the "referral source." In the 2003 paper, the "participants" became the topical focus for the sentence, and agency is removed from the referral source ("All of the
subjects, not the referral source, called the author").

These shifts suggest that criticisms that initially emerged within media orders
of discourse affected how this study was recontextualized within a scientific order
of discourse. "Non-scientific" contextual concerns, such as Spitzer's historical role
in revising the DSM, discussions with activists, and considerations of political implications, are silenced, while micro-rhetorical shifts in describing the criticized
subject selection process transitioned the subjects from playing passive to active
roles in choosing to participate.

Macro-rhetorical argumentative strategies

Besides the recruitment of subjects, another major criticism of Spitzer's study in
2001 was his reliance on self-report measures, rather than on presumably more
objective physiological methods. Spitzer acknowledges that his research "would
have greatly benefited by also using objective measures of penile or vaginal pho-

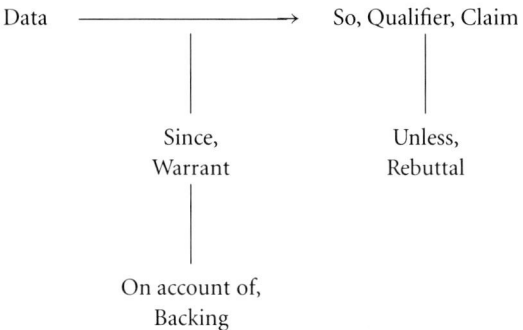

Figure 1. Representation of Toulmin's (1958) argument scheme

toplethysmography," but "this was judged to be not feasible as funds were not available …" (412). He further acknowledged that, "Using a prospective design, in which participants were evaluated before entering therapy and then many years later, would provide much more information than the design that was used. However, such a study was not feasible" (412).

Therefore, Spitzer must justify the validity of his self-report data and its relevance to his conclusion. I use Toulmin's (1958) model of argument, specifically the notion of Warrant, to analyze Spitzer's argument strategy (Figure 1). I also use Toulmin's model to characterize the overall debate that takes place in the *Archives of Sexual Behavior.*

In Toulmin's scheme, Data are the reasons offered in support of a Claim. Warrants are "general, hypothetical statements, which can act as bridges" that link reasons to claims in an argument, and "may normally be written very briefly (in the form 'If D, then C')" (Toulmin 1958:98). Warrants often are not explicitly stated in arguments, but are instead appealed to implicitly (100), similar to a suppressed premise in an Aristotelian enthymeme. Qualifiers such as *most likely* or *probably* "[indicate] the strength of the bearing of W[arrant]" on the relationship between Data and Claim, while the Rebuttal "[indicates] circumstances in which the general authority of the warrant would have to be set aside" (101). The Backing is evidence to support the Warrant, and is "field dependent" in Toulmin's scheme, meaning that different fields, like jurisprudence or science, might require different kinds of Backing to support Warrants, for example, legal precedent or empirical validation.

Spitzer addresses the criticism that the self-reports in his study are compromised as scientific evidence in excerpt (6) below:

(6) Are the participants' reports of change, by-and-large, *credible or* are they *biased* because of self-deception, exaggeration, or even lying? This critical issue deserves careful examination in light of the participants' and their spouses'

high motivation to provide data supporting the value of efforts to change sexual orientation. Again, it is impossible to be sure, but comparing the actual results to the results that might be expected if such systematic bias were present suggests (at least to the author) that, by-and-large, this is not the case. Several such comparisons follow (412).

Spitzer sets up an implied contrast between "credible" (i.e., true) self-reports and "biased" self-reports (i.e., "self-deception, exaggeration, or even lying"). He offers six arguments to support his contention that the reports are credible, rather than biased. In five of these, Spitzer explicitly states the Warrant that links his reasons to his claim, that the self-reports are not biased.[9] These arguments are presented in the following excerpts, with the Warrants in *italics* and the Data underlined. The Claim, in each case, is: So, the self-reports are (likely) unbiased.

(7)   *If there was significant bias, one might expect that many participants would report complete or near complete change in all sexual orientation measures at POST.* Only 11% of the males and 37% of the females did so.

(8)   *[If there was significant bias], One might also expect that many participants would report a rapid onset of change in sexual feelings after starting therapy.* In fact, participants reported that it took, on average, a full 2 years before they noticed a change in sexual feelings.

(9)   *If there was bias, one would expect that participants would be reluctant to admit any use of gay pornography.* In fact, 24% of the males and 4% of the females acknowledged that at POST they had used gay pornography.

(10) *If systematic bias was present, one would expect that the magnitude of the bias for females would be similar to that for males.* However, marked gender differences were found.

(11) *If their [the married couples'] reports of marital adjustment were biased to show how helpful the therapy was for their marriage, one would expect that the married participants would report a level of marital adjustment higher than that of the normative reference group of the Dyadic Adjustment Scale.* . . . However, they did not report a current level of adjustment higher that that of the normative reference group for this instrument (412–413).

Explicitly stating Warrants suggests that the relationship between these reasons and claim are not obvious (Booth, Colomb, & Williams 1995). This strategy makes the arguments more intelligible to a potentially skeptical audience, but it also creates an opening for attacking the arguments. In particular, it suggests openings in terms of the Backing for the Warrants, as well as Rebuttals, that is, conditions

---

9.   This strategy represents another shift between the 2001 and 2003 representations of this study. In 2001, Spitzer offered similar arguments, but without explicitly stated warrants.

under which the Warrants would have to be "set aside." In this case, Backing could have been established through parenthetical citations, pointing to studies that "establish" the relationships in the Warrants; the Warrants could be attacked similarly, by pointing to research that contradicts these Warrants. Rebuttals could include arguments that suggest that Spitzer's data are unreliable or invalid, suggesting that expected relationships between what subjects report and what can be inferred would have to be set aside.

To summarize, in the 2001 controversy over his study, Spitzer was sharply criticized for his reliance on self-report data. In his 2003 journal article, Spitzer makes very explicit arguments to bolster the credibility of this data, in particular, by expressly stating the Warrants that link his reasons to the Claim that the self-reports are likely credible, and not biased. At least 10 of the 26 peer commentators attack these Warrants, either by citing research (i.e., Backing) that suggests other Warrants are more likely, or by suggesting that methodological problems in Spitzer study offer Rebuttal conditions that negate the relevance of his Warrants. These critiques offer compelling reasons for rejecting Spitzer's claim that his data show that some people change their sexual orientation through reparative therapy.

However, while Spitzer explicitly states his Warrants in his arguments that the self-reports are valid, the Warrants for his overall argument that his subjects have changed their sexual orientation are left unstated. This argument can be represented as in Figure 2. The Warrants underlying this argument, such as, "Since gay men and lesbians who 'repair' broken gender development will tend to change their sexual orientation," or "Since gay men and lesbians who accept Christ as their savior will tend to change their sexual orientation," and the backing for these assumptions, such as, "On account of Psychoanalytic models of sexual development," or "On account of The Bible," are glossed in the introduction, and are otherwise unstated and uncommented upon.[10] Most of Spitzer's critics focus their arguments on relatively narrow empirical questions, namely, whether this self-report data constitutes reliable and valid evidence for sexual orientation change. Such critiques then leave aside those assumptions (Warrants and Backing) that are central to the representations of gay men and lesbians in discourse about reparative therapy and to the ideological and theoretical commitments of those who advocate it.

Within this scientific order of discourse, the *Archives of Sexual Behavior,* the debate about reparative therapy is largely limited to the empirical questions of whether the "treatment" is "efficacious." As shown in the preceding analyses, the arguments that attempt to establish reparative therapy as a psychotherapeutic

---

10. Some critics argue that Spitzer does not and cannot address questions of causation in his research design, which addresses the role of Warrants in argument in a general sense, but does not open up a specific critique of these Warrants.

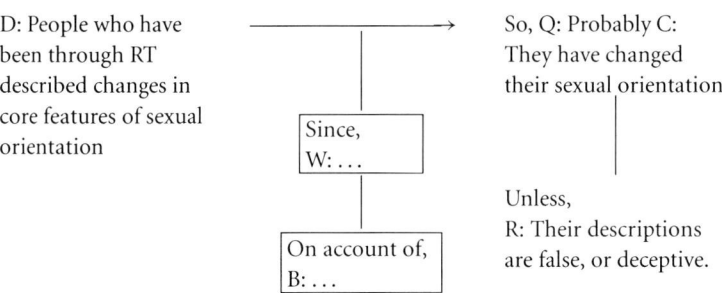

Figure 2. Representation of Spitzer's argument using Toulmin's scheme

practice are merely glossed rather than debated; social and political aspects of the debate are declared irrelevant and excluded from explicit consideration, even as they exert an influence on the discourse. However, as I discuss in the next section, a few respondents attempt to redefine the discursive boundaries for this debate to make present the role of social and political orders of discourse within a scientific order of discourse.

Peer commentaries

The majority of those peer commentaries critical of Spitzer's research addressed problems of methodology and research ethics (e.g., informed consent), but either do not address or only tangentially address the broader political or historical context in which Spitzer's study is situated. In other words, Spitzer's *Archives* critics attempted to expel Spitzer's study from the realm of "good science" on scientific criteria, but for the most part, they did not problematize the demarcation between "science" and "non-science," even thought the controversy regarding Spitzer's research comprised not only scientific, but political, religious, and personal orders of discourse. Although these scientists wish to disqualify Spitzer's study as "good science," they do not in their commentaries attempt to redraw discursive boundaries that would disqualify "science" from being able to make authoritative claims about reparative therapy in particular or homosexuality in general. Indeed, some critics praise Spitzer for initiating an empirical investigation and for cautioning against mixing scientific and moral concerns. For example, Strassberg (2003) says "Spitzer is to be congratulated on trying to 'light a candle' rather than continuing to 'curse the darkness'" (452), while Rust (2003) warns that "[it] is important . . . to distinguish methodological criticisms from criticism of Spitzer's underlying moral perspective, and to refrain from using the former to undercut the latter" (449).

As mentioned in the previous section, many of the peer commentaries on Spitzer's journal article were critical of his reliance on self-report data, some going into extensive detail about both Spitzer's collection and interpretation of this data. Some address directly the Warrants that Spitzer offers. For example, Hill and DiClemnti (2003) argue that "distortion never occurs in a form where all individuals skew their reports perfectly in line with the desirable standard" and that gender differences may obtain when there is deception, "*especially* with respect to sexuality" (441). Rind (2003) suggests that these self-reports reflect the resolution of the subjects' "cognitive dissonance" between their actual and desired sexual orientation, and thus would not result in "perceptions of complete and rapid change" (448). Others address more general methodological problems, which bear on whether Spitzer's Warrants are relevant. For example, Herek (2003) notes that Spitzer did not "make even minimal attempts to assess the data's reliability (e.g., by assessing internal consistency within interviews and through follow-up interviews) and validity (e.g., through third party ratings or independent personal interviews with the respondent's spouse)" (438–439). In sum, much of the critique of Spitzer's study can be characterized as addressing either the lack of Backing, by pointing to evidence that suggests his Warrants are invalid, or by making criticisms that act as Rebuttals, which could be represented as "unless the data lack reliability or validity," in which case Spitzer's Warrants would have to be "set aside."

However, some critics, rather than focusing on methodological issues, situate Spitzer's study and their critiques in the broader, non-scientific context(s), allowing, at least, that the boundary between science and non-science is not as brightly drawn as others would have. The commentaries that do this kind of work are Jack Drescher's (2003) "The Spitzer study and the culture wars," John H. Gagnon's (2003) "The politics of sexual choices," and Marcus C. Tye's (2003) "Spitzer's oversight: Ethical-philosophical underpinnings of 'reparative therapy.'" Drescher is a psychiatrist, head of the APA's Committee on Gay, Lesbian, and Bisexual Issues, and a frequent commentator in the media. Gagnon is an emeritus professor of sociology who researches AIDS prevention and has edited a book of "post-modern" approaches to sex research. Tye is a clinical psychologist who researches LGBT issues and legal issues in psychology. I show how these commentaries position Spitzer, his study, or the topic of sexual orientation change outside the discursive boundaries of science.

Drescher (2003) argues that "reparative therapy" is not properly bounded with the realm of science because its arguments have moved from the scientific to the socio-political: "the clinical argument that homosexuality is an illness meshed seamlessly with a social-conservative, political message: Heterosexuality is the only normal expression of human sexuality and accepting homosexuality is harmful to society" (431). Because of this meshing of the technical with the social, the "reparative therapists" arguments are no longer "clinical," but antigay and directed toward non-scientists, who take up their arguments as "recitation" and "mantra." Drescher strengthens the demarcation of NARTH and its members as outside the boundaries of science by associating their tactics with those of creation scientists and by citing examples of NARTH's members intervening in public (e.g., op-eds) and legal (e.g., affidavits) discourse to oppose gay civil rights.

Drescher places Spitzer in the same position to NARTH as NARTH is to anti-gay political groups (that is, as a source of "scientific" arguments and *ethos*). Because of his role in "revamping the American psychiatric diagnostic system in the DSM-III," Spitzer brought "a standing among the international scientific community that no sexual conversion therapist has ever achieved" (431). Therefore, Drescher argues, "antihomosexual social forces now seek to harness Spitzer's reputation – and the media attention he attracts – to legitimize their own [political position]" (431). The significance of Spitzer's study is not his findings, but the "use" to which Spitzer's personal story is put by "conservative political groups." Drescher notes that this use began even before the official presentation, and is thus an implicit critique of Spitzer's scientific practice (suggesting that his results were disseminated through political rather than scientific channels).

Drescher's discursive placement of Spitzer within the bounds of politics rather than science is not complete, however. In discussing Spitzer's response to citations of his work in the Finnish Parliament's debate over whether to extend same-sex marriage rights, Drescher dissociates Spitzer's research from politics.

(12)   However, the question has been raised whether researchers should consider any potential social harm which might arise from their scientific research (Byne, Schuklenk, Lasco, & Drescher 2002). To his credit, Spitzer has been willing to speak out against political misuse of his study.

Here Drescher suggests that, although "social harm" may be the result of "scientific research," he does not go so far as to say in this case that the research itself was a social harm; rather, it is the "political misuse" of science, in this case Spitzer's study, which is the (at least proximal) cause of "social harm." Drescher ends his commentary writing, "With the publication of his study, one can only hope that when Spitzer's 'rockets' land elsewhere, he will find ample time and opportunity to respond to those situations as well" (p. 432).

Unlike Drescher, both Gagnon and Tye explicitly bracket criticisms related to Spitzer's scientific arguments. Gagnon states, "I will not discuss the methodology or substance of the article in any detail. This will undoubtedly be the topic of a number of other commentaries" (434), whereas Tye states, "Although I do not question Spitzer's science, there is a glaring oversight in the article: a failure to examine the ethical and philosophical underpinnings of sexual orientation modification (SOM)" (542). Instead, both of the commentators argue that the questions raised by reparative therapists are not amenable to scientific investigation because they are fundamentally political or ethical.

Gagnon argues that the political context with respect to reparative therapy is similar to that of Jewish people, who face potential discrimination and pressure to convert (e.g., "Jews for Jesus") from the majority cultures in which they reside, and that, more generally, that change in sexual practices is similar to conversions in cultural practices from religion (as in the case of Jews) or national identity (as in the case of immigrants to the United States). Gagnon argues that sexual practices are not best understood in terms of essentialist "orientations" and genetic causality. Instead, like preferences for other cultural practices, "the complex of sex practices is learned in a particular historical or cultural situation" (436). Gagnon positions Spitzer's findings as completely expected and uninteresting from a scientific perspective:

(13)   It is clear from the Spitzer study that some persons who have long (and perhaps exclusive) histories of sex with same gender partners move, often with religious and other 'therapeutic' supports, to lives in which they have sex with persons of the other gender. From prior studies, we know that substantial numbers of persons who have had long (and perhaps exclusive) lives with partners of the other gender have voluntarily (sometimes describing the experience as finding their true selves) and sometimes with therapeutic support [moved] to lives in which they have sex exclusively or nearly exclusively with persons of the same gender. This movement back and forth in partner preferences is not unexpected given the general movement of humans from one to another deeply seated and 'un-chosen' life way or practice (436).

The almost exact parallelism between the description of Spitzer's findings and that of "prior studies" helps reinforce the idea that what Spitzer found is simply what "we know" about people moving from one sexual orientation to another, and is thus "not unexpected," but rather commonplace. Thus, Gagnon concludes that the debate about Spitzer's study is not over science, but over politics: "Whether such change should happen, what direction it should take, whether it should be encouraged, and who should decide whether it is a good or bad thing for either individuals or communities is the political question" (436).

Tye seeks to place the debate within the ethics of medical practice (as opposed to medical research), explicitly rejecting empirical argumentation in favor of hypothetical ethical reasoning, stating that "[t]he ultimate issues regarding SOM are ethical-philosophical ones and not empirical ones. It is not whether sexual orientation *can* be changed, but whether it *should* be changed" (452, emphasis in original). This demarcation then shifts the focus from whatever the data might show, but to the presuppositions of reparative therapists.

(14)   It is not really client autonomy that is the basis of reparative therapy, but therapist autonomy to change clients, based chiefly on a therapist preference for
heterosexuality. This is ultimately a value judgment and not something that
can be fruitfully addressed through further empirical research (453).

Both Tye and Gagnon construct arguments that place questions of sexual orientation change outside the discursive realm of science. Although Spitzer's study
was sharply criticized by many respondents on its scientific merits, such critiques
reinforced the authority of science to answer questions.

Conclusion

The analysis of the publication of Spitzer's reparative therapy study shows how
a media controversy over a contested scientific study can influence subsequent
technical discourse about the study. Specifically, it shows how an element of news
discourse practice, the conflict frame, is also evident in scientific discourse about
a controversial topic. Further, it shows how criticisms of science that emerged in
a socioscientific controversy may influence subsequent technical discourse about
that science – by deleting references to sociopolitical context, by changing descriptions of critiqued methodology, and by using explicit argumentation to justify
technical claims. Nevertheless, despite this influence, the discursive boundaries between science and non-science were policed by the journal's editor and by Spitzer,
and they were largely successful in maintaining this demarcation. However, some
critics were able to challenge these discursive boundaries, even working within a
scientific order of discourse. It should not be assumed that the technical discourse
on "reparative therapy" preceding the media controversy was somehow untouched
by "non-scientific" discursive influences. As some of Spitzer's critics argued, along
with such science scholars as Condit (1996), Fausto-Sterling (2000), and Longino
(1990), scientific practice in research on topics such as gender, race, and sexuality,
is always embedded within broader social beliefs and practices. As I have shown in
this chapter, critical discourse analyses of scientific texts are crucial to understanding how social and political discourse influence scientific discourse as well as the
converse.

References

American Psychiatric Association. 2000. *Therapies Focused on Attempts to Change Sexual
Orientation (Reparative or Conversion Therapies)*. APA Document Reference 200001.
Washington, D.C.: Author.

Bayer, R. 1981. *Homosexuality and American Psychiatry: The Politics of Diagnosis*. New York: Basic Books.

Beckstead, A. L. 2003. "Understanding the Self-Reports of Reparative Therapy 'Successes'". *Archives of Sexual Behavior* 32. 421–123.

Beacco, J.-C., Claudel, C., Doury, M., Petit, G., & Reboul-Touré, S. 2002. "Science in Media and Social Discourse: New Channels of Communication, New Linguistic Forms". *Discourse Studies* 4. 277–300.

Bennett, W. L. 2003. *News: The Politics of Illusion, 5th ed.* New York: Longman.

Booth, W. C., Colomb, G. G., & Williams, J. M. 2003. *The Craft of Research,* 2nd ed. Chicago: University of Chicago Press.

Condit, C. 1996. "How Bad Science Stays That Way: Brain Sex, Demarcation, and the Status of Truth in the Rhetoric of Science". *Rhetoric Society Quarterly* 26: 4. 83–109.

Drescher, J. 2003. "The Spitzer Study and the Culture Wars". *Archives of Sexual Behavior* 32. 431–432.

Fairclough, N. 1992. *Discourse and Social Change*. Cambridge.: Blackwell.

_____. 1995a. *Critical Discourse Analysis: The Critical Study of Language*. London: Longman.

_____. 1995b. *Media Discourse*. London: Arnold.

Fausto-Sterling, A. 2000. *Sexing the Body: Gender Politics and the Construction of Sexuality*. New York: Basic Books.

Fetner, T. 2005. "Ex-Gay Rhetoric and the Politics of Sexuality: The Christian Antigay/Pro-Family Movement's 'Truth in Love' Ad Campaign". *Journal of Homosexuality* 50. 71–95.

Gagnon, J. H. 2003. "The Politics of Sexual Choices". *Archives of Sexual Behavior* 32. 434–436.

Gieryn, T. F. 1999. *Cultural Boundaries of Science: Credibility on the Line*. Chicago: University of Chicago Press.

Goffman, E. (1986). *Frame Analysis: An Essay on the Organization of Experience*. Boston: Northeastern University Press.

Goodnight, G. T. 1982. "The Personal, Technical, and Public Spheres of Argument: A Speculative Inquiry Into the Art of Public Deliberation". *Journal of the American Forensic Association* 18. 214–227.

Herek, G. M. 2003. "Evaluating Interventions to Alter Sexual Orientation: Methodological and Ethical Considerations". *Archives of Sexual Behavior* 32. 438–439.

Hill, C. A., & Diclementi. 2003. "Methodological Limitations do not Justify the Claim that Same-Sex Attraction Changed Through 'Reparative Therapy'". *Archives of Sexual Behavior* 32. 440–442.

Kang, J. 2004. "Reconfiguring Argument Fields: Towards a Dynamics of Discursive Public Spheres". Paper presented at the National Communication Association Convention, Chicago, November 2004.

Longino, H. E. 1990. *Science as Social Knowledge: Values and Objectivity in Scientific Inquiry*. Princeton, NJ: Princeton University Press.

Myers, G. 2003. "Discourse Studies of Scientific Popularization: Questioning the Boundaries". *Discourse Studies* 5. 265–279.

Nicolosi, J. 1992. *Reparative Therapy of Male Homosexuality*. Northvale, NJ: Jason Aronson, Inc.

Pan, Z., & Kosicki, G. M. 1993. "Framing Analysis: An Approach to News Discourse". *Political Communication* 10. 55–75.

Paul, D. 2004. "Spreading Chaos: The Role of Popularizations in the Diffusion of Scientific Ideas". *Written Communication* 21. 32–68.

Rind, B. 2003. "Sexual Orientation Change and Informed Consent in Reparative Therapy". *Archives of Sexual Behavior* 32. 447–449.

Rust, P. C. R. 2003. "Reparative Science and Social Responsibility: The Concept of A Malleable Core as Theoretical Challenge and Psychological Comfort". *Archives of Sexual Behavior* 32. 449–451.

Spitzer, R. L. 2001. "200 Subjects who Claim to have Changed their Sexual Orientation from Homosexual to Heterosexual". Paper presented at the American Psychiatric Association Convention, New Orleans, May 2001.

_____. 2003. "Can Some Gay Men and Lesbians Change their Sexual Orientation? 200 Participants Reporting a Change From Homosexual to Heterosexual Orientation". *Archives of Sexual Behavior* 32. 403–417.

Stewart, C. O. 2005. "A Rhetorical Approach to News Discourse: Media Representations of a Controversial Study on 'Reparative Therapy'". *Western Journal of Communication* 69. 147–166.

Strassberg, D. S. 2003. "A Candle in the Wind: Spitzer's Study of Reparative Therapy". *Archives of Sexual Behavior* 32. 451–452.

Tannen, D. 1993. *Framing in Discourse*. New York: Oxford University Press.

Taylor, C. A. 1996. *Defining Science: A Rhetoric of Demarcation*. Madison: University of Wisconsin Press.

Toulmin, S. 1958. *The Uses of Argument*. New York: Cambridge University Press.

Tye, M. C. 2003. "Spitzer's Oversight: Ethical-Philosophical Underpinnings of 'Reparative Therapy'". *Archives of Sexual Behavior* 32. 452–453.

Wainberg, M. L. et al. 2003. "Science and the Nuremberg Code: A Question of Ethics and Harm". *Archives of Sexual Behavior* 32. 455–457.

Wilcox, S. A. 2003. "Cultural Context and the Conventions of Science Journalism: Drama and Contradiction in Media Coverage of Biological Ideas About Sexuality". *Critical Studies in Media Communication* 20. 225–247.

Zucker, K. L. 2003. "The Politics and Science of 'Reparative Therapy.'" *Archives of Sexual Behavior* 32. 399–402.

CHAPTER 11

Controversy as a media event category

Peter A. Cramer
Simon Fraser University

Introduction

As a function of their periodic nature and their value of timeliness, newspapers present news stories as new and unique events. However, journalists do not report each story as if it were without precedent. They must find ways to connect their reporting of new developments in ongoing news narratives to the previous events in the narrative and to the prior text of the reporting. Without cohesive links, news readers would not necessarily understand how today's story represents a development from a related story published yesterday, last week, or last year (Bell 1991: 169; Trew 1979b: 141). One way that journalists establish cohesion among news stories is by introducing category terms that classify the ongoing event that they are reporting. Not only does this classifying help to link together separate news stories about the same ongoing event, but it also serves to define the event itself. That is, the classifications that journalists make have more than a text- or coverage-cohesive function; the lexical items that iterate the classifications are not semantically or referentially empty. They carry meaning that inflects the representation of the event and glosses the details of the event (Glasgow University Media Group. 1976a: 355; Trew 1979a: 99, 1979b: 123; Tuchman 1980: 190). Of course, beyond their role in media texts, category terms perform a key cohesive and classifying function in discourse generally (Eggins 2004: 37; Halliday 1978: 125; Kress & Hodge 1979: 62; Martin 1992: 140; Trew 1979b: 141).

In this paper I build on research about classification from Critical Discourse Analysis and functional linguistics by investigating the event categories that journalists use to refer to an ongoing event that is, ostensibly, a controversy: the conflict over Chris Ofili's *The Holy Virgin Mary*, a painting that appeared in the *Sensation* exhibition at the Brooklyn Museum in the Fall of 1999. My object of study is a corpus of news texts that report on this event. "Event categories" are a special case of classification, one that is particularly important in news where journalists must consistently cast the recent and sometimes distant past in language. In this way, my study contributes to research in critical discourse analysis and functional linguistics on classification, especially in analyses of media texts. This study builds on that research by focusing squarely on the language of events and by investigating a specific discourse feature across a large corpus of media texts. I find that "controversy" is an event category that is consistently used to indicate a large-scale, amorphous event involving ill-defined parties when compared to related categories, like "battle," which is used to indicate a localized event involving known parties. The results suggest a ladder of discreteness and agency among event categories, a ladder that descends from the amorphousness and causal opacity of natural events down through the relative discreteness and causal transparency of cultural events. These relationships among event categories and their transformations suggest that even when describing an event that presumably involves a discursive conflict among human beings, journalists use a number of event categories in a variety of transformations that complicate our commonsense assumptions.

"Controversy" as an event category

"Controversy" is a particular event category that journalists sometimes use to classify events. Of course, journalists are not the only writers who use this event category. Scholars also use the term "controversy" to classify a variety of public and professional conflicts. Scholars use the term to denote conflicts within their own professional communities, like the "null hypothesis testing controversy," conflicts that seem to cross professional boundaries, like a the "repressed-memory controversy," and those that seem decidedly public, like the "global warming controversy," a conflict that animates research in several fields, demands government policies, and routinely generates news coverage for a general readership (Froyn 2005; Goodman et al. 2003; Krantz 1999). Anecdotal examples from medicine (Ghali et al. 1999; Lefering & Neugebauer 1995), business (Ayanian 1983; Jensen 1986), policy studies (Hajer 1993), statistics (Krantz 1999; Senn 2000), and psychology (Goodman et al. 2003; McNally 2003) suggest that this sort of denotation is not unusual in scholarship and research in general. Journalists use the term to denote a variety of public conflicts. Consider some anecdotal examples from the news: an "abortion controversy" (O'Hanlon 2004); a "flag controversy" (Hartsell 2005; Wattie 2004); an "art controversy" (Kalette 2005); a "steroids controversy" (Kepner 2005). Research on popular scientific writing has found that controversy plays an important role in bringing expert discourses to public audiences (Gregory & Miller 1998; Nelkin 1995).

    To observe that scholars and journalists use the term "controversy" to denote professional and public conflicts is to state what is intuitive to most readers and users of English. What may be surprising, however, is that scholars do not seem to use the term in a proprietary, technical way. Unlike the terms of art on which scholars typically build their theories and arguments, "controversy" seems to be an ordinary word with no technical meaning. It does not seem to be part of what Halliday and Martin call "scientific English" (Halliday & Martin 1993:4). This is not a criticism of the scholars who use the word; not all the language used in a report of research can or should be proprietary and technical. It only serves to illustrate the extent to which scholars feel a proprietary, technical definition is unnecessary for their purposes. To refer to a "controversy" is not to refer to a substantive object of study; it is a convenient way to make a metadiscursive comment about their field or about the world of law, policy, or culture beyond it.

Rhetoric scholars, however, do make "controversy" one of their central objects of study. Rhetoric research abounds with argumentative, stylistic, or dialectical analyses of controversies (Benoit & Hanczor 1994; Bjork 1995; Darling-Wolf 1997; Dowling & Ginder 1995; Fielding 1995; Foss 1979; Gouran 1995; M. A. Hasian, Jr. & Nakayama 1997; M. Hasian, Jr. 2000, 2003; Hauser 1995; Keehner 1995; Kennedy & Benoit 1997; Matthews 1995; Moore 1993; Olson 1989, 1995; Olson & Olson 1995; Oravec 1984; Palczewski 1995; Railsback 1984; Winkler 1995; Young & Launer 1995; Zarefsky 1984). Among controversies examined by rhetoric scholars, for example, are the "spotted owl controversy", the "breast implant controversy," the "controversy over Reagan's visit to Bitburg." Although controversy is an object of study that is central to rhetorical analysis, rhetoric scholars typically use the word in a conventional way, much like other scholars and journalists. Goodnight (1991) has identified this as a problem. He points out that even rhetoric texts that purport to instruct students about controversy seem to regard its meaning as simple and obvious. He takes as an example of Glen Mills' book, *Reason in Controversy*, which briefly defines "controversy" on page 1; then, as Goodnight says, "The remaining 383 pages of the book is devoted to discussing how to make sound, persuasive arguments and to criticize bad ones" (G. Thomas Goodnight 1991:2). Goodnight himself has aimed to develop a more careful technical understanding of controversy (G. T. Goodnight 1992; G. Thomas Goodnight 1999; Olson & Goodnight 1994), and other scholars from rhetoric and argumentation have also addressed the problem (Dascal 1990; McKeon 1990; Phillips 1999). In these cases, scholars have developed technical definitions based on their knowledge of the rhetorical and the philosophical traditions, on public sphere theory, and on pragmatics. While the majority of rhetoric scholars seem to accept the conventional meaning of "controversy," a few have seen this as a problem and have sought to craft a more careful technical understanding.

Many of those who seek a technical definition take an etic viewpoint on "controversy." According to Kenneth Pike, when a scholar takes an etic viewpoint, that scholar "studies behavior as from the outside of a particular system, and as an essential initial approach to an alien system." A scholar with an emic viewpoint, on the other hand, is "studying behavior as from inside the system" (Pike 1967: 37). Pike emphasizes that these terms name a pair of standpoints rather than a binary pair. The scholars who theorize "controversy" based on the rhetorical and philosophical traditions, on public sphere theory, or on pragmatics are emphasizing an etic viewpoint because they locate "controversy" in the theoretical apparatus that lies outside of the social and linguistic system in which controversies occur. Most other rhetoric scholars do not theorize "controversy" at all, even as they examine and comment on specific cases.

In this paper, I develop an emic analysis of "controversy." Rather than asking, "What is controversy?" and then producing an *a priori* answer based on theories of rhetoric and argumentation, I ask "How do journalists categorize an ongoing event?" and then present an *a posteriori* answer based on an empirical investigation of a news corpus. That is, my viewpoint in this paper is emic because I aim to describe how insiders (i.e., journalists) use particular terms within their profession (i.e., news writing). In this investigation, I use discourse analysis to discover how journalists categorize the conflict over Chris Ofili's *The Holy Virgin Mary*, which appeared in the *Sensation* exhibition at the Brooklyn Museum in the Fall of 1999. Here is how *New York Times* writer Michael Cooper describes the conflict in a 2003 article in which he recounts the event:

> Chris Ofili, the British artist, came to be spoken of as a something of a public enemy around City Hall after his painting "The Holy Virgin Mary" – adorned, memorably, with elephant dung – appeared at the Brooklyn Museum of Art in 1999. Rudolph W. Giuliani, who was then the mayor, called the work "sick stuff," tried to pull city funds from the museum and established what became known as a decency commission to establish standards for all publicly funded museums.
>
> (Cooper 2003)

I take the event to be an *ostensible* controversy because of my encounters with scholarly work that classifies it such: (Becker 2001; Dubin 1999; Ellison 2003; Fraser 2001; Halle 2001; Knowles et al. 2002; Levine 2000). While this offers an interesting starting point – a hypothesis – my discovering that a number of scholars call the event a "controversy" does not explain how the event was apprehended by a broad audience at the time it was unfolding and does not settle the question of how to define the event, in principle. However, by examining the ways that journalists at widely circulating newspapers characterized the event in their reporting, I can document the event categories that they used, shedding light on the mediating work of some primary sources of public information. While I do not provide an empirical account of how readers consumed, comprehended, and interpreted news these news texts at the time, I do examine the texts themselves, texts that had wide circulation in the New York City media market.

For most newspaper readers, news coverage is isomorphic with the event. Readers understand the coverage to be the event because they tend to use news as a "veridical account of social life" (Tuchman 1980:203). That is, news readers, by and large, accept that what they read in the news is factual, that the events reported there did actually happen, and that they have significance. Having read, seen, or heard a report about the event, they routinely speak as if they know what happened. They do not focus on the mediating work of news texts – the linguistic choices or the generic, editorial, and financial constraints (Bennett 2004:132; Tuchman 1980:196). This is not to say that readers have no ability or knowledge that might enable them to recognize the mediating work of news. It speaks instead to the ways that readers use news texts, along with their own constraints of time and attention, and the extent to which news discourse remains seamless with dominant cultural assumptions.

Events in media texts

Studies of media discourse have used "event" as a unit of analysis, especially as a narrative macrostructure (Bell 1991:164; Dijk 1988:42). In his analysis of news stories, for instance, Bell (1991) makes "event" a part of a story grammar, a framework that the analyst can use to map the overall structure of an individual news story. As he analyzes a news story called "Troops take over Lithuanian office," for example, he codes each individual sentence within the story according to which of six "events" it reports. He summarizes these events in his own words, for instance, "1. Occupation of the prosecutor's office" and "4. Bush's note to Gorbachev" (Bell 1991:165). And in his work on news schemata, van Dijk (1988) identifies "Main Event" and "Previous Event" as two of the macrostructures at work in the news story genre. Van Dijk positions "event" as a "macrostructure" rather than a "microstructure" of discourse. Macrostructures, for van Dijk, go beyond "sounds, words, sentence patterns, and their meanings"; they provide "a description at a more comprehensive, global level, that is of whole parts of discourse, or of entire discourses" (Dijk 1988:26).

Terms for events in media texts

Other researchers work at a smaller grain size than Bell and van Dijk, asking questions about lexical items rather than about the structure of narrative. Among these are sociologists of media and critical discourse analysts. In the first case, the analysis of terms and language is a small part of a much larger and more ambitious project examining the professional, financial, social, and ideological production and reception practices of media. For the second, language is a primary object of study and analysts extend their claims about language out to ideology and social practice. Many critical discourse analysts study media texts as a way to illustrate claims about ideology and language, but unlike sociology of media, critical discourse analysis does not limit its focus to media. For critical discourse analysis, media discourse seems to be a special and important case of discourse in general: For instance, compare Fairclough's work on media discourse with his work on discourse and power more generally (Fairclough 1989, 1995). For critical discourse analysis, the tendency to gravitate toward media texts as examples is a predictable outcome of its theoretical commitments to the critique of ideology, given the traditional importance of media to public information and political decision making in modern democratic societies.

The sociology of media

Some sociologists of media observe the categories that journalists use to classify events, pointing out that particular categories have significant ideological and constitutive functions (Fishman 1978, 1988; Glasgow University Media Group. 1976b; Roshco 1975; Tuchman 1980). Tuchman, for instance, uses the term "riot" as an illustration: "news reports transform *a* riot as an amorphous happening into *the* riot (this particular riot) as a public event and public concern" (Tuchman 1980: 190). The Glasgow Media Group illustrates the function of categories in the news by presenting a segment of broadcast news discourse where the term "unrest" is used. They interpret it this way:

> In this piece of news talk, the category "unrest" is used simultaneously to gloss such diverse phenomena as different strikes, shortened work hours, and a conspiracy case. The preferred hearing is clearly that we see (since we are talking of television) all of these as merely cases of "unrest."
>
> (Glasgow University Media Group. 1976: 355)

In both cases, Tuchman and the Glasgow Media group show how journalists use a category to stitch together disparate phenomena into a common category term for a single, specific historical occurrence, and to define the event for their readers.

Although the sociology of media recognizes the importance of category terms in ideology, language remains a sidelight to its primary concerns about institutions, professions, and social practices. Fishman's analysis of "crime waves" provides an example of the ambiguous role that language seems to play for sociologists of media. On the one hand, Fishman observes anecdotally the way that the language of media helps to construct the "crime wave" as an event. He notes that the way the media presents this event could effect a "public definition of a new type of crime" and his on-again off-again use of scare quotes around the term "wave" suggests that he is taking a critical attitude toward that term as it is used in media coverage (Fishman 1978:532). On the other hand, Fishman often uses the phrase "crime wave" as if it refers unproblematically to the historical event he is studying. For instance, he introduces the case by writing, "In late 1976, New York City experienced a major crime wave" (Fishman 1978:531). From the perspective of discourse analysis, this presents an ambiguity and would seem to beg the question. If the phrase "crime wave" is problematic and ideological on the one hand, how can the analyst use it to refer to his object of study, on the other? The generous answer to this question concerns the priorities of Fishman's study, and the priorities of sociology of media in general. Language is simply not the primary focus of this research. Fishman draws conclusions not about media *texts* but about the "news production system" – the judgments of the various media organizations, journalists, and public officials involved in covering the case (Fishman 1978:531).

Critical Discourse Analysis (CDA)

Where sociologists of media mention the ideological functions of category terms as a small part of a much larger analysis of professional, financial, social, and ideological practices of media, critical discourse analysts focus on category terms in media as a way to exemplify their claims about the ideological functions of language more generally. Although some CDA studies have limited their scope specifically to media texts (Fairclough 1995; Trew 1979a, 1979b), others gravitate toward media examples even when their conclusions are more general, concerning discourse and language broadly (Fairclough 1989; Kress & Hodge 1979).

  Critical discourse analysis provides a richer theoretical and methodological framework for investigating linguistic categories than does the sociology of media. Unlike sociologists of media, critical discourse analysts ground their analyses primarily in textual data. When it comes to analyzing classification in a culture or subculture, for instance, Kress and Hodge argue that language is the appropriate object of study because it "provides the major access for individuals into the classification system of their society" (Kress & Hodge 1979:63). And unlike sociologists of media, critical discourse analysts focus on the ways that linguistic classifications limit and inflect writers' and speakers' reports about the world. Following Whorf and Sapir, Kress and Hodge investigate categories in the language in order to make claims about the culture and worldview of the speakers and writers of that language. They suggest that classifications produce control and hegemony: "A classification system constrains thought, giving a basic unity to everything expressed within it, whatever its content, and making alternative systems of classification seem incommensurable" (Kress & Hodge 1979:64).

  Trew (1979) and Fairclough (1995) apply this concern with classification from critical discourse analysis specifically to media texts. Trew, for instance, analyzes the media coverage of the 1977 Notting Hill Carnival, revealing, among other things, the variety of category terms that journalists use to refer to the events and the people involved (Trew 1979b: 126–127). While Trew is particularly concerned with the terms that journalists use to describe people, noting such categories as the "British people," "Blacks," "mob," and "police," he does examine the ways that journalists refer to events. For example, he mentions "riot" and "violence in the streets" (Trew 1979a: 99; 1979b: 123). In reference to a "riot" reported in a newspaper, Trew suggests that classifications provide "a framework for explaining what happened," and to this functional analysis, he adds a critical one: "It is also description which legitimizes police intervention, because riot is by definition civil disorder requiring police action" (Trew 1979a: 99). Trew emphasizes that this research is a "work in progress" and that it is "pointing towards the questions that need to be asked, even it cannot answer them" (Trew 1979a: 116; 1979b: 154).

"Event categories" in the media

In this paper, I build on Trew's research – and other research about classification from critical discourse analysis and functional linguistics – by investigating the category terms that journalists use to refer to events. I call these items "event categories" in order to emphasize that they are a special case of classification, one that is particularly important in news where journalists must consistently cast the recent and sometimes distant past in language. Event categories in media texts function at three levels: the lexicogrammatical, the textual, and the generic. They form *topical reference chains* that *classify events*:

- Generic: Event categories are *topical* because they tend to appear in heads and leads (i.e. titles and summaries) of media texts.
- Textual: Event categories are a kind of *reference chain* because they perform a cohesive function within and across texts.
- Lexicogrammatical: They are used to *classify events*, uniting complex collections of actions and processes with a single category term.

In this paper, I focus primarily on the lexicogrammatical level, showing how journalists deploy particular event categories to refer to and categorize an ongoing event. Following the methods of critical discourse analysis, I analyze lexicogrammatical transformations, examining event categories within the context of a sentence. I draw conclusions about their meaning and function based on the features of the phrases and clauses in which they appear.

The generic level

Event categories are fundamental to contemporary news writing practice. They warrant attention as a particular feature of media discourse (as distinguished from larger projects in the sociological study of news, and from generalized studies of discourse). This follows from the generic structure of news stories themselves. Because journalists observe the "inverted pyramid" principle, they condense descriptions of complex events into brief headlines and leads at the top of news stories. This professional custom requires them to exploit special lexical resources that can gloss particulars while maintaining a meaningful reference function for readers.

Journalists did not always use the inverted pyramid to structure news stories. Because of this, news stories from the nineteenth century, for instance, would likely depend less on event categories than contemporary ones. Bell (1991) provides an example of a news story from 1876 as a way to illustrate the way that news was written before the advent of the inverted pyramid. He points out that before the turn of the century, news stories typically reported events in chronological order, without the summary function of headline and lead that readers expect today. In the 1876 article that Bell reproduces, even the headline (1) is chronological, and the lead sentence (2) reports from the chronological origin of the story:

(1) A Man Jumps From a Lighting Express, but Lights on his Head and is not Hurt.

(2) On Monday night a man named Schwartz took passage at Cincinnati for New York.

In (3), Bell offers his own translation of the lead into contemporary news writing style:

(3) A drunken man survived a jump from the Cincinnati-New York express.

Bell's contemporary lead nominalizes "jump" from its verbal usage in the original headline. In this, Bell transforms "jump" from a specific action being performed by a specific news actor at a specific moment into a category noun, a general class of event that this particular news actor happens to iterate in this particular case. Kress and Hodge analyze nominalizations in media texts, emphasizing the ways in which these transformations elide agency (Kress & Hodge 1979:26).

The textual level

Event categories contribute to textual coherence both within and among individual articles. They are particularly important in the reporting of ongoing news events because they help create *coverage* by reiterating a category term for the event across multiple texts. As they are used across coverage, event categories establish a particular kind of *reference chain* that contributes to event cohesion (Eggins 2004:37; Martin 1992:140). Some of the event categories in the news are particularly episodic and local, like "bombing" and "warning" in headlines (4) and (5) from the *New York Times:*

(4)   Bombings in India Raise Fear of Sectarian Violence

(5)   White House Issues Warning on Iran's Nuclear Ambitions

Others describe long, protracted, emerging events, like "campaign", "war" and "case" in headlines (6)–(8) from the *New York Times:*

(6)   Under Shadow of Sharon, Israeli Election Campaign Begins

(7)   Translator in Iraq War Lied In Citizenship Bid, U.S. Says

(8)   Court Suspends a Ruling in Satmar Case

By reporting on episodic events, like a "bombing" or a "warning," within the context of longer, more protracted, and emerging events, like a "war" or a "campaign," journalists help readers place today's news into the context of an ongoing news event. Event category terms like "war," "campaign," and "case," are among the linguistic resources that journalists use to achieve a sense of coherence in the news, giving readers a sense of an ongoing news event. One of the effects of these category terms is that they present an ongoing news event as if has discrete boundaries. This should be no surprise. In order to write stories that will communicate effectively and efficiently with newspaper readers, journalists must make a number of assumptions about the boundaries of events. One of the ways that journalists do this is by slotting events into event categories.

The lexicogrammatical level

Event categories are typically realized in text as individual lexical items, so the lexicogrammatical level of analysis is crucial to understanding them. At the lexicogrammatical level, event categories are a kind of general noun (Halliday & Hasan 1976) that speakers and writers use to classify complex collections of actions and processes under a single category term (Kress & Hodge 1979; Trew 1979b). Halliday and Hasan define "general nouns," as "superordinate members of major lexical sets" (Halliday & Hasan 1976:274–275). They describe several classes of general noun, including, for example, human nouns, action nouns, inanimate abstract nouns, and place nouns. Event categories are a particular variety of inanimate abstract noun. "Business," "affair," and "matter," are the three examples of inanimate abstract nouns that Halliday and Hasan provide, and event categories are best exemplified by "affair." As past events are the primary resource of news, it should be no surprise that many of the general nouns, especially those used in headlines and leads, are event categories.

The notion of the sentence transformation deployed by critical discourse analysts presents lexicogrammatical morphology as a series of choices made by a writer or speaker – choices that impact the foregrounding and backgrounding of participants and processes. Unlike Chomsky, who explains transformations as variations in surface structure against the substance of the underlying grammar, critical discourse analysts view transformations as having a substantive impact on the way a text is understood by readers (Kress & Hodge 1979: 37). The brief analysis of Bell's nineteenth-century newspaper in examples (1)–(3) above provides an example. There, the verb "jump" was nominalized in Bell's contemporary rewrite. So instead of performing the verbal function within a clause as it does in (1), in (3), "jump" is used as a noun. The nominalization of "jump" disconnects the participant who did the jumping in (1) – "a man" – from the action that he performed by condensing that transitive relationship from the clause into a single, general noun. This example of nominalization illustrates the sort of transformation that generates many event categories in the news.

Design and method

In order to discover how an ongoing news event is categorized by journalists, I counted and ranked various terms that journalists used in referring to the ostensible "Brooklyn Museum Controversy." I constructed a corpus of news texts about the event from the top three circulating newspapers in New York City, and I read and coded all of the texts in the corpus for categories that journalists used to describe the ongoing event. This human reading and coding of the corpus generated a catalog of terms. Working from this catalog, I searched the corpus electronically for each term to discover how many times it was used by journalists in each of the three newspapers represented in the corpus. I searched for each of the terms, collecting each instance along with its sentence context.

I checked each instance for its relationship to the Brooklyn Museum event. For example, if the word "battle" in a particular article referred to the Senate race between Giuliani and Clinton, or the word "controversy" referred to the event over the NEA in the 1980's, I excluded it from the results. The only instances that qualified were those that referred to the conflict between the City of New York and the Brooklyn Museum over the Sensation exhibit. The vast majority of cases did refer to the Brooklyn Museum event. Like many corpus projects, this study delivers both quantitative and qualitative results. In order to deliver the quantitative results, I counted the frequency of various event categories. For the qualitative results,

I performed a lexicogrammatical analysis of the top three most frequent event categories as they are used in sentences by journalists.

The corpus

In order to construct the corpus, I used three LexisNexis Guided News Searches, targeting the *New York Post*, the *New York Times*, and the *Daily News (New York)*. In order to have been included in the archive, the headline or lead paragraphs of a text must have contained the term "brooklyn museum" along with one or more of the following terms: "sensation," "virgin mary," or "dung." These are the most appropriate search terms because they identify the name of the institutional site of the event, the name of the exhibit in question, the title/subject of the painting in question, and the unusual material used in the painting. Since three of the four terms are proper names, and since the one common noun is rare, these terms are highly proprietary to the event, especially in combination. Together, the three searches produced a corpus containing 273 texts and totaling 204, 203 words.

Results and analysis

Quantitative results and analysis

Journalists used a large range of terms to refer to the event, from the clinical "incident" to the playful "to-do." One way to explain this large range by would be to say that journalists are varying their vocabulary in order to enliven their prose or by suggesting that the category of the event was unclear and underwent definition over time.

Table 1 below presents the results of this study, ranked and sorted by newspaper.

Although the list has a large range, the most frequently used terms form a relatively coherent group, as seen in Table 2.

"Controversy" appears as the first most common event category in the *New York Post* and the *Daily News*, and the second most common in the *New York Times*. This result supports the conclusion that the event at the Brooklyn Museum in 1999 was a "controversy" in the eyes of many New York City journalists, and that it was presented to readers as such. "Battle" was the second most common event category in both the *Post* and the *Daily News*, and the first most common in the *Times*. In the *Times*, "dispute," "controversy," and "battle" all rank very closely together at the top. In the *Post* and the *Daily News*, the three most common terms are less closely grouped, with "war" (along with "fight" in the *Daily News* case) a distant third behind "controversy" and "battle."

Table 1. All terms referring to the event

NYT	NYP	DNNY
battle (27)	controversy (33)	controversy (30)
controversy (23)	battle (18)	battle (20)
dispute (21)	war (14)	war (8)
war (16)	flap (7)	fight (8)
fight (13)	uproar (6)	dispute (7)
furor (13)	fight (6)	flap (6)
debate (9)	furor (6)	fuss (4)
uproar (8)	debate (5)	debate (3)
fuss (7)	scandal (3)	furor (3)
skirmish (6)	brouhaha (3)	uproar (3)
outcry (4)	fuss (2)	hoopla (2)
fury (3)	fury (1)	brouhaha (2)
ruckus (3)	feud (1)	feud (2)
debacle (2)	tussle (1)	dustup (2)
standoff (2)	ruckus (1)	brawl (2)
to-do (2)	contretemps (1)	skirmish (1)
commotion (2)	boondoggle (1)	tizzy (1)
dust-up (2)	fiasco (1)	ruckus (1)
incident (1)	debacle (1)	circus (1)
circus (1)		confrontation (1)
conflict (1)		fury (1)
assaults (1)		
squabbling (1)		
upheaval (1)		
rancor (1)		
maelstrom (1)		
affair (1)		
fiasco (1)		

Table 2. The most common terms referring to the event

NYT	NYP	DNNY
battle (27)	controversy (33)	controversy (30)
controversy (23)	battle (18)	battle (20)
dispute (21)	war (14)	war (8)
		fight (8)

Qualitative results and analysis

"Controversy," "war," "battle," "dispute," and "fight" were the event categories most often used in newspaper coverage of the event at the Brooklyn Museum, but how were the terms used within sentences? This study examines sentences in which journalists used these terms, and asks how differences at the lexicogrammatical level can illuminate our understanding of these terms as they represent the event for readers. For example, what difference might it make that a journalist refers to the event as a "controversy" rather than a "battle"? What are the patterns of use for each term? Given the patterns of use, what does each term suggest to readers about the kind of event that occurred?

In much of the CDA research on classifications, the analyst examines a small number of whole texts in great detail. However, if I were to analyze only a few texts in great detail, then, among the many other features of the text, I would encounter a small number of event categories and a very limited number of instances. With only a few examples to account for, I could provide a detailed discussion of each. In contrast to this sort of CDA study design, my study examined a single feature over many instances and across large corpus of texts. In order to deliver a meaningful discussion of the various instances of the feature, I sorted them by the particular lexicogrammatical transformation that they displayed. I then compared each event category across each transformation. I use the term "transformation" in the sense developed by critical discourse analysts who theorize classifications (Kress & Hodge 1979: 36–37).

Five patterns of lexicogrammatical transformation emerged from the coverage:

– unqualified event
– possessed event
– categorized event
– dialectical event
– emergent event

The first four of the cases in the list have in common the fact that the event categories are being used in various ways as count nouns. The fifth category, "emergent event" features the term used as a mass noun. It is an "emergent event" because, in its use as a mass noun, the category represents the event as if it is amorphous, lacking distinct boundaries. Compare examples (9) and (10), both from news texts not included in the Brooklyn Museum corpus:

   (9)   Developer Rusty Hyneman is back in the thick of *controversy*, this time over the sudden death of a champion walking horse. (Perrusquia 2006)

   (10)   The continuing *controversy* over cartoon depictions of the prophet Mohammad in Danish newspapers is not a clash of civilizations but 'a clash of the uncivilized,' a group of religious leaders declared here Monday in announcing a new Islam education campaign. (Parker 2006)

In (9) the writer uses "controversy" as a mass noun, and in (10) as a count noun. (9) uses "controversy" to describe a general state of affairs that Hyneman finds himself in. Grammatically, the event, the "sudden death of a champion walking horse," has not been classified as a "controversy" as it might be in later news reports, with the following sort of transformation: "the walking horse controversy." In (9) the writer presents just such a transformation by categorizing an ongoing event as a "controversy." Here, "controversy" is used as a count noun, representing the ongoing event as if it had distinct boundaries and shape. Of course, there are many more lexicogrammatical features at work in these examples, features that contribute to this effect. Beyond the count/mass distinction, articles, modifiers, prepositions, and possessives all contribute to the transformations. The following analysis will expand on the role of these features. Within results of this study, one of the most interesting discoveries is that journalists use "controversy" in both count and mass transformations. Table 3 shows the results of the analysis of "controversy" in coverage:

Table 3. Transformations of "controversy"

transformations of "controversy"	examples	DNNY	NYP	NYT	total
unqualified event	"refused to speak about the controversy" "when this controversy began"	16	12	12	40
possessed event	[Giuliani's controversy]	0	0	0	0
categorized event	"the controversy over the painting"	7	8	2	17
dialectical event	[the controversy between the Museum and the City]	0	0	0	0
emergent event	"generated controversy" "sparked controversy" "stirred up controversy" "in the thick of controversy" "in a storm of controversy" "at the center of controversy" "plunged into controversy"	7	11	8	26

The instances of "controversy" are concentrated in the uncategorized and categorized event transformations, along with the emergent event transformation. In the way that journalists use the term to refer to the Brooklyn Museum event, "controversy" does not seem to qualify as the kind of conflict that agents possess – "the museum's controversy" – or the kind of conflict that thematizes its participants – "the controversy between the Mayor and the museum." Here is an example of the use of the term in its sense as an unqualified event, from the *Daily News*:

(11)   The *controversy* finds the Republican mayor in a familiar spot: brawling over the First Amendment. (Casimir et al. 1999)

Because it is a count noun with a definite article, (11) suggests that the event is discrete and particular, having achieved a certain coherence. Journalists also use the term in its sense as a categorized event. This transformation features the term modified by a category definition that is not possessive. Here is an example of the use of the term in its sense as an categorized event, from the *New York Times:*

(12)   Patrick J. Buchanan used the *controversy* over the "Sensation" exhibit to rally his troops at a Manhattan restaurant yesterday. (Roane 1999)

The other common transformation for "controversy" is as an emergent event. In this case, journalists use "controversy" to indicate a state of affairs, a place, or a medium. They use "controversy" as a mass noun, suggesting something amorphous. Naturally, the mass noun cases lack the characteristic count articles, "a" or "the." They tend toward metaphors of natural phenomena. Here is an example from the *New York Post:*

(13)   An exhibition with a blood-filled head, oversized sex organs, a religious portrait caked in elephant dung and real animals in formaldehyde has plunged the Brooklyn Museum of Art into *controversy.* (Turner 1999)

Here "controversy" suggests a body of water into which the museum is being "plunged." In this sort of construction, "controversy" is temporally durable, general, and unfortunate. It seems to represent a circumstance that anyone might stumble into spontaneously, given certain conditions. In its emergent event transformation, "controversy" is not something that agents control, and it does not suggest an event that is discrete or has achieved coherence. Although the Museum, the exhibit, or the painting seem to have come into contact with "controversy," in these cases, that term is not being used as the durable category reference for a discrete event involving them.

The other common event categories contrast notably with "controversy." In particular, "controversy" is distinguished from the others by its emergent event transformations. None of the other event categories are used in this way. In addition, "battle" and "war" are both rarely used as unqualified events, and they are commonly used as possessed and dialectical events, precisely the opposite clustering from "controversy." In general, these patterns suggest a trend that favors agency in the case of "battle," and "war," and disfavors it in the case of "controversy."

As Table 4 shows, the characteristic transformations for "battle" are the possessed event, the categorized event, and the dialectical event. Here is a case of "battle" as a categorized event from the *New York Post:*

(14)   The *battle* over the Brooklyn Museum of Art's controversial 'Sensations' show is a rematch between First Amendment lawyer Floyd Abrams and city Corporation Counsel Michael Hess. (Kuntzman 1999)

Here the journalist categorizes the "battle" by modifying it with a prepositional phrase with "over," indicating that the exhibit is the topic of the controversy. In-

Table 4. Transformations of "battle"

transformations of "battle"	examples	DNNY	NYP	NYT	total
unqualified event	[has refused to comment on the battle] [the battle began]	0	0	3	3
possessed event	"his battle"	4	4	5	13
categorized event	"court battle" "legal battle" "battle over 'Sensation'"	14	12	18	44
dialectical event	"battle between" "battle against" "the two sides are set to do battle"	4	5	10	19
emergent event	[sparked battle] [at the center of battle]	1	0	0	1

stances of "battle" as a possessed event and as a dialectical event tend to co-occur. Here is another example from the *New York Post*:

(15)   Mayor Giuliani threw in the towel yesterday in his fierce *battle* with the Brooklyn Museum of Art. (Hardt & Massarella 2000)

In this example, the "battle" is not only possessed by the Mayor, but the prepositional phrase following it indicates a dialectical exchange with the museum.

In general, journalists use "battle" to refer to a particular kind of event when the participants are known and named. Many of the categorized event instances of "battle" indicate the Federal Court case, with examples like "legal battle" and "court battle." The possessed and dialectical event instances of "battle" emphasize agency by indicating that a particular party owns the event, "the museum's battle," or that the battle features two named parties "his battle with the museum." Compared to their instances of "controversy," journalists tend to use "battle" to indicate a more well-defined and agent-driven event. Journalists tend to use "war" in much the same way that they use "battle," as a categorized, possessed, and/or dialectical event. Since it is a synonym, perhaps this should be no surprise. Table 5 shows are the results for "war."

As with "battle," "war" is commonly used as a categorized event, but the categories differ. Journalists routinely use "battle" to indicate the legal arena, with "legal battle" or "court battle". However, "war" is less often used with legal modifiers. Journalists seem to categorize "war" in the terms of culture or religion, with "holy war," "culture war," and "art war." Here is an example of a categorized event use of "war" from the *New York Post*:

Table 5. Transformations of "war"

transformations of "war"	examples	DNNY	NYP	total
unqualified event	[would not comment on the war]	0	0	0
possessed event	"the BMA's war"	2	1	3
categorized event	"holy war" "culture war" "art war"	5	6	11
dialectical event	"has declared war on them"	2	4	6
emergent event	[sparked war] [diving into war]	0	0	0

Table 6. Transformations of "dispute"

transformations of "dispute"	examples	NYT
unqualified event	"the dispute continued to reverberate" "since the dispute began last week"	10
possessed event	[the museum's dispute]	0
categorized event	"museum dispute" "lease dispute"	8
dialectical event	"settling the dispute between"	3
emergent event	[created dispute] [fallen into dispute]	0

(16)   Giuliani used each interview to lash out at his opponents in the art *war*, branding them 'First Amendment hysterics'. (Topousis et al. 1999)

While only the *New York Times* uses "dispute" as one of its most common terms for discursive conflict, that term presents an interesting case of a usage that contrasts with "controversy" and "battle/war" (see Table 6).

New York Times journalists most commonly use "dispute" to indicate an unqualified event and categorized event. While this makes "dispute" similar to the cluster of use for "controversy," journalists do not seem to use dispute in the emergent event sense that we see with "controversy." Here is an example from the *New York Times* of "dispute" as a categorized event:

(17)   And while he was invited to the shows primarily to discuss the Brooklyn Museum *dispute*... (Herszenhorn 1999)

Table 7. Analysis summary

event category	transformation	location	discreteness	agency
"controversy"	emergent event	nature	less discrete	less agentive
"controversy"	categorized event unqualified event	culture	↑	↑
"battle"	dialectical event possessed event	conversation		
			more discrete	more agentive

Here is an example of "dispute" as an unqualified event:

(18)   For the first time since the *dispute* began last week, other museums and arts groups in New York City spoke out in support of the Brooklyn Museum. (Barstow 1999)

As with the count transformations of "controversy," these count transformations of "dispute" suggest that the event is discrete and particular, having achieved a certain coherence.

Among the most common event categories in the coverage, "controversy" stands apart from "battle" and "war" in that it deemphasizes agency. While "battle" and "war" are both commonly used with named parties who either present two sides of it or own it, "controversy" is more commonly a general term for the event, either in its discrete sense, as an unqualified event, or in its amorphous sense, as a emergent event. If the common transformations of "battle" involve a localized event with known parties, "controversy" is a large-scale, amorphous event with ill-defined parties.

The results of this study present a ladder of discreteness and agency among event categories used in coverage. Whereas "controversy" in its emergent event transformation has the least discrete event boundaries and lowest agency, "battle," dominated by dialectical and possessed event transformations, has the most discrete event boundaries and the highest agency. And when "controversy" is used in its categorized and unqualified event transformations, it falls somewhere in the middle on these scales. Table 7 displays these comparisons.

In order to make this ladder of discreteness and agency more concrete, I have designated a location for each collection of transformations in the table. By location, I mean that the particular transformation of a given event category indicates a site where the event takes place. For instance, when "controversy" is used in its emergent event transformation, it presents the event as if it were a natural phenomenon or force. So when journalists say that something has "generated controversy" or that someone is "in the thick of controversy" or "in a storm of controversy," it alternately seems to emanate like electricity or to embody a swamp or storm. Although I am tempted to describe all of these constructions as metaphorical, following the notion of "grammatical metaphor" from functional linguistics (Thompson 1996: 163), the final example represents a very conspicuous weather metaphor. As it locates events in forces of nature, the emergent event transformation presents an event as amorphous and backgrounds human beings.

While the emergent event transformation locates events in nature, the categorized and unqualified event transformations locate events in culture. They make the events more discrete as they add definite articles and modifiers that further specify the particular site or topic of the event. These locate the event in culture because they fix it in a given place and time, contextualizing it against prior text and the backdrop of the reader's knowledge and experience of the world. So when a journalist writes, "he refused to speak about the controversy" or mentions "the controversy over the painting," he or she is placing that event in the cultural milieu of the reader. Not only does it exist as an ongoing event for a given community, it is characterized by discrete topics, sites, and concerns that are particular to that community.

The conversation transformations (possessed and dialectical events) are more discrete and agentive than the others because not only do they marshal the features from the culture transformations (unqualified and categorized events), but they also foreground named or implied individual agents. The possessed and dialectical event transformations locate events in conversation using names, pronouns, and prepositions. The prepositions "between," "against," and "with" are common in the dialectical event transformation, and the possessed event regularly uses a possessive pronoun along with one of these prepositions. Note the way that examples like "battle between" and "his fierce battle with," for instance, locate the event in conversation and imply agents. Compared to the nature and culture transformations, the conversation transformations place the event in a very local situation with specific characters participating.

By noting the ways that particular event categories are most often used in certain transformations and then by describing the kind of location implied by each of these, I want to show not only how journalists use event categories to classify events, but also to show how their particular transformations inflect the sort of event described. In the movement from "controversy" as a large-scale, amorphous event involving ill-defined parties to "battle," which suggests a localized event involving known parties, I have traced a ladder of discreteness and agency that descends from the amorphousness of nature down through culture to the more discrete conversation. These relationships among event categories and their transformations suggest that even when describing an event that presumably involves a discursive conflict among human beings, journalists use a number of event categories in a variety of transformations that complicate our commonsense assumptions. Did the conflicts at the Brooklyn Museum emerge from nature, like a storm? Were they figured in the culture, like a zeitgeist? Were they rooted in conversation between two parties, like a debate? At various times in the coverage, journalists used event categories and their transformations to suggest all of these things.

Discussion

In this study I have shown how the most frequently used event categories that journalists used to refer to the ongoing event around the Brooklyn Museum in 1999 differ in their degrees of agency and discreteness. In particular, I discovered that "controversy" is unique among the most frequently used event categories in its emergent event transformation. Although this study was limited to a lexicogrammatical analysis of a single feature across a large corpus focused on a single ongoing event, the results provoke hypotheses about how event categories are generated and how clusters of event categories function in relation to one another, textually and historically.

In her example of "riot," Tuchman emphasizes the role of news in transforming an amorphous event into a discrete one. Although she does not pursue a lexicogrammatical analysis, Tuchman seems to recognize that linguistic transformations – like the definiteness of articles – play a part in the particular way that news reports achieve this transformation of the representation of the event. In my analysis of Bell's nominalization of "jump" in example (3), I draw similar conclusions about the way in which this transformation affects the amorphousness and discreteness of the event representation. And in the results of the study of the Brooklyn Museum corpus, I found that "controversy" is distinct from other event categories in that journalists used in the emergent event transformation, a transformation that emphasizes amorphousness. The results of this study suggest that the amorphousness/discreteness distinction is a common one in the deployment of event categories, and that certain lexicogrammatical transformations support these representations of events.

The results of this study suggest that event categories can vary across a ladder of discreteness and agency which descends from the amorphousness of nature down through culture to the more discrete, local, and anthrocentric scenario of a conversation. These relationships among event categories and their transformations suggest that even when describing an event that involves a discursive conflict among human beings, journalists use a number of event categories in a variety of transformations that extend far beyond the bounds of dialog and conversation.

In this study, the results are divided by newspaper and by type of transformation. This provides a picture of the overall frequency of event categories in the corpus, but it does not provide chronological results that could, for instance, reveal patterns of historical development across the corpus. This presents a question: How do event categories affect the discreteness of event representations over time and text? I would offer the following hypothesis: In their coverage of an ongoing event, journalists will begin with event categories and transformations that indicate amorphousness and move toward those that indicate discreteness. The Brooklyn Museum corpus presents anecdotal evidence supporting this hypothesis. During the first week of coverage, they refer to the event as a "controversy," often using the emergent event transformation, and later shift to count transformations of "controversy" along with "battle" and "war," neither of which are used in the emergent event transformation.

Conclusion

Journalists used a wide range of event categories in order to categorize the Brooklyn Museum event. While this study illuminates the differences among the event categories on the axes of discreteness and agency, it does not directly address questions about how theorists should categorize the Brooklyn Museum event, let alone resolve those problems. However, these results are useful as a foundation for understanding how rhetoricians and argumentation theorists might categorize events that do not qualify in traditional categories such as "argument" or "debate." The ordinary discourse of journalists points to a key problem for theorists: How do we define and categorize ill-defined and emergent events, where interlocutors' exchanges are asynchronous and conspicuously mediated? This study of event categories in the coverage of the Brooklyn Museum controversy highlights problems of agency and event discreteness, factors that become more complicated as we move farther from well-defined and institutionalized events, such as debate.

Although controversy is an object of study that is central to rhetorical analysis, rhetoric scholars typically use the term in a non-technical, ordinary sense, much like other scholars and journalists. In those cases where scholars have developed technical definitions, they have done so based on their knowledge of the rhetorical and the philosophical traditions, on public sphere theory, and on pragmatics. The emic approach that I have taken in this study – examining the discourse behavior of journalists – does not conflict with these. Instead, it provides a alternative approach to the problem.

It finds that journalists use "controversy" differently than they use related event categories and that this difference rests on agency and event discreteness. This finding may shed some light on the problem of controversy as an object of study for rhetorical critics and other analysts. Many analysts begin their work by assuming that controversy is a dyadic exchange akin to dialectic or conversation. Others locate controversy in culture, beyond the level of individual exchanges among interlocutors or parties. The fact that journalists describe the same event as a "controversy," or "battle," for instance, would seem to parallel this tradeoff that exists for analysts. Those researchers who have begun to investigate and theorize controversy are struggling with this same tension between locating controversy in culture and locating it in conversation. By foregrounding the specific language practices of journalists who are covering controversy, this paper shows that the problem for researchers is, to a great extent, reflected in the basic ambiguities in the term as it is used in ordinary discourse. Without a careful understanding of the language of event categories – how they are used in ordinary discourse – it may be difficult for researchers to develop a distinct and productive technical definition of "controversy" which will be adequate for rhetorical studies.

References

Ayanian, Robert. 1983. "The Advertising Capital Controversy". *the Journal of Business 56* (3), 349–364.

Barstow, David. 1999. "Brooklyn Museum Sues to Keep Mayor from Freezing its Funds". *The New York Times,* September 29. P. 1.

Becker, C. 2001. "The Brooklyn Controversy: A View from the Bridge". In *Unsettling "Sensation": Arts-Policy Lessons from the Brooklyn Museum of Art Controversy,* L. Rothfield (Ed.), New Brunswick, NJ: Rutgers University Press.

Bell, Allan. 1991. *The Language of News Media.* Cambridge, Mass.: Blackwell.

Bennett, Lance. 2004. *News: the Politics of Illusion,* 6th Ed., New York: Longman.

Benoit, William L., and Hanczor, Robert S. 1994. "The Tonya Harding Controversy: An Analysis of Image Restoration Strategies". *Communication Quarterly 42* (4), 416.

Bjork, Rebecca S. 1995. "Public Policy Argumentation and Colonialist Ideology". In *Warranting Assent: Case Studies in Argument Evaluation,* E. Schiappa (Ed.), 211–236. Albany: State University of New York Press.

Casimir, Leslie, Lombardi, Frank, Santiago, Roberto, and Blood, Michael R. 1999. "Kill Exhibit, Guiliani Tells B'klyn Museum Sez He'll Give Board the Ax". *Daily News,* September 25. P. 4.

Cooper, Michael. 2003. "Some Bloomberg Money, But No Dung in Venice". *The New York Times,* July 23. P. 2.

Darling-Wolf, Fabienne. 1997. "Framing the Breast Implant Controversy: A Feminist Critique". *The Journal of Communication Inquiry 21* (1), 77.

Dascal, Marcelo. 1990. "The Controversy about Ideas and the Ideas about Controversy". In *Scientific and Philosophical Controversies,* G. Fernando (Ed.), 61–100. Lisboa: Fragmentos.

Van Dijk, Teun Adrianus. 1988. *News as Discourse.* Hillsdale, NJ: L. Erlbaum Associates.

Dowling, Ralph E., and Ginder, Gabrielle A. 1995. "An Ethical Apprasial of Ronald Reagan's Justification for the Invasion of Grenada". In *Warranting Assent: Case Studies in Argument Evaluation,* E. Schiappa (Ed.), 103–124 Albany: State University of New York Press.

Dubin, Steven C. 1999. *Displays of Power: Controversy in the American Museum from the Enola Gay to Sensation*: New York University Press.

Eggins, Suzanne. 2004. *An Introduction to Systemic Functional Linguistics* (2nd Ed.). New York: Continuum.

Ellison, Jennifer. 2003. "Re-Visioning the Media, Museums & Controversy: A Preliminary Case Study". *Open Museum Journal 6: New Museum Developments & the Culture Wars*, 1–27.

Fairclough, Norman. 1989. *Language and Power*. London; New York: Longman.

_____. 1995. *Media Discourse*. London; New York: E. Arnold.

Fielding, Ian. 1995. "Examining An Argument By Cause: The Weak Link Between Pornography and Violence in the Attorney General's Commission On Pornography Final Report". In *Warranting Assent: Case Studies in Argument Evaluation*, E. Schiappa (Ed.), 211–236. Albany: State University of New York Press.

Fishman, Mark. 1978. "Crime Waves As Ideology". *Social Problems 25* (5), 531–543.

_____. 1988. *Manufacturing the News*. Austin: University of Texas Press.

Foss, S. K. 1979. "Equal-Rights Amendment Controversy: Two Worlds in Conflict". *Quarterly Journal of Speech 65* (3), 275–288.

Fowler, Roger, Hodge, Robert, Kress, Gunther, and Trew, Tony. 1979. *Language and Control*. London; Boston: Routledge & K. Paul.

Fraser, Andrea. 2001. "A 'Sensation' Chronicle". *Social Text 19* (2), 127–156.

Froyn, Camilla Bretteville. 2005. "Decision Criteria, Scientific Uncertainty, and the Global Warming Controversy". *Mitigation and Adaptation Strategies for Global Change 10* (2), 183–211.

Ghali, William A., Saltz, Richard, Sargious, Peter M., and Hershman, Warren Y. 1999. "Evidence-Based Medicine and the Real World: Understanding the Controversy". *Journal of Evaluation in Clinical Practice 5* (2), 133–138.

Glasgow University Media Group. 1976a. "Bad News". *Theory and Society 3* (3), 229–262.

Glasgow University Media Group. 1976b. *Bad News*. London; Boston: Routledge & K. Paul.

Goodman, G. S., S., Ghetti, Quas, J. A., Edelstein, R. S., Alexander, K. W., Redlich, A. D. et al. 2003. "A Prospective Study of Memory for Child Sexual Abuse: New Findings Relevant to the Repressed-Memory Controversy". *Psychological Science 14* (2), 113–118.

Goodnight, G. T. 1992. "Habermas, the Public Sphere, and Controversy". *International Journal of Public Opinion Research 4* (3), 243–255.

_____. 1991. "Controversy". In *Argument in Controversy: Proceedings of the Seventh SCA/AFa Conference On Argumentation*, D.W. Parson, Speech Communication Association., American Forensic Association & University of Utah. (Eds.), 1–13. Annandale, VA: Speech Communication Association.

_____. 1999. "Messrs Dinkins, Rangel, and Savage in Colloquy on the African Burial Ground: A Companion Reading". *Western Journal of Communication 63* (4), 511.

Gouran, Dennis S. 1995. "The Failure of Argument in Decisions Leading to the 'Challenger Disaster': A Two-Level Analysis". In *Warranting Assent: Case Studies in Argument Evaluation*, E. Schiappa (Ed.), 57–77. Albany: State University of New York Press.

Gregory, Jane, and Miller, Steve. 1998. *Science in Public: Communication, Culture, and Credibility*. New York: Plenum Trade.

Hajer, Maarten A. 1993. "Discourse Coalitions and the Institutional Practice: The Case of Acid Rain in Britain". In *The Argumentative Turn in Policy Analysis and Planning*, F. Fischer & J. Forester (Eds.), 43–76. Durham, N.C.: Duke University Press.

Halle, David. 2001. "The Controversy over the Show Sensation at the Brooklyn Museum, 1999–2000". In *Crossroads: Art and Religion in American Life*, A. Arthurs, G. Wallach, Center for Arts and Culture & Henry Luce Foundation. (Eds.), 139–188. New York: New Press: Distributed By W.W. Norton.

Halliday, M. A. K. 1978. *Language as Social Semiotic: The Social Interpretation of Language and Meaning*. London: Edward Arnold.

_____. 1985. *An Introduction to Functional Grammar*. London: Edward Arnold.

_____ and Hasan, Ruqaiya. 1976. *Cohesion in English*. London: Longman.

_____ and Martin, J. R. 1993. "General Orientation". In *Writing Science: Literacy and Discursive Power*, M.A.K. Halliday & J.R. Martin (Eds.), 2–21. London: Falmer Press.

Hardt Jr., Robert, and Massarella, Linda. (2000, 3/28). "Rudy Drops Legal Battle With 'Dung Art' Museum". *The New York Post,* March 28, P. 2.

Hartsell, Jeff. 2005. "Flag Issue Not Yet On Socon Agenda". *The Post and Courier*. March 5.

Hasian, Marouf A., Jr., and Nakayama, Thomas K. 1997. "The Empires Strike Back: The Sokal Controversy and the Vilification of Cultural Studies". *The Journal of Communication Inquiry 21* (2), 45.

_____. 2000. "Colonial Re-Characterization and the Discourse Surrounding the Eyre Controversy". *The Southern Communication Journal 66* (1), 79.

_____. 2003. "The "Hysterical" Emily Hobhouse and Boer War Concentration Camp Controversy". *Western Journal of Communication 67* (2), 138.

Hauser, Gerard. 1995. "Constituting Publics and Reconstructing Public Spheres: The Meese Commission's Report on Pornography". In *Warranting Assent: Case Studies in Argument Evaluation*, E. Schiappa (Ed.), 283–310. Albany: State University of New York Press.

Herszenhorn, David M. 1999. "With Art Battle in Spotlight, Mayor Revels in the Glare". *The New York Times,* October 4. P. 3.

Jensen, Michael C. 1986. "The Takeover Controversy: Analysis and Evidence". *Midland Corporate Finance Journal 4* (2).

Kalette, Denise. 2005. "Art Director Fired After TV Discussion of Graphic Work on Bush". *The Associated Press State & Local Wire*. July 22.

Keehner, Mary. 1995. "Arguing About Fetal 'Versus' Women's Rights: An Ideological Evaluation". In *Warranting Assent: Case Studies in Argument Evaluation*, E. Schiappa (Ed.), 193–210. Albany: State University of New York Press.

Kennedy, Kimberly A., and Benoit, William L. 1997. "The Newt Gingrich Book Deal Controversy: Self-Defense Rhetoric". *The Southern Communication Journal 62* (3), 197.

Kepner, Tyler. 2005. "Giambi to Meet Media On Yankees' Terms". *The New York Times*. February 10.

Knowles, Alison, Heartney, Eleanor, Monk, Meredith, Montano, Linda, Ehn, Erik, and Marranca, Bonnie. 2002. "Art As Spiritual Practice". *PAJ: A Journal of Performance and Art 24* (3), 18–34.

Krantz, David H. 1999. "The Null Hypothsis Testing Controversy in Psychology". *Journal of the American Statistical Association 94* (448), 1372–1381.

Kress, Gunther R., and Hodge, Bob. 1979 *Language As Ideology*. London; Boston: Routledge & Kegan Paul.

Kuntzman, Gersh. 1999. "A Rematch for First Amendment Legal Eagles". *The New York Post,* September 30. P. 4.

Lefering, Rolf, and Neugebauer, Edmund. 1995. "Steroid Controversy in Sepsis and Septic Shock: A Meta-Analysis." *Critical Care Medicine 23* (7), 1294–1303.

Levine, Peter. 2000. "Lessons from the Brooklyn Museum Controversy". *Report from the Institute for Philosophy and Public Policy University of Maryland Volume 20* (2/3).

Martin, J. R. 1992. *English Text: System and Structure*. Philadelphia: John Benjamins Pub. Co.

Matthews, Gray. 1995. "Epideictic Rhetoric and Baseball: Nurturing Community through Controversy". *The Southern Communication Journal 60* (4), 275.

McKeon, Richard. 1990. "Dialogue and Controversy in Philosophy". In *The Interpretation of Dialogue*, T. Maranhão (Ed.), 25–46. Chicago: University of Chicago Press.

McNally, Richard J. 2003. "Progress and Controversy in the Study of Posttraumatic Stress Disorder". *Annual Review of Psychology 54*, 229–252.

Moore, M. P. 1993. "Constructing Irreconcilable Conflict – the Function of Synecdoche in the Spotted Owl Controversy". *Communication Monographs 60* (3), 258–274.

Nelkin, Dorothy. 1995. *Selling Science: How the Press Covers Science and Technology* (Rev. Ed.). New York: W.H. Freeman.

O'Hanlon, Martin. 2004. "Abortion Controversy again Boils to Surface of Campaign". *Kamloops Daily News,* June 9. P. A10.

Olson, K. M. 1989. "The Controversy over President Reagan's Visit to Bitburg – Strategies of Definition and Redefinition". *Quarterly Journal of Speech 75* (2), 129–151.

_____. 1995. "Aligning Ethicality and Effectiveness in Arguments: Advocating Inclusiveness Percentages for the New Lutheran Church". In *Warranting Assent: Case Studies in Argument Evaluation*, E. Schiappa (Ed.), 81–102. Albany: State University of New York Press.

_____ and Goodnight, G. Thomas. 1994. "Entanglements of Consumption, Cruelty, Privacy, and Fashion: The Social Controversy Over Fur". *The Quarterly Journal of Speech 80* (3), 249–276.

_____ and Olson, Clark D. 1995. "Ideology and Argument Evaluation: Competing Axiologies in the Sanctuary Trial". In *Warranting Assent: Case Studies in Argument Evaluation*, E. Schiappa (Ed.), 155–191. Albany: State University of New York Press.

Oravec, C. 1984. "Conservationism vs Preservationism – the Public-Interest in the Hetch Hetchy Controversy". *Quarterly Journal of Speech 70* (4), 444–458.

Palczewski, Catherine Helen. 1995. "Survivor Testimony in the Pornography Controversy: Assessing Credibility in the Minneapolis Hearings and the Attorney General's Report". In *Warranting Assent: Case Studies in Argument Evaluation*, E. Schiappa (Ed.), 257–281. Albany: State University of New York Press.

Parker, Michael J. 2006. "Faiths Unite to Counter Clash of the Uncivilized". *San Antonio Express-News,* February 21. P. 3B.

Perrusquia, Marc. 2006. "Hyneman Sued Over Horse Trade". *The Commercial Appeal,* March 23. P. B1.

Phillips, Kendall R. 1999. "A Rhetoric of Controversy". *Western Journal of Communication 63* (4), 488.

Pike, Kenneth Lee. 1967. *Language in Relation to a Unified Theory of the Structure of Human Behavior* (2d, Rev. Ed.). The Hague: Mouton.

Railsback, Celeste Condit. 1984. "The Contemporary American Abortion Controversy – Stages in the Argument". *Quarterly Journal of Speech 70* (4), 410–424.

Roane, Kit R. 1999. "Buchanan Visits Art Exhibit in Brooklyn and Doesn't Like It". *The New York Times,* November 6. P. 5.

Roshco, Bernard. 1975. *Newsmaking.* Chicago: University of Chicago Press.

Senn, Stephen. 2000. "Consensus and Controversy in Pharmaceutical Statistics". *The Statistician, Journal of the Royal Statistical Society – Series D 49*, 135–176.

Thompson, Geoff. 1996. "Grammatical Metaphor". In *Introducing Functional Grammar*, G. Thompson (Ed.), 163–178. London; New York: Arnold.

Topousis, Tom, Graham, Jessica, Mosconi, Angela, and Graves, Neil. 1999. "Galleries Jammed As Rudy Sounds Off". *The New York Post,* October 4. P. 4.

Trew, Tony. 1979a. "Theory and Ideology At Work". In *Language and Control*, R. Fowler, R. Hodge, G. Kress & T. Trew (Eds.), 94–116. London; Boston: Routledge & K. Paul.

_____. 1979b. "'What the Papers Say': Linguistic Variation and Ideological Difference." In *Language and Control*, R. Fowler, R. Hodge, G. Kress & T. Trew (Eds.), 117–156. London; Boston: Routledge & K. Paul.

Tuchman, Gaye. 1980. *Making News: A Study in the Construction of Reality*. New York, London: Free Press; Collier Macmillan.

Turner, Megan. 1999. "Is This Art? Butchered Animals, a Dung-Smeared Virgin Mary and Giant Genitalia Spark Outrage At the Brooklyn Museum". *The New York Post,* September 21. P. 57.

Wattie, Chris. 2004. "Duceppe Pitches Amicable Divorce". *The Star Phoenix,* November 13. P. B6.

Winkler, Carol K. 1995. "Narrative Reframing of Public Argument: George Bush's Handling of the Persian Gulf Conflict". In *Warranting Assent: Case Studies in Argument Evaluation*, E. Schiappa (Ed.), 33–55. Albany: State University of New York Press.

Young, Marilyn J., and Launer, Michael K. 1995. "The Evaluative Criteria for Conspiracy Arguments: The Case of KAL 007". In *Warranting Assent: Case Studies in Argument Evaluation*, E. Schiappa (Ed.), 3–32. Albany: State University of New York Press.

Zarefsky, David. 1984. "Conspiracy Arguments in the Lincoln-Douglas Debates". *Journal of the American Forensic Association 21* (Fall), 63–75.

CHAPTER 12

Analyzing everyday talk about social issues

Susan Gilpin
Marshall University

Introduction

Speaking publicly and freely on political issues and matters of social concern is one of Americans' most cherished rights, and, some argue, a civic duty. With access to over 1,450 daily newspapers, roughly 1,300 news/talk radio stations, ever increasing publishing opportunities on the Internet, and a seemingly endless series of public opinion polls, citizens can make their will known at any time, on any issue, to all who care to notice. However, this abundance of one-to-many public discourse is a concern for the many cultural observers who decry Americans' practices of civic discourse. In particular, following Habermas (1989), they criticize citizens' inability or unwillingness to discuss social issues publicly in ways that reflect traditional rhetorical norms of rational-critical argument and deliberation. This perceived dysfunction impedes progress at every level of civic life and fosters declining civic participation.

Moreover, there is the charge that it is just as well that the public has disconnected, because it is too thoroughly dominated by the media to be an effective body for the grassroots working of participatory deliberative democracy. As I write this in the months preceding the 2008 national elections in the United States, I frequently read and hear the complaint that candidates' speeches and ersatz debates do not engage issues and audiences in meaningful ways; rather, such talk is crafted for public spectacle and media consumption. Many believe that this absence of public dialogue is putting the future of our democracy at risk.

Despite such criticism, there is also evidence that ordinary citizens do feel a need to make sense of complex issues and to form opinions about them. One of the ways they do this is through spontaneous, unplanned conversations woven through their daily activities. Thus, when critics focus on formal discursive structures and public discourse, they overlook or discount other less formal yet important forms of civic rhetorical activity. Studies of talk about politics or social issues in spontaneous, informal social groups are few, and fewer still look at the unplanned conversations in which citizens participate from day to day with people outside their immediate social circles. Although the professional literature is fairly silent as to why these particular kinds of conversations take place, it does speak to burgeoning interdisciplinary interest in relatively private modes of civic discourse. One finds a need for a richer understanding of how Americans create meaning discursively in complex social issues and practice citizenship in what Michael Schudson terms "the microprocesses of social life" (1998:298).

Two useful concepts for thinking about such discursive enactments are entextualization and social network theory. Entextualization is the practice in which interlocutors "take some fragment of discourse and quote it anew, making it seem to carry a meaning independent of its situation within two now distinct co(n)texts" (Silverstein & Urban 1996:2). When ordinary citizens attempt to discern meaning in contemporary political complexities, they may practice entextualization in unplanned conversation, sharing their relevant experiences with an issue as well the experiences of others that they have heard or heard about. Their conversational partners may do the same. In this scenario, entextualization can result in new, more nuanced, and possibly shared interpretations of what the issue means. Further, Huckfeldt and Sprague's research may be appropriated to suggest an extension of entextualization via social network theory. Drawing on survey and interview data, these political scientists investigated social influence in a political campaign and "the manner in which citizens' political choices become interdependent" (1995:13). In their analysis, they draw on insights from Granovetter's (1973) social network theory and the different ways that information travels in social groups with weak ties or strong ties. Extrapolating from Granovetter's conclusions, Huckfeldt and Sprague make this argument:

> Social communication regarding politics does not only occur among intimates, and this fact is important for several reasons. . . Information that is conveyed only through intimate social ties does not travel well. The friends of my friends are quite frequently my friends too, and thus information conveyed through intimates tends to feed back on the source, thereby minimizing its spread. In contrast, *information conveyed through casual social ties tends to keep traveling, and thus its spread is maximized* (emphasis added). Not only have we seen that information is conveyed through casual contact, but casual acquaintances are no less influential than intimates. (1995:288)

Drawing on entextualization and social network theory, I theorized a discourse practice I call *heuretic engagement* and designed a study to learn more about the contexts that facilitate its practice and its meaning for participants. In this chapter I describe heuretic engagement and discourse analytic findings from the study that define the contexts for its practice.

Theorizing heuretic engagement

Heuretic engagement, as I define it, is everyday talk that functions as a nonargumentative dialogue related to mutual concerns about a social issue.[1] I am employing Tracy's (2002:5) definition of everyday talk: "the ordinary kinds of communicating people do in schools, workplaces, shops, and at public meetings, as well as when they are at home or with their friends." I have appropriated the now rare term *heuretic* (from Greek roots meaning inventive, ingenious; to find) as an adjective to denote a particular kind of discourse. For the purposes of this study, heuretic engagement is everyday talk in which individuals participate for the purpose of discovering or creating meaning in topics of social concern, as illustrated in this observation adapted from my larger study (Gilpin 2004):

> I was waiting my turn for a haircut in a discount hair salon shortly before America's invasion of Iraq in March 2003. It seemed that the possibility of war was on everyone's mind: some were opposed to war under any circumstances, while others were convinced that the United States had no choice but military action, and debates were raging nationwide. But in spite of the abundance of public debate and mediated expert commentary about the issue, many still were troubled by questions about what an invasion of Iraq might mean. In the salon, three hair stylists and their customers, all women and men between about twenty-five and fifty years old, were chatting either quietly in pairs or not at all when one customer asked in a raised voice, "Do you think we'll go to war?" Immediately, all six were engaged in a serious *exploration* of what the threat of war was all about and what it might mean if the threat were carried out. Everyone spoke at least once. No political party line was advanced, and no media personalities were quoted. Instead, these six assembled as a public, sharing stories from friends and relatives with connections to the military, reflecting on the Vietnam era, and speculating about a future with and without Iraq and her oil. I had the strong impression that the opportunity for that conversation was important to them all, and it is easy to imagine fragments of that group conversation becoming part of other conversations with different partners while the participants continued to search for meaning in the issue. It is doubtful that those six ever would be together in the same place at the same time again. (31–32)

I hypothesized that participants in this unplanned talk were momentarily and opportunely acting from the footing (Goffman 1981) of "citizen." If this were so, then an investigation of this talk from a rhetorical perspective would reveal the agency of the individual civic rhetor, a core component of the heuretic engagement construct and a condition previously overlooked or obscured by other approaches. By rhetorical perspective, I intend to signal rhetoric's traditional concerns with the

---

1.   I thank Kenneth R. Williams, Professor Emeritus, Marshall University, for his help with this formulation and his valuable comments on this chapter.

individual rhetor in public forums and with the act of persuasion. In this case, the persuasion in heuretic engagement results in meaning making, a pre-requisite for argument, deliberation, and opinion formation. I also draw on the construct of the rhetorical situation (Bitzer 1968), which foregrounds exigence, audience, and constraints. The rhetorical exigence that gives rise to heuretic engagement is the felt difficulty Dewey (1933) has described as initiating inquiry. I also draw on the traditional rhetorical concept of *kairos* (Covino & Jolliffe 1995:62), or the opportune moment for speech, in an effort to understand the contexts that make heuretic engagement possible.

Design of the study

Much of the inquiry into everyday political talk to date has been conducted by sociolinguists, sociologists, and political scientists using research designs that reflect the standard for the creation of knowledge in their disciplines.[2] Although a review of interdisciplinary political communication literature reveals a growing recognition among researchers that everyday talk is significant, nothing to date fully explains what I have observed. The research into civic discourse includes both quantitative and qualitative methods, and mixed methods studies are increasingly valued. The studies by rhetoricians, in contrast, generally favor the interpretative theories and close reading techniques of rhetorical criticism and literary studies over systematic empirical methods.[3] Believing that the interdisciplinary effort underway called for more explicit methods and robust analyses from rhetoricians, I designed a project that would draw on strengths from both traditions of qualitative research. That is, I sought a way to provide careful yet flexible readings of texts coupled with systematic methods of analysis sometimes lacking in interpretive work on discourse (Johnstone 2008:270).

Adopting an ethnographic approach to data collection, I functioned as a participant observer in public settings, principally in the waiting areas of two Pittsburgh hair salons. During the course of the study, I observed and noted people's conversations in a variety of public settings such as coffee shops, bars, family restaurants, medical facilities, ball games, church gatherings, and hair salons. Without intending initially to focus on one particular location or type of location, I soon identified hair salons as the richest of the field sites for several reasons. First, the hair salons I visited attracted a demographically diverse clientele.

---

2.   See, for example, Duneier (1992), Eliasoph (1998), Gamson (1992), Harris-Lacewell (2004), Hausendorf and Bora (2006), May (2001), Myers (2004) and Walsh (2004).

3.   See, for example, Cushman (1998), Hauser (1999), and Lindquist (2002).

In additional, the open physical arrangement of the salons allowed conversations to be easily observed and joined by nearly anyone in the salon. As another practical benefit, most salon patrons would come and go in relatively brief periods of time, so that in ninety minutes or so (about the length of time I could stay intently focused on the activity) I could observe about eight service encounters and participants' interactions with others in the salon, thus increasing the likelihood that I would observe something significant for my research. Also important was the hair salon environment itself and the way "close-contact service encounters" stimulate talk among "mutually captive" audiences members (McCarthy 2000). Finally, the "participation framework" (Goffman 1981:3) of the salons minimized the impact of my presence on the observation and satisfied ethical concerns about my activity as a participant observer.[4]

Since I was interested in understanding contexts for heuretic engagement, I was careful to interfere with the field site as little as possible. Moreover, since I could not know in advance which conversations would emerge as relevant to my research, obtaining participants' permission in advance and recording every conversation on the floor was neither desirable nor practical. Therefore, even though some research on shop talk in hair salons does draw on audio and video tapes of participant interaction, mine does not.[5] My project findings draw on field observations of heuretic engagement that I was able to follow up with semi-structured interviews of hairdressers and patrons. During the interviews, which I recorded with participants' prior consent, I shared part of my field notes to confirm that my accounts or interpretations of the observations corresponded with theirs. This practice of data collection has received interdisciplinary acceptance in similar recent investigations of discursive and other social activities that occur in public gathering places where audio recordings are not possible or appropriate.[6]

I analyzed only contextualized data relevant to the practice I identified as heuretic engagement, the working definition of which I refined over three months of field-testing techniques of observation, recording, and analysis. The project data set was comprised of field notes of direct observation, transcripts of recorded,

---

4. As Goffman argues, "When a word is spoken, all those who happen to be in perceptual range of the event will have some sort of participation status relative to it" (1981:3).

5. Jacobs-Huey (2006), Majors (2007), McCarthy (2000), for example, use transcripts of salon recordings. Jacobs-Huey and Majors collected audio and video recordings of salon activity. They do not describe how permissions were obtained or equipment was used. McCarthy analyzes transcripts from the Cambridge and Nottingham Corpus of Discourse in English corpus (http://www.cambridge.org/elt/corpus/cancode.htm), a collection of spoken English collected in Britain.

6. In this regard, I was especially influenced by the data collection methods of Harris-Lacewell (2004), Lindquist (2002), and Walsh (2004).

semi-structured interviews with participants soon after the observations, and a series of e-mail messages I exchanged with one participant. To achieve the flexible yet systematic analysis I desired, I employed three analytic methods to answer questions about heuretic engagement, its contexts, and its meaning for participants: the first is a series of questions I posed to the transcripts of participants' post-observation interviews; the second, which is the focus of this chapter, applies the Johnstone (2008) discourse analytic heuristic to interview transcripts and field notes of the observational contexts; and the third is an activity analysis of interview transcripts, e-mail messages, and the observational context notes.

I turn now to the project's discourse analytic findings. Following Johnstone, I employed discourse analysis not "centrally focused on language as an abstract system," but instead "interested in what happens when people draw on the knowledge they have about language . . . to do things in the world" (2008: 3). The Johnstone analytic heuristic (10) provided an explicit and rigorous approach to and process for answering my research question about contexts for heuretic engagement. The heuristic enabled a systematic analysis of the relationships between talk and context, particularly the ways in which each shapes the meaning of the other. In addition, it revealed the roles of rhetorical agency and *kairos* in heuretic engagement. The discourse analytic findings served as complementary supplements to the findings of the other analyses in the study.

To analyze one interactional context of heuretic engagement, I adapted the Johnstone heuristic and applied it to field notes of one observation and a transcript of a participant's reflection during a follow-up interview. As Johnstone notes, "the procedures of a heuristic do not need to be followed in any particular order, and there is no fixed way of following them. . . A heuristic can be compared to a set of tools for thinking with" (10). Another way of thinking about these tools is as a set of claims that focus one's attention to specific aspects of discourse and context. With this in mind, I chose to systematically probe one observation of heuretic engagement for additional insights into its contexts with these tools from the Johnstone heuristic (10):

- Discourse is shaped by the world, and discourse shapes the world.
- Discourse is shaped by participants, and discourse shapes participants.
- Discourse is shaped by prior discourse, and discourse shapes the possibilities for future discourse.
- Discourse is shaped by its medium, and discourse shapes the possibilities of its medium.
- Discourse is shaped by purpose, and discourse shapes possible purposes.

My aim was to use these probes to reveal details about the context that may otherwise have gone unnoticed. The following sections illustrate the value of discourse analysis to this project. I begin with the larger context for the observation and provide an overview of the observation itself.

The observation

On Sunday, February 1, 2004, a professional football championship game, Super Bowl XXXVIII, aired on national television during early evening family viewing time. An unexpected halftime event, which eclipsed discussion of the game itself, sparked a public response and controversy across America. By Monday afternoon, over 200,000 complaints had been filed with the Federal Communications Commission (Crigler 2004). These two news articles, one from an AP wire report that appeared in the *Pittsburgh Post-Gazette* and another less objective account from *The New York Times* online readers' forum, provide a backdrop for the scene I observed in a hair salon the following Tuesday. (See Figures 1 and 2)

Super Bowl Notebook: CBS apologizes after airing overexposed Janet Jackson
Monday, February 02, 2004
By The Associated Press

HOUSTON – CBS apologized for an unexpectedly R-rated end to its Super Bowl halftime show, when singer Justin Timberlake tore off part of Janet Jackson's top, exposing her breast. "CBS deeply regrets the incident," spokeswoman LeslieAnne Wade said after the network received several calls about the show.

The two singers were performing a flirtatious duet to end the halftime show, and at the song's finish, Timberlake reached across Jackson's leather gladiator outfit and pulled off the covering to her right breast.

The network quickly cut away from the shot and did not mention the incident on the air.

Timberlake said the incident was unintentional, calling it a "wardrobe malfunction."

Wade said CBS officials attended rehearsals of the halftime show all week, "and there was no indication any such thing would happen. The moment did not conform to CBS' broadcast standards and we would like to apologize to anyone who was offended."

The Super Bowl halftime show, which also featured Puff Daddy, Nelly and Kid Rock, was produced by MTV, CBS' corporate cousin in Viacom.

"We were extremely disappointed by elements of the MTV-produced halftime show," Joe Browne, NFL executive vice president, said. "They were totally inconsistent with assurances our office was given about the content of the show."

"It's unlikely that MTV will produce another Super Bowl halftime."

Figure 1. Associated press story

February 5, 2004
DEBATES

Busted
NYTIMES.COM

Have you heard? Something scandalous happened during the Super Bowl halftime show.

It wasn't the get-out-the-vote montage that was immediately turned into a farce by Jessica Simpson overriding the call to civic duty with the order to "Party!" Nor Nelly's unprecedented amount of crotch-grabbing or across-the-board lip-synching of hoary hits. The big surprise of the night was when Justin Timberlake tore off part of duet partner Janet Jackson's costume, revealing her breast.

At first, there was reason to believe that the N.F.L./CBS/MTV nexus was in on the deal, both because Ms. Jackson looked adorned for the occasion and the act seemed choreographed to Mr. Timberlake's lyric "better have her naked by the end of this song." But then the apology/blame-game began, with MTV Networks chairman Tom Freston saying, "We were really ripped off. We were punk'd by Janet Jackson." Ms. Jackson, left holding the bag, issued an apology. She said that her red lace undergarment was torn away accidentally, resulting in the unexpected nakedness.

Figure 2. *New York Times* story

Viewer comments in the NYTIMES.COM "Readers' Opinions" (online forum highlights about the halftime show that appear on the "DEBATES: Busted" web page) illustrate the general public framing of the issue that had begun to take shape when I was observing in the hair salon two days after the event:

Position 1: The event was offensive, if not indecent. Sample post:

Firinci: "I found the Super Bowl halftime show extremely indecent; one of the rappers kept grabbing his genitals, the final duet had very suggestive acts and the very final thing was the ripping of Janet Jackson's bra, flashing a breast (real or fake) for a second or so. This was happening as part of the most-watched and most expensive event, at 8:30 EST, when thousands of kids were still awake and watching. Are CBS and MTV (both of Viacom) so much in need of such cheap, tasteless and indecent stuff?"

Position 2: The event was not indecent, and the furor over the event is not justified. Sample posts:

Aribendavid: "Big deal, a breast is flashed for a second on national television in a live broadcast. Intentional or not, who cares? If your little kids haven't seen a breast yet they will soon enough. I just wish the American people would grow up and worry about the real obscenities out there, like Bush's crimes against humanity in Iraq!"

Forrest.gump: "Even if people know what to expect when a woman exposes her nipples (because they've seen men's pecs), they still insist that the nipples not be shown. That's a bit silly, dontcha think?"

Figure 3. Super Bowl issue framing

On the Tuesday after the Super Bowl, I was observing interaction in a discount chain hair salon in the late afternoon, a time often favored by clients from a cross-section of the population. Located in a small neighborhood strip mall, the salon was convenient for patrons from area schools and hospitals. In spite of the freezing temperatures and icy roads, the salon was full, with an especially rich mix of ages and ethnicities: from middle school to about 60; women and men; African-American, Asian, Indian, Middle Eastern, white. In my field notes I wrote at 6:05 P.M., "A real multicultural shop right now!" I had been making notes of the interactions between the hairstylists Patricia and Beth and their clients in particular, as they were the ones working closest to where I was seated.

I had noted that in about a half an hour, Patricia and her female client, who appeared to be a high-school student, had carried on lively discussions about the reality television shows they both were watching: *Average Joe, Survivor,* and *Road Rules.* At one point, Patricia had exclaimed, "What's the point of public confessions? What's *wrong* with these people!" During much of this time, Beth, working at the next chair, was completely absorbed with disentangling the round hairbrush that her client had snarled in her long wavy hair. Patricia finished with her high-school client and had begun taking care of Lynn, a no-frills, pleasant-looking middle-aged woman. "She looks like an academic," I wrote. They greeted each other at the reception desk and out of my hearing. As they approached Patricia's chair, I heard Patricia say, "Well, you can do the work you love or you can make money, but you can't combine the two." When I asked Lynn later in an interview what that comment was about, she said that Patricia had asked her even before she was seated what work she did. Lynn replied (from the interview transcript) "I had told her that I was an editor and I said that there's no money in it but it's wonderful work and it's my observation that, uh, *(chuckle)* that you get one or the other … It's hard to get both." Apparently the comment I heard from Patricia was affirming the observation Lynn made during their greeting.

Lynn initiated conversation about the halftime performance at the Super Bowl and asserted, "that was not for families." She said that she did not watch much television as a child and that she had tried to limit the amount of television her children watched. As a consequence, they did not often watch together as a family. She understood from her friends, however, that watching football on Sunday afternoon is a family tradition in some households. She asked Patricia directly, "How do you feel about it?" Beth, who has children younger than Lynn's children, was paying attention to this exchange, and appeared eager to join in. Patricia replied, "I don't watch much TV. It seems so inane" – quite a different stance than the one she had assumed with a younger client a few minutes earlier. Beth jumped in: "TV is dictating what's normal. It's our fault as parents when we let them watch."

Lynn then described how she had disabled certain channels, and MTV in particular, from their cable service and how her children quickly had figured out how to get around it: "Kids are so smart!" Beth commiserated with her about how difficult it is to monitor everything one's children see. Then Patricia, who is in her late thirties and does not have children, spoke up: "My dad was all about freedom of speech. He let us see about anything we wanted to see." "It didn't seem to hurt us" was her implication. Lynn was quick to reply that freedom of speech and parental responsibility are different things. From there, the conversation went on to consider briefly the pros and cons of censorship and whether a parent's job is to shield children from particular messages or to help them interpret them. Patricia was relatively quiet. As mothers, Lynn and Beth supported each other, though Lynn's tone was that of the older and more experienced of the two. Both Lynn and Beth initially strongly disapproved of the half time show, but neither was sure what the appropriate response should be. I wondered if Patricia's reference to the First Amendment tempered their critical opinions. In any case, nothing was resolved and the uncertainty remained. In about fifteen minutes Lynn's hair was cut, and she prepared to leave the floor to pay the receptionist. "Wait a minute!" Beth called out. "Don't you have any advice for me?"

When I recounted this episode from my field notes for Lynn early in our interview, she said, "Oh, there's nothing anybody can do. I wish I knew." Later, when I thought the interview was over and I'd turned off the tape recorder, she said that after talking about her concerns, "I feel closer to an answer. I feel relieved somehow."

Findings: Contexts for heuretic engagement

I identified this conversation as heuretic engagement. What insights into its interactional context do the discourse analytic probes yield? First, when we ask how discourse in this observation is shaped by the world and how discourse shapes the world, we discover how the context for heuretic engagement is linguistically constructed. That is, the context is created and sustained by what is said and left unsaid. For example, Lynn opened with a description of the halftime show as a certain kind of experience "that was not for families." She followed with comments that repeated what she had heard – but had not experienced herself – of families gathering to watch football together on television. Successive comments from Patricia and Beth kept parental values at the center of the conversation. Reflecting on the conversation during her interview, Lynn said she "would definitely agree" that the conversation had been more about problems in parenting related to entertainment media more generally than it was about the content of the halftime show in particular, though participants attempted to wrest meaning from both. For Lynn and Beth, Janet Jackson's "wardrobe malfunction" indexed an extensive category of media images and messages they found offensive and wished to keep from their

Table 1. Participant power relationships

Name	Age	Role	Children	Married	TV Fan	Control
Lynn	>50	Patron	2	Yes	No	Yes
Patricia	>40	Sr. Stylist	0	No	Yes/No	No
Beth	>40	Jr. Stylist	2	Yes	Yes	Yes

children. Patricia, in contrast, perceived their concern as unduly protective, possibly even an affront to the way she had been raised, and reframed the issue as one of freedom of expression, a framing that Lynn and Beth did not adopt.

This context also was shaped by what was not said – indeed, could not have been said – because of the way Lynn introduced the subject. Imagine that the high-school girl who liked reality TV and had been in Patricia's chair earlier had been the one to introduce the topic with a statement such as, "Wasn't that halftime show awesome? Janet and Justin were great!" Patricia would probably have agreed, and Beth's concern about parenting probably never would have been raised because a well-trained hairdresser knows that the customer is always right.[7] Thus we learn that heuretic engagement requires an interactional context that permits all participants to have a chance to shape through language the aspect of the world under discussion.

A second use of a discourse analytic probe related to contexts for heuretic engagement asks how discourse is shaped by interpersonal relations among participants and how discourse shapes participants' interpersonal relations. Consider the context of this observation in terms of the power relationships among the participants, as shown in Table 1.

Lynn had authority in the conversation by virtue of being the salon patron, the oldest woman, and the person who introduced the topic and its framing. Married with children, she was clearly a stakeholder in the discussion. Lynn attempted to level the playing field and create a bond with Patricia right away by disclosing, even before she was in Patricia's chair, that she was not well paid for her work. In her interview, Lynn said of Patricia (who had cut her hair once before), "I could see that she was a bright, communicative person and ... I wanted her opinion." However, Lynn was not especially attuned to popular culture – the topic of conversation – and thus was not well qualified to judge when entertainment fell

---

7.   This hair salon's employee manual instructs hairdressers to refrain from discussing topics related to sex, politics, religion, or anything potentially controversial. Interestingly, during the interviews following observations of conversations that I identified as focused on controversial social issues – all of which are to some extent political – participants claimed they rarely discussed "politics," and never in public places or with people they didn't know well.

out of the bounds of cultural norms. Plus, she had what some would consider an outdated, controlling style of parenting.

Though the two hairdressers were nearly the same age, Patricia was a senior stylist to Beth and was skillful at reading her clients and presenting an appropriate persona. When talking with the high-school student, Patricia had been quite knowledgeable about reality TV and had discussed it enthusiastically, even if somewhat disparagingly. With Lynn, though, she claimed she watched little TV, declaring it "inane." Even so, Patricia had the broadest exposure to the relevant cultural context. Also, what Beth may have known but Lynn did not is that Patricia had an M.F.A. in creative writing. She was extremely bright and articulate – something Lynn had picked up on in an earlier experience as Patricia's client. But Patricia was unmarried and without children, and lacked credibility when the discussion expanded from the appropriateness of the halftime show as family entertainment to problems in parenting more generally. Patricia further diminished her credibility with the group when she endorsed her father's *laissez-faire* style of parenting.

Beth interjected herself into a conversation in which she shared Lynn's status as a stakeholder. Her credibility as a mother, enthusiasm for the topic, and outgoing personality compensated for her lower status as a junior hairdresser and as an uninvited latecomer to the conversation. Her motivation for joining the conversation appeared credible, as hers was the clearest expression of "Help!" in the attempt to make meaning of the discussion. By this logic, a condition for the interactional context for heuretic engagement is a balance of social authority, credible prior experience, and appropriate motivation among participants. From a rhetorical perspective, participants in the interactional context must successfully negotiate dimensions similar to those of the Aristotelian concept of *ethos*: wisdom, virtue, and goodwill.

The third probe, which asks how discourse is shaped by prior discourse and how it shapes the possibilities for future discourse, reveals additional features of this interactional context. Though Lynn did not cite prior discussions about the topic during the salon conversation, in her interview she said that in the two days between the event and her conversation in the salon, she had heard differing opinions from several people: some co-workers, her husband, her seventeen-year-old son, and his girlfriend. These conversations had complicated her initial response that the show was completely inappropriate. For example, referring to her son, Lynn said, "He didn't think it was a big deal, and he thought that my husband and I were old fogies." Without this prior discourse and the cognitive dissonance it had created, the topic of the halftime show would not have emerged as the focus of heuretic engagement. Lynn would not have asked Patricia directly, "How do you feel about it?" The traces of the conversation in the salon doubtless appeared in future conversations Lynn had about the topic. As Lynn describes the circumstances:

These are probably things that people can't resolve. How can Patricia and I know or Beth the other stylist resolve this except perhaps in our own minds whether we are for or against it. But, um, I think people have conversations like this because they're a little worried. They see these things that don't fit into their worldview, or in some way bother them, or seem inappropriate, and, uh, they carry them around with them all day maybe in the back of their minds, and when they see someone who seems to be a reasonable person who might be able to … help them understand this a little better, then they talk. This is what people do, people talk especially women I believe they talk. Especially when it comes to parenting. And I do believe this is a parenting issue. This is a society versus parents (*chuckle)* issue almost.

Lynn appears to be a beleaguered parent in search of support. As noted earlier, Beth does, too, and it is reasonable to expect that traces of this conversation appeared in the three-hour conversation about children and families Beth reported having some weeks later with another mother she met in a fast-food restaurant play area. Moreover, in this observation, MTV and cable TV emerged as indexing "society" in the "society versus parents" framing Lynn proposes above, even though the Super Bowl was broadcast on network television. For Lynn and Beth, anyway, it is likely that MTV will in future conversations index the entire segment of popular culture they find inappropriate for their children. Finally, not only did the salon conversation shape what might be said in future conversations, but it also shaped how Lynn at least would introduce and frame the topic in future conversations. That is, as a result of this conversation, she reports having moved from asking whether or not the show was appropriate for children (a bogus question, because she had already made up her mind that it was not), to asking the question that was troubling her deeply: What do good parents do when personal values, popular culture, and parental responsibility are in conflict? This analysis illustrates how interactional contexts for heuretic engagement function similarly to those of other discourse contexts: heuretic engagement admits prior discourse and situational frames and gives them the play and power to influence future discourse.

A fourth discourse analytic probe focuses on the role of medium in shaping discourse and the ways discourse shapes the possibilities of its medium. In this case, the medium is face-to-face interaction, which is the ideal medium for heuretic engagement. This talk cannot happen without the immediacy of a perceived appropriate partner. So, while the medium is not the message, it does make possible a particular kind of message and its multiple layers of meaning. Compared to contexts such as online discussions, letters to the editor, citizen presentations to city councils and school boards, or radio and television call-in shows, dialogic face-to-face interaction offers participants in heuretic engagement the opportunity to process and create meaning not only from language but also from a host of visual, aural, and kinesthetic cues and to adjust one's discourse immediately.

Meaning derived from these cues, which are available from the interactional context, shapes what is said and what might be said in the physical presence of an interlocutor. It is possible to imagine heuretic engagement taking place within a telephone conversation or in a chat room, but because of the relative impoverishment of these communication environments, I do not consider them here. My many observations of Patricia in my role as a researcher and in my dozen or more times as her client are a case in point. I know her mannerisms well enough to know when she is saying something important to her or when she is working to connect ideas that she cares about communicating carefully. When conversation is light and meandering, her work as a stylist continues apace: combing, talking, cutting, laughing, styling all seem part of one activity. An observer might reasonably conclude that she and her client are engaging in social chitchat. But when Patricia is particularly earnest about a point she is making or choosing her words with special care, she stops her work behind her clients, rests her hands on their shoulders, and makes eye contact via the mirror in front of them. After making her point, she may hold this pose while she listens to a response; then she returns to her work. In my observations, Patricia's stopping her work is a signal that what is about to happen may be worth attending to. The medium of face-to-face interaction imbues talk with meaning available only through that medium. Likewise, discourse like heuretic engagement extends the possibilities for meaning-making in face-to-face interaction.

The final heuristic considered here proposes an examination of the relationship between discourse and purpose. This relationship is especially significant to this study because heuretic engagement is everyday talk that is defined by its purpose: discovering meaning in topics of social concern. For heuretic engagement to take place, the interactional context must present at least two interlocutors interested in pursuing a topic for the purpose of understanding it better or, to use Lynn's expression, discovering a "logic I can live with." We looked earlier at the conditions that facilitate and constrain heuretic engagement. To the extent that those are present in an interactional context, the opportunity for this purposive talk is enhanced or diminished. In the context of the observation under discussion here, we also can note strategic moves the participants made to achieve their own purposes, which initially may have been unrelated to heuretic engagement but certainly helped it emerge. For example, during their greeting, Lynn chose to express solidarity with Patricia as an underpaid worker "to get an interesting conversation out of it." With Lynn as her client, Patricia chose to change her earlier stance as an enthusiastic, regular television viewer to a critic of television, possibly to present herself as a more cultured person for a different kind of conversation with Lynn. Beth, silent for too long with her present client, moved quickly to join uninvited a conversation that had special salience for her concerns as a parent. Both individual purposes and the purpose of heuretic engagement shaped the discourse in this interactional context, and this conversation shaped the purpose of future similar conversations for each participant.

In summary, I borrowed from Johnstone's set of "tools for thinking with" (2008: 10) to discover what might be said about the relationship between the discourse of heuretic engagement and its interactional contexts by looking closely at one observation and its related interview. With these tools, I probed a stable definition of heuretic engagement in unstable contexts and learned that when citizens work to make meaning of social issues together, "the internally persuasive word is half-ours and half-someone else's," as Bakhtin reminds us (1981: 345). More particularly, heuretic engagement takes place in interactional contexts where the following conditions are present:

- Interaction shapes through talk the world under discussion in a way that resonates with participants' own experience of it.
- Interaction takes place among participants who share authority and perceive each other as credible. Participants may attempt to negotiate their individual ethos to enhance others' perceptions of them.
- Interaction elicits participants' personal experiences and situational frames.
- Interaction ideally occurs in face-to-face contexts, rich with the interpersonal cues that imbricate meaning.
- Interaction can take place only among individuals whose discursive purposes are congruent with the purpose of heuretic engagement: discovery. Participants with other goals or whose minds are made up may redirect the conversation or be dropped from it.

The findings suggest that heuretic engagement emerges from everyday talk when a particular complex of conditions is present and when participants are able to successfully negotiate the changes that occur once the mode of discourse emerges. The findings also illustrate how context, including individual characteristics of participants, enables, constrains, and disables the process.

Conclusion

This study has engaged scholarship about idealized civic discourse and the critiques of contemporary practice while seeking to understand heuretic engagement, an everyday civic discourse practice largely neglected by both. I observed how small publics take up a broad range of topics, occasionally working to find meaning in perplexing local manifestations of broader social issues. In this chapter, I have illustrated how discourse analysis plays a key role in understanding how the mode of discourse I call heuretic engagement helps citizens explore meaning. This study complements other recent investigations into public civic discourse, such as

Harris-Lacewell's (2004) ethnographic study of everyday political talk in African American communities, Hausendorf and Bora's (2006) edited collection of essays that bring a variety of analytic perspectives to civic public participation on one social issue, Myers's (2004) detailed study of personal and public opinion formation and reportage, and Walsh's (2004) analysis of informal political talk within strong-tie social groups.

Looking beyond the findings of these and related studies of civic discourse, my study adds a voice to the calls for rethinking doxic views of civic discourse in scholarship and teaching. A new formulation would accept, as Wyatt, Katz, and Kim suggest, that "democracy can be enriched if the role of informal political conversation is appreciated and such conversation encouraged along with other forms of political discourse" (2000:72). Similarly, Asen contends, "discourse practices present potentially accessible and powerful everyday enactments of citizenship" (2004:207). My research suggests that citizens themselves do not view heuretic engagement as a significant civic activity. Instead, they believe that the real work of "political" talk takes place in contexts they actively seek to avoid because they are too public, unacceptably contentious and unpleasant, or because they have little confidence in their speaking skills.

As the discourse analytic probes reveal, everyday talk I call heuretic engagement is a rhetorical act; thus, it shares with rhetoric the characteristic of being an art that can be taught and practiced. I argue for an informed and deliberate effort to translate a theory of heuretic engagement into praxis for programs of liberal learning. Such an agenda is especially appropriate for interdisciplinary civic education, action research, and service learning – areas in which I am attempting to carry this research in my teaching. Rhetoricians, in particular, because of our specialized training and expertise, are called to teach not only performance and analysis of public speech, but also civic engagement in its full breadth of opportunity across disciplines. Research that supports the teaching agenda suggested above (what *is* the role of the citizen orator?) and includes systematic analyses of contextualized talk, such as that offered by discourse analytic techniques, can assist rhetoricians and their social science colleagues in finding common ground for interdisciplinary inquiry.

As we have seen, present research into everyday talk about social issues neglects not only civic practice, but also civic opportunity. A theory of heuretic engagement invites a re-visioning of both.

Appendix

Patricia illustrates the promise of practice and opportunity. After concluding my field work and writing up my findings, nine months after making the observation that has been the focus of this chapter, I took advantage of a less hectic schedule and went to the discount hair salon for a long overdue haircut. I had made it a point to arrive when I knew that Patricia would be working. I was moving away to accept my present position, and I wanted to thank her again for her help in gaining access to her salon and to her friend's salon where I also had collected data. Patricia congratulated me on my new job and said that she would miss me as a customer. The rest of the conversation came as quite a surprise, and I recorded it in my field notes shortly after leaving the salon. I present it here as I recorded it:

Susan:	So, you're one of the stars in my write up. I didn't use your real name or give the name of the salon, of course, but you're there!
Patricia:	Really? Well! That's so cool ... So, did you write about everything you heard?
Susan:	No, I focused on two conversations. One here, one at Carmen's place.
Patricia:	You didn't by chance write about that woman – oh, you remember? The older woman, real conservative. She was freaked out by the Janet Jackson thing. She had brown kind of curly hair.
Susan:	(*laughs*) I don't believe it. Yeah, I did. You remember that conversation?
Patricia:	Oh, yeah, I sure do. I've thought about it a lot. I've wondered why she was so interested in that. I mean, her kids were almost grown up.
Susan:	Do you remember that Beth joined the conversation, too?
Patricia:	Right ... Beth's kids are younger.
Susan:	So, when you thought about the conversation, what did you think? I mean, why did it stay with you?
Patricia:	I wondered why it even mattered to this woman. I tried to think what I would have been thinking if I'd had kids. *Patricia paused, put her hands on my shoulders, and caught my eye in the mirror.* I'll tell you what else I've thought: she's what happened to the election.
Susan:	What do you mean?
Patricia:	Well, I couldn't understand how Bush could be re-elected. I mean, what were people thinking of? Who *were* these people who voted for him, anyway? And then I thought of her. She's a nice person; she's smart. She's a writer, remember? But she's scared of some things, and so, you know. I mean they say that people who voted for Bush were voting for the status quo. I'll bet she voted for Bush. Everybody I know voted for Kerry. But we think pretty much alike, and so it seemed obvious. So when I tried to figure out what went wrong, she came to mind. Kerry's people should have been thinking of people like her, too.
Susan:	She was here in early February. Have you seen her since then?
Patricia:	No. Haven't seen her. If she's been here it was when I wasn't working. I'd know her if she came in. I hope she does. I'd like to talk to her again.

References

Asen, Robert. 2004. "A Discourse Theory of Citizenship". *Quarterly Journal of Speech* 90: 189–211.

Associated Press. 2004. Super Bowl Notebook: CBS Apologizes After Airing Over-Exposed Janet Jackson. 2 February 2004. http://www.Post-Gazette.com/Pg/04033/268388.stm.

Bakhtin, Mikhail M. 1981. *The Dialogic Imagination: Four Essays by M. M. Bakhtin*. Michael Holquist (Ed). Caryl Emerson and Michael Holquist (Trans). Austin: University of Texas Press.

Bitzer, Lloyd. 1968. "The Rhetorical Situation". *Philosophy & Rhetoric* 1: 1–14.

Covino, William A. and Jolliffe, David A. 1995. *Rhetoric: Concepts, Definitions, Boundaries*. Boston: Allyn and Bacon.

Crigler, John. 7 February 2004. Interview on *Washington Journal*. Washington, DC: C-SPAN.

Cushman, Ellen. 1998. *The Struggle and the Tools: Oral and Literate Strategies in an Inner City Community*. Albany: State University of New York Press.

Dewey, John. 1933. *How We Think: A Restatement of the Relation of Reflective Thinking to the Educative Process*. Boston: D.C. Heath.

Duneier, Mitchell. 1992. *Slim's Table: Race, Respectability, and Masculinity*. Chicago: University of Chicago Press.

Eliasoph, Nina. 1998. *Avoiding Politics: How Americans Produce Apathy in Everyday Life*. Cambridge: Cambridge University Press.

Gamson, William A. 1992. *Talking Politics*. Cambridge: Cambridge University Press.

Gilpin, Susan. 2004. Heuretic Engagement: Everyday Talk about Social Issues. Phd Diss., Carnegie Mellon University.

Goffman, Erving. 1981. *Forms of Talk*. Philadelphia: University of Pennsylvania Press.

Granovetter, Mark. 1973. "The Strength of Weak Ties". *American Journal of Sociology* 78: 1360–1380.

Habermas, Jürgen. 1989. *The Structural Transformation of the Public Sphere: An Inquiry into a Category of Bourgeois Society*. T. Burger (Trans). Cambridge, MA: MIT Press.

Harris-Lacewell, Melissa Victoria. 2004. *Barbershops, Bibles, and BET: Everyday Talk and Black Political Thought*. Princeton, N.J.: Princeton University Press.

Hausendorf, Heiko and Bora, Alfons (Eds). 2006. *Analysing Citizenship Talk: Social Positioning in Political and Legal Decision-Making Processes*. Amsterdam: John Benjamins.

Hauser, G. 1999. *Vernacular Voices: The Rhetoric of Publics and Public Spheres*. Columbia: University of South Carolina Press.

Huckfeldt, Robert and Sprague, John. 1995. *Citizens, Politics, and Social Communication: Information and Influence in an Election Campaign*. Cambridge: Cambridge University Press.

Jacobs-Huey, Lanita. 2006. *From the Kitchen to the Parlor: Language and Becoming in African American Women's Hair Care*. Oxford: Oxford University Press.

Johnstone, Barbara. 2008. *Discourse Analysis*, 2e. Malden, Mass: Blackwell.

Lindquist, Julie. 2002. *A Place to Stand: Politics and Persuasion in a Working-Class Bar*. Oxford: Oxford University Press.

Majors, Yolanda. 2007. "Narrations of Cross-Cultural Encounters as Interpretive Frames for Reading Word and World". *Discourse and Society* 18(4): 479–505.

May, Ruben A. Buford. 2001. *Talking at Trena's: Everyday Conversations at an African American Tavern*. New York: New York University Press.

McCarthy, Michael. 2000. "Mutually Captive Audiences: Small Talk and the Genre of Close-Contact Service Encounters". In *Small Talk*, Justine Coupland (Ed), 84–109. London: Pearson.

Myers, Greg. 2004. *Matters of Opinion: Talking about Public Issues.* Cambridge: Cambridge University Press.

NYTIMES.COM. 2004. Debates: Busted. 5 February 2004. http://www.nytimes.com/2004/02/05/Readersopinions/05DEBA.Html.

Schudson, Michael. 1998. *The Good Citizen: A History of American Civic Life.* New York: The Free Press.

Silverstein, Michael and Urban, Greg. 1996. "The Natural History of Discourse". In *Natural Histories of Discourse*, Michael Silverstein and Greg Urban (Eds), 1–17. Chicago: University of Chicago Press.

Tracy, Karen. 2002. *Everyday Talk: Building and Reflecting Identities.* New York: Guilford Press.

Walsh, Katherine Cramer. 2004. *Talking about Politics: Informal Groups and Social Identity in American Life.* Chicago: University of Chicago Press.

Wyatt, Robert O., Katz, Elihu, and Kim, Joohan. 2000. "Bridging the Spheres: Political and Personal Conversation in Public and Private Spaces". *Journal of Communication* 50: 71–92.

Index

In the series *Discourse Approaches to Politics, Society and Culture* the following titles have been published thus far or are scheduled for publication: